A VERY PRINCIPLED BOY

A VERY PRINCIPLED BOY

The Life of Duncan Lee, Red Spy and Cold Warrior

MARK A. BRADLEY

BASIC BOOKS
A Member of the Perseus Books Group
New York

Books published by Basic Books are available at special discounts for bulk purchases in the United States by corporations, institutions, and other organizations. For more information, please contact the Special Markets Department at the Perseus Books Group, 2300 Chestnut Street, Suite 200, Philadelphia, PA 19103, or call (800) 810-4145, ext. 5000, or e-mail special.markets@perseusbooks.com.

Designed by Trish Wilkinson
Set in 11.5 point Minion Pro

Library of Congress Cataloging-in-Publication Data
Bradley, Mark A. (Mark Andrew), 1956
    A very principled boy : the life of Duncan Lee, Red spy and cold warrior / Mark A. Bradley.
        Pages   cm
    Includes bibliographical references and index.
    ISBN 978-0-465-03009-5 (hardback) — ISBN 978-0-465-03665-3 (e-book) 1. Lee, Duncan Chaplin, 19-1988. 2. Moles (Spies)—United States—Biography. 3. Intelligence officers—United States—Biography. 4. United States. Office of Strategic Services—Biography. 5. Communists—United States—Biography. 6. Espionage, Soviet—United States—History. 7. World War, 1939–1945—Secret service. 8. Cold War—Biography. I. Title.
E748.L46B73   2014
940.54'8673092—dc23
[B]

                                                                          2013045461

10 9 8 7 6 5 4 3 2 1

To Daniel Patrick Moynihan,
who gave me the idea,
and to Liza, who made it possible.

We have two lives . . . the life we learn with and the life we live with after that.

—Bernard Malamud, *The Natural*

Why isn't he in jail?
They can't get him, old sport. He's a smart man.

—F. Scott Fitzgerald, *The Great Gatsby*

Contents

Prologue
Helen

As he did on most days, Duncan Lee rose early in his small apartment in Georgetown. He put on his US Army uniform and walked to work at the Office of Strategic Services (OSS), the forerunner of today's Central Intelligence Agency (CIA). Anyone who noticed him on the morning of May 21, 1943, would have seen a studious-looking twenty-nine-year-old man of medium height, with brown hair and gray eyes framed by round spectacles. Lee could have passed easily for just another soldier on his way to work in wartime Washington. Instead, he was the highest-ranking military officer inside the OSS's headquarters who was also a Soviet agent, one of the best-placed spies the Kremlin's communist spymasters ever had inside any US intelligence agency.[1]

When he arrived at 25th and E Streets, NW, Lee showed his identification card to the armed guards, walked through the gates, and headed down the slope to his office in the Secretariat, the OSS's communications hub. His desk was in Room 226, one floor above that of William "Wild Bill" Donovan, the OSS's colorful head and his mentor. Lee was one of the intelligence chief's personal gatekeepers for secret reports and cables from all over the globe, and Donovan kept the Yale- and Oxford-educated Rhodes scholar close. Lee was also one of the newly appointed general's favorites.[2]

On May 21, as Lee leafed through hundreds of cables and reports that streamed in from the OSS's overseas stations and the State Department, one in particular—a secret interoffice memo dated that very day from Whitney Shepardson, head of the spy agency's Secret Intelligence

Branch—caught his experienced eye. Addressed to "Captain Lee, Secretariat," the memo explained that attached were two secret documents from London "which General Donovan wishes to see."[3]

One of the documents, "SA 4489, British Government Reactions to Russo-Polish Crisis" from the OSS's London station, was dated April 30, 1943, and discussed the growing rift between the Soviet Union and the exiled Polish government in London over determination of their nations' postwar boundaries. It also highlighted the differences this tension was causing between British prime minister Winston Churchill and Anthony Eden, his foreign secretary. Before he passed Shepardson's sheaf of papers to Donovan, Lee sat at his desk and read SA 4489 over and over until he had memorized it.[4]

Sometime within the next week, a tall, large-boned woman with short, curly brown hair visited him at his apartment. When he opened the door, Lee invited the woman he knew only as "Helen" into his small living room. He had been expecting her because she regularly came to see him every two weeks.[5]

Perhaps after some brief pleasantries, Lee motioned to his couch and sat down next to Helen. Speaking barely above a whisper for fear that the Federal Bureau of Investigation (FBI) had bugged his apartment, he meticulously and slowly recited Shepardson's reports.[6]

Almost a year earlier, when Lee had first agreed to pass the OSS's secrets to the People's Commissariat for Internal Affairs (NKVD), the Soviet Union's intelligence service, he told his handlers that he could not take classified documents home; instead, he would memorize any useful reports and recite them back to his controller. Lee had good reason to take such precautions, despite the OSS's notoriously poor security: he knew he could be executed if caught.[7]

Helen was in fact Elizabeth Bentley, a seasoned courier for the People's Commissariat of State Security (NKGB)—the NKVD had changed its name in April 1943—who had been educated at Vassar and Columbia. She knew better than to press the nervous and high-strung Lee for documents. He was too valuable to her Soviet masters to risk losing. Instead, Bentley listened intently and absorbed the information he relayed. Only later, after she had said good-bye and hurried to Union Station to catch her train back to New York, would she write down what he had said.[8]

Lee's code name was "Koch." On June 9, 1943, the Soviet Consulate in New York sent an encrypted cable to Lieutenant General Pavel Fitin, the Moscow-based head of the NKGB's Foreign Intelligence Directorate. "Koch reports that the OSS has received from its [branch] in London two confidential reports," the cable stated. "One of them from April 30 says that Eden is inclined to side with the Poles but Churchill takes a more moderate position proposing to cede [Belarus] and the Ukraine to the USSR and Eastern Prussia to Poland."[9]

This was the same secret information that Lee had read in SA 4489 on May 21. Joseph Stalin, the Soviet Union's iron-fisted dictator, eagerly sought this kind of intelligence; he wanted the British and Americans to agree to allow his country to keep all the land it had forcibly wrested from Poland in 1939. He was enormously interested in any window his spies could open onto what Churchill or President Franklin Roosevelt, his two wartime allies, might be plotting with regard to the Soviet Union's borders after the fighting with Adolf Hitler ended.[10]

Lee's secret information from London highlighted his great potential as a spy and underscored his access to valuable intelligence headed directly for Donovan. As early as September 8, 1942, the NKVD's files on Lee in Moscow trumpeted that "agent reports from Europe and all over the world go through him. He chooses among them and shows them to Donovan for his consideration."[11]

Most Americans have heard of Aldrich Ames and Robert Hanssen—one a CIA turncoat, the other a traitor working for the FBI—but not of Duncan Lee. The son of missionaries and the descendant of famous Americans, this husband and father spent three years fighting Nazi Germany and imperial Japan in the cause of democracy and freedom. At the same time, he was spying for the Soviet Union.

Unlike Ames and Hanssen, Lee did not commit espionage against the United States out of greed or egotism. Rather, he chose his political leanings and conscience over his country and government, even though doing so meant breaking its laws and betraying the very men who had recruited him into its intelligence service. Behind bars for life, Ames and Hanssen are still paying for what they did, but Lee got away. This book tells the story of why he spied, how he eluded his pursuers, and the personal and national consequences of his actions.

The stomp of fascists' jackboots and the Great Depression's economic misery had radicalized Lee in the mid-1930s. He decided that only Soviet-style communism could counteract these twin evils. By the time William Donovan recruited him into the OSS in 1942, he had been a member of the Communist Party of the United States of America (CPUSA) for three years. All the same, Lee easily passed the OSS's cursory background investigation and was admitted to its highest echelons. His elite education and illustrious background blended perfectly with the OSS's gentlemen's club ethos of personal trust and shared values among social equals.

Lee started passing the OSS's secrets to the Soviets almost as soon as he began working in the Secretariat, but he set the terms, keeping his two lives strictly separate. That arrangement worked until his carefully constructed worlds began collapsing into each other. Just before the spring of 1945, with the war's end in sight, Lee's idealism had dissolved into sleep-destroying nightmares about being discovered, arrested, and shot.

His last meeting with a Soviet intelligence officer took place in early March 1945. Terrified, he begged his controller to leave him alone. Although never exactly happy with Lee as a source, considering him too independent, difficult, and problematic, his Moscow spymasters did not want to let him go. They hoped to use him as a talent spotter inside the OSS.

Their plans evaporated in November 1945 when Elizabeth Bentley, haunted by her own demons, defected to the FBI and outed Lee and the other spies she handled. Now free of the Soviets, Lee found himself on a collision course with FBI director J. Edgar Hoover, the most feared man in Washington. Neither man was completely prepared for the shock waves generated by Bentley's disclosures.

Rocked by allegations that, unbeknownst to him, Soviet spies had infested wartime Washington, Hoover launched the largest espionage investigation in the FBI's then almost four-decade history. Lee was an especially attractive target: the suave, urbane Ivy Leaguer represented everything the provincial and conservative Hoover was not and despised. Better yet, Lee was a top aide to William Donovan, Hoover's most hated rival for control of the US postwar intelligence empire, then in its infancy though already a rich prize for whoever became its czar.

The all-or-nothing chess game Lee and Hoover played entailed moves and countermoves often dictated or influenced by domestic and international events that neither man could control or evade. Each also recruited to his side powerful allies who played the game out of self-interest. The stakes could not have been higher. Hoover played to purge the United States of a dangerous spy and subversive; Lee played for his life and freedom. A conviction for espionage committed during wartime meant death or a life sentence in a federal prison.

Later, in what was most likely a bid to atone for what he had done for the Soviets and strengthen his anticommunist credentials, Lee joined with a small band of freebooters led by World War II hero Claire Chennault, who gave the United States its first Cold War victory in East Asia by denying Mao Zedong ownership of seventy-one airplanes the communist leader planned to use to invade Taiwan. Lee's actions in Hong Kong, applauded in Washington's shadowy backrooms, meant nothing to the Ahab-like Hoover.

Determined to bring Lee to justice, Hoover pulled out all the stops. The lessons he learned and the conclusions he drew from his hunt of Lee and the others named by Bentley helped catalyze his no-holds-barred crusade against communism and the political left inside the United States. The methods Hoover used and the targets he selected would eventually play a leading role in destroying his reputation and reining in the FBI's illegal activities.

Lee's espionage also inflamed Washington's already tense political climate. In the summer of 1948, Bentley's allegations against him and her other sources became public. The Republicans, more concerned about partisan politics than investigating an astonishing breach of national security, tried to use them in a series of sensational House Un-American Activities Committee (HUAC) hearings to tar President Harry Truman, already an underdog in that November's presidential election. Just as vehemently, the Truman administration attacked Bentley's mental stability and ridiculed her claims. Neither side bothered itself with the best interests of the American people.

The HUAC's ultimate failure to trap Lee and the others fingered by Bentley left Truman's political foes feeling deeply bitter and frustrated. The Soviets' explosion of their first atomic bomb in August 1949, followed by a high-profile series of criminal convictions—in 1950 of Alger Hiss, a former State Department official who had accompanied President Franklin Roosevelt to Yalta in February 1945, for lying about passing classified State Department papers to Whittaker Chambers, a Soviet military intelligence courier; and a ring of atomic spies that included Harry Gold and Klaus Fuchs for espionage; in 1951 of Julius and Ethel Rosenberg also for espionage—only aggravated these feelings and added to conservatives' belief that subversives had undermined the United States from within.

An obscure Republican US senator from Wisconsin named Joseph McCarthy capitalized on this paranoia and charged that the Democrats could not be trusted with protecting the country from communism's threat. McCarthy would use this claim to propel himself to fame and then to infamy. Before the Senate finally tired of his brutish antics and censured him at the end of 1954, he had bullied the Democrats into believing that they could never again appear soft on national security. Although McCarthy does not bear the sole responsibility— Soviet aggression and American fears of appeasement also played starring roles—his cutting accusations that the Democrats could not be relied on to protect the country helped push the United States into the Korean War, the Bay of Pigs, and the Cuban missile crisis, and into escalating its disastrous military involvement in Vietnam. The repercussions of McCarthy's accusations and his ghost still make themselves felt in Washington today.

Lee's treachery had personal consequences as well. It fractured his family, derailed his once promising career, and forced him to live an elaborate lie for the rest of his life. He went to his grave in 1988 still denying that he had spied for the Soviets. His story is emblematic of the morally shaded, highly compartmentalized black, white, and gray worlds that spies inhabit and of the awful costs they ring up.

This is the first biography of Duncan Lee. To write it, I have used his personal papers and thousands of pages of declassified documents, many of which I have gotten by using the Freedom of Information

Act, from the FBI, CIA, National Security Agency (NSA), and State Department. I also relied heavily on the eight notebooks of Alexander Vassiliev, a former Committee of State Security (KGB) officer and a journalist, which focus on Soviet espionage inside the United States from the 1930s through the 1950s. Vassiliev filled these notebooks by hand between 1993 and 1996 while he had access primarily to the NKVD's and NKGB's archives as part of an approved SVR (Russia's external intelligence service) book project. His White Notebook #3, in particular, contains extracts, lengthy quotations, and summaries of Lee's NKVD and NKGB files in Moscow. In 2009, Vassiliev donated his notebooks to the Library of Congress. In addition, I have mined other archived material about Lee and his times that I found in a host of libraries and collections. I have used all these sources to assemble a mosaic of Lee's fascinating, though deeply conflicted, life.[12]

ONE

BORN TO SERVE

The CIA has a preternatural interest in those who spy against their own countries. The agency understands the enormous damage these agents can cause not only to its own operations but to those of its enemies. Years of experience—much of it hard won, some of it painful—have taught the CIA's counterintelligence experts that most of these spies share two characteristics: they spring from psychologically fertile soil, and the right set of circumstances will push them to act. Duncan Lee's highly unusual background and his visceral reaction to the economic and political catastrophes of the 1930s supplied him with both.[1]

The seeds of Lee's psyche sprouted in the fertile soil of Virginia and New England over two and a half centuries before his birth. He took tremendous pride in his dual heritage: it had produced scores of unflinching men and women who had dedicated their lives to serving causes they deemed much greater than themselves. Yet their often larger-than-life examples also haunted him throughout his own life.[2]

Through his father, he descended from the "Lees of Virginia," a family that, as John Adams observed in 1779, has "more men of merit in it than any other." Several of the family's more famous members had made taking long odds and high risks a way of life.[3]

The Lees' long history in Virginia began in late 1639 or early 1640, when Richard Lee left the English Midlands to settle in Jamestown,

1

Virginia. By the time he died in 1664, he owned 13,000 acres, making him one of the richest men in Virginia. His descendants leveraged his wealth and standing to increase their holdings, establishing themselves as one of the colony's most powerful and distinguished families.[4]

In 1776 and again in 1861, the Lees rebelled against their governments. Duncan Lee's most famous direct ancestor was Revolutionary War leader Richard Henry Lee. On June 7, 1776, he rose at the Second Continental Congress in Philadelphia to introduce the resolution that "these united colonies are, and of right ought to be, free and independent states." Shortly thereafter, he and Francis Lightfoot Lee, both British subjects, became the only brothers to sign the Declaration of Independence. As Duncan Lee wryly observed in "My Family: A Memorandum for My Children and Grandchildren," a memoir he wrote near the end of his life, "The signers would . . . have been the first to be hanged, had the Revolution failed. Success or failure in a revolution makes the difference between hero and traitor."[5]

Duncan's great-grandfather's first cousin had been Robert E. Lee, the most renowned of all Lees, who followed Virginia and his principles out of the Union and into the Confederacy in 1861. By the next summer, his Army of Northern Virginia had developed into the most dangerous military threat the American government had faced since the British burned Washington in 1814.[6]

The Lee who most influenced Duncan's psychological development was Edmund Jennings Lee IV, his missionary father. A powerful and mystical figure, Edmund provided his son with a role model, one to emulate and, ultimately, to run from.

Born on September 5, 1877, in Shepherdstown, West Virginia, Edmund Lee graduated from the University of Virginia at age nineteen with a master's degree and a Phi Beta Kappa key. More than his family's name and his keen intellect separated this introspective, gray-eyed young man from his peers who eagerly flocked after graduating to join banks and railroads in what Henry Grady, managing editor of the *Atlanta Constitution*, called the "New South." Instead of following them, Edmund entered the Virginia Theological Seminary to become a foreign missionary for the Episcopal Church. Intoxicated with the Gospel, he was determined to take the Christian message to remote lands.[7]

While finishing at the University of Virginia, he had fallen under the spell of the Student Volunteer Movement for Foreign Missions (SVM), an evangelical, pre- and postmillennial tidal wave then washing over the country's college campuses and seminaries. Formally organized in late December 1888, the SVM aspired, in the words of its breathtaking manifesto, to bring about "the evangelization of the world in this generation."[8]

Protestant student leaders founded the SVM to reenergize and mobilize their churches, then suffering a crisis of purpose after the Civil War. After four years of bloody sacrifice, the war had rubbed out slavery, the republic's greatest stain, but it had also triggered a staggering rate of industrialization and the opening of the West. Both brought to the United States millions of Irish and southeastern European Catholic immigrants, who looked to Rome for their salvation. The American Protestant churches, already reeling from an earlier blow to the Christian faith dealt by Charles Darwin's theory of evolution, were groping for ways to make themselves relevant again and to reinvigorate their congregations. They achieved these goals by summoning followers to wage a new crusade aimed at nothing less than saving and improving mankind.[9]

The SVM intended to pave the way for Christ's Second Coming by preaching God's word abroad to those who had never heard it and by spreading American ideals. By the time Edmund joined the movement's ranks, American imperialism was approaching its zenith. Infused with the spirit of Manifest Destiny, the United States annexed Hawaii in 1898 and the Philippines, Puerto Rico, and Guam after the Spanish-American War formally ended in 1899. Protestant church leaders believed that these territorial acquisitions confirmed Americans as a chosen people preordained to triumph over adversity and wickedness, specially picked by God to redeem the world and its foreign heathens. America was Puritan leader John Winthrop's City on a Hill, with a divine mission to bring light and truth to the world.[10]

Only a few thousand missionaries from the United States were then serving overseas; more were needed. Scores of the country's best and brightest college graduates, fired up with evangelical rhetoric and radiant visions of moral heroism and noble sacrifice, enlisted as Christian foot soldiers in the SVM. Among them was Edmund Lee. On February 7, 1902, after serving more than a year as a traveling SVM recruiter, he sailed for Shanghai. China was an unsettled and embittered country just emerging from the Boxer Rebellion, a nationalist movement against foreign imperialism and Christianity that took place between 1900 and 1901. The Boxers killed over two hundred Protestant and Catholic missionaries and their children. They also murdered nearly 30,000 Chinese converts, whom they branded traitors. Western powers, including the United States, crushed the rebellion, publicly executed its ringleaders, saddled the country with $333 million in reparations, and forced additional business concessions—acts that enraged the Chinese for generations to come.[11]

Despite this turmoil, Edmund never doubted the value of spending his life bringing Christ to China. When questioned about his exotic plans, he answered unblinkingly, "Anything I may do at home will be done by someone else if I do not do it; but anything I do in China will probably not be done unless I do it."[12]

China was a key target for missionaries, who believed that millions of Chinese were dying without hearing God's message. American imperialists were also beginning to fear that the massive, badly fractured country might become a Russian or Japanese dominion. With its deeply entrenched xenophobia, cultural history far older than that of Pericles, and eclectic religious practices, China presented a formidable challenge to the evangelicals. To meet it, Protestant churches summoned their most educated, committed, and dedicated young missionaries.[13]

Edmund stopped first in Nanjing for two years of intensive language training. By 1904, when he sailed for Anqing, a Yangtze River port about four hundred miles west of Shanghai, he was fluent enough that he could preach in Mandarin and use Chinese translations of the Bible, the *Book of Common Prayer*, and the Episcopal hymnal. In his spare time, he forgot about theology and hunted wild game outside the city's centuries-old walls. He also enjoyed watching boxing matches, playing tennis, telling clean jokes, and reciting poetry. For his first nine years in China, he lived a bachelor's life with a cousin who was a minister and medical missionary.[14]

In 1910, while attending a tea hosted by fellow missionaries in the mountainous resort of Lushan, Edmund met Lucy Chaplin. As part of an around-the-world tour financed by her father, she had come to participate in a missionary Bible conference. Edmund was immediately smitten, but Lucy was not. Unimpressed when her hosts told her that the austere-looking missionary was from the aristocratic Lee family of Virginia, she dismissively declared after the tea, "He is exactly the type of Episcopal clergyman I can't stand." She especially disliked his practice of attaching his pince-nez spectacles with a black ribbon.[15]

Although Lucy certainly did not realize it that day, she was the perfect mate for Edmund. Her family had been in America even longer than his. As importantly, its members had dedicated themselves to serving their God as soon as they had come ashore. The first Chaplin came to Maine in 1638 from Yorkshire and engendered an almost unbroken chain of earnest clergymen. No fewer than fifteen members of Lucy Chaplin's immediate family were men of the cloth.[16]

Even though Duncan Dunbar Chaplin, her father, had broken with the family tradition of ascending to the pulpit and instead entered the wool business in New York City, he too devoted money and time to his church. He also taught a Bible class at a Christian mission in the Bowery. There he met his wife, Fanny Myers, a fellow Bible teacher and direct descendant of the Mayflower passengers John and Priscilla Alden. Lucy was born on January 22, 1884, in New York City.[17]

Like many women of her background, she did not graduate from high school or college. Her father did not neglect her education, however, sending her to the exclusive Masters School at Dobbs Ferry, New York, one of the most respected finishing schools in the state. Eliza Bailey Masters, its stern Presbyterian founder, instilled Calvinist virtues in her girls and instructed them to pursue "useful, orderly lives based on truthfulness, integrity, and responsibility." She also demanded that her charges follow the school's biblical motto: "Whatever thy hand findeth to do, do it with all thy might." Each of the school's students had to perform useful social work.[18]

Lucy, though, did not graduate from the Masters School; instead, she left before the start of her senior year to tour the great museums of Europe. After returning from this trip in 1904 and making her debut into New York society, Lucy began volunteering at the Christodora House, one of the first Christian settlement houses in Manhattan's overcrowded Lower East Side slums. Founded in 1897, Christodora was a product of the Social Gospel movement, which grew out of a rising fear of labor unrest in the last quarter of the nineteenth century. Educated middle-class Protestants espoused the movement's goals, believing their churches had to play an active role in combatting the country's growing ghettos, bloody labor strikes, and chronic cycles of economic depression after the Civil War. Its followers ministered to America's growing proletariat, teaching its members about God's grace and the wonders of cultural assimilation.[19]

At Christodora, Lucy instructed residents in how to read and write in English, a hands-on experience that reinforced her strong sense of noblesse oblige and ardent Christian socialism. She would pass on both to Duncan. Her belief in action over talk shaped him profoundly and played just as decisive a part in his psychological development as the remarkable heritage his father passed on.

Edmund's charm and persistence overcame Lucy's reservations and doubts. She admired his deep commitment to his work and quiet moral strength. They were engaged six weeks after they met and married on June 29, 1911, at her home in Ridgewood, New Jersey. He was thirty-three years old; she was twenty-seven. Lucy, with her heightened sense of the practical, realized what she was asking of herself by moving to China. Her part-time Social Gospel work in New York City's slums had not required her to make any great personal sacrifices or to remake her own life. She knew marrying Edmund would force her to do both.[20]

In late September 1911, after a brief honeymoon in Shanghai, the newlyweds boarded a British river steamer to Anqing. Their three-day journey up the muddy Yangtze carried them slowly past hundreds of Chinese fishing villages with thatched roofs and mud-walled houses. She later remembered this trip as "the final days when my husband and I could be together without the alarms and responsibilities which were waiting for us in Anqing."[21]

The ancient city of Anqing was a gray, tile-roofed outpost with high, crenelated walls surrounded by a deep moat. Marauding warlords and plundering river pirates regularly threatened its roughly 45,000 residents. The city's four stout gates were often kept locked. Another wall encircled the sixteen-acre missionary compound, which stood inside the northeast corner of the city wall. Inside were a hospital, a large boy's high school, a middle school for girls, sports fields, churches, and missionary houses. Twenty-three other adult missionaries, some with young children, joined the Lees inside the compound.[22]

Life in Anqing was difficult. Dysentery, typhoid fever, and cholera were constant dangers. All water had to be boiled, and there was no fresh milk. Fresh vegetables, common fare in the United States, were inedible because the Chinese used human waste for fertilizer. But physical risks were not the only hardships. The Lees were also entering an emotionally isolated world, far from their families and closest friends; the Episcopal Church allowed its missionaries only one paid six-month visit home every four years.[23]

The newlyweds were immediately exposed to Anqing's Wild West–like violence. Shortly after they arrived, they slept one night on the floor with their mattresses up against their windows to protect themselves from the gunfire of Sun Yat-sen's revolutionaries, who were attempting to overthrow the ruling Manchus.

The city's commanding general, who became Lucy's friend, routinely displayed the severed heads of executed river pirates on pikes over the city's gates as grisly deterrents. Once, her servants complained to her that the general had taken fifteen whacks with his dull sword to sever a pirate's head. Horrified, Lucy, in an extreme application of her Social Gospel training, persuaded the general to buy a sharper sword. She later wrote that "it seemed a small victory on my part, and probably none of the brutes who died by the new sword knew that their deaths were perhaps made a little more merciful because of the anger of an American woman."[24]

On a river journey with another missionary, Edmund watched in horror as a Chinese laborer fell into the churning water. The Chinese captain went back for the drowning man only after Edmund and his companion pleaded with him to turn around. They were too late. As the two missionaries labored on deck to revive the drowned man, several of the other passengers crowded around and complained bitterly about the delay.[25]

The Lees also faced personal tragedies. On May 9, 1912, Lucy gave birth to Edmund Jennings Lee V. He died eleven months later of spinal meningitis. Similarly, Maxwell Chaplin, her medical missionary brother, would die of cholera in 1926 while treating China's sick. Such cruel and heartbreaking experiences never weakened the Lees' unswerving faith.[26]

Some of their sorrow over the loss of their first child eased with Duncan Chaplin Lee's birth on December 19, 1913, at 11:50 a.m. in Anqing's American Church Mission. Siblings Armistead and Priscilla would follow in 1916 and 1922. Thanks to money from Edmund's older brother and Lucy's father, the family had enough to build a sweeping, two-and-a-half-story stone house, with eight large rooms and two porches designed to catch the Yangtze River's breezes, inside the compound. A portrait of Robert E. Lee in a Confederate uniform hung in the living room.[27]

Although often away, Edmund was a loving, if distant, father. Sometimes he showed his affection to Duncan in confusing ways. Once, when the little boy was constipated, his father gave him a vile mixture of castor oil and port wine to solve his digestive problems and put him off alcohol forever. The cure was only partly successful. Duncan later became an alcoholic, but his father's home remedy prevented his ever developing a taste for port wine.[28]

For entertainment, the family often read aloud to one another. Charles Dickens was a favorite author. They also enjoyed listening to music on a wind-up Victrola. The two Lee boys spent most of their time with other missionary children but occasionally played soccer with young Chinese boys.[29]

Edmund made only $2,000 a year, the equivalent of $40,000 a year now. Because labor was so cheap, however, he was still able to hire four Chinese servants to cook, clean, and watch the children. He also hired an American teacher to educate the young Lees and built a bungalow in Lushan so that his family could escape the worst of the summer heat and the health dangers it brought.

Having servants allowed Lucy to concentrate on learning to speak Mandarin—her first teacher held an orange to his nose because he believed all foreigners smelled bad—and to put to use her Social Gospel training. In 1914, she returned to New York City on home leave and enrolled in the socialist Rand School. There, she learned how to organize cooperatives. When she came back to China later that year, she started what became known as the Anqing Colored Cross Stitch Society, which eventually employed over one hundred local women in a profitable sewing enterprise. Lucy ensured that they kept all the money they earned.[30]

Spending long periods away from home, Edmund continued with his evangelical ministry. He often set out alone on his bicycle or on foot in the bandit-infested countryside, armed with only a Bible and a pistol. Lucy believed danger exhilarated him. He built and administered five churches and schools in and around Anqing. He also recruited and trained Chinese clergymen to help him spread his message about Christ's imminent return.[31]

Edmund studied Buddhism, Taoism, and Confucianism and jousted regularly with the Chinese intellectuals who questioned his Christian teachings. He held regular Sunday night salons with local scholars to debate and discuss religion and philosophy. Duncan missed none of this. He venerated his father as a mystic who had dedicated his life to serving humanity in the finest traditions of his famous family. At the same time, his father's mysticism and spirituality left the young boy with mixed feelings of awe and alienation.[32]

Duncan was educated inside the missionary compound until he was eleven years old. In 1925, he sailed to the United States with Lucy and attended school in Ridgewood, New Jersey. When he returned to China a year later, his parents sent him to Lushan to attend the American school there. With its intentional, almost total detachment from China, this school provided an education that would allow students to return to the United States for university training. Duncan remained at the American school until the spring of 1927.[33]

In May 1927, Lucy and her three children left China. Chiang Kai-shek's efforts to unify the country had targeted Westerners and ignited antiforeigner demonstrations. His troops attacked and looted Christian missions. Missionaries fled in droves, but Edmund insisted on staying to salvage what he could, not understanding that his Chinese neighbors viewed him as just another Western intruder. As she was leaving Anqing for Shanghai, Lucy heard the locals cry out, "Kill the foreigners."[34]

The family, dressed in their Sunday best, boarded a US Navy destroyer and sailed upriver to Jiujiang. There, they boarded a Chinese boat with other Western refugees. Large rats in the bedding forced them to sleep on deck, surrounded by crates piled high to shield them from snipers lying in wait along the river's banks. After several weeks in Shanghai, Lucy and her children boarded the SS *President Grant* and sailed for New York. After drinking spoiled milk that the ship's steward insisted was buttermilk because of its sour smell, Duncan and his brother contracted dysentery and nearly died on the long crossing.[35]

Battling amoebic dysentery himself and finally having given up hope, Edmund abandoned China in 1928. He had converted few Chinese by the time he left—since their arrival in the 1830s, Western missionaries had converted less than a fraction of 1 percent of the Chinese to Christianity. Still, his and Lucy's single-minded dedication to a cause they felt was much greater than themselves, together with their willingness to sacrifice everything for it, made an indelible impression on Duncan. He revered his parents and the uncommon lives they pursued.[36]

Duncan would credit Edmund in particular with fostering his idealism; at the same time, he blamed his father for triggering the self-reproach he felt at his inability to live up to his parents' expectations that he would devote his life to serving causes greater than himself. In his family memoir, he brooded at length on his long-dead father: "He was a mystic and a saint, and I was only too aware I was neither. I knew that my inability to share fully his religious faith was a great disappointment to him. It gave him a sense of failure and gave me a deep sense of guilt."[37]

The son would spend the next decade, the 1930s, searching for a way to erase these feeling of inadequacy and preparing to live up to his noble heritage.

While Lucy and her children waited for Edmund to return from China, they started their new life in Washington, DC. In the fall of 1927, she enrolled Duncan in the St. Albans School, on the grounds of the Washington National Cathedral. Edmund joined his family early the next year and began rebuilding his life. For months he traveled widely, sharing his experiences in China with church groups. He also interviewed for jobs at several vacant Episcopal parishes.[38]

In the summer of 1928, he accepted an offer from the Diocese of Southern Virginia to become both the principal of the Chatham Hall School, a preparatory school for girls, and rector of the Emmanuel Episcopal Church in Chatham. Because he had no experience educating girls, he hesitated in taking the position. He decided to assume the challenge after Beverly Dandridge Tucker, rector of St. Paul's Church in Richmond, assured him with a flourish of pseudosociology that American girls were psychologically similar to Chinese boys.

When the Lees came to Chatham Hall, their first task was deciding whether running the small school made sense at all. It was moribund: falling tobacco prices had depressed the local economy, and the consequent decline in enrollments had pushed the school to the brink. Edmund saved the school from bankruptcy by soliciting a gift of $5,000 from the Craddock-Terry Shoe Company in nearby Lynchburg. He and Lucy then stopped the cadets from the neighboring Hargrave Military Academy from roaming the hallways of Chatham Hall's dormitories, tightened security patrols on campus, and built a chapel on school grounds to prevent the same cadets from ogling the girls as they walked to the town's Episcopal church.[39]

Gradually, by offering cheaper tuition than its northern counterparts and raising its academic standards by hiring better faculty, the Lees transformed Chatham Hall into one of the country's finest girls' boarding schools. Lucy's social connection to some of New York City's wealthiest families, coupled with the fame of the Lee name, enabled the school to raise money and build its endowment.[40]

They also improved the lives of African Americans in the racially divided town of Chatham. Edmund persuaded its white leaders to build a community center for the town's sizable black population. He also overcame his own racist feelings and took the lead in integrating the meetings of the Southern Virginia Diocese of the Episcopal Church.[41]

Similarly, Lucy established the Social Gospel–oriented Service League at Chatham Hall, which forced the school's pampered girls to help the town's poor. The northern native also refused to bow to Chatham's Old South racial conventions. Much to the disgust of the small town's white residents, Lucy insisted that all her black visitors use her front entrance instead of the back door.[42]

Edmund was absolutely convinced that he was furthering God's will at Chatham Hall. Once again, he credited his and Lucy's success to the power of prayer and divine guidance. He believed God had found another use for two of his instruments.[43]

After the family moved to Chatham, Edmund decided to send Duncan to the Woodberry Forest School, his alma mater, near Orange, Virginia. Captain Robert Walker, who had served as one of Confederate colonel John Singleton Mosby's Rangers during the Civil War, had founded the boarding school in 1889. His original purpose was modest—to turn a dozen or so local boys each year into what he called "educated gentlemen"—but after visiting the stately Groton School in Massachusetts, he became more ambitious, expanding Woodberry's campus and revolutionizing its curriculum.

Under his guidance and later that of his son, J. Carter Walker, the headmaster when Duncan attended, the school emphasized English, mathematics, history, modern languages, and laboratory sciences. This was a dramatic shift from the traditional preparatory school focus on Latin and Greek. The South needed practically educated men to rebuild the region after the Civil War, and the Walkers were determined that Woodberry Forest would play a leading role in its resurgence. Above all, they believed that their school's greatest purpose was to inspire its students to serve others. Their commitment to providing a modern, practical education and building a Christian character appealed to Edmund and his son.[44]

As a missionary's child, Duncan understood that he had neither independent wealth nor a comfortable family business to retreat into once he finished his studies. His family's enterprise, such as it was, was saving and improving mankind, not earning money and acquiring wealth. To support himself and live up to his parents' high expectations that he equip himself for a life of service, he knew he needed to excel.

Duncan quickly established himself as one of Woodberry Forest's top students. He made the most of his three years there, ranking first in

Latin grammar and translation and in solid geometry. He also honed his leadership skills through extracurricular activities. He joined the debate team, played football, edited the school newspaper, acted in drama club plays, and served on the Board of Prefects, the school's all-important honor court.[45]

As he entered adolescence, he began showing the first glimmer of the self-righteous man he would become. In a precocious letter to his moralistic father, he confided that he was planning to write his term composition on the "ignorant, bigoted spirit in the proletariat, which finds its voice in the Ku Klux Klan."[46]

From his perch at Chatham Hall, Edmund prescribed an additional regimen of study to expand his son's spiritual development beyond the classroom. Duncan read his Bible every day and studied an outline his father had carefully prepared for him. Revealing his independence, however, the boy defiantly set his own agenda for self-improvement. He pushed himself relentlessly and created a rigorous program for himself: "daily exercises and outdoor work, moderate smoking only, read Norman Thomas and *The Nation*, and get from Mother book[s] on Russia and India."[47]

Despite flashes of independence, the boy still very much believed in his parents' Christian teachings. In one of the many letters he wrote to his mother during this time, he mentioned that he had read the Koran and Charles Darwin's *On the Origin of Species*, but he ended his letter contemptuously: "Mohammed and Darwin were great figures in just about the same field—that of deception."[48]

Duncan's stellar academic record at Woodberry Forest made him a strong candidate for admission to many elite colleges. He originally planned to matriculate at the University of Virginia like his father, but the school's well-deserved reputation for alcohol abuse offended him. Lee then considered Princeton University, the alma mater of several Chaplins, including Maxwell, Lucy's beloved dead brother. Princeton's strong ties to the Presbyterian Church appealed to Lucy's deep Masters School roots but not to her Episcopalian son.[49]

In late March 1931, Duncan Lee visited Yale University and fell in love with the school's old campus. Family ties also drew him to New Haven. A first cousin had married Myres Smith McDougal, a Rhodes scholar from Mississippi and a Sterling Fellow at the Yale Law School from 1930 until 1931. Lee applied and was accepted. By then, Woodberry Forest had an established relationship with Yale's undergraduate admissions office. When he arrived in late September 1931, he would be one of thirteen Woodberry Forest students studying in Yale's undergraduate college. Lee's outstanding record at Woodberry Forest— he stood fourth in his class of fifty-one students—led Yale to award him a Southern Alumni Association Scholarship for his freshman and sophomore years. In fact, he received financial aid for all four years.[50]

Before Duncan left for New Haven, Edmund summoned him to his study and warned him about the twin pitfalls of liquor and women. He quoted Robert E. Lee's admonition that the Lees had no head for strong drink and should avoid it. He also told his son that he was absolutely sure that none of his own male first cousins had ever had sex outside marriage. Although Edmund's warnings added to his son's feelings of guilt, they would not stop him from either engaging in premarital sex or drinking alcohol.[51]

Lee entered Yale at a glittering time. Even during the depths of the Great Depression, the New York Times routinely covered the school's athletic, social, and academic events, treating them like major news. Who was elected to Yale's Phi Beta Kappa chapter or captained its football team was just as important to the newspaper as who starred in the latest Hollywood movie or acted in the newest Broadway play. The Yale of the 1930s was also a university in transition. Although it remained strikingly provincial, catering to social and economic elites from the Northeast and the Midwest, with no shortage of swells in attendance, the school had overhauled its curriculum and repositioned itself to remain one of the premier training grounds for America's ruling elites. James Rowland Angell, Yale's president from 1921 to 1937, spearheaded the efforts to transform the university. During his tenure, Angell launched a massive building campaign, greatly enhanced the university's graduate and professional schools, and established Yale's residential college system. This system, based on those at Oxford, Cambridge, and Harvard, aimed at fostering a more intellectual life for Yale's undergraduates. In September 1933, Lee would be among the first residents of Pierson College, one of seven of Angell's new residential colleges.[52]

Lee was among the 846 members of the freshmen class that President Angell personally welcomed to Yale on October 1, 1931. By then, the Great Depression was entering its third year. Even Angell, who shared President Herbert Hoover's beliefs in free enterprise and individual liberty, was moved by the widespread economic and social devastation. In his speech to Lee's class, he reminded its privileged sons that their country was in the throes of an unprecedented economic collapse and that millions of Americans were out of work. Angell appealed to their sense of noblesse oblige: "Nothing we can do to relieve their need must be omitted and nothing that we can learn to do to prevent the recurrence must be left undone."[53]

The Great Depression reached its lowest point during Lee's first two years at Yale. The American economy was disintegrating as the booming era of industrial expansion that had powered it since the Civil War ground to a halt. More than 5,000 banks failed between October 1929 and March 1933, wiping out billions in personal assets. A quarter of America's workforce sat idle by 1933. Even Yale was not spared the Depression's seismic shocks. By September 1933, more than 46 percent of the 704 students listed on that fall's Yale honors list in the *New York Times*, including Lee, had registered at the university's Bureau of Appointments for work-study jobs.[54]

But most of Yale's undergraduates were barely inconvenienced by their country's economic distress. They continued to live financially insulated lives, sprinkled with weekends spent sailing in the Hamptons and summers devoted to perfecting their forehand topspins on country club tennis courts.[55] Unlike many of his classmates, however, Lee was far from wealthy. He tracked every nickel and sent long letters home discussing his tight finances. Academic scholarships, campus jobs waiting tables and shelving books, and money from his parents did give him enough financial freedom to attend football games at the Yale Bowl and debutante balls in New York City. It was a golden time to be at Yale, and he enjoyed it immensely. Senator William Proxmire of Wisconsin, who graduated from the university in 1938, later spoke about the campus's lighthearted mood during the mid-1930s: "If you wanted to be happy, it was a great time to be a Yalie. If you wanted to be serious—you had to wait."[56]

Lee did not want to wait. After Angell's speech, he wrote Lucy that he planned to maximize his time at Yale by using its academics, athletics, and extracurricular offerings to advance his career prospects. He had already set his sights on winning a Rhodes scholarship to Oxford. He closed his letter to his mother with an assurance: "Of course, I needn't say that all through this, I am aiming at spiritual development and a mature stability of thought (however radical)."[57]

Radical thinking did not garner much of Lee's time and attention, however. Instead, he focused on winning as many of Yale's honors as he could. He dove into the school's rich offerings. During his first year, the slight, 5'10", 140-pound Lee played on Yale's freshmen football team (in his senior year, he played for Pierson College's intramural football team), wrestled for the freshman squad (he later wrestled two years for the varsity), joined the debate team, acted in a drama club play, waited on tables in the dining hall, and commenced winning a string of dazzling academic awards.[58]

Lee spent part of his freshman year examining Christianity's ability to meet the country's growing social ills. He also followed Edmund's wishes: in 1931 he had joined the university's principal Protestant student organization, Dwight Hall. He found it disappointing, however, especially its dull meetings led by "earnest, heavy, young men" who believed that prayer could arrest society's ills, and resigned at the end of his third year.[59]

As he continued at Yale, he turned his energies to serving as the debating club's vice president and writing for the *Harkness Hoot*, one of Yale's more outspoken student publications. He also helped found the Yale Political Union to combat the university's apathetic political culture, joined the university's Liberal Club, and served as the head librarian of Pierson College.[60]

What should have been Lee's crowning moment came on May 10, 1934, when Berzelius, one of Yale's six senior societies, tapped him to become a member. His induction was bittersweet. Skull and Bones, the most elite of the six, did not select him, even though the *New York Times* noted that he was "considered to be the best orator at Yale." His disappointment lingered long after he had graduated.[61]

Lee's dedication to his outside activities matched the energy he devoted to his academic efforts. He began his time at Yale with the second-highest grade on his class's Latin entrance examination. In February 1933, he won the Parker Dickson Buck Prize "for the best oration on a subject of a patriotic nature." He went on to win two academic scholarships, as well as all but one of the university's debating and oratory awards, and to collect, like his father, a Phi Beta Kappa key.[62] By the time Lee graduated in 1935 as a scholar of the second rank with an eighty-seven average, he had done honors work in modern European history on the causes of World War I with Professor Harry Rudin, the History Department's premier scholar of European diplomacy. He had also won or been honorably mentioned for six prizes.[63]

Interestingly, his academic prowess was on the same high level as that of several other Soviet-controlled spies of his generation. Guy Burgess, John Cairncross, Anthony Blunt, Harold Adrian Russell "Kim" Philby, Donald Maclean (all members of the NKVD's Cambridge University–recruited Magnificent Five spy ring), and Americans Alger Hiss and Donald Wheeler were all gifted students. By the mid-1930s, the NKVD understood that education, even more than money and social standing, opened the door to the rapidly expanding British and American governing bureaucracies. The Kremlin's spymasters were attracted to academic high fliers as much as those high fliers were attracted to them.

Lee's search for his identity also shaped his academic experience at Yale. Throughout his undergraduate years, he wrestled with weighty philosophical and political questions. While a freshman, he wrote to his mother that "the one certain thing that I have found is that one must do his own thinking in all things, and regarding all his tastes. . . . Remember this, that being your son, I could never be content with a life of selfish culture."[64] In another letter to Lucy, he told her that he was composing an essay about jingoistic patriotism. The essay posed the question "Do you acknowledge any consideration higher than the social duty of supporting your country, right or wrong, in any course she might take?" In a strikingly accurate forecast of his choice in 1942, Lee answered that in a conflict between his conscience and his country, he would follow his conscience.[65]

There were other faint but clear inklings at Yale of what the future held for Lee. For example, he supported Norman Thomas, the Socialist Party's presidential candidate in 1932, but doubted that socialism would work in the United States. Even then, he was adept at compartmentalizing his life and masking his true thoughts and feelings from all but Lucy. Dr. John Scully, his roommate for two years in Pierson College, remembered him as conservative, solemn, and religious but never "anti-Roosevelt."[66]

Despite his flirtation with socialism, Lee left Yale as unpoliticized as when he entered. He had been far more obsessed with winning and attaining academic and social honors than interested in studying Karl Marx or worrying about Adolf Hitler.[67]

Lee's political apathy mirrored that of many other young American men of his generation. He was not yet four years old when the United States brushed aside George Washington's warning about European entanglements and sent its soldiers to fight in Belleau Wood and on the Marne. Before the ink had dried on the principal treaty that ended World War I, the Americans had retreated behind their two vast oceans. On November 19, 1919, the US Senate rejected the Treaty of Versailles and with it President Woodrow Wilson's hope that his country would play a leading role in postwar international affairs. This return to isolationism and self-absorption meant that the United States would not act as a stabilizing force in a Europe that had just witnessed the disintegration of the Austro-Hungarian, Ottoman, and Hohenzollern empires and the overthrow of Russia's Romanovs or in an Asia that faced a militant Japan determined to become the equal of any Western power.

The worst economic crisis the world had known since the Industrial Revolution had followed the Americans' disastrous about-face. While the United States was preoccupied with its own economic collapse, Japan invaded Manchuria in 1931, and Adolf Hitler became Germany's chancellor in 1933. This shocking turn to the right in Japan and Germany jolted those Americans who paid attention to international affairs and convinced them that a new dark age was breaking over Europe and Asia. Lee was about to join their ranks.[68]

As his time at Yale drew to a close, Lee focused on winning a Rhodes scholarship, named for Cecil John Rhodes, the British imperialist and Kimberley diamond baron. When Rhodes died in 1902, his final will established a scholarship program at his alma mater, the University of Oxford. Its terms allotted the United States thirty-two scholarships for two or three years of study at Oxford.

Rhodes's criteria for the winners of his scholarships were as eccentric as the man himself. Unconventionally, Rhodes sought scholars who were "not . . . merely bookworms" but all-around men—women were not eligible to apply until 1976—chosen for their intellectual and personal qualities, including their scholastic attainments, character, interest in their fellow students, leadership instincts, and physical vigor. Above all, Rhodes wanted his scholars to be the best men for what he called the "world's fight." By 1935, this meant choosing applicants who did not believe that isolationism was an acceptable policy for a country as powerful and important as the United States. Lee, with his honors work on the causes of World War I, other academic and social awards, athletics, and inherited idealism, was a natural candidate. He understood well the scholarship's allure and cachet, and he carefully planned his activities at Yale to make himself a likely winner. But despite his considerable efforts, he did not succeed on his first try.[69]

Lee reapplied in the autumn of 1934. In his essay for the scholarship, he wrote that he wanted to study law at Oxford so that he could make himself "something more than the ordinary practitioner with a scrap-bag full of uncorrelated fragments of information." His seven letters of recommendation were solid endorsements. Myres McDougal wrote the chairman of the Virginia Rhodes scholarship selection committee that his relative by marriage had a first-class mind, an unusual gift of expression, and a pleasing personality. He also pointed out that Lee had been raised in "an atmosphere of culture and altruistic public service." Leonard W. Labaree, an assistant professor of history at Yale, noted that although not brilliant, Lee's work with him had been marked by "interest, initiative, independence, and faithful accomplishment of a superior order." Another of his Yale professors pointed out that Lee was a "thorough gentleman, earnest, high-minded, tactful, clean, and honorable, and a man of unusual intellectual power and promise."[70]

On January 8, 1935, Lee was one of four Rhodes scholars selected from Yale. Three days later, Edmund congratulated him: "The world certainly needs just the things you should have to offer, and while we must take a modest estimate of the particular point of vantage at which you will apply your lever, I have no doubt that it will be a real force and will be exerted in the right direction."[71]

Many years later, when Lee brooded over his time at Yale, he focused on neither his remarkable scholastic achievements nor his enviable social record. Instead, he dwelt again on how often Edmund's legacy had shadowed him during those developmentally critical years: "All through my early years, including my years at Yale, I was ridden by a sense of guilt that I could not share the quality of my father's faith or emulate his life of service or even the high standards of personal conduct, which he observed and expected of his children."[72]

Although a sense of inadequacy and guilt may have been hidden leitmotifs during his four years at Yale, the university did inculcate many things in Lee. Above all, it taught him to question. For the first time in his life, Lee began questioning Christianity's infallibility and its power to arrest and solve the mammoth social and economic problems spawned by the seeming collapse of capitalism.

As importantly, Yale gave him the means to win a Rhodes scholarship and to study at Oxford. There, he would meet his first wife, travel to a militarized Nazi Germany, see firsthand the wonders of Joseph Stalin's workers' paradise, and encounter the precipitating circumstances that would lead him to spy against his own country. At a highly politicized Oxford, he would select his own way to exorcise his deep guilt and to contribute to mankind's salvation.

TWO

"A NURSERY OF SOMEWHAT REVOLUTIONARY IDEAS"

On September 25, 1935, Duncan Lee boarded the SS *Washington* in New York Harbor and sailed for the English port city of Plymouth. As the luxury steamer pitched and rolled during its seven-day crossing of the gale-swept Atlantic Ocean, Lee and his fellow Rhodes scholars exchanged bits of wisdom about Oxford gleaned from books or learned from members of their selection committees.[1]

Lee's class was as geographically and economically diverse as any of the twenty-seven classes of American Rhodes scholars before it. His thirty-one classmates came from all over the United States, including Colorado's sugar beet fields, North Dakota's plains, and Virginia's Piedmont. One member had grown up in a Washington State tent house with no running water or electricity. Another was the son of an immigrant shoemaker. The class also included three Jews. Despite this diversity, nine members had graduated from Ivy League universities; several more had graduated from exclusive American preparatory schools.[2]

After a week of sightseeing in London, Lee went "up" to Oxford on October 8. From his readings, Lee knew that the university comprised a number of colleges. While still at Yale, he had written Beverly Tucker, his father's old mentor and a Rhodes scholar from the

Class of 1905, to ask which he should attend. Tucker recommended Christ Church, his own college and Oxford's most aristocratic.[3]

Christ Church assigned Lee to Room Number 2, Staircase I, in the Meadow Building, its least fashionable student housing. Arnold Cantwell Smith, a Canadian Rhodes scholar, lived in the same building and was Lee's closest friend at Oxford. Later, Smith served as a diplomat in the Canadian embassy in Moscow during World War II. Afterward, in an ironic twist, he acted as secretary to the 1946 Kellock-Taschereau Royal Commission, created by Mackenzie King, Canada's prime minister, to investigate the Soviets' penetration of the Canadian government during the war.[4]

After eating his habitual college breakfast of eggs and sausages, Lee routinely attended lectures in jurisprudence, rowed in one of Christ Church's boats on the River Isis, a tributary of the Thames, and prepared a weekly essay on a legal topic for his tutor, who recorded that Lee "is very keen and has plenty of industry and good sense. He reached a good B standard and is most pleasant to work with." During his first week, Lee joined the left-leaning Labour Club as well as the right-leaning Conservative Association to sample Oxford's political life to the fullest. He also joined the Oxford Union, the university's premier debating society.[5]

Lee's three years at Oxford were the most formative of his life. While he learned how to think at Woodberry Forest and Yale, he learned what to think at Oxford. He arrived in the autumn of 1935 searching for himself and what to believe. He found both at an Oxford more politicized that it had been at any other time in its nearly seven-hundred-year history. The choices he made in this highly charged atmosphere determined the course of his life.

If, on its surface, the Oxford Lee attended between 1935 and 1938 seemed the same idyllic place it had always been, it assuredly was not. Unlike at Yale, the Great Depression's economic devastation and fascism's march had gotten the attention of even Oxford's most self-absorbed students. While most remained on the political sidelines, safely wrapped in the Conservative Party's grouse moor complacency, a conspicuous minority proved more venturesome and outspoken. This was especially true for those on the political left and for the Rhodes scholars.

None of this was lost on the shrewd warden of Rhodes House, Carleton Kemp Allen, an Oxford graduate and veteran of World War I's trenches. In his 1935–1936 annual report to the Rhodes Trustees, he lamented that many Rhodes scholars found Oxford "a nursery of somewhat revolutionary ideas." He believed the American Rhodes scholarship selection committees were in the habit of sending him left-wing troublemakers. And yet, in an admirable display of realism and tolerance, the buttoned-down Allen later admitted to one of the trustees, "We cannot help it if Rhodes scholars become Communists and it is perfectly certain in the present state of affairs that an increasing number of them will do so. . . . It is not a circumstance which is palatable to oneself, but clearly we can do nothing and ought to do nothing about it."[6]

Allen understood that Rhodes had expected his scholars to participate fully in Oxford's intellectual life, which by 1935 was decidedly red. When Lee arrived in Oxford, the university was only seventeen years removed from the blood-soaked battlefields of World War I. That horrible experience and its echoes had converted the ancient university into the perfect petri dish to nurture Lee's questioning of his Christian faith and growing need to find his own way to serve mankind. Lee's exposure to this milieu transformed him from a mild, mostly apolitical socialist into a future communist willing to spy against his own country.

Between 1914 and 1918, Oxford's constituent social elites had been shot to pieces in four years of massive-scale annihilation. Not since the fifteenth century's Wars of the Roses had England's leading families seen so much bloodshed. By the November 11, 1918, armistice, one in four British and Irish peers had perished in the conflict.[7]

Oxford and Cambridge suffered especially numbing losses. Expected to lead from the front, the British army's Oxbridge-educated junior officers were far likelier to be killed going "over the top" than the working-class men they led. An Oxford or Cambridge student's odds of dying in the war were at least five times greater than those of the common soldier. Many of these junior officers simply disappeared into the mass graves that dotted such killing fields as the Somme and Passchendaele.[8]

Just over 29 percent of the young men who matriculated at Oxford between 1910 and 1914 had lost their lives on the western front. All told, the university lost 2,569 men over the course of the war at a time when its yearly undergraduate population never exceeded 3,000 students. Survivors of this "Lost Generation" had grown bitterly disillusioned with the lingering Edwardian values they blamed for this massive carnage.[9]

In the 1920s, Oxonians had retreated from this bloodletting into intense bouts of nihilism and hedonism; students became strikingly apathetic about anything other than athletics and aesthetics. The 1930s, however, brought a different political climate to the university's dreaming spires. By then, the aftershocks of Wall Street's 1929 crash had smashed with full force into Britain's economy. The Great Depression laid bare the country's intrinsic economic weaknesses. Imperialism had allowed successive British governments to ignore their country's international competitors, even while their German and American rivals industrialized at a dizzying pace. As late as 1938, a third of the British people still lived below the poverty line, while another third barely kept their heads above it. The last third, however, lived quite comfortably.[10]

This paradox of poverty amid plenty stoked the fires of political discontent. Hundreds of the privileged sons of Oxford and Cambridge, who had benefited the most from capitalism's excesses, became its harshest critics. Becoming so-called traitors to their class eased their gnawing personal guilt and produced a keen sense of moral superiority. On some level, their apostasy also satisfied an emotional need to rebel against an economic and class system that had greatly favored them.[11]

In 1931, communist cells formed at Cambridge and the University of London. Their members vowed to save Britain by following the teachings of Karl Marx and Vladimir Lenin. Oxford soon followed; two years later, by 1933, its communist October Club counted roughly three hundred members. That same year the Oxford Union, still reflecting World War I's devastating impact on the university, voted 275 to 153 "that this House will in no circumstances fight for its King and Country."[12]

Political disillusionment and capitalism's seeming collapse contributed partially to communism's draw. For those who believed that a new dark age had dawned, the great democracies' failure to curb fascism's bottomless appetite for violence answered any lingering questions about communism's merits. Foreign aggression went unchallenged. In March 1935, Hitler announced his intention to rearm Germany and violate the 1919 Treaty of Versailles. Italy's dictator Benito Mussolini invaded Ethiopia seven months later. In March 1936, Hitler remilitarized the Rhineland.[13]

But it was the Spanish Civil War that electrified Oxford and Cambridge, carrying for many students all the romantic overtones of a crusade. Virginia Woolf called their obsession with Spain "a fever in the blood of the younger generation." The Spanish olive groves pulled them as strongly as the Grecian groves had pulled Lord Byron in 1823, when he went to fight the Ottoman Turks in Greece's war of independence. It was chic to care about the happenings in Spain in the mid-1930s. Events there enthralled Lee and pushed him to the left.[14]

By the summer of 1936, Spain, a country that had not counted for much on the international scene since it became Napoleon's "bleeding ulcer" during his 1808–1814 Peninsular Campaign, was ground zero in the struggle between democracy and fascism. Earlier that year, a wobbly coalition of various Spanish socialist, communist, and liberal parties had eked out a very narrow election victory over an amalgam of right-wing parties. The new Republican government never found its balance because of internal rifts and waves of political assassinations.[15]

On July 17, 1936, right-wing generals, including General Francisco Franco, the hero of Spain's Catholic Church and its conservative middle class, attempted to overthrow the Republicans. Germany and Italy immediately backed this coup for their own internal reasons and sent arms and troops to promote its success. Hitler and Mussolini's actions transformed a provincial civil war, with causes deeply rooted in the tangled underbrush of Spanish history, into a twilight struggle between good and evil. Many on the left believed the Spanish Civil War represented their best chance to stop fascism in its tracks.[16]

In sharp contrast with Germany and Italy, Britain, France, and the United States remained neutral. Only the Soviet Union rallied to the Republicans' side, sending arms and military advisers. Its Communist International (Comintern) also sponsored and recruited international brigades of foreign fighters. Stalin's actions enormously raised the Soviet Union's prestige in the eyes of the left. Although some on the left—such as novelist and essayist George Orwell, who wrote an account of his experiences fighting for the Republicans—understood Stalin's intent after seeing Spain for themselves, most who cheered the Soviet dictator's actions did not grasp that he was using the civil war to burnish his international image, shift attention away from his own internal purges, murder Trotskyists, and test his generals' field tactics.[17]

Lee did not become a Soviet spy while at Oxford, but his experiences there prepared him for recruitment later on. Although his mother Lucy had no way to know this, she worried about Oxford's sway over her impressionable son. In early March 1936, feeling uneasy, she wrote to ask how the university was influencing his philosophy and morality and reminded him of his inexperience and immaturity. Lee fired back testily that he was "very much in the throes of intellectual maturity," adding, "You must realize that in finding my experience and working out my salvation, I can no longer turn to anyone but myself."[18]

That stance changed two months later. At a dance in late May 1936 at the Ruskin School of Drawing and Fine Art, Lee met and was immediately drawn to Isabella Mary Ann Scott Gibb, a willowy young woman with chestnut hair and piercing blue eyes. After she told him of her interest in the American Civil War, he boasted of his blood ties to Robert E. Lee. The next day, he sent her a note, formally addressed "Dear Miss Gibb," inviting her to see Shakespeare's As You Like It at Stratford-upon-Avon. That August, they were engaged.[19]

Isabella's influence on Lee at Oxford was just as profound as his parents' in China a decade before. At the same time that he offered his fiancée a new life in the United States, she pointed him toward a new path that turned sharply to the left.

Ishbel, as her family called her, was born on October 12, 1913, in Allahabad, India. Thomas Gibb, her Scottish father, was a commissioner in the Excise Service. Katherine Scott Gibb, her mother, was the headstrong daughter of a Scottish estate manager and a justice of the peace.

Ishbel's childhood was typical for a British child raised in the early twentieth-century Indian Raj. On Sundays, a phalanx of armed British soldiers accompanied her and her family to Church of Scotland services. This weekly escort underscored to the young girl that she was an unwelcome foreign occupier.[20]

She saw Motilal Nehru, her family's neighbor and father of Jahawarlal Nehru, India's first prime minister, arrested and tried after he refused to pay his taxes to the British government. Her father testified against him. She also was in India when Mohandas Gandhi started his Non-cooperation Movement, aimed at peacefully boycotting British-made goods.[21]

Although Ishbel was too young for these events to make a large impression, another one did. She became enraged when she saw bored British soldiers, high atop their Moghul fort, shooting for entertainment at partially cremated Indian corpses floating in the Ganges River. When she was ten years old, her family sent her back to Scotland for school. She later read modern history at Oxford's Somerville College, then one of its four all-women's colleges.

Between her weekly history tutorials and lectures, Ishbel immersed herself in Oxford's left-wing politics. She spent her time at the university searching for independence and forgetting the scenes of her childhood. She joined the Labour Club and the Oxford Union. Ishbel was in the audience that heady night when the union voted not to fight for king and country. She also raised money for the Republicans in Spain, believing that the best way to keep Britain out of another world war. She graduated with second-class honors in 1935 and went to work at Selfridges department store in London. Her job allowed her to visit her mother, who lived in Oxford, on weekends.[22]

In a letter home, Lee described Ishbel to his mother, praising her values and "very genuine ideal of service," then admitting that she was not as socially sophisticated as American girls. He also noted her intensity: "She can get utterly absorbed in a conversation and spill ashes over herself without noticing."[23]

In many ways, Lee and Ishbel meshed perfectly: both were in revolt against their respective missionary and colonial pasts and in rebellion against their fathers' unyielding faiths. Lee knew he could never share Edmund's unquestioning belief that Christianity would save the world from all evils, and he wanted to rely on his own intellect and experiences instead. Similarly, Ishbel did not share her father's unshakeable belief in the British Empire's goodness and grace. Only the left seemed to offer her a replacement for it.

There was another, more fundamental, attraction: Lee was drawn to strong-willed and intellectually confident women. Lucy had been his sounding board, his priest, and his confidant since he was a small boy, but she was now 3,000 miles away. He needed another independent-minded woman in whom to confide, and he chose Ishbel to satisfy this psychological need. Although he never admitted certain things to either of them, he gave these two women, more than anyone else, access to his inner self. Neither woman would betray Lee's confidences, no matter how much he disappointed or hurt them.

Ishbel also offered him sexual liberation. This did not make his mother happy. Lucy and Edmund came to Oxford in the summer of 1936 to tour England and meet Ishbel, who clearly appeared to be spending a great deal of time in their son's Christ Church rooms. In London, Lucy lectured the young couple for a day and a night on responsibility and respectability. In a frank letter thanking her, Ishbel told Lucy that her words had fallen on deaf ears: "I'm afraid you will be disappointed that we have decided to go on as we were doing before."[24]

In that same letter, she divulged Lee's growing attraction to socialism: "I am tremendously interested in this new interest he is taking in Socialist theory and practice. I was afraid he would always be too cautious and broad-minded to be a thoroughgoing Socialist, but now he is convincing himself so thoroughly, it will be twice as valuable as too great readiness—so many people in Oxford are all enthusiasm and no knowledge."[25]

She was not the only force pulling him in that direction. In 1936, Lee visited Germany twice. He went to Munich that April, right after Hitler remilitarized the Rhineland, the region of Germany controlled by France after World War I. Back in January 1935, the Saarland had voted by plebiscite to rejoin Germany. In March 1936, Hitler occupied it with 3,000 troops, despite its still being a demilitarized zone under the Treaty of Versailles. In a letter to Lucy from Munich, Lee commented worriedly on the country's growing militarism and what he called its "great glorification of the soldier."[26]

He took Ishbel to Germany that summer after his parents' visit to Britain. On a hike near Hitler's mountain retreat at Berchtesgaden, they encountered two Nazis. The men approved of her light, sun-bleached hair but chastised him as decadent after he mentioned loving American jazz.[27]

In an undated letter to his mother that summer from Bavaria, Lee announced that despite his admiration for Hitler's deft handling of Germany's economy, "I am hating fascism more and more. . . . Its renunciation of intellectualism, internationalism, and civil liberties simply aren't worth it." He also informed her that Ishbel had gotten a new job teaching Latin, English, and history at Langdon Grove, a school in Malden, Essex, alleging that her radical politics might make for a brief stay. "I strongly suspect," he confided, that "she intends to make communists out of the whole lot of them, and I hope she does not get tossed out for her pains."[28]

When Lee returned to Oxford in the fall of 1936, he decided to visit the Soviet Union before the school year ended, though he didn't actually go until late the following summer. A trip there, he wrote Lucy, was "about as important a matter as any contribution to my experience here that I can think of." Another of his letters home sharply criticized the British government, denouncing its neutrality in the Spanish Civil War as "wholly indefensible." That same fall, Ishbel shared with Lucy Lee's growing infatuation with communism and his talk of joining the Communist Party. Lee's attacks on Christianity were almost as disturbing to his parents, who supported the Episcopal Church and the mild brand of socialism advocated by Norman Thomas, the six-time presidential candidate of the Socialist Party of

America. While still in Germany, he jolted Edmund by writing that the Christian Church suffocated human nobility under a "whole body of dogmatic teachings" and that he was about "to read the Gospels from the point of view of Christ as a humanitarian and socialist."[29]

Lee's letters home in the first half of 1937 continued to reflect his growing radicalism and Ishbel's influence, containing news of Spain and discussions of the ills of capitalism, his fading belief in his parents' God, and the British Empire's obsolescence. On January 3, he wrote his mother that Ishbel had returned extremely agitated from a weekend in Cambridge spent in meetings about Spain. He reported that she had cut down her cigarettes to only five a day to save money for the Republicans and that "this is not as trivial as it sounds. It is not an altogether academic question when several men you know have been killed in action." Although Ishbel and Lee were committed to the Republicans, their devotion was intellectual and emotional. Neither considered fighting in one of the international brigades or driving an ambulance. One of Lee's Rhodes scholar classmates was more daring: Donald Wheeler became a communist and went to Paris, where he served as a Republican courier.[30]

Spain was not Lee's only concern. On May 10, he wrote Lucy about *Time*'s publication of photographs of a lynching in Mississippi. Although he applauded the magazine's decision to showcase these brutal pictures, he warned that America's race problem would remain unsolved until the country's capitalist institutions were overthrown. Two months later, he acknowledged having become a "qualified agnostic," preaching that "a man must go through the mill of Marxist discipline and emerge a bit further on."[31]

Disillusioned with God and capitalism, Lee looked to Karl Marx and the Soviet Union for answers. In April 1937, he wrote to the Society for Cultural Relations with the USSR, asking it to introduce him to a Soviet law student. The society, always on the lookout for intellectuals interested in visiting the Soviet Union, directed him to a lawyers' tour to Leningrad and Moscow that Dudley Collard, a well-known barrister who often represented the Communist Party of Great Britain (CPGB), was leading that August. In 1937, Collard had penned a shameless apology for that January's show trial of seventeen

"Old Bolsheviks," whom Stalin had charged with conspiring with Leon Trotsky to overthrow him. Collard ridiculed as "pure nonsense" the notion common among Soviet exiles that Stalin was "polishing off his old associates." He also pronounced the sentences handed down—thirteen defendants were shot and four were sent to die in labor camps—"as proper." Collard's stamp of legal approval gave this sham trial and those that followed a patina of legitimacy that eased the troubled consciences of rank-and-file CPGB members uncomfortable with the savage outcomes.[32]

While waiting to leave for the Soviet Union, Lee sat for his examinations in jurisprudence. Although consumed by his growing political awareness and with finding his own path, he never abandoned his work ethic. He took his legal studies very seriously, and his tutors had high expectations for him, convinced he would receive first-class honors, the university's highest level. Instead, Lee matched Ishbel's performance and that of most other Rhodes scholars, receiving a respectable second-class honors degree.

In a July 1937 report to the Rhodes scholarship selection committee that had chosen Lee, Carleton Allen, the Rhodes House warden, pinpointed Lee's undoing: "His industry was almost too great, and I suspect he may have worked himself into a somewhat stale condition for his final examinations." Despite this, Allen noted that Lee's second-class degree "was very sound and creditable, and that he has a marked aptitude for the law." He volunteered that Lee's character was "full of admirable qualities" and that his classmates generally liked him.[33]

The results disappointed Lee but were academically good enough to secure a third year at Oxford at Cecil Rhodes's expense and an opportunity to read for a postgraduate bachelor of civil law (BCL) degree, then widely considered the best general law degree in the British Empire. Another year at Oxford also meant more time with Ishbel.[34]

Before commencing his third year, Lee wanted to see the Soviet Union. On August 8, 1937, he and Ishbel went to the London Bridge and boarded the *Andrei Zhdanov*, a small Soviet steamer. That same day, Lee wrote to Lucy on the steamer's hammer-and-sickle stationery, describing their fellow passengers as an "odd mixture of tourists and Red intellectuals." This mixture included Daniel Boorstin, a Rhodes scholar from the Class of 1934, a future member of the American Communist Party, and later a conservative historian and Librarian of Congress, and Willie Gallacher, the CPGB's first elected member of Parliament. Lee assured Lucy that "Collard seems to know his stuff and should make a good leader."[35]

They arrived on August 12 in Leningrad, where their Soviet handlers deposited them at the luxurious Hotel Europa. Later that day and the next, their guides from Intourist, the Soviet state-run travel agency, gave them a whirlwind tour of the city's vast treasures, including the Winter Palace and the Hermitage. On the night of August 13, Lee and Ishbel took a special train to Moscow, pulled by a wood-burning locomotive that spewed sparks and ashes into the warm summer air. Their train had comfortable sleepers and no crowds, luxuries beyond the dreams of the average Soviet citizen. Lee's first postcard home was besotted: "Moscow surpasses all expectations. Perfectly unbelievable."[36]

Many Western intellectuals who took these carefully shepherded pilgrimages had the same giddy reaction to this "workers' paradise." Making this all the more remarkable, by the late summer of 1937 Stalin's "Great Terror" was in full hemorrhage. When Lee and Ishbel stepped off their train in Moscow, blood was flowing in the cells of the city's Lubyanka Prison and in the gloomy forests on its outskirts. Stalin, in the throes of crazed paranoia and violent counterrevolutionary zeal, had set out to rid himself of any real or imagined internal threats. His NKVD henchmen executed 750,000 Soviet citizens between 1936 and 1938. His People's Courts sentenced another 750,000 to die in frozen Siberian gulags.[37]

The Intourist hosts kept Lee and Ishbel well away from Stalin's stockyard-like killing machinery. Installed in Moscow in another first-class hotel, this one directly across the river from the Kremlin, they visited Lenin's tomb and house, where they heard a recording of his voice. They also watched three judges of Moscow's City Court preside over some minor cases and interviewed a group of Soviet attorneys at Moscow's Collegium of Lawyers. Afterward, Ishbel and Lee attended a vodka-soaked reception with several of the lawyers "defending" a handful of those fingered by Stalin as traitors. Lee reported in a letter to Lucy that the reception's food was "unnecessarily sumptuous."[38]

Lee's group visited the Bolshevo Penal Settlement, a Potemkin village, whose mayor, a former rapist and murderer, lectured the group about mankind's need for proper work and wages. Lee was amazed when the mayor claimed to need no guards and no fences to keep the settlement's inmates from escaping; instead, he bragged, he relied wholly on the threat of expulsion to keep the inhabitants in line.[39]

Ishbel toured a maternity hospital and interviewed a social worker who sent periodic postcards to local prostitutes, reminding them when it was time for their venereal disease tests. As on their first date, Ishbel and Lee saw a Shakespeare comedy, this time at the Bolshoi Theatre. Completely captivated, they arrived back in London on August 30.[40]

The NKVD's documents on Lee contain no evidence that its officers assessed and recruited him while he visited the Soviet Union. On the surface, this seems odd. The NKVD traditionally used these boat trips to screen potential recruits. They had relied on a similar trip in August 1935 to assess American Michael Straight, a Cambridge student and the scion of a wealthy family that ran the *New Republic* magazine. Anthony Blunt, one of the NKVD's infamous Magnificent Five spies, traveled with Straight. Blunt would recruit him in 1937 to penetrate the US government.[41]

No one recruited Lee in Moscow because the NKVD and the Chief Intelligence Directorate (GRU), its military counterpart, were in bloody tatters. Stalin had turned the NKVD loose on itself in March 1937 as part of his campaign to purge the Soviet Union of counter-revolutionaries. By that year's end, 3,000 of the commissariat's most experienced officers lay buried in mass graves. Even if the NKVD had evaluated Lee that August, it had almost no experienced officers left to enlist him.[42]

Shortly after his return, Lee wrote Lucy that the Soviet Union had exceeded his "wildest dreams." In his next letter, he stunned his parents by announcing that he and Ishbel were planning to join the Communist Party of Great Britain.[43]

In a mixture of scripted lecture and outright rebellion, Lee explained to his parents that he was embarking on a new path toward his own spiritual salvation. After cutting them to the bone with his declaration that he had found his own religion in communism—"I find the Communist Party a far nearer embodiment of what I regard as genuine Christianity than any organized church"—he shocked them even further with his plan to join the party's secret underground. This, he claimed, would allow him to maintain "some security" while engaging in "Party work denied to an open member." (Whether he understood that this work might include espionage is unclear.) Not joining the party at all, he warned, would force him into what he labeled as "ineffectual armchair pinkness," a cowardly option he could no longer live with.[44]

On September 19, 1937, Lee declared in another letter to his mother that he was renouncing his parents' pacifism. He admonished Lucy that only force could counter fascism and predicted a coming revolution. He also reminded her, in language Karl Marx would have applauded, that "the possessing class shows everywhere that it will defend what it has with massacres, suicidal war, anything. . . . We are merely discovering the means of resistance and self-defense."[45]

Ishbel wrote to Lucy that same day, bubbling that the Soviet Union was "a paradise for mothers and children." She confirmed that Lee planned to join the Communist Party. "I think," she ventured, "that is the very best thing he could do at the moment on which to focus the social impulses that Russia has stimulated so much in both of us."[46]

Appalled, Lucy and Edmund cabled their son immediately, pleading with him not to ruin his brilliant future. When Lee replied, he blamed fascism for driving him into the Communist Party's arms: "The trip to Russia, the Spanish Civil War, and the horrors of what is going on inside China have just brought matters to a head. It is simply delusion to imagine there is any possible middle choice between Hitler and Stalin. . . . The Communists are the only ones with the slightest grip on realities, and because they have found the realities they are in a position to offer the most effective opposition to the menace of Fascism." And in words that Edmund himself might have spoken before he left for China, Lee told his father, "Any other course than joining would be a complete betrayal of myself. . . . It is a case of must and nothing short of that."[47]

His parents refused to give in. Although excited by their son's trip to the Soviet Union, they had never expected him to come back a convert to communism and a disciple of Karl Marx. Lee wanted their approval; instead, they were horrified.

By mid-October, he and Ishbel had agreed not to join the Communist Party until they could support themselves financially. Lee made it clear to his parents, however, that "Isabella and I both feel that the necessity of eventually joining the CP is pretty inescapable." He then tried placating them in another letter with a lie: "I rejoice at what for the moment I can regard as an honorable excuse for staying out of the Party," he wrote Lucy. "I never *wanted* to join, you know."[48]

On the surface, Lee was as much drawn to communism as Edmund had been to the Student Volunteer Movement over three decades before. Both father and son wanted to save and remake mankind. Belief that only the Gospel, preached by him and others, could liberate heathen peoples from sin weighed on Edmund much as a personal call to rescue the world from enslavement by advancing fascism weighed on his son. The self-sacrifice and the righteousness of their causes aroused both men. Their family's bold heritage, showcased in the American Revolution and Civil War, of taking great risks and making bold stands demanded no less of them.

Lee's embrace of communism also filled a critical psychological need. Under Ishbel's tutelage, he finally had broken free of his parents' gravitational pull and struck out on his own. He must have understood that true communism aimed to destroy Edmund's church and religion. Still Lee believed that his father's God was too weak to stop Adolf Hitler's hypnotic rants or root out capitalism's ingrained rot.

Only the Soviet Union seemed to offer a way forward. Lee had now found a means to erase his feelings of guilt and inadequacy. Mankind's fate hung in the balance, and he would enlist in the only cause he thought could save it. Communism also offered him, just as the Social Gospel gave Lucy, a hands-on way of acting.

Yet Edmund's faith in Christianity differed from his son's faith in communism in a key way. Edmund truly believed that God had called him to become a priest, a missionary, and a schoolmaster. Lee had come to communism with Ishbel's help and, as she observed in one of her letters to Lucy, by "convincing himself so thoroughly." Whose faith was stronger and more resilient would become clearer in the years ahead.

Lucy finally buckled under the strain. Living with Edmund in a small, rural Virginia town with a Confederate monument in front of its courthouse had been challenging enough. Now one of her children had decided to become a communist. He also had decided to get married. On April 24, 1938, Lee and Ishbel's formal engagement announcement appeared in the *Danville Register*, his parents' local newspaper. That June, a physically and emotionally exhausted Lucy underwent psychiatric treatment at the Austen Riggs Foundation in Stockbridge, Massachusetts. While they would remain close, Lee never again wrote to his mother with the same frequency or deep intimacy.[49]

Six days after his engagement announcement appeared, Lee proudly marched with Oxford University's delegation in London's May Day celebration. In an undated letter to her shortly after the march, he predicted a fascist coup d'état in France and a "black night of barbarism all over Europe." All this, he concluded, is "enough to make you weep." Lee also defended Stalin's show trials. In a letter that would have made Collard proud, he castigated his brother Armistead for his "liberal revulsion at the Executive's strong arm."[50]

As at Yale, however, Lee did not share his political beliefs with his Oxford classmates. Only Daniel Boorstin, who had traveled with him and Ishbel to the Soviet Union, knew about his communist leanings. Once, though, his new creed percolated to the surface. In early May 1938, he joined a busload of Rhodes scholars on a trip to Cliveden, Lady Nancy Astor's country home. No longer able to restrain himself publicly, Lee chided her in front of at least two classmates, commenting that Cliveden would make "a wonderful rest home for the workers." The American-born Astor's retort was as witty as her speeches in Parliament: "Yes, when you Bolshies take over, I hope someone will get some rest. I certainly don't get any now."[51]

Two months before this confrontation, Lee learned that the Yale Law School had awarded him a Sterling Fellowship for its 1938–1939 school year. By then, university President Angell had improved and modernized the law school's faculty and curriculum. Both now emphasized the importance of social forces for legal precedents. Angell also had given the law school a new building. Myres McDougal, Lee's Rhodes scholar relative, persuaded him that he needed to spend a year studying American law as a graduate student at Yale before he "tackled Wall Street."[52]

When he offered this advice, McDougal knew nothing about his relative's plans to join the Communist Party. He did know that Lee still depended on Lucy and Edmund for money and that the Yale Law School funneled a large number of its graduates into New York City's top-paying law firms. McDougal's advice convinced Lee that a Wall Street practice would provide excellent legal training. In similar financial straits and with a new wife, Alger Hiss, later one of the Soviets' spies inside the State Department, made the same choice: in 1932, he briefly joined a New York City law firm with several Wall Street clients.[53]

Lee found it difficult to reconcile his dreams of working for what he called the "cause" and practicing law on Wall Street. He confided to Lucy, "I am haunted by the specter of the Babbitt-brained lawyer and all he stands for." Despite this, he would never leave the Establishment. He wanted to have it both ways. In this, he was no different from the Soviets' Cambridge spies, who were unwilling to abandon their comfortable backgrounds and became prominent figures in the British Broadcast Corporation, the Foreign Office, and the intelligence services. Not until absolutely at the end of their ropes did Guy Burgess, Donald Maclean, and Kim Philby flee to Moscow's drab apartments and cheap vodka. Only one thing set them and Lee apart from their ruling-class peers: they spied against their countries.[54]

In June 1938, Lee took his BCL examinations and received another solid second-class honors degree. He then married Ishbel on June 18 in a religious ceremony at a small Presbyterian church in Oxford. He had reluctantly bowed to Edmund's wishes for a religious ceremony after his father warned "that a failure to have the service, to the extent it was known, would injure your influence. This, taken with your radical beliefs, if known, would cause you to be regarded as a 'Godless Communist,' which would tend to reduce greatly any influence you may be able to assert in the cause you have at heart."[55]

Still, Lee brooded over this capitulation. In a letter to his mother, he told her, "We most certainly do not want to build up any reputation for 'god-less communism' on non-essentials which do not prejudice the basic integrity of our position. That, of course, is where life will always be so hard. . . . It is going to be so terribly easy to start in on a course of minor retreats which will end up in the impotence of parlour radicalism."[56]

The couple spent a modest honeymoon in Amberley, on the edge of the Cotswolds, near Oxford. Lee returned to Chatham Hall that July, and Ishbel followed him to southern Virginia that August. In September, they moved to New Haven. They were now ready to take the "pretty inescapable" step he had warned his parents about after he returned from the Soviet Union.[57]

THREE

THE PARTY

On August 27, 1940, a tall, strapping woman walked into the FBI's New Haven field office. Katharine Robb Rawles Nangle had come to warn J. Edgar Hoover's agents about Duncan and Ishbel Lee, her two former tenants. She would give the FBI its most complete picture of the Lees' immersion in New Haven's radical politics and their earliest days as members of the Communist Party of the United States of America.

Katharine Nangle was one of thousands of well-meaning citizens who flooded the bureau that summer with reports about suspected Nazi and communist subversives. By then, Hitler and Stalin had dismembered Poland. The Nazi leader had also conquered Denmark, Norway, the Low Countries, and France. Many Europeans believed that so-called fifth columnists had undermined these countries' defenses and made Hitler's lightning-quick victories possible.[1]

There was some truth to this. Although Hitler's armed forces easily pulverized any resistance, the Nazis had used covertly organized sympathizers in Austria in 1938 and Czechoslovakia in 1939 to help annex both countries. And in 1940, Norwegian politician Vidkun Quisling sabotaged his country's mobilization against Germany's invasion and set up a puppet government.[2]

All this shook President Franklin Roosevelt. On May 26, 1940, he unnerved his fellow Americans with news of subversives in one of his fireside chats: "We know of new methods of attack. The Trojan Horse. The fifth column that betrays a nation unprepared for treachery. Spies, saboteurs and traitors are the new actors in this tragedy." The president's radio broadcast triggered a brief wave of hysteria. On a single day in late May, the FBI received nearly 3,000 reports from jittery Americans about suspected acts of sabotage.[3]

Three months after the president's broadcast, as the Battle of Britain raged in the skies over England, Katharine Nangle decided to go to the FBI. She had given the government information before. In 1923, while returning to her home in Indiana after serving for a year as a missionary nurse in China, she took photographs of Tokyo's harbor from her passenger ship's porthole and sent them to the US Navy. Nangle's experiences in China convinced her that Japan was a threat to the United States. She now suspected that the Lees planned to harm her country.[4]

She informed the interviewing agent that the Lees were communists. She knew this, she said, because she and her husband had gotten to know the young couple well when they rented the third floor of the Nangles' house at 23 Livingston Street in New Haven between 1938 and 1939. Ishbel, in particular, was radical and preached communism's virtues whenever she could.

The Lees' close proximity had given Nangle an ideal opportunity to talk with them and observe their daily activities. From the outset, she noticed that they owned several travel posters bearing the hammer and sickle and many books on communism. When Nangle asked Ishbel why the Lees read these books, she replied that she had always been a socialist and could not see much difference between socialism and communism. Ishbel's comments horrified Nangle, a confirmed elitist and the daughter of an Indiana University business school professor.[5]

At the end of her interview, Nangle handed the FBI agent a list of fourteen people who knew the Lees in New Haven. Each one, she explained, was probably a communist. She had either talked with them herself or overheard them talking with the Lees. In colorful language, she described these conversations as "decidedly pink" if not definitely "red."[6]

After listening to her, the agent typed out a report, which he titled "Attorney and Mrs. Duncan Lee, Communist." On October 10, 1940, the agent sent his report to the FBI's New York City field office, where a clerk filed it with thousands of others on suspected fascists and communists. This key evidence against Lee would not resurface for more than a decade, long after he had quit spying for the Soviets.[7]

In the spring of 1952, the FBI again interviewed Katharine Nangle, this time with her husband, Benjamin Christie Nangle. The Nangles amplified the allegations Katharine had passed on almost twelve years before. Katharine, in particular, still remembered the Lees vividly. The Nangles reported that the couple had moved into their home in September 1938. Although the FBI's summary does not explain how the young couple came to live at 23 Livingston Street, Lee likely first met Benjamin Nangle in 1934, when the professor was a fellow at Yale's Pierson College and Lee was an undergraduate residing there.[8]

Both men shared a missionary heritage. Benjamin Nangle had graduated from Yale in 1921 and joined the university's Yale-in-China program. Now an associate professor in Yale's English Department, he helped pay the mortgage on his three-story, white clapboard house by renting its third floor for $20 per month. This floor contained a small front room, a kitchen, one bedroom, and a bathroom.[9]

At first, the Nangles found the Lees attractive. They often saw and talked with the young couple because the Lees had to walk through the family's main hallway and past their front parlor to reach the stairs leading to the third floor. These warm feelings chilled, however, after the Lees plunged into New Haven's antifascist politics and Katharine concluded that they were communists.[10]

The Nangles volunteered that the Lees were very active in the American League for Peace and Democracy (ALPD) and the North American Committee to Aid Spanish Democracy (NACASD). Founded by a coalition of left-wing and communist groups in 1933, the ALPD trumpeted the dangers of fascism and publicized the need for collective security with the Soviet Union and other nonfascist countries. It claimed 20,000 members in 1939. Similarly, the NACASD, established by communists, socialists, and liberals in 1936, was the largest of the pro–Spanish Republican humanitarian organizations. The Lees' membership in the NACASD reflected their Oxford-bred passion for the Republicans' struggle against Franco.[11]

Duncan and Ishbel made telephone calls for both groups, distributed literature, held NACASD meetings in their apartment, took part in various strikes and pickets, and rushed off, according to the Nangles, to unidentified meetings with strangers. Lee spoke at an ALPD demonstration sponsored by the league's Yale chapter. He also made a memorable impression at the law school but not for his grasp of legal principles. In 1955, a Yale Law School professor told the FBI that Lee had been his most radical student during the 1938–1939 school year. Ishbel was also a member of the Industrial Relations Club of New Haven, which lobbied for better working conditions in New Haven's factories, especially for women.[12]

Benjamin Nangle remembered that his two former tenants helped organize a pro–Spanish Republican rally in a local hall that demonstrators disrupted by blocking the entrance. The couple and the other organizers finally held their rally over a garage. Nangle did not know that this incident cost Ishbel her job as a field hockey coach at the all-women's Albertus Magnus College, which was not far from the Yale campus. Although the Catholic college's nuns had initially agreed to let the Lees use their hall for this rally, the Knights of Columbus lambasted the sisters for helping "the reds." Soon after, college administrators folded under the Knights' pressure and fired Ishbel.[13]

At the beginning of the fall semester, the Nangles had occasionally invited the Lees to dinner. After the meal, the two couples would discuss international and domestic politics. These invitations stopped because the Lees always defended the CPUSA's policies, especially those centered on the public ownership of property, the struggle of workers, and social justice. One conversation with Ishbel particularly upset Katharine. After Ishbel preached that "the hope of the world is the class struggle," Katharine stared at her and said, "I think you are a communist." Rather than deny it, Ishbel declared, "I must admit that I think nothing is more important than the class struggle." Katharine also recalled that the Lees liked to play a card game called Privilege. In this game, the black cards represented the pope and Wall Street while the red cards, which counted for more, stood for what Katharine recalled as "socialistic institutions or ideas."[14]

Both Nangles agreed that Ishbel dominated Lee and was the prime mover in all of the couple's political activities. Katharine, though, refused to characterize Lee as a mere acolyte. She pointed out that he never disagreed with anything his wife said and subscribed to the same beliefs.[15]

Katharine Nangle was right about Lee. The NKVD's files reflect that he and Ishbel joined the Communist Party in 1939, the same year Franco defeated the Republicans in Spain, while he was at Yale. By then, the Communist Party of the United States of America had almost 100,000 members. Although it still retained some of its earliest characteristics—roughly 40 percent of its members lived in New York City, and nearly half were Jews—the party, as it became known, had come a long way since its founding twenty years before.[16]

As early as August 1918, Lenin had exhorted American workers, "Rise up and take things in your own hands." Within the year, his disciples had launched revolutions in Poland, Germany, Hungary, Latvia, and Finland. In March 1919, he summoned delegates from thirty-seven countries under the umbrella of the Third Communist International and made them commit to worldwide revolutions.[17]

In this intoxicating atmosphere, breakaway members of Eugene V. Debs's Socialist Party of America founded two communist parties in 1919: the Communist Party of America and the rival Communist Labor Party. Together, they claimed 34,000 members, fewer than 4,000 of whom spoke English. This did not change until the mid-1930s, when most party members were native-born Americans.[18]

In the meantime, the Comintern forced the two feuding American communist parties to merge in 1921 and form the new Communist Party of America. This edict came in the midst of a crackdown on communism in the United States. Between 1919 and 1922, local, state, and federal authorities rounded up and deported thousands of foreign-born communists for advocating the violent overthrow of the US government. They also arrested and even briefly imprisoned scores of American citizens. These heavy-handed actions drove the Communist Party underground and triggered a steep decline in its membership.[19]

The Comintern poured money into the movement's coffers to keep it afloat. Moscow's gold kept American communism on life support, but at a steep price. The aid cost the movement its independence. Slavish devotion to the Kremlin ultimately undercut any chances communism had of playing more than a bit role in American politics. The Comintern effectively governed the party from Moscow through its American Commission. In 1929, Stalin, who emerged as Lenin's successor after a bitter struggle with Leon Trotsky, ordered the party to purge all Trotskyists from its ranks. By then, a renamed Communist Party of the United States of America had only 7,500 members.[20]

Perhaps communism's most serious problem was most Americans' intense dislike for it. President Woodrow Wilson had refused to establish diplomatic relations with Lenin's new government and even sent troops to help overthrow it in 1918. His anti-Soviet stance stemmed from the long countersubversive US tradition reaching back to at least the 1798 Alien and Sedition Acts, which were strong reactions to the excesses of the French Revolution. Communism's basic tenets clashed with Americans' fundamental faith in God, upward mobility, and individualism. They believed in Christianity, private property, and free enterprise as much as Soviets did in Marx, public ownership, and a planned economy. Similarly, communism's reliance on class solidarity did not appeal to a racially and ethnically divided American working class.[21]

The Great Depression and fascism saved the CPUSA and refashioned it into a comfortable intellectual home for the Lees. It was the first political party to organize nationwide demonstrations against widespread unemployment. Its cadres spearheaded strikes from Kentucky's coal mines to North Carolina's textile mills. The CPUSA also championed highly visible social causes, such as freeing the Scottsboro Boys, unfairly accused of rape in Jim Crow Alabama, and women's rights.

Communism appealed to clusters of America's most prominent intellectuals, just as it did to many of Britain's leading thinkers. Still, most Americans remained highly suspicious of anything that smacked of it. They backed their president and their system of government. The CPUSA did not help its cause by dismissing the New Deal as

"American fascism" and a desperate ploy to save capitalism. The party leaders had done so, of course, on the Comintern's instructions, which they followed to the letter.[22]

Americans' highly critical view of the CPUSA softened in 1935 after the Comintern muffled the CPUSA's attacks and pushed the Popular Front movement against fascism. The CPUSA's *Daily Worker* had called for a "United Front to Fight Fascism" as early as March 1933 after Hitler destroyed the German Communist Party. Stalin needed allies to hold the Nazi leader in check, and he looked to the West to find them. He realized by then that the Great Depression was not going to trigger a communist-led revolution in the United States. In an astonishing about-face, the Comintern ordered the CPUSA to support the New Deal. This policy shift coincided with President Roosevelt's tilt to the left as he looked for allies to build support for his programs. In 1936, Earl Browder, the CPUSA's general secretary, declared, "Communism is twentieth-century Americanism."[23]

Stalin's aid to the Republicans in the Spanish Civil War won the support of many leading American intellectuals. As in Britain, it also deflected any criticisms of his purges. Although Stalin's "Great Terror" was no secret in the United States, very few Americans understood its mammoth scope and scale. Not a few apologists agreed that if Stalin did not have so many enemies, he would not have to spend so much time protecting his government and limiting personal freedom.[24]

The CPUSA tried to take full advantage of Stalin's popularity to extend its own appeal, but the Soviet leader himself undermined this effort on August 23, 1939, when the foreign ministers of Germany and the Soviet Union signed their nonaggression pact. Under its terms, Stalin and Hitler agreed not to attack each other for ten years. They also agreed in secret protocols to divide eastern Europe: as part of this bargain, the Soviet Union annexed half of Poland, a sixth of Romania, and all of Lithuania, Latvia, and Estonia. The protocols did not become publicly known until 1945.[25]

The nonaggression pact forced the CPUSA to drop its Popular Front policies and openly criticize President Roosevelt for his support of Europe's democracies. Most CPUSA members, despite their bewilderment at this seismic shift, stayed in the party. The Lees were among them. American communists claimed that Stalin had entered into this agreement to buy time to prepare the Soviet people for Hitler's inevitable invasion. Spain had fallen to the fascists in March 1939, and many CPUSA members worried that the Soviet Union would be next. Perhaps one-third of the party's members quietly left in disgust as their former leaders campaigned against President Roosevelt's reelection in 1940.[26]

For those who remained, loyalty to the Soviet Union and to the goal of overthrowing the US government trumped all else. Members learned never to question the party's authority. Allegiance to it and to its teachings overrode all other considerations, including country, family, and friends. This core commitment to the party and to the cause made stealing secrets much easier for those recruited for the task.[27]

Although the NKVD's files are silent about where the Lees joined the CPUSA, they probably did so in New York City. Not only is New Haven a short train ride from New York City, but membership in one of New York's many units gave them far better security and greater anonymity. In 1939, probably as few as eight or nine hundred communists lived or worked in Connecticut. A report in the NKVD's files from Donald Wheeler—Lee's Rhodes scholar classmate and fellow CPUSA member and another of the Soviets' spies inside the OSS—confirms their New York City membership. So does Mary Price, Lee's first NKVD handler, who told Elizabeth Bentley that the Lees were members of the party in New York City.[28]

The Lees always denied having joined the CPUSA. Although the NKVD's documents disprove their denials, they probably were never formal, card-carrying members. The party did issue membership cards to those who wanted them, but leaders realized that many lawyers, doctors, and intellectuals wanted no traceable ties to the organization—open membership could harm their professional standing. As Lee once observed, "One didn't ask a friend about membership anymore than one would ask a friend today about being a closet gay." To protect its members, the CPUSA kept its rosters of professionals in secure locations and ensured that they contained only party names or pseudonyms. Elizabeth Bentley told the FBI that Lee's party name was "Pat."[29]

The CPUSA's obsession with secrecy made it an ideal partner for the Soviet Union's intelligence services. The most senior of these services, the NKVD, would recruit Lee in 1942. The NKVD's history and mission explain why he was such an attractive and important target.

As early as February 1920, Lenin had asked why he had no intelligence agents operating in the United States. That same year, the Comintern, at its Second World Congress in Petrograd and Moscow, spelled out twenty-one conditions that national communist parties had to meet to be admitted into its ranks. The third condition required the national parties to establish a secret underground that would aid the coming revolution. The underground that American communists set up during the country's first Red Scare between 1919 and 1922 provided the building blocks that the NKVD used to recruit scores of Americans, including Lee, during World War II.[30]

We can trace the origins of Lenin's question and the Comintern's response to the Soviet leader's unshakeable belief in using espionage and covert action to root out and destroy his foes. On December 20, 1917, Lenin created the All-Russian Extraordinary Commission for Combating Counterrevolution and Sabotage (Cheka). Lenin tasked the Cheka with murdering or imprisoning his domestic enemies. It established its Foreign Department in 1921.

While the Cheka and its successors never stopped stalking those who wanted to strangle the revolution, they also sought to steal Western technology in order to boost the Soviets' planned economy and drag it into the twentieth century. In May 1924, the Soviet government formed the Amtorg Trading Corporation in New York City to expedite commerce with the United States. The company employed between seven and eight hundred people by the early 1930s. These workers stole American technology and military secrets. Amtorg also provided commercial or business cover for Soviet spies.[31]

The Soviets built on this success when they established World Tourists Inc. in 1927, with offices in New York City's Flatiron Building at 175 Fifth Avenue. World Tourists served as the American agent for Intourist, the Soviet Union's official travel agency. In addition to sending American delegations and individuals to the Soviet Union for Comintern events and tourism, World Tourists collected the birth certificates of dead Americans. The Unified State Political Directorate (OGPU), which succeeded the Cheka in 1923, used these birth certificates to apply for US passports to create false American identities for its officers.[32]

Despite these efforts, the United States was an intelligence backwater for the Soviets in the 1920s and early 1930s. They directed their espionage efforts primarily at collecting military and technical information from Britain, France, Finland, Germany, Japan, and Poland. The GRU, the Soviet military's intelligence arm established in 1921, joined the OGPU in these tasks.[33]

The OGPU and GRU gradually shifted their priorities in 1933 when the United States formally established diplomatic relations with the Soviet Union. The Roosevelt administration recognized the Soviet Union for economic reasons. America's producers needed new markets to help loosen the Depression's viselike grip. By 1933, the Soviet Union was already America's seventh-largest trading partner and its largest customer for heavy machinery. But closer ties with the Soviets served a strategic purpose as well. President Roosevelt envisioned a friendly Soviet Union working with him to temper Japan's territorial ambitions in Asia. Similarly, Hitler's rise to power in 1933 showed Washington and Moscow that fascism was a growing threat to Europe. Lastly, Roosevelt fell for Stalin's false promise to refrain from aiding the CPUSA.[34]

The OGPU immediately capitalized on the Americans' recognition and placed most of its officers in the Soviet Union's new embassy in Washington, DC, and its consulates in New York City and San Francisco. These were the OGPU's three "legal" stations, where its officers served under diplomatic cover. These three stations complemented an "illegals station," based in New York, for officers who used false identities and often worked under commercial cover. These deep-cover officers had no open contact with the other three stations.[35]

By the mid-1930s, the OGPU had become the NKVD, as well as the world's largest and most powerful intelligence service. As World War II neared, it had ninety-two sources—Americans the Soviets had recruited to pass them sensitive information—scattered throughout the US government and in private industry. At least three of these operated inside the State Department, one inside the Department of Justice, and one—a congressman—in the House of Representatives. Similarly, its lead officer inside Amtorg recruited several key sources inside various industries. In 1939, these commercial spies gave the NKVD 18,000 pages of technical documents, 487 sets of technical designs, and fifty-four new samples of technology.[36]

Remarkably, Stalin himself brought an end to this intelligence bonanza. Most Soviet espionage stopped after he carved huge, bloody slices out of the NKVD and the GRU between 1937 and 1938. By the time he had exorcised his paranoia, he had ordered the murders of 20,000 of his most senior intelligence officers and nearly 23,000 of his army's most skilled officers. Scores of the NKVD's top overseas officers, including those who headed its American stations, were among the casualties. Stalin's massacre of the Soviet army similarly devastated the GRU. No revolution in history, not even the blood-drenched French Revolution, consumed its own children with such unrestrained ferocity and bottomless stupidity. Years of institutional memory and hard-won operational experience were now buried in the dreary woods outside Moscow or locked away in frozen gulags. The purges also triggered the defections of two senior NKVD and GRU generals and of David Whittaker Chambers, an American working for the GRU as a courier, who would later accuse the State Department's Alger Hiss of being a Soviet spy.[37]

Stalin's killing spree drastically reduced his ability to collect American intelligence. By April 1941, the NKVD had just fifteen officers left in the United States. Only two of these had any experience working in America, and only four spoke English reasonably well. Most of the NKVD's ninety-two American spies were now dormant.[38]

As the world lurched closer to war, the gravely wounded NKVD turned to the CPUSA for help. For its collection of intelligence inside the United States, the party relied heavily on the enigmatic Jacob Golos, the man who would orchestrate Lee's recruitment. In the late 1930s and early 1940s, he served as the CPUSA's liaison with the NKVD. Standing only 5'2", Golos had straight auburn hair, an oval, freckled face, and eyes that never looked directly at anyone. Despite his unimposing physical appearance, he quickly emerged as the pillar of the NKVD's espionage operations in the United States after the purges.[39]

Jacob Golos, whose real name was Yakov Raisin or Tasin, was born on April 23, 1890, in the Ukraine. He entered the Russian revolutionary movement in 1904. Three years later, he was sentenced to hard labor in Siberia for operating an underground printing press for the Bolsheviks. Golos escaped, made his way to Japan and China, and arrived in the United States in 1909. He became a naturalized US citizen and joined the Socialist Party of America in 1915. In 1919, he helped found the Communist Party of America and adopted "Jacob Golos" as his party name.[40]

In the 1920s, Golos was on the move, working on several party publications and organizing in Chicago and Michigan, while also living in the Soviet Union for nearly four years. In 1930, CPUSA leaders appointed him to the party's Central Control Commission, its internal disciplinary board. By then, the NKVD was referring to him in reports as "our reliable man in the USA."[41]

By 1932, Golos was the president of World Tourists. From there, he laundered money for the NKVD while helping it obtain American passports. Many of these came from Americans he recruited to fight in Spain for the Comintern: on arriving in Spain, they handed their passports over to their battalion leaders for safekeeping. The NKVD shipped roughly 2,000 of these passports to Moscow. Golos had also developed extremely close personal ties to Earl Browder, the CPUSA's general secretary. He used this relationship to screen and recruit CPUSA members for intelligence work.[42]

But even Golos was not shielded from Stalin's paranoia. By April 1938, his intelligence service file in Moscow noted that he knew six NKVD officers arrested for treason. Soon after, the NKVD's Moscow Center, its hulking headquarters on Lubyanka Square, began investigating Golos as a suspected Trotskyist, concluding by the summer of 1940 that he was in fact a dangerous subversive. Center agents arranged for his family to ask him to return to the Soviet Union.[43]

Ironically, a rising tide of anticommunism in the United States saved Golos. By 1938, President Roosevelt's economic policies had generated a backlash, as a conservative coalition consisting of Republicans and southern Democrats formed in Congress. This coalition believed that Roosevelt intended to impose socialism, or worse, on the United States. It gained strength from his failed plan to pack the US Supreme Court in 1937, a series of violent sit-down labor strikes that same year, and a deepening economic recession.

This powerful backlash, coupled with Nazi Germany's political union with Austria on March 13, led to the creation of the Special House Un-American Activities Committee on May 26 and triggered a torrent of anticommunist and antifascist legislation, including the 1938 Foreign Agents Registration Act (FARA). The FARA required anyone who issued propaganda on behalf of a foreign government to register with the US Department of State.[44]

In the wake of Stalin's 1939 pact with Hitler, allegations that party general secretary Earl Browder had traveled on a fraudulent passport led to an FBI investigation and indictment. The bureau then opened a FARA investigation into World Tourists and searched its offices that October. After reviewing the corporation's books, the US Attorney's Office for the Southern District of New York charged the company and Jacob Golos with violating the act.[45]

Moscow Center closely followed World Tourists' legal proceedings and periodically briefed Stalin on them. The CPUSA's Central Committee ordered Golos, as the corporation's principal officer, to plead guilty. Neither the party nor the NKVD wanted a lengthy trial or an extended FBI investigation into World Tourists' shadowy finances. Thanks to a CPUSA mole inside the Department of Justice, the center knew that the FBI did not know about Golos's ties to the NKVD. Golos did what he was told, pleaded guilty in 1940, and received a $500 fine, a suspended jail sentence of four to twelve months, and probation. Ironically, the conviction probably saved his life because the State Department refused to issue him a passport to travel to the Soviet Union afterward.[46]

Hitler's invasion of the Soviet Union on June 22, 1941, ended the center's investigation of Golos. Now locked in a death struggle with Germany, the Soviet Union needed accurate and timely intelligence to support its war efforts. The NKVD's leaders once again turned to

Golos for help, despite the risk of relying on him: Golos had been trained to support the NKVD's operations, not to run them. His tradecraft was amateurish and at times reckless. He had mingled sex with business by seducing Elizabeth Bentley, his chief courier; he had refused to resign from World Tourists, even though the FBI remained interested in its ties to the Soviet Union; and he had declined to break up his untrained, highly idealistic CPUSA recruits into small, discrete cells. But the NKVD had no choice: Stalin had already bled it white, and it had no one else on American soil to turn to.

In the meantime, Earl Browder had been convicted of passport fraud and sentenced to four years in prison. On March 25, 1941, he surrendered to federal marshals. Before he left for the Atlanta penitentiary, he had transferred several members of the CPUSA's underground to Golos.[47]

One of Browder's most important transfers was Mary Wolfe Price, who would become Lee's first handler and his lover. The tenth child of impoverished North Carolina tobacco farmers, Price was born on March 3, 1909, in Madison, a town whose rural economy was built on exploitation: the tobacco buyers took advantage of the farmers, and the farmers did the same to their tenants.[48]

Price's parents believed in God's mercy and in education's power. The young girl had no use for God, but she did for education. She graduated from the University of North Carolina at Chapel Hill, where she studied journalism and, according to her FBI file, developed an interest in leftist movements. After a short stint as a proofreader at a newspaper in Greensboro, she left North Carolina in the spring of 1933 and moved to New York. Price worked briefly for a management company and then took a job as an in-house editor for the Insurance Brokers Association of New York City.[49]

In 1936, Price accompanied her sister Mildred on a trip to Europe that included almost three weeks in the Soviet Union. The Price sisters toured Leningrad, Moscow, and Stalingrad. Both women marveled, as the Lees did a year later, at the Soviets' experiment in creating a classless society far different from the highly stratified one they had known growing up in rural North Carolina. The FBI later learned that Mary Price vocally supported the Soviet Union after she returned from her trip and had attended meetings of the Young Communist League, the CPUSA's youth arm.[50]

The Price sisters also commenced a secret relationship with the NKVD. Mary, 5'7" and 135 pounds, with gray eyes and wavy black hair, would become an especially key operative. By September 1939, she had two NKVD code names: "Kid" and "Dir." Mildred's work for the NKVD may have started even before her trip to the Soviet Union. A FBI source reported in 1941 that she had been "engaged in research or secret service work for the Communist party for over ten years."[51]

The well-educated and urbane Price sisters were exactly the kind of CPUSA recruits the NKVD wanted. By 1938, the Soviets had started to de-Russianize their American spies, rejecting potential agents who spoke broken English with Russian accents. Moscow Center was especially interested in recruiting unmarried American women adept at shorthand who could find jobs in the federal government and private offices. They could also be used as sexual lures—"honey traps"—to blackmail unwilling sources.[52]

Iskhak Akhmerov, head of the NKVD's illegals station from late 1937, had particularly high hopes for Mary Price, especially after she became Walter Lippmann's private secretary and stenographer on July 10, 1939. Lippmann, then working for the *New York Herald Tribune*, was the country's most famous political columnist and a well-known Washington insider, with almost unlimited access to the American capital's corridors of power. But when the NKVD recalled Akhmerov to Moscow that same year, Mary Price was deactivated because no one was left to handle her. This changed in February 1941 after Earl Browder, who was about to go to federal prison, passed her name to Jacob Golos. Before long, she began supplying him with documents and correspondence she copied from Lippmann's private files.[53]

In 1939, while the NKVD was still reeling from Stalin's massacre of its most experienced officers, Lee was finishing his year at Yale Law School and looking for a job. He had no set course of study. As a Sterling Fellow he could take any of the law faculty's classes he wanted. But he had not come to Yale to write a thesis or earn a degree, of which he already had three. He had enrolled to learn enough American law to pass the New York State bar examination.

Lee's extreme political views did not restrain him from looking for a job on Wall Street, the epicenter of finance capitalism. He needed the money and saw no contradiction between his radical politics and his choice of a traditional job. More than one communist lawyer spent his days working on Wall Street and his nights plotting to collectivize its wealth. Although Lee interviewed with several other prestigious New York City law firms during the spring of 1939, he ultimately chose Donovan, Leisure, Newton, and Lumbard.[54]

William Joseph Donovan, a charismatic war hero and Donovan, Leisure's principal partner, had started the firm in the summer of 1929 after winning the Distinguished Service Cross and the Medal of Honor in World War I, then serving as an assistant attorney general in the US Department of Justice's criminal and antitrust divisions. He left the Department of Justice after President Herbert Hoover backed out of his promise to nominate him for attorney general.

Donovan's law firm specialized in antitrust, tax, corporate, and appellate cases. With the stock market crashing within months of the firm's opening, it soon was handling many of the complicated business bankruptcies and mergers the financial collapse spawned. By 1939, it was one of New York City's finest law firms. Occupying two floors at 2 Wall Street, it brought in more than $800,000 a year—over $13 million in 2013 dollars—and had over forty associates on its payroll.[55]

Lee started working at the firm as a law clerk in September 1939, the same month that Hitler invaded Poland and ignited World War II. He was certain that the firm's sophisticated practice would sharpen his legal skills and perhaps pave the way for a career in politics.[56]

He and Ishbel settled into a top-floor apartment at 531 East 84th Street. Lee worked at Donovan, Leisure during the day and studied for the New York bar examination at night and on weekends. Edmund sent the young couple $30 a month to help with rent and expenses. They needed the subsidy, especially after Gavin Dunbar Lee, their first child, arrived on December 23, 1940.[57]

Ishbel worked part-time for Professor James Marshall Osborn of Yale's English Department. Osborn and Benjamin Nangle were colleagues, collaborating on an index of the *Gentleman's Magazine*, an eighteenth-century British publication. Osborn hired Ishbel to do research for him in the New York Public Library because she had specialized in that period of British history at Oxford.[58]

During 1939 and 1940, Ishbel also worked as a volunteer for the Yorkville Tenants Association (YTA), which campaigned for affordable housing. The CPUSA supported it. The May 1, 1939, *Daily Worker* listed the association among the marchers in that year's annual May Day parade.[59]

Ishbel disclosed her membership in the YTA on the alien registration form she executed on September 28, 1940. The Alien Registration Act—more commonly called the Smith Act—required all resident aliens to register with the federal government and be fingerprinted. The act also outlawed teaching or advocating the overthrow of the United States by force or violence. The Voorhis Act, its companion legislation, required all groups with foreign affiliations to register with the federal government. That act also allowed the federal government to deport aliens belonging to any foreign-controlled organization that pushed for the violent overthrow of the United States.[60]

After the Voorhis Act became law in January 1941, the CPUSA received permission from Moscow to disassociate itself from the Comintern and step out from underneath its umbrella. The CPUSA also dropped from its rolls 7,500 members who had not applied for American citizenship, thereby sparing these people from facing deportation proceedings. Bentley later told the FBI that Ishbel was among those the CPUSA dropped. Although she had considered naturalizing, Ishbel never applied for citizenship because she feared that an investigation into her background might uncover her CPUSA membership. This decision would come back to haunt her in an extraordinarily painful way.[61]

Lee's letters to Edmund in 1939 and 1940 were strikingly apolitical. Perhaps he wanted to conceal his and Ishbel's membership in the CPUSA from his parents, though he did let his pro-Soviet sympathies show in one letter. The day after the September 27, 1940, Tripartite Pact among Germany, Italy, and Japan established the Axis alliance, Lee wrote to Edmund, "You may have noted in today's papers that for the first time since the signing of the German-Soviet pact, the Axis is taking an openly hostile tone towards the USSR."[62]

Lee did not pass the New York State bar examination on his first try. He did on the second and was admitted to the New York Bar on February 10, 1941. At the Donovan firm, he worked mostly on anti-trust and corporate matters. He did not like his work and, like many other young lawyers in large firms, complained about the long hours: "[I] have just spent the most villainous week yet at the office," he wrote his father, "getting home only one night before 11:00 pm, excluding Saturday."[63]

Grumble as he might, Lee's work ethic impressed the firm's partners as much as it had his Oxford tutors. In April 1941, the US House of Representatives Committee on Military Affairs hired Donovan's firm to assist in its investigation into the nation's military readiness. Donovan dispatched Otto C. Doering Jr., one of his partners, to help the committee for eight weeks. Doering chose Lee to be his chief assistant.[64]

Despite working long hours, Lee did find time to satisfy his social conscience by doing voluntary legal work for the China Aid Council (CAC) and Russian War Relief (RWR). Both organizations were humanitarian, and the Donovan firm had no objections. The HUAC would later accuse the CAC of having strong communist ties. Lee worked on the CAC's merger with another charitable organization. By 1942, he had a seat on the CAC's executive committee, where his legal work favorably impressed Mildred Price, now the CAC's head and a member of its executive committee. Under her leadership, the CAC gave direct economic aid to Chinese organizations tied to the Chinese Communist Party.[65]

Lee found his voluntary work far more satisfying than defending corporations. Through it, he met RWR chairman Edward Carter (Louis Budenz, former managing editor of the *Daily Worker*, later claimed that Carter was a CPUSA member). Lee was soon a member of RWR's board of directors and its general counsel. He also acted as its assistant secretary. RWR primarily funneled private funds and supplies to the Soviet Union, which had been fighting Hitler since the Nazi leader's attack during the early morning hours of June 22, 1941.[66]

Mildred Price introduced Lee to her sister sometime in the spring of 1942. Theirs was not an accidental meeting. The NKVD had been pushing Mary Price "to find someone new," and Mildred helped her sister by introducing her to Lee. Mary and Duncan, two southerners, were drawn to one another instantly. Although Mary lived and worked in Washington, she came to New York often to visit her sister. While there, she also saw Lee.[67]

Golos, not knowing Donovan himself approved of Lee's work for the CAC and RWR, decided that the young lawyer's open work for the two organizations might destroy his future usefulness. Sometime in the spring of 1942, he told Mary Price to make Lee a member of the CPUSA's secret underground. In the 1930s and early 1940s, the term "underground" was synonymous with heroism, self-sacrifice, and moral purity.[68]

In the late spring or early summer of 1942, Mary Price advised Golos that Lee would be following Donovan to Washington to join his new intelligence service. Golos immediately ordered her to recruit Lee as a spy.[69]

FOUR

MY LEAGUE OF GENTLEMEN

In early March 1941, like millions of other young American men, Lee completed a questionnaire for his country's first peacetime draft. Because he had two dependents, the draft board granted him a deferment. In the meantime, while waiting to see whether the United States would plunge into the fighting, he continued to practice law, volunteered for the China Aid Council and Russian War Relief, and cared for his young family.[1]

Although most Americans opposed Adolf Hitler in early 1941, they opposed fighting Nazi Germany themselves even more. They had learned their lesson in World War I. That abattoir had brought them little but disillusion and a desire to steer well clear of any future global conflicts. A deep isolationism mingled with pacifism had gripped the nation during the 1930s. Many alleged that bankers and armament manufacturers such as J. P. Morgan Jr. and Pierre Du Pont had pushed the country into World War I in order to make millions selling munitions to the US Army and its allies. Blinkered by the suggestion of such a conspiracy, Americans wanted nothing more than to retreat between their oceans and focus on their own affairs.[2]

President Franklin Roosevelt, sensitive to public opinion and unwilling to cross swords with the isolationists in his governing coalition, sided with the prevailing sentiment during most of the 1930s. When he took the oath of office as the country's thirty-second president on

March 4, 1933, the United States was in the depths of the worst economic catastrophe in its history. Americans had elected him to pull
them out of their financial misery, not to entangle them in international crises. Roosevelt's first inaugural address reflected this powerful,
pervasive conviction. He devoted only one paragraph of the speech to
foreign affairs.[3]

Japan's brutal escalation of its invasion of China in the summer of
1937, followed by Germany's seizure of Austria in March 1938 and
its annexation of Czechoslovakia's Sudetenland late that September,
convinced Roosevelt that isolationism and appeasement would not
prevent another global clash. His certainty intensified after France
fell to the Germans in June 1940. By then, most Americans deemed
Adolf Hitler a threat to the United States; still, they were not ready to
fight another world war. By the time the Germans captured Paris, the
US Army was smaller than Belgium's. It still relied heavily on horses
and asked for 20,000 more that fall. Although Roosevelt had pushed
the $1.5 billion Naval Expansion Act through Congress in 1938 and
called for the production of 10,000 combat airplanes that same year,
most of the ships and airplanes were still under construction in 1940.
The country had no large-scale arms industry.[4]

The United States also lacked a centralized way to collect and evaluate
foreign intelligence. Before the summer of 1941, essential intelligence-
gathering responsibilities were parceled out among the State Department, the Office of Naval Intelligence (ONI), and the US Army's
Military Intelligence Division (MID). Their methods and means belonged more to the nineteenth century than the twentieth. The critical
need for a modern intelligence service led President Roosevelt eventually to create the Office of Strategic Services, which in turn enabled
the NKVD to recruit Lee as a spy.

In 1940, the State Department had only seven hundred Foreign
Service officers stationed around the world (there are at least ten
times that number today). None of them collected intelligence clan-
destinely; instead, they gathered political and economic information
from open sources. They seldom analyzed and understood even this
intelligence beyond what diplomats needed to address very specific

problems. This was graphically demonstrated just before Japan's bombs began falling on Pearl Harbor, when Stanley Hornbeck, in charge of Chinese affairs for the State Department since 1928, wrote a memorandum confidently predicting that "the Japanese government does not desire or intend or expect to have forthwith armed conflict with the United States."[5]

Similar problems with collecting and understanding foreign intelligence plagued the US Navy and Army. The navy established ONI in 1882 but had only twenty-four officers and eighteen clerks serving in it fifty years later, focusing on the technical characteristics of foreign navies and relying heavily on naval attachés posted at US embassies. ONI did not make analysis an official function until 1937, barely four years before Pearl Harbor.

The army had followed the navy's lead and created MID in 1885. The War Department immediately showed its lack of interest in the new division by allotting it only four men. Ambitious officers quickly realized that careers went to MID to die, not thrive. MID had only sixty-six enlisted men and officers working for it in 1936, with most officers assigned as attachés to American embassies abroad. Almost none understood the function and importance of military intelligence in modern warfare. This was true even though, by 1940, US Army and Navy cryptologists could read Japanese diplomatic messages between Tokyo and its embassy in Washington.

A host of other US agencies and departments, ranging from the FBI to the Treasury Department, also collected foreign intelligence. They rarely made sense of information gathered for their own limited purposes or shared it outside their very narrow internal channels.[6]

Frustrated to the point of despair, Roosevelt turned to other sources. William Bullitt, his ambassador to France, sent him intelligence reports from the Deuxième Bureau, that country's military intelligence service. Similarly, his ambassador in Poland dispatched reports from the Polish intelligence bureau. Roosevelt also relied on firsthand accounts from foreign correspondents and from an informal but trusted network of lawyers and businessmen who traveled overseas. But much of their reporting contained no more than hearsay or rumor.[7]

By the spring of 1941, this lack of coordinated and evaluated foreign intelligence left the United States functionally blind. This was an especially dangerous time because Congress had passed the Lend-Lease Act that March, acting on the president's call to make the United States "the great arsenal of democracy." As a steady stream of British ships carried American war supplies to an embattled Britain, Roosevelt moved to protect them from Hitler's roving packs of U-boats. German submarines were torpedoing over 500,000 tons of British shipping per month in the North Atlantic. To be effective, Lend-Lease supplies needed the US Navy's protection.[8]

Despite the growing dangers in the North Atlantic, no one in the US government could answer Roosevelt's most pressing question: Where would Hitler strike next? On May 27, 1941, the president, convinced of the Nazi dictator's determination to conquer the world, did the only thing he could do: he declared a state of unlimited national emergency.[9]

Roosevelt was no stranger to extraordinary crises. He had faced little else since his swearing in. Only Abraham Lincoln had taken office under graver circumstances. But like Lincoln, Roosevelt had an almost mystical faith in the federal government's power to solve problems. During his first term, he created scores of New Deal agencies, stocking them with brilliant policy makers and gifted administrators. These men and women revolutionized how the federal government oversaw and regulated the American economy. President Roosevelt applied the same tactic to revolutionize how the United States collected and analyzed foreign intelligence.

On July 11, 1941, FDR signed an order that would reverberate through Lee's life for decades to come. The order created the Office of the Coordinator of Information (COI), the country's first peacetime, civilian, freestanding intelligence organization. The COI was among the most novel and unusual of the 136 separate war agencies that Roosevelt would establish by 1945. In his dual role as president and commander in chief, FDR authorized the COI to collect, analyze, and disseminate to him and all his pertinent department heads all the national security information the federal government collected.[10]

Roosevelt chose William J. Donovan, Lee's mentor, to lead the COI. Although they had started out in the same Columbia University

Law School class—Donovan graduated; Roosevelt did not—they did not know each other well. Donovan was an Irish Catholic from Buffalo who had once seriously considered becoming a priest. Roosevelt was a Protestant patrician descended from Hudson River valley money and a refined product of Groton and Harvard. He was also a distant cousin of Theodore Roosevelt, the country's twenty-sixth president. As consequentially, Roosevelt was a Democrat, and Donovan was a Republican: in 1932, Donovan had run unsuccessfully for governor of New York, and he had campaigned for Herbert Hoover's reelection against Roosevelt at the same time.[11]

Despite these major social and political differences, both men shared a sophisticated view of the world and America's place in it. They sensed their country's greatness and its need to play a much larger role in international affairs. And each saw something he liked in the other. Roosevelt knew that Donovan was a genuine war hero; he also sensed that Donovan was absolutely fearless, afraid of neither Hitler nor Washington's bureaucrats. Donovan, intensely ambitious and very socially conscious, admired Roosevelt's regal personality, his effortless self-confidence, and his aristocratic bearing.[12]

Both men also possessed charismatic personalities that inspired those they led to face the murderous fire of embedded machine guns or the economic ravages of the Great Depression. This same charisma also triggered deep feelings of hate and jealousy among their bitter and frequent detractors.

Roosevelt, in an effort to gain bipartisan support for his increasingly bold stands against Germany and Japan, had invited Republicans Henry Stimson and Frank Knox to join his cabinet in 1940 as secretaries of war and the navy, respectively. Knox reintroduced Donovan to Roosevelt that summer. By then, Donovan was a national figure. In January, Warner Brothers had released *The Fighting 69th*, a movie featuring some of Donovan's courageous World War I exploits.[13]

After the British army was rescued from the beaches of Dunkirk and France fell in June, Roosevelt followed the advice of his newly appointed war and naval secretaries and asked Donovan to travel to England to gauge its chances of holding out against Hitler's ruthless air campaign. FDR had received dozens of pessimistic reports from

Joseph P. Kennedy, his ambassador in London, who supported former prime minister Neville Chamberlain's appeasement policy. Roosevelt, doubting Kennedy's inclination to share an honest assessment, wanted Donovan to give him an independent evaluation.[14]

Always intellectually and physically restless, Donovan was delighted to take another absence from his Wall Street practice. Winston Churchill, Chamberlain's successor as prime minister, was anxious to win America's support and gave Donovan unprecedented access to many of Britain's most sensitive defense and intelligence secrets. His openness paid off. On returning that August, Donovan told Knox and Roosevelt that the British could hold out if they got the war supplies they needed from the United States.[15]

Impressed with this trenchant assessment, Roosevelt next endorsed the plan for Donovan to make a strategic evaluation of the war's Mediterranean theater in December 1940. By the time he returned in mid-March 1941, Donovan had visited over a dozen countries and battlefields in Libya and Albania. Through it all, he had kept Knox and the White House updated with lengthy and detailed reports.[16]

On April 26, Donovan acted on Knox's suggestion and put together a detailed study on how the British collected and assessed foreign intelligence information. In his "Memorandum of Establishment of Service of Strategic Information," sent to Roosevelt on June 10, Donovan highlighted what had troubled the president since at least the spring of 1941: "Although we are facing imminent peril, we are lacking an effective service for analyzing, comprehending, and appraising such information as we might obtain (or in some cases have obtained), relative to the intentions of potential enemies and the limit of the economic and military resources of those enemies." Roosevelt, better than anyone, knew that Donovan was correct. With subtle and not so subtle prompting from Knox and the British, who desperately wanted to share and coordinate intelligence with the United States, the president established the COI in July with Donovan as its head.[17]

Roosevelt's decision ignited a firestorm in the FBI and the US military. Both, following the worst traditions of Washington's entrenched bureaucracies, feared Donovan's encroachment on their territories and his access to the Oval Office. Roosevelt, in response, prohibited the COI from operating, except in very limited ways, inside the United States, where the FBI reigned supreme, and from interfering with MID's and ONI's core missions. Despite reassurances, J. Edgar Hoover belittled the COI as "Roosevelt's folly." General George C. Marshall, the icily reserved chief of staff of the army, linked arms with Secretary of War Stimson to block the awarding of the major general's stars—or any military rank—that FDR had dangled before Donovan to lure him into the job. Stimson also ensured that Donovan would not receive payment for his service as the head of COI. Although the COI's independence from any cabinet department gave Donovan wide latitude, it also guaranteed that his new organization would never be without bitter bureaucratic rivals.[18]

Although not one to back down from his enemies, Donovan concentrated on the mammoth task of building the COI from scratch. Whatever his foes believed, he knew that Roosevelt had given him a broad mandate to protect the United States. In September, the mission of COI expanded further when it absorbed ONI's and MID's small espionage units—the navy and army no longer wanted them—and won access to unvouchered funds from Roosevelt's discretionary spending account. Donovan could now pay for secret operations outside the purview of the Bureau of the Budget's auditors.[19]

Donovan immediately set out to hire the right kind of people to carry out the COI's far-flung missions. Barred from recruiting from the military and the FBI, and temperamentally unwilling to do so anyway, he sought men and women cast from the same mold as he. To find them, he turned to his legal, business, political, and social circles, from which those he trusted most—lawyers, industrialists, bankers, and academics—reached out in turn to their own contacts in law firms and board rooms, on Wall Street, and in the more prestigious universities and colleges.[20]

Donovan had a tribal, almost British-upper-class attachment to the institutions to which he belonged and the values they represented. He believed that those who went to the best schools, belonged to the right clubs, backed the same political party, held similar jobs, and were financially well-off would never dream of betraying their country. He built his new organization on trust. It was inconceivable to him that those he selected to join him could choose another country over their own. Donovan expressed his deep faith in this insularity by dubbing his inner circle inside the OSS "my league of gentlemen."[21]

Although he relied heavily on the eastern Establishment to fill the COI's highest echelons, Donovan did not confine his recruitment exclusively to it. John Paton Davies, a Foreign Service officer who served in China with Lieutenant General Joseph Stilwell, later vividly described Donovan's hires as "a pungent collection of thugs, post debutantes, millionaires, professors, corporation lawyers, professional military, and misfits, all operating under high tension and in whispers." Donovan was just as likely to hire a communist who had fought in Spain against Franco as he was to hire a stockbroker from Wall Street—if that person could help him win the war. He once boasted, "I'd put Stalin on the OSS payroll if I thought it would help defeat Hitler." In some ways, he did. After World War II, the FBI and the National Security Agency would identify at least twenty-two women and men, including Lee, who were Soviet sources inside the OSS. While it is impossible to be exact, anywhere from fifty to one hundred OSS employees belonged to the CPUSA. Despite this, Donovan told the *New York Herald Tribune* in August 1948 that he believed none of the OSS's secret information "was ever turned over to any one not authorized to receive it."[22]

Donovan's strengths lay in leading, not in managing a sprawling bureaucracy that grew to 13,000 employees. Privately, even his admirers admitted that he earned the moniker "Wild Bill" not for his battlefield heroics but because he allowed the wildest, loosest kind of administrative and procedural chaos to develop. Following his habit of relying on those he trusted most, Donovan reached back to his law firm for help in running his new organization.[23]

To bring some semblance of order to the COI's daily affairs, Donovan hired Otto "Ole" Doering, his scholarly law partner and another of Lee's mentors, as his general counsel. The White House suggested the State Department's Alger Hiss for this position, but Donovan wanted Doering, who came from a wealthy Chicago family and had degrees in engineering and law from Cornell University. Doering's calm temperament and patient approach to problem solving were perfect foils for Donovan's fire-in-the-belly attitude and frenetic pace.[24]

In the spring of 1942, Doering and Donovan asked Lee to join the COI. He jumped at the chance to serve under his old bosses and do such stimulating and exciting work. There is no evidence that the Soviets asked him to apply to the OSS. On May 1, Lee interviewed with the COI's John J. McDonough, who later served as an OSS counterintelligence officer in New Delhi. That same day, McDonough drafted a memorandum conveying his certainty that the young man was an ideal recruit because of his exceptional background and education. McDonough, clueless about Lee's CPUSA membership, was especially impressed with the young Rhodes scholar's ability to help the Russian War Relief and China Aid Council services while working full-time for Donovan's demanding law firm.[25]

Lee applied to the COI's New York City branch the next day. He relied on his Yale connections. In his personal history statement, he listed Henry Sloane Coffin, a member of Yale's Class of 1897 and president of the Union Theological Seminary, and Myres McDougal, his relative, mentor, fellow Rhodes scholar, and Yale Law School professor, as two personal references. McDonough interviewed the former within the week, reporting that Coffin "had known the Lee family for three generations . . . and [has] great confidence in young Lee, and says that he is clever, ambitious and [that] he very heartily recommends him to us."[26]

On May 21, Allen Welsh Dulles, a prominent New York City lawyer (and future head of the CIA) who ran the COI's Rockefeller Center office, forwarded Lee's file to Washington with a small note attached: "Our impression was most favorable." Eight days later, McDonough wrote Watts Hill, an administrator in the COI's Washington office, echoing Dulles: "This young man looks like an excellent prospect as his record will indicate."[27]

On June 13, 1942, Franklin Roosevelt signed an order renaming the COI the Office of Strategic Services and placing it under the jurisdiction of the military's Joint Chiefs of Staff. By then, the United States had been fighting Japan and Germany for five months. Donovan knew that the COI needed the military's support and resources to play a meaningful role in winning the war, and Roosevelt agreed. Donovan also thought that his organization's new name better reflected its mission to provide strategic intelligence to Roosevelt and the Department of War. His critics complained that OSS really stood for "Oh So Social" because of the number of bluebloods within its ranks. The president elevated Donovan from civilian status to OSS director with the military rank of colonel.[28]

On July 1, 1942, Lee completed Standard Form No. 57, "Application for Federal Employment." He described himself as twenty-eight years old, 5'10", and 160 pounds, with myopia and astigmatism. He also claimed to be a loyal American. In his application and an accompanying signed affidavit, he denied belonging to any organization that advocated the overthrow of the US government. That same day, Lee appeared before a notary public and swore to support and defend the US Constitution against all enemies foreign and domestic.[29]

Lee was hired the next day as an aide-de-camp and assistant general counsel in the director's office for the duration of the war. His duties ranged from routine administrative legal matters—drafting and reviewing contracts, leases, directives, and briefs—to liaising with attorneys from the Department of Justice and other government agencies. Otto Doering, now a US Army captain, was his supervisor. The director of personnel underscored Doering's and Donovan's faith in Lee in a report written that same day: "Since the work of this position includes much of a special and highly confidential nature, it is particularly desirable to appoint the candidate herein submitted. . . . Mr. Lee has been closely associated in his legal work with both Colonel Donovan and Captain Doering with whom he will work, giving them a complete knowledge of his character and integrity."[30]

Lee began working in the director's office on July 2, but his appointment was conditional. He had to pass a perfunctory Civil Service Commission background check to keep his job. After Pearl Harbor, the FBI had taken on the task of conducting background investigations for all COI hires. By the late spring of 1942, however, the bureau was overburdened with Hatch Act investigations of federal employees whose loyalty had been questioned, in addition to its other wartime responsibilities, so the Civil Service Commission took over the job of vetting COI and then OSS applicants. But the Civil

Service Commission's resources were stretched as thinly as the FBI's because the war's outbreak had triggered another explosion in federal hiring. It cleared Lee eight days after he began working in Donovan's office.[31]

In 1952, the FBI would retrace the Civil Service Commission's hasty investigation of Lee and reinterview George C. Seward, one of his neighbors at 531 East 85th Street in New York City. Seward, a graduate of the University of Virginia's law school and an attorney at the Wall Street law firm of Shearman and Sterling, told the FBI in 1952 that Lee and Ishbel had very liberal political views, which had not concerned him until after a Civil Service investigator questioned him about his neighbor's loyalty to the United States. Shortly after that interview, Lee had asked Seward if anyone had been checking on him. When Seward said yes, Lee offhandedly replied that Seward's favorable endorsement had probably put him "beyond the reach of the FBI." Seward admitted in 1952 that this odd remark made him uneasy and that he had come to regret giving Lee a positive reference. Curiously, he added that Lee had a strong character and "would not do anything unless he was convinced that it was the correct course to follow." The FBI also discovered that the Civil Service Commission had not interviewed the Nangles, the Lees' former landlords, or any Yale Law School professors.[32]

On July 6, Lee completed a War Department questionnaire and applied for a reserve commission as a first lieutenant in the US Army. Donovan found military slots for many of the civilians who joined the OSS, although most of them never spent a day in basic training. Lee gave the army a list of blue-chip character references. These included Donovan, Doering, and Coffin, as well as Carl Newton, another partner in Donovan's law firm and a Rhodes scholar, and Allen Wardwell, a leader of the New York City bar and a member of Yale's Class of 1895. Coffin and Donovan also wrote letters on Lee's behalf. With their enthusiastic backing, he became a first lieutenant three weeks later.[33]

In the meantime, Mary Price's recruitment efforts had succeeded. Lee had agreed to become a spy. On September 8, 1942, Moscow Center received its first detailed report from Jacob Golos about Lee. Excitedly, Golos noted, "Telegrams going to the State Depart[ment] go through him. He chooses among them and shows them to Donovan for his consideration. In addition, agent reports from Europe and all over the world go through him. . . . Koch [Lee's code name] wants to work with us and provide us with any information he can get. He cannot take any documents out of his department, but he will memorize them as much as possible and then write them down and give them to Dir [Mary Price's code name]."[34]

The Soviets did not know that Lee was also sleeping with Price. Moscow Center prohibited sex between its spy handlers and their agents, fearing it could cloud both parties' judgment and create biased assessments. Their sexual relationship had blossomed in the late spring of 1942, when she recruited him into espionage. It most likely started in Washington. In an April 17, 1947, interview with the FBI, Price confessed that Donovan's new hire had stayed with her for "a week or two" when he had come to Washington to look for an apartment for his family.[35]

An old FBI adage says that there has never been an espionage case in which sex did not play a part. Although this is not strictly true, Price's sexual charms probably played an important role in erasing any lingering doubts Lee might have harbored in 1942 about providing classified information to the Soviets. Their illicit relationship went hand in hand with his new, secret double life. Lee's affair with Price also represented more than just a willingness to indulge his physical desire. It showed that he was going to make and play by his own rules and could compartmentalize.

Lee did not agree to commit espionage to have sex with Price, however. Although their intimate hours together made doing what she asked easier for him, they did not motivate him to spy for the Soviets. Rather, he did so because he knew that his hour had arrived. Others in his family had experienced similar life-altering epiphanies: Richard Henry Lee in 1776, Robert E. Lee in 1861, and Edmund in 1902. In 1942, Lee knew that the great Soviet experiment, with its promise to usher in a new kingdom on earth, was fighting for its very life. Chance and ability had brought Lee into the OSS. He could not pass on this stunning opportunity to help what he deemed the best hope for the future of mankind. The red star had replaced the Christian cross.

From the start, the NKVD realized Lee's enormous potential, which only increased when, on February 6, 1943, Doering asked him to become the assistant chief of the Secretariat, the OSS's nerve center. Lee described the Secretariat in a memorandum to all OSS employees as the "channel for all papers requiring the approval of the Director and Assistant Directors." This position gave him unlimited access to the OSS's most sensitive matters and secret operations. A month later, the army promoted Lee to captain. Doering had given him an "excellent" efficiency rating—the OSS's highest—with "outstanding" marks in twenty different areas, including "dependability" and "ability to make decisions."[36]

Lee doubled as the secretary of the OSS's executive committee and signed the minutes of its meetings. Among its other tasks, this committee decided the fates of OSS employees determined to be security risks by the Civil Service Commission. On April 30, 1943, the committee ordered that all OSS applicants had to pass a full security check before they were hired. Lee was lucky to have joined the OSS when he did: even with Donovan's full support, he probably could not have survived a rigorous background investigation that included interviews with the Nangles and his professors at Yale Law School.[37]

In the meantime, by September 1942 Lee had started passing the OSS's secrets to Price. They met at her apartment or at his. Ishbel often participated in their meetings. She knew that her husband was giving Price classified information; she did not know that he was also sleeping with her.[38]

The secret information he passed orally to Price covered a wide spectrum of political intelligence. On May 13, 1943, the NKVD's Moscow Center summarized the intelligence he had given to her and Golos so far. It ranged from Chinese Nationalist leader Chiang Kai-shek's plans to meet with Chinese Communist Party leaders to a report from the US ambassador in Moscow about rumors circulating there that Churchill had told Stalin that the Allies would not open a second front against Germany until the USSR declared war on Japan.[39]

Lee also told Price about a State Department cable from Carlton Hayes, the US ambassador to Spain. A secret interoffice memorandum Lee wrote and addressed to Donovan on October 5, 1942, summarized this cable, which discussed Argentina's attempts to persuade Pope Pius XII to negotiate an end to the fighting with Hitler. The memo contained abstracts of the most important political intelligence the OSS had received in September. Under the subhead "Catholic Resistance," Lee wrote about the Vatican's stiffening attitude toward the Axis and cited, "Particularly State Department cable from Ambassador Hayes dated 9/8/42 quoting the Argentine envoy to Spain as saying that in rejecting Argentine peace feelers the Pope declared that Nazi defeat is required and will be achieved." Hayes's information was of keen interest to the NKVD because Stalin wanted to know about any peace negotiations with Hitler—he was terrified that Britain and the United States would conclude a separate peace with Germany, leaving him to face Hitler alone. At the same time, the Americans and the British worried that Stalin would do the same to them.[40]

Although Lee had given the NKVD valuable snippets of intelligence, Moscow Center complained about his lack of focus. The center blamed Price's inexperience in handling agents and suggested that she be replaced with a more seasoned handler. A month later, it also demanded that Lee be given specific questions to answer, especially about the OSS's structure and personnel. On May 13, 1943, the center voiced its frustration again over the failure of its New York station to manage Lee properly: "As of now, K[och] is not giving info based on our assignments. . . . He is of great interest to us. As of yet there is no information from the station that his recruitment has been made official."[41]

By then, the NKGB (the NKVD changed its name in April 1943) was under enormous pressure from Stalin to collect accurate and timely intelligence. A year before, with Hitler's troops driving toward Moscow, he had decided to penetrate the COI and the OSS. He directed his secret agents to collect American intelligence in four main areas: Hitler's plans for the Soviet Union; Roosevelt's and Churchill's secret war aims, especially their planning for a second front that would divert Hitler's attention and resources away from the Soviet Union; any hint of his western allies' secret peace negotiations with the Nazi leader; and any American scientific and technological advances that his agents could steal or copy.[42]

Lee, as one of Donovan's most trusted aides, was in an ideal position to help the Soviets. But Price's inexperience was only one reason why he was not living up to the NKGB's expectations. Lee recognized that he had a far better chance of surviving if he selected what to give to her and left no paper trail in doing it. He did not need his Yale and Oxford degrees to understand the difference between tempting and steering fate.

More than survival, however, motivated him to control his relationship with the Soviets. Lee was wrestling with a deeply ingrained character trait: his intellectual and emotional inability to give himself fully, be it to his father's religion, his marriage, his country, or communism. He may also have felt ambivalent about his divided loyalties to Donovan and the OSS and to Price and the Soviet Union.

In April 1943 Price's health collapsed under the strains of working simultaneously for such demanding bosses as Walter Lippmann and the NKVD. She was not only handling Lee but also receiving secret information from Maurice Halperin, then chief of the Latin American Division of the OSS's Research and Analysis Branch. Overwhelmed and exhausted, she went to New York City to recover from viral pneumonia. She stayed there for eight weeks. Jacob Golos immediately replaced her with Elizabeth Bentley, his lover and most trusted courier.[43]

FIVE

A CRISIS OF CONSCIENCE

On the surface, Elizabeth Bentley was the perfect handler for Duncan Lee. Her family had been in the United States even longer than his, and she had just as many demons. Mirroring each other in background and personality, Bentley and Lee would face personal crises in 1944 and 1945 that would shatter their faith in communism and in each other.

Although Bentley lied to the Soviets about being descended from the *Mayflower*'s pilgrims and from Roger Sherman, a signer of the Declaration of Independence, both her parents did come from old New England stock. Her father was an itinerant dry goods merchant who campaigned against the evils of alcohol. Her mother was a schoolteacher, heavily influenced by the Social Gospel movement and its call to help the urban poor.[1]

Bentley, born on January 1, 1908, in New Milford, Connecticut, was her parents' only child. Her father's chronic attempts to establish himself in a stable business forced him to uproot his small family several times. She told the NKGB in 1944 that her upbringing had been overly strict and painfully lonely.[2]

In 1926, Bentley won an academic scholarship to Vassar College. She was neither academically nor socially prepared to attend one of the era's most elite American women's colleges. She studied mostly French, Italian, and English but managed only a C+ average.[3]

Socially, she fared even worse. By the time she entered Vassar, she was nearly 5'9" tall, with a large frame and long neck. Former FBI agents described her as "not pretty, but not unattractive." Bentley later told the Soviets that she dated no men because she could not afford a nice dress, although this probably was not true. One of her classmates later described her harshly as "kind of sad sack, plain, dull, very teacher-like. She didn't have a single boyfriend, as I recall. Everyone who knew her just called her Bentley. She was a sad and lonely girl." In her junior year, her loneliness deepened when her mother died.[4]

After graduating from Vassar in 1930, she went to Europe and had her first sexual experience. A year later, the exclusive Foxcroft School, an all-girls boarding school near Washington, DC, hired her as a teacher. She traveled to Perugia, Italy, that summer to study Italian. While there, she slept with a much older Hungarian army officer.[5]

She left the Foxcroft School in 1932 and enrolled as a graduate student in Columbia University's Italian Department that fall. Her father died in April 1933. Now completely alone, Bentley returned to Italy to spend an entire year studying at the University of Florence. Unmoored and freed from her parents' moral constraints, she had sex with many men, including one of her professors, who, captivated by the tall, sexually liberated American, forced one of his assistants to write Bentley's master's thesis on a fourteenth-century poem. Plagiarism was the least of her problems. While in Florence, she became addicted to alcohol and flirted with fascism.

After failing one of her courses, Bentley tried to kill herself by swallowing poison. By the summer of 1934, however, she had tamed her demons enough to return to Columbia to complete her master's degree. She arrived back in New York City a confirmed alcoholic and a practiced liar.

Bentley also returned to a shattered economy. Unable to find work in her field, she enrolled in a secretarial course to learn how to type and take shorthand. She also rented a small apartment near Columbia. Lonely and depressed, she accepted a neighbor's invitation during the fall of 1934 to attend a meeting of a local chapter of the American

League Against War and Fascism (ALAW&F), a communist front group. The chapter immediately enrolled her as a member, and she became its resident expert on the dangers of Italian fascism.[6]

Enamored with her new role, Bentley took the next step in March 1935 and became a member of the Communist Party of the United States of America, which assigned her to its Columbia University cell. In a nod to her embellished New England roots, she took "Elizabeth Sherman" as her party name. Her CPUSA membership stabilized her life and gave her, at long last, direction and purpose. While she worked at a string of dead-end jobs to survive during the day, she volunteered as an organizer and educational director for the party at night.[7]

She immediately attracted the GRU, the Soviets' military intelligence service. Her Vassar and Columbia degrees, coupled with her fluency in Italian, made her a choice recruit for underground work in Italy. Shortly after Bentley joined the CPUSA, the executive secretary of the ALAW&F introduced her to Juliet Stuart Poyntz, a Barnard College– and Oxford-educated spotter for the GRU. Poyntz specialized in recruiting women, whom she expected to use whatever means they could, including sex, to collect secret information.[8]

Bentley, though, was not willing to become a "honey trap" for the GRU. After failing to recruit Bentley, Poyntz, who had become increasingly disillusioned with communism after she visited Moscow and witnessed the start of Stalin's purges, vanished from her New York City hotel room. Jacob Golos later told Bentley that Stalin's henchmen had liquidated her.[9]

In June 1938, Columbia University's placement office found Bentley a job as a researcher and secretary at the Italian Library of Information, an arm of Benito Mussolini's Ministry of Propaganda. Straightaway, she alerted the CPUSA and offered to hand over whatever useful information she could take or copy. The party accepted her offer. After she complained to a CPUSA leader that no one was taking her efforts seriously, he introduced her to Jacob Golos on October 15, 1938. Golos instantly recognized Bentley's potential, detached her from the open party, and placed her in the CPUSA's underground. During a snowstorm that December, he also seduced Bentley in his car.[10]

In March 1939, the head of the Italian library learned about Bentley's membership in the ALAW&F and fired her. Bentley then took a series of clerical jobs and did research for Golos on such diverse topics as Herbert Hoover and Mexican politics. She also began learning how to spy and handle sources.[11]

Golos's espionage system depended heavily on the CPUSA and Earl Browder, its general secretary, for recruits. As the party's head, Browder screened potential sources and then referred those with the best access to sensitive information to Golos. The diminutive Golos relied on what the FBI called the sponge method to collect information: he accepted any type of material from any source he could get. He also spent very little money to run his spy networks. Golos received between $2,000 and $3,000 every two months from the Soviets. He used almost none of this money to pay his sources. They spied because they believed they were helping the Soviet Union survive, especially after Hitler's June 1941 invasion.[12]

Golos taught Bentley not only how to handle Moscow's money frugally but also how to detect if she was being followed. She learned to look for drugstores and rest rooms with two exits, to cross and recross the street, to walk against traffic on one-way streets when she suspected a car was trailing her, and to turn and follow her pursuers if she could not elude them. He schooled her in how to erase clues about where she was from by removing store tags from her clothes, to destroy incriminating evidence by burning it or flushing it down the toilet, and to pass bulky reports to others in his networks by leaving them inside lockers at railroad and bus stations. He also educated her in how to discover whether someone had secretly entered and searched her apartment and how to service mail drops.[13]

Golos taught Bentley all these things because he needed her to serve as more than his lover. By 1940, he had an FBI file and a criminal record and was the target of a House Un-American Activities Committee investigation. He was also very sick. Although he was barely over fifty years old, several different doctors told him in early 1941 that he had developed arteriosclerosis—hardening of the arteries—and warned him to slow down.[14]

In March 1941, Golos introduced Bentley to Mary Price. That spring, Bentley traveled to Washington, DC, once a month to help her comb through Walter Lippmann's files and copy his voluminous corre-spondence with leading American and international political figures.[15]

In April, Golos used funds from the CPUSA to establish the United States Service and Shipping Corporation (USSSC). World Tourists, his original front company that had provided money, cover, and passports to the NKVD, was little more than a shell after the FBI's 1939–1940 investigation. He set up USSSC as World Tourists' corporate overseer and to give Bentley a new cover for her espionage work. She became its first vice president.[16]

By the late spring of 1941, Bentley was functioning as Golos's right hand. Her expanded role coincided with his deteriorating health and the June 22 march of Hitler's troops into the Soviet Union. Bentley later told the NKGB that Golos had taken the invasion very hard and worked around the clock to help the USSR. With Earl Browder in prison for passport fraud, he had to invest more time coordinating his espionage activities with CPUSA functionaries he did not respect. Moreover, he had to manage a rapidly expanding stable of agents who wanted to help the Soviets, now locked in a struggle to the death with Hitler.[17]

Among these sources was a loose confederation of US govern-ment employees headed by Nathan Gregory Silvermaster, a longtime communist, Russian émigré, and economist working for the Farm Security Administration and the Board of Economic Warfare. Wil-liam Ludwig Ullmann, the scion of a wealthy Missouri family and a Harvard Business School graduate, led the group with Silvermas-ter. Ullmann, who lived with the Silvermasters and also slept with Gregory's wife, Helen, worked in the Treasury Department and at the Pentagon. At full strength, the Silvermaster Group consisted of four-teen agents and subagents.[18]

The group's members, civil servants scattered across the federal government and even inside the White House, provided Golos and Bentley with a vast array of valuable intelligence to send to the Soviet Union, including secret information on American aircraft produc-tion, statistics on high-octane aviation fuel production and tank pro-duction, profiles of US Army Air Corps officers, data on Germany's armed forces and their locations, a confidential report to Roosevelt from presidential adviser Harry Hopkins on his summer trip to

Moscow in 1941, and very sensitive documents on Anglo-American financial assistance to the Soviet Union.[19]

Golos oversaw this ring until the spring of 1942, when Silvermaster became the focus of four separate federal investigations because of his suspected ties to the CPUSA. Alarmed, Moscow Center ordered Golos to break off all contact with the group for two months. When the NKVD ordered him to resume contact, Golos turned to Bentley for help.[20]

On May 4, 1942, the NKVD's New York station reported to Moscow Center that "Clever Girl," Bentley's code name, had contacted Silvermaster on March 30 and would be seeing him once or twice each month. Within four months, the group's productivity had soared to such an extent that Silvermaster and Ullmann built a darkroom in the basement of their home at 5515 30th Street, NW, for photographing secret documents. Bentley was returning to New York every two weeks on the Friday night *Congressional Limited* carrying a knitting bag bulging with rolls of microfilm and carbon copies of government documents. She was also collecting secret information from fifteen other spies in Washington who were unaffiliated with any group. Duncan Lee was one of them.[21]

Elizabeth Bentley did not completely replace Mary Price as Lee's handler until the fall of 1943, but she first met him in December 1942 or January 1943. Price was hospitalized that January in New York City with pleurisy. Under relentless pressure from Moscow to squeeze more out of Lee, Golos finally sent Bentley to Washington to meet him. She walked up to his Georgetown apartment and introduced herself as Helen; later, she confirmed Price's earlier evaluation that Lee had access to the OSS's most closely guarded secrets.[22]

Golos quickly arranged to meet him in New York City, but Lee failed to make a good first impression. On February 9, 1943, the NKVD's New York station glumly reported to Moscow Center that Golos had found him wanting as a committed CPUSA member and willing conduit. Despite this, the report underscored, "He hasn't dropped the work, however, and continues to provide oral information. He refuses to pass information in writing to Dir [Mary Price]."[23]

When Price fell ill again in April 1943, Bentley stepped in and began handling Lee as her own source. She met with him every two weeks until approximately June 1943, when he left Washington to go overseas on an OSS mission. On May 26, the NKGB's New York station had sent an encrypted message advising Moscow about Lee's upcoming mid-June trip to China with a US Army colonel to have a firsthand look at OSS operations there. A week later, Moscow Center learned that Lee had discussed his trip with Golos and promised to do better work for him when he returned.[24]

Before Lee left for China, Bentley cross-examined him about Donald Wheeler, Lee's close friend and a fellow Rhodes scholar and CPUSA member who worked for the OSS researching German man-power issues. Golos wanted to recruit Wheeler and found Lee's de-scription of him as a "really progressive person" reassuring. By 1944, Wheeler would emerge as the NKGB's most productive and enthusi-astic spy inside the OSS.[25]

On June 16, 1943, Donovan signed a secret memorandum request-ing the Pentagon to schedule flights for Lieutenant Colonel Richard P. Heppner, a future assistant secretary of defense, and Lee to Chongqing, China, with extended layovers in London and Cairo. Donovan wanted to expose his protégé to some of the problems in the OSS's foreign stations.[26]

Donovan asked Heppner and Lee to look into one of the OSS's most pressing problems: its tortured relationship with Tai Li, Chiang Kai-shek's cunning intelligence chief. Tai Li had used OSS-provided weapons and military supplies to fight the Japanese and Mao Ze-dong's communists and to consolidate his own racketeering empire. Yet he had shared very little valuable intelligence with the Americans. He had also limited their independent operations against the Japa-nese. Lee received extensive briefings on the OSS's difficulties with Tai Li before he left Washington on June 29, 1943—information he passed on to Bentley just before he departed.[27]

Lee would never meet Tai Li. On August 2, he and twenty other passengers and crew members boarded a twin-engine Curtiss-Wright C-46 Commando in Assam, India, for a 2.5-hour flight over the

"Hump," the jagged eastern end of the Himalayas between India and China. In 1942, the Japanese had captured Rangoon and cut off the Burma Road, which the British had used to supply Chiang Kai-shek's Nationalist troops with weapons, medicine, and food from India. Now the Allies were forced to supply Chiang's armies by air. By the time Lee boarded the C-46, American pilots had ferried tons of war supplies and thousands of Nationalist soldiers back and forth over the Hump in what those who flew the planes and had to clean them out dubbed "Operation Vomit."[28]

At 8 a.m. that August morning, Lee strapped on a parachute, sat down in one of the plane's aluminum bucket seats, and opened a book. Eric Sevareid, a CBS reporter and protégé of Edward R. Murrow, sat beside him, scribbling notes for a dispatch from China. John Paton Davies, a US Foreign Service officer and political adviser to Lieutenant General Joseph Stilwell, the Allies' commander of the China-Burma-India theater, was also on the flight. After an hour in the air, the C-46 lost power in its left engine and began corkscrewing downward. As the plane pitched sharply on its side, Lee grabbed a pistol, pulled a bottle of Carew's gin out of his bag, which he kicked out the door, and jumped. He had never parachuted from an airplane. The gin landed safely with Lee, who shared it with his comrades that first night in the jungle.[29]

He landed near Davies on a hillside in waist-high grass. They had dropped into the Naga Hills, a lush jungle region straddling the border between India and Burma and infested with leeches, razor-sharp grass, Japanese patrols, and headhunters. Since that January, one nearby village of headhunters had boiled over one hundred heads taken from neighboring tribes. As Davies and Lee staggered to their feet, four muscular, tattooed men dressed only in G-strings and carrying knives and spears encircled them.[30]

Sevareid faced the same threat several miles away. When headhunters surrounded him, he raised his palm as if in a Saturday morning western and mumbled, "How." It was no worse than anything else he could have said. Before the men had taken off, the US Army had given them a sheet of paper with emergency sentences in the wrong language.[31]

Luckily for Lee and his companions, the headhunters disliked the Japanese more than they did the Americans. With their help and daily supply drops from Assam, Lee and the others eluded Japanese army patrols and walked out of the jungle twenty-six days later. Photographs of Lee, who was not identified as a member of the OSS, and the others he had been marooned with quickly spread around the world.[32]

Sevareid wrote about his time in the Naga Hills for *Reader's Digest* in 1943 and in a memoir published in 1946. In his book, he described Lee as a "boyish, highly intelligent agent of the OSS . . . who had been a Rhodes scholar at Oxford." Davies, whose own career in the State Department was cut short almost a decade later because of unfounded charges that he had undermined his government's policies in China, praised Lee in a letter addressed to Donovan. "Captain Lee's conduct throughout the crisis and during the several weeks which followed, while we were in the jungle and making our way out, was entirely exemplary. Although this was Captain Lee's first venture into the field, he showed a maturity of judgment, a sense of responsibility and a willingness to take the initiative whenever necessary."[33]

Lee had little time to relish his jungle adventure. He returned to the United States on October 4, 1943, to a shaky marriage, an angry mistress, and a worried Jacob Golos. While he was away, Ishbel had somehow discovered his affair with Price. The fallout was immediate: she had flown into what Bentley described to the Soviets as "jealous fits" in front of Price, who had returned to Washington that fall. Unable to cope with this, Price decided that she could no longer work with Lee.[34]

All this had rattled Golos, forcing him to come to Washington to confront the Lees. Although gravely ill, he could not risk losing a spy who sat at Donovan's right elbow. He and Bentley socialized with the Lees on an October evening at the 823 Club, a German beer cellar, on 15th Street. Lee chose this location because he expected not to run into anyone he knew there. Bentley later explained to the FBI the reason for this meeting: "Lee had become quite involved with Mary Price and . . . this situation was causing Ishbel considerable distress. Part of the purpose was having Ishbel take an active part in the operations of the espionage apparatus in so far as it concerned Duncan Lee."[35]

A master at handling high-strung American recruits and their personal problems, Golos calmed Ishbel and explained the importance of her wayward husband's work to the party. His strategy succeeded. Bentley later used Ishbel to encourage Lee to continue spying.[36]

The meeting also gave Golos an opportunity to evaluate Lee's physical and mental health after Burma. The NKVD's New York station passed to Moscow Center Golos's assessment that "wandering around the Burmese jungles had worn [Lee] down badly, and it will take some time before we can once again involve him in act[ually] work[ing] for us."[37]

The jungle had drained Lee, but not enough to stop him from sleeping with Price, who had fallen in love with him. She hoped he would divorce Ishbel and marry her. Price was also looking for a new career because she had quit her job with Walter Lippmann.[38]

When she returned to Washington in September from an extended vacation in Mexico, Price moved back into her apartment at 2038 I Street, NW, and, under instructions from Golos, applied for jobs with the OSS, the State Department, and the US Army Signal Corps at Arlington Hall Station. Eight months earlier, at Arlington Hall, the army had begun its top-secret effort to decipher the Soviet Union's encrypted diplomatic traffic between Moscow and its American-based embassy, consulates, and trade missions. Price got none of these highly sensitive jobs. Though impressed by her ability, the OSS questioned her loyalty to the United States because of her "extremely leftist views and associations." This time, the agency managed to prevent a dangerous agent from gaining direct access to its secrets.[39]

After Lee resumed his job at the Secretariat that fall, Bentley tasked him with finding out why the OSS had rejected Price. Uncharacteristically, he followed her instructions and examined Price's security file. He told Bentley that Price had been turned down for having past ties to known communists. His report not only answered the NKVD's question but also highlighted his access to the OSS's highly classified security files. Bentley instructed Lee to keep his eyes open for any information in these files that might be of interest.[40]

On November 24, 1943, the NKGB's New York station cataloged what Lee had discussed with Bentley since his return from Burma: the OSS's relationship with the Polish intelligence service inside the United States, the possibility of a Finnish-Soviet peace treaty, Bulgarian politics, a meeting between the US ambassador in Britain and the head of the Polish government-in-exile in London, and rumors of a Japanese invasion of the Soviet Union. He also shared with Bentley the OSS's plans to rescue downed American airmen in Greece. In fact, the Secretariat had sent a memorandum from Donovan to President Roosevelt that trumpeted the spy service's success in rescuing fourteen of them.[41]

On December 13, 1943, the army promoted Lee to the rank of major. A little over a month later, he became the chief of the OSS's Secretariat, a position he held officially until November 20, 1944. He also began to meet regularly with Bentley at his apartment. Lee later admitted to one of his closest friends that he had slept with her.[42]

Bentley faced the same problems with Lee that Price had confronted. He refused to give her any OSS documents and did not allow her to take notes as he reported the information he had collected. Like Price, she had to memorize what he said until she could write it down after she had left. And except on very rare occasions, he decided what information he would pass to her rather than following any instructions she gave him.[43]

Although Golos seemed to attach great significance to his information, Bentley considered Lee a difficult and even spineless source. She later described him to the FBI "as a rather weak individual who was impressed with being a descendant of General Lee and most of the time I saw him he was nervous and emotionally upset." From their very first meeting, she tried to reassure him that his information would go only to Earl Browder and the CPUSA. Bentley told the same lie to several of her other sources.[44]

The fiction that their information went only to Browder and the CPUSA was important for Golos and his American sources. Knowing how close he had come to execution during the purges, Golos believed telling his Moscow masters that his American sources would only pass their information to other Americans made him indispensable to the NKVD's operations and shielded him from harm or removal. It also allowed many of his sources to deny to themselves that they were giving their country's secrets to the Soviet Union. This self-deception may have salved those consciences troubled by the betrayals. Bentley reinforced this myth by collecting her sources' CPUSA dues and giving them party literature to read. She later admitted to the FBI, however, that she had told Lee that Golos was the head of their particular espionage group, and "after a while he realized that such information was actually destined for Russian intelligence." It is improbable that Lee ever believed that the classified intelligence he was passing to Price and Bentley was going just to the CPUSA. He was too smart and sophisticated not to understand that his secret information—for instance, about the OSS's problems with Tai Li, the head of Chiang Kai-shek's secret service, or classified reports on Bulgarian politics—was going to Moscow's spymasters. Bentley also speculated that Mary Price probably told Lee who Golos really was, the pillar of the NKVD's operations in the United States.[45]

Whatever he pretended to believe, Lee continued to supply Bentley with oral summaries of classified OSS reports that flowed in and out of the Secretariat. These summaries detailed Hungary's intrigues for a separate peace with the United States, the opening of an OSS station in India, and the OSS's problems in Spain with American ambassador Carlton J. Hayes—Lee personally directed his staff in the Secretariat to send to Donovan in New Delhi the secret "Memorandum of Understanding Between [the] Embassy and OSS in Spain" that solved this crisis.[46]

In early March 1944, Lee disclosed to Bentley his belief that Donovan's upcoming trip to Europe in April probably signaled the approach of the long-promised Allied invasion of France. He predicted that the landing would take place between mid-May and the beginning of June and pointed out that Donovan had been present at the start of all major US military operations. Bentley knew that Lee was especially agitated by Britain's and America's chronic delay in launching a second front—Roosevelt and Churchill had promised Stalin at their conference in Tehran in late 1943 that the cross-channel invasion of France would take place in May 1944—and would not make this prediction unless confident in his own judgment.[47]

On April 20, 1944, the British and American military missions in Moscow informed Stalin that Operation Overlord would begin in early June. Stalin, however, remembered that Roosevelt and Churchill had sworn to cross the English Channel in 1942 and 1943; instead, they had invaded North Africa and Italy. Lee's information added to the evidence that Stalin's other spies were collecting in Britain that General Dwight Eisenhower was indeed preparing to invade France.[48]

Despite Lee's efforts, Moscow Center continued to complain that most of his information was still too vague.[49]

But Lee was already losing his nerve. Insomnia driven by nightmares of being caught and executed had started several months before in December 1943 when Donovan traveled to the Soviet Union after Roosevelt, Churchill, and Stalin's meeting in Tehran. The purpose of his trip was to establish an intelligence-sharing partnership between the OSS and the NKGB, but Lee feared Donovan might accomplish more and uncover his spying.

Donovan understood the Soviet military's enormous killing power and wanted to help it kill as many Germans as possible. Also aware that the NKGB operated in countries and regions where the OSS had little presence or insight, he wanted whatever intelligence about these blind spots the Soviets would hand over. He had flown to the Soviet Union with an offer to post a small OSS team in Moscow in exchange for a small NKGB team posted in Washington. Pavel Mikhailovich Fitin, the youthful chief of its foreign intelligence directorate, readily agreed. Fitin, who knew all about Golos's networks and Lee, seemed more interested in Donovan's offers of technical assistance than in exchanging intelligence.[50]

Donovan left Moscow on January 6, 1944, convinced that he had engineered a major breakthrough with the Soviets. Both Averell Harriman, the US ambassador to the Soviet Union, and the Joint Chiefs of Staff supported an open exchange with the Soviets. But Donovan's project petrified Lee. Bentley, in her highly dramatic 1951 memoir, vividly described how much the proposed exchange with the Soviets frightened him. She claimed that Lee had taken to crawling around on the floor of his apartment looking for the FBI wiretaps on his phone and that one night he had begged her to come to his home where, drenched in sweat, he excitedly declared that the exchange would finish him: "They'll come to call on me, and when I let them in, they'll shake my hand and say, 'Well done, comrade.'"[51]

Lee followed the progress of the proposed exchange closely and shared what he heard and read about it with Bentley. He told her that Donovan had been completely open with Fitin but that FBI director J. Edgar Hoover loathed the plan. By 1943, Hoover was just beginning to see the outlines of the Soviets' systematic and long-standing espionage efforts against the United States. Lee reported to Bentley in January 1944 that Donovan had called Hoover "a fool" after hearing that the FBI director opposed the exchange and maintained that the Soviets had had spies in the United States since the 1924 establishment of Amtorg. Donovan fumed that Hoover was "uninformed" about Soviet espionage.[52]

Lee also explained to Bentley the bitter rivalry between the FBI and the OSS and how their bureaucratic warfare was intensifying as each jockeyed to become the dominant American intelligence agency. Growing agitated, he blurted out that the FBI would like nothing more than to arrest a disloyal OSS officer.[53]

Fortunately for Lee, Hoover marshaled the combined voices of Attorney General Francis Biddle, influential presidential adviser Harry Hopkins, and FDR's chief of staff Admiral William Leahy to table Donovan's proposal. Biddle especially feared that conservative Republicans would use Donovan's exchange to attack Roosevelt in the 1944 presidential election. In early March, Lee divulged to Bentley that Hoover had warned the president about an unfavorable public reaction to Donovan's plan. Roosevelt vetoed the proposed exchange on March 15, 1944.[54]

Despite this, Lee was sure he was about to be exposed. That March, the NKGB's New York station reported to Moscow Center that he had given Bentley the names of OSS major Murray Gurfein and Angel Kouyoumdjisky. Gurfein, from his post in Istanbul, Turkey, was working with Kouyoumdjisky, a wealthy Bulgarian émigré and OSS asset living in New York City, to detach Bulgaria from its military alliance with Hitler. Later that same month, Lee told Bentley in a panic that Donovan had received a cable from the US Army's mission in Moscow saying that Vyachelsav Molotov, the Soviet Union's foreign minister, knew who Kouyoumdjisky was and what he was trying to do. A horrified Lee had no doubt that the OSS would discover him to be the insider who had passed the Bulgarian's name to Moscow.[55]

As his feet got colder, Lee failed to keep appointments with Bentley at least twice during the spring of 1944. Even Mary Price could not persuade him to meet with her. Finally, Bentley went to the Lees' apartment and convinced Ishbel to prod him to rendezvous with her in a public park. She and the Lees talked for three hours, during which Lee told her that he feared being executed for treason. Despite his evident terror, Lee yielded to her and Ishbel's pressure and agreed to continue spying. His work for Bentley even improved briefly.[56]

On June 9, the New York station cabled Moscow Center Lee's oral summary of the OSS's debriefing of Father Stanislaus Orlemanski, a Catholic priest from Springfield, Massachusetts, who had met with Joseph Stalin that spring in Moscow about the future of Poland. He also continued to supply Bentley with oral summaries of cables between the State Department and the OSS. All the while, he worried constantly about being caught.[57]

To further protect himself, Lee stopped meeting Bentley regularly at his apartment. The FBI was not his only worry. That July, the Lees moved into their new home, a house at 1522 31st Street, NW. They needed more room for their growing family. John Lightfoot Lee was born on November 15, 1943, and shortly thereafter, Ishbel's mother, Katherine Gibb, came to help her daughter. She ended up staying for five years. Lee told Bentley that he feared her regular visits would arouse Gibb's suspicions.[58]

Occasionally, though, when his family was away, Lee let Bentley come to his house. They would spend two to three hours together. When his family was home, he met her at either of two drugstores in his Georgetown neighborhood. He would enter one of the stores, glance around nervously, buy a pack of cigarettes, and then walk out. She would follow behind for a half block to make sure no one was trailing him, and then they would walk around the neighborhood, discussing the information that he had brought her.[59]

Lee's fears spiked again in the summer of 1944 after he learned about an internal OSS hunt for communists. On July 6, the Secretariat, acting on Donovan's instructions, sent a memorandum to Archbold Van Beuren, head of the OSS Security Office, asking him to draft a report that "would indicate the number of persons employed in the agency who were definitely Communists, those who were suspected of being Communists, and those who were felt to entertain Communist beliefs." The memorandum also asked Van Beuren to recommend how the OSS should deal with those named. Donovan may have been responding to a recommendation from the head of the army's military intelligence wing to purge all officers who were also CPUSA members.[60]

Two weeks later, the OSS's Security Office sent Donovan and Doering a memorandum titled "Special Cases" that identified forty-seven employees suspected of being communists or harboring communist beliefs. The memorandum went on to assert confidently that "there were no proven Communists employed by the OSS" and that "no known member of the Communist party has ever been given a security approval recommendation by this office for employment by this agency." Donovan knew this could not be true. The OSS had recruited Milton Wolff, the last commander of the Abraham Lincoln Battalion, and other Spanish Civil War veterans because of their guerrilla warfare experience. Donovan knew they were all communists, but he needed men who had fought behind enemy lines and organized partisan bands. In a dramatic display of his "ends-justify-the-means" mind-set, he later lied to a congressional committee in 1945 about the communist ties of four of his officers serving in Italy, including Wolff. He told the committee that he had personally investigated all four and found they were not communists.[61]

Donovan had also refused to fire Lee's fellow Rhodes scholar Donald Wheeler, one of the OSS's foremost experts on German manpower and one of the Soviets' most important spies inside the organization, after the FBI told him, as part of a Hatch Act loyalty investigation in

1942, that Wheeler was pro-communist and a suspected emissary of the Comintern. The FBI had uncovered nothing, however, to indicate that Wheeler was a spy. Neither his membership in such leftist organizations as the Washington Committee for Democratic Action and the Washington Bookshop Association nor his subscription to the *Daily Worker* meant anything to Donovan. Much more importantly, three other OSS officers vouched for Wheeler and spoke highly of his work calculating German war deaths for the agency.[62]

Although his own name was not on the "Special Cases" list, Lee reacted immediately: he refused an assignment from Bentley to hand over the names and job titles of all OSS employees in Moscow. He did tell her, however, about the Security Office's list, claiming that he had stumbled on it. On September 15, 1944, the New York station sent an encrypted message to Moscow about the OSS's list. Because the compilation was too long for Bentley to memorize, Lee, in the only known instance of his transmitting handwritten information to her, handed her a version of the list that contained twenty-six names. One week later, the New York station forwarded it to Moscow. The suspects included Donald Wheeler and Maurice Halperin, who had both been sources for Price and Bentley. Moscow Center ordered an immediate temporary halt to all contact with Wheeler, which lasted until March 1945. Up until then, he had been stripping the OSS's files and passing a treasure trove of OSS reports to the Soviets. From his position on the editorial board of the Research and Analysis Branch, he had delivered batches of classified OSS assessments to the NKGB, including one that discussed casualties in the German armed forces.[63]

Meanwhile, on October 1, 1944, Lee requested a transfer from the Secretariat to the OSS's Secret Intelligence Branch, its clandestine intelligence-gathering wing. He was named chief of its Far Eastern Division's Japan-China Section seven weeks later. Since August, he had been thinking about how to make money after the war. He knew China would have to be rebuilt after the fighting and that he would be an attractive hire for any American company looking to expand there. Edmund, sensing his son's unlimited postwar options, cautioned him not to "burn any bridges" and to be in Washington when the "post war plums [were] handed out."[64]

Lee had another reason for returning to China that his father knew nothing about: he wanted to get away from Bentley and the NKGB. By then, he was sure that the Allies would win the war. He had done his part to save the great Soviet experiment, but he had never planned on dying for it. He did not want to press his luck with the OSS's tightening security.

Even though he reported to Bentley in late September about a possible trip to India and China, then again in October about an OSS officer working with a group of communists in China who were planning to use Korean communists to infiltrate Japan, he claimed that most of the reports he saw were of no use to her. Following these meetings, the New York station sent a scathing report on Lee to Moscow: "At pres., K[och] only has access to reports on Japan that, according to him, are of no interest. . . . [He] requires special guidance—he is one of the 'weakest of the weak sisters'; nervous and frightened of his own shadow."[65]

Bentley had far more to worry about than a scared spy. Her life was falling apart around her. Its collapse, which had started a year before, changed the course of Lee's life.

On November 25, 1943, Golos came to Bentley's Brooklyn apartment and took her to a Thanksgiving Day dinner and an early movie. Bentley noticed how pale and tired Golos looked. For almost a year, he had engaged in a losing tug-of-war with Vassily Zarubin, the short and beefy new chief of the NKGB's North American operations, for control of his American networks. Zarubin had arrived in the United States in January 1942 as the Soviet embassy's third secretary. One of his most important missions was to learn about all of Golos's sources, professionalize them, and then break his networks into smaller cells. To do this, he had to push Golos out of the way.[66]

Zarubin specialized in running over people. He had joined the Cheka in 1920 and served in the OGPU and NKVD as an illegal and legal officer in Manchuria, Denmark, France, Germany, and the United States. He had survived the purges and risen to become one of the NKVD's most experienced and ruthless officers. He also may have played a role in the Soviets' massacre of thousands of captured Polish officers in the Katyn Forest in April and May 1940.[67]

As Golos lay napping on Bentley's couch after they returned to her apartment, he made horrible choking sounds and died of a massive heart attack. His refusal to slow down and his struggles with Zarubin had finally killed him. He had fought tenaciously to hold onto his networks, but Zarubin's relentless pressure had worn him out. Before he died, he had finally given ground and let the Soviets peel away Julius Rosenberg's cell of fellow engineers, who were stealing secrets about radar and airplane designs, and several members of the Silvermaster Group.[68]

Golos's sudden death crushed Bentley, but with Earl Browder's blessing—President Roosevelt had pardoned and released him from federal prison in 1942 as a goodwill gesture to the Soviets—she stepped into his shoes and succeeded him. When the Soviets discovered this, as well as that she had been Golos's partner in espionage and sex, they were shocked. He had lied to them, claiming she was only his courier.[69]

On November 29, 1943, Bentley met with "Bill," whom she later described as being of "medium height, [with] dark, round eyes [and] blue- or purple-colored lips, and who was always a sharp dresser." Bill was Iskhak Akhmerov, former head of the NKVD's illegals station in the United States in the late 1930s. He had returned to the United States in December 1941 to revive the station's work and to help Zarubin take over Golos's networks. His return, along with Zarubin's, signaled that Stalin now viewed the United States as his most important intelligence target.[70]

During his first meeting with Bentley, Akhmerov demanded operational control of Mary Price. Reflexively, she resisted his power grab. Despite her pushback, she impressed Akhmerov with her quick intelligence and Vassar-bred manners. He thought he could work with her. On December 19, 1943, Zarubin sent a message to Moscow Center that his New York station would shortly begin to take over Bentley's spies. First, he wanted Lee and Maurice Halperin, now head of the Latin American Division in the OSS's Research and Analysis Branch. Four months later, Akhmerov was still trying to persuade Bentley to hand them over.[71]

She proved no more cooperative than her lover Golos had been, balking at Akhmerov's request to at least meet her sources. She parried with the lie that they were only willing to give their information to her and the CPUSA. Akhmerov also noted a not-so-subtle anti-Soviet streak. Presciently, he reported to Moscow, "Sometimes I sense from the remarks that are made that deep down she dislikes us."[72]

Meanwhile, in early 1944 Earl Browder asked Bentley to manage yet another ring of spies who worked for the federal government in Washington and had made contact with Golos just before he died. Victor Perlo, an economist and statistician with the War Production Board, was this group's leader. Its other eight members came from the OSS, the staff of the Senate's Subcommittee on War Mobilization, the Foreign Economic Administration, the Treasury Department, and the United Nations Relief and Rehabilitation Administration.[73]

The Soviets remained determined to take over all of Bentley's sources. They had already begun looking ahead and had made stealing American technology and gathering information on Washington's plans for the postwar period their top priorities. To accomplish these goals, the NKGB planned to increase its penetration of the State Department, the Foreign Economic Administration, the War Production Board, and the OSS. It also wanted to infiltrate agents into the FBI and the Department of Justice's War Division, which offered legal advice on war-planning policies and alien control. The NKGB knew that it needed highly trained spies to run its new networks. It no longer needed American amateurs like Elizabeth Bentley.[74]

In particular, Moscow Center worried about her erratic personality and realized that her networks, although enormously productive, were riddled with gaping security holes that could bring them down at any moment. The NKGB was appalled that so many of Bentley's sources knew each other and worked so closely together. Zarubin pressured Earl Browder to make her give up her spies.[75]

In November 1944, Bentley met a Soviet agent named "Al," tasked with taking her completely out of the NKGB's American operations, at a Georgetown pharmacy. Al was Anatoly Gorsky, the new first secretary of the Soviet's embassy in Washington, who had replaced Zarubin the previous August as the NKGB's top officer in North America. Before that, he had handled the Magnificent Five spy ring in Britain. Moscow Center had sent him to the United States to follow Donald Maclean, one of the ring's most important members, who had been promoted that spring to the post of first secretary of the British embassy in Washington. Gorsky continued Zarubin's policy of shifting the epicenter of the NKGB's operations from New York City to Washington.[76]

Bentley later sketched Al as "maybe 5'3" or 5'4", broad shouldered, stocky, fat, nearsighted, with rimless glasses . . . [with] two extra teeth jutting out, overlapping each other, like tiger teeth, in the upper front. . . . He is the kind of person that instinctively makes shivers run up and down your spine." Later in November, at another meeting in New York City, Gorsky told her that the Supreme Presidium of the Union of Soviet Socialist Republics had awarded her the Order of the Red Star. He solemnly explained that this prestigious award meant privileges: she was now entitled to a monthly salary, preferential living quarters in Moscow, all-expense-paid vacations, and free streetcar rides. He also offered to send her to Moscow, where the NKGB could train her to manage sources properly.[77]

Bentley was not impressed. Rather, her mood worsened in December after Gorsky told her that she had to give up her well-paying job at the United States Service and Shipping Corporation and start training her NKGB successor to run the company. He fretted about reports that the FBI was beginning to look into USSSC's finances and feared that the bureau's rooting around in the corporation's records might lead its agents to Bentley's espionage activities. He also instructed her to vacate her brownstone apartment in Brooklyn because too many of her former sources knew where she lived. Gorsky forced Bentley to move into a room in the Hotel St. George in Brooklyn. Depressed, she began drinking even more heavily than before.[78]

By early 1945, she was no longer handling any sources, not even Lee. The Soviets had instructed her to tell her spies that she was leaving to have her appendix removed and that they could expect to meet her replacement soon. Bentley had her last conversation with Lee in January 1945. They met at Longchamps Restaurant in New York City, but OSS secrets were not on the menu. Instead, he begged her for help with Price, who was pressuring him to leave Ishbel. Bentley refused to get involved. Price's demands were coming at a particularly bad time because Lee was about to become a father for the third time. Edmund Jennings Lee VI was born on January 25, 1945.[79]

The NKGB tried several strategies to mollify Bentley after taking away all her sources. Akhmerov, dismissing her as just another American who craved consumer goods, offered her a fur coat and an air conditioner. For good measure, Gorsky asked Moscow Center to find her a suitable husband, suggesting that it send "a Polish or Baltic refugee to South America or Canada. We'll take care of the rest."[80]

As Bentley's life was disintegrating, so was Lee's will to continue spying. While she contended with the Soviets, he began meeting with "Jack," whose real name was Joseph Katz, one of the NKGB's most seasoned American agents. Originally from Lithuania, he had become a US citizen, studied aeronautical engineering, and joined the CPUSA in 1932. The NKVD recruited him in 1937 or 1938. One of the New York station's most versatile operatives and troubleshooters, Katz specialized in establishing businesses for commercial cover while mastering espionage's black arts of safecracking, lock picking, wiretapping, fighting in close quarters, and using firearms.[81]

Bentley described Katz as about 5'9" with very broad shoulders, kinky hair, very heavy eyebrows, bright blue eyes, and a face that was "always very, very gray." She claimed that he suffered from bleeding stomach ulcers and walked with a limp.[82]

Katz was also a superb case officer who exuded friendliness and compassion. He understood that sources were more likely to confide in those they trusted and liked than in those they feared and despised. Katz succeeded in developing a rapport with Lee and managed to coax his terrified source to meet. During their meeting, Lee confessed his fear.

On February 3, 1945, Katz reported on his first meeting with Lee to Moscow Center. It had not gone well: "After beating himself up over how cowardly he had been, how much he regretted this etc., he told me that he has to stand by his decision to leave. . . . He is absolutely terrified and has lost heart. He is plagued by nightmares where he sees his name on lists, where his life has been ruined, etc."[83]

Lee baffled the Soviets. In Moscow, the NKGB's spymasters pored over his background and looked for any clues that might explain his emotional collapse. They fixated on his CPUSA background and his association with Russian War Relief. They could not understand why the OSS had hired him in the first place after his work for a communist-dominated relief agency or how he had risen so high in Donovan's agency. Marinated in a culture that made paranoia a professional virtue, they feared that he might be a double agent.

Moscow Center was oblivious of two facts: no one in the US government knew Lee was a communist, and the OSS actually valued his extra efforts for Russian War Relief as showcasing his work ethic and highlighting his interest in international affairs. The Soviets also had no idea that Donovan had permitted Lee to work for the charity during his association with the spymaster's law firm.

Katz, though, perhaps sensing a professional challenge, refused to give up on Lee. Once more, he coaxed him into meeting. Again, it went badly. On March 20, 1945, Gorsky sent a message to Moscow describing Katz's two appointments with his spooked and guilt-ridden spy. Lee had come to both so frightened that he could not even hold a cup of coffee in his shaking hands. He complained of chronic nightmares and assured Katz that the FBI was waiting for the war to end before its agents pounced on him and the other communists who had spied for the Soviets. He also complained about Bentley's "big mouth" and "indiscretion." Lee apologized for acting so cowardly, but he made it clear that he wanted out—"that he could not lead a 'double life,' that he had a 'guilty' conscience for 'deceiving the USA,' and that he was constantly having a crisis of conscience, and so forth."[84]

Fear played a starring role in Lee's decision to abandon spying for the Soviets, but it was not his only motivation. Believing Katz truly understood his predicament, Lee confessed that shards of his missionary-bred conscience had finally worked their way to the surface; the guilt they dragged up with them had become impossible to live with. His betrayal of his country and of the men who had given him the opportunity and means to serve it had overwhelmed the chilly righteousness he had felt when he agreed to spy for the Soviets in 1942.

Lee's vision of himself as a savoir of mankind from fascism, following in the bold and heroic footsteps of his illustrious family, had collided head-on with the much darker image of his execution. Wracked by fear and remorse, he was emotionally spent and wanted out. Looking back at her time with him, Bentley later told the FBI that Lee always "appeared to be troubled by a severe conflict of ideas."[85]

In his personal torment, Lee was not alone. Bernard Schuster, organizational secretary of the CPUSA's New York District and a talent spotter for the NKVD, complained openly to Bentley about the high emotional costs the risks and stresses of their double lives exacted from his recruits. Several of them, completely unprepared for what they were getting into, had been emotionally gutted by their work for the Soviets and needed psychiatric treatment.[86]

During the first week of April, Moscow Center ordered Gorsky to break off all contact with the self-accused coward. Still, the center hoped to salvage Lee in the future as a talent spotter and an insider who could monitor the progress of the OSS's counterintelligence investigations.[87]

Lee did not give them an opening. On July 25, he went with Donovan to Kunming, China, on an inspection of OSS stations. He was still there when the United States dropped its atomic bombs on Hiroshima and Nagasaki. Although the NKGB knew about his trip, there is no indication that any of its agents in China tried to contact him.[88]

Still, he could not leave his past completely behind, and his behavior never disturbed some compartments of his conscience. Lee remained a ladies' man and captivated women with his wit and charm. Adultery remained a private pastime. Walter Pforzheimer, later the CIA's first legislative counsel, who had known him since their undergraduate days together at Yale, claimed that Lee always "screwed more than a silkworm." He had an especially ill-fated affair with an OSS secretary from Pennsylvania while in Kunming. Its consequences proved fatal: she later killed herself in New York City because he refused to leave Ishbel.[89]

In his public life, however, Lee received continued recognition. The OSS promoted him to lieutenant colonel on September 11, 1945. He was named the Secret Intelligence Branch's executive officer two months later, after serving as chief of the Japan-China Section. By then, he had been transferred to the War Department's Strategic Services Unit. On August 23, 1945, Donovan had received word from

President Harry Truman's Bureau of the Budget that the OSS faced disbandment. Donovan had feared this eventuality because, as a wartime agency, it had always been in danger of elimination as soon as the fighting ended. Franklin Roosevelt's death on April 12, 1945, ensured this fate. President Truman, no supporter of Donovan, signed Executive Order 9621 on September 20, 1945, abolishing the OSS as of October 1. The old warrior returned to his law firm as a retired major general.[90]

Before he left Washington, Donovan wrote a personal letter to Lee, praising his wartime service: "From the early days when you added to the smooth functioning of the secretariat until these recent months when you were planning and staffing and implementing operations in China, your results have always been superior. You have reason to be proud of what you have done, and we are proud of you."[91]

In his forty months of service, Lee had become one of Donovan's most relied-on aides. James Murphy, the OSS's chief counterintelligence officer, told the FBI in 1954 that the agency's top officers trusted Lee completely. He had also amassed a distinguished war record. By the end of the fighting, Lee had received an Asiatic Pacific Campaign Medal with two bronze battle stars; a European, African, Middle Eastern Campaign Medal; an American Campaign Medal; and a World War II Victory Medal. To top it off, the secretary of war awarded him a US Army Commendation medal.[92]

Lee's value to the OSS was underscored in another, more secret way. After the OSS disbanded, S. Peter Karlow, who had served as one of its officers in Algiers and lost a leg for Donovan's intelligence service off the Italian coast, compiled an index on November 5, 1945, of all the OSS's key personnel. Donovan, who wanted President Truman to establish a permanent intelligence agency using the OSS's staff, probably asked Karlow to do this. This core list contained the names of all those who would be considered for rehiring once a new intelligence agency replaced the OSS. Lee's entry described his area specialty as "Far East–General Intelligence." Under the box "Recommendation" one word appeared: "Highly."[93]

Two days after Karlow made his notation about Lee, Elizabeth Bentley caught a subway train that let her out near New York's Foley

Square. In her hand, she carried a magazine, a signal to the man in the dark double-breasted suit and white shirt waiting for her on the platform that she was the woman he had spoken to on the telephone the day before. As they both emerged into the late afternoon's fading light and onto the street, the man whisked her into the hulking federal building that overlooked the square. Bentley had come to tell the FBI about her life as an NKGB courier and spy ringleader.[94]

SIX

GREGORY

By the time Elizabeth Bentley slipped through the side door of the FBI's New York City field office in early November 1945, her commitment to communism was as threadbare as Duncan Lee's. But there was one stark difference between the two: he wanted to forget, whereas she wanted to confess. The fallout from her decision contaminated both their lives.

Bentley would soon learn that she had defected to an FBI that reflected the personality and background of J. Edgar Hoover, its larger-than-life director. Since 1924, he had methodically hammered the bureau into his own image. His obsessions and preoccupations, coupled with strategic decisions made by Franklin Roosevelt's White House, would give the Soviets a huge head start over his G-men and pave the road for Lee's getaway.

Ironically, the Soviets were more responsible for her defection than the FBI. The NKGB had unraveled her devotion to its cause by stripping Bentley of her self-worth, her mission, and her home. Anatoly Gorsky, with his vast experience in handling foreign agents on two continents, had sensed her growing anger and smoldering resentment over her mistreatment by the NKGB. Still, he could not persuade Moscow Center that she was rapidly morphing into a lethal threat to the Soviets' most important American spy networks. Even the streetwise Gorsky failed to grasp that Bentley's work with Jacob

Golos had infused her life with a profound sense of purpose that she now believed had died with him.

The Soviets also did not understand that her loneliness and isolation were causing her to drink more and more and to spend her days and nights brooding over a future that seemed to be leading nowhere. She was a powder keg waiting to explode.

The match that set her off flickered to life on an April afternoon in 1945, when she picked up a man she was having a drink with in her hotel's bar. With his thinning red hair and blue eyes, Peter Heller looked enough like Golos that she struck up a conversation with him. After a few more drinks, she took him upstairs to bed.[1]

Still reeling from Golos's death, Bentley fell madly in love with Heller. She rejoiced to her colleagues at the United States Service and Shipping Corporation that she planned to marry him. But just as quickly as they had fallen into bed, Heller vanished. When he returned several weeks later, he startled her with the claim that he was a "big shot Government spy." Bentley immediately suspected that she had walked into a trap. Her worst suspicions seemed to be confirmed when she combed through Heller's wallet one night while he slept. In it, she found what looked like an identification card emblazoned with a shield.[2]

Stricken, Bentley feared that Heller was working for either the FBI or the NKGB. She decided not to tell Gorsky or Joseph Katz about him but to wait for more clues about his true mission. Her strategy worked until her ecumenical sexual appetite got the better of her. Sometime during that late spring, Bentley made a pass at Rae Elson, the woman the Soviets had chosen to replace her at USSSC because they worried that the FBI knew the corporation was a front for espionage. Elson complained bitterly to Gorsky about Bentley's sexual advances, which she said surprised her because Bentley had a male lover. Gorsky sent Katz to interrogate Bentley about this new man in her life. After Katz pressed her, she told him and then Gorsky about Heller's amazing claim. They warned her that he was almost certainly an FBI or US Army counterintelligence agent and that she had to break off their relationship. Being too lonely, she refused.[3]

During the first week of June 1945, Bentley met Gorsky in a small movie theater in Washington, DC. As they sat together in the dark, he whispered that she was now in extreme danger and had to leave her job at USSSC at once. He urged her to go to Mexico or Canada. From there, he assured her, the NKGB could smuggle her into the Soviet Union. She was noncommittal.[4]

They met again ten days later. Gorsky immediately pressed her to go to Moscow for what he called special training. After that, he suggested, the NKGB could dispatch her to Latin America or Canada or even back to the United States under an alias. In a show of goodwill, he promised to send her on a paid vacation in the seaside resort at Old Lyme, Connecticut, before she left to begin her new life. He merely managed, however, to frighten and unbalance Bentley even more. She remembered Juliet Poyntz's disappearance and murder eight years before.[5]

Insomnia and paranoia preyed on Bentley at night, robbing her of rest and clouding her judgment. Instead of sleeping, she wandered the streets around her hotel, weighing her increasingly poor options. When she finally drifted off, a recurring nightmare about a firing squad shooting Mary Price, Gregory Silvermaster, or herself haunted her sleep. The dream's ending disturbed her particularly: "As I stood there, rooted to the spot with horror, the victim would suddenly wheel around and point his finger at me. Traitor, he would cry out. It is you who have killed me. A volley of shots would ring out and it would seem as if all of them had entered my own body."[6]

Elizabeth Bentley was collapsing under the weight of her fear and despair, just as Duncan Lee had five months before.

On her NKGB-financed vacation in Old Lyme, Bentley finally decided to act. She later claimed in her autobiography that she experienced a religious epiphany while sitting in a pew of the old artists' colony's Congregational church. She also wrote that she'd had a crisis of conscience, like Lee, as she sat alone in the kind of simple New England church her stern forebears might have founded: "Oh God, I cried out desperately, help me to find the strength! . . . And then, in the empty church, the voice of my conscience seemed to ring out loudly: You have no right to be here—yet. You know now that the way of life you have followed these last ten years was wrong; you have to come back where you belong. But first you must make amends!"[7]

Before atoning, Bentley wanted to uncover the truth about Peter Heller and whom he was really working for. Fearing she might be on the verge of exposure, she decided to approach the FBI in a sounding-out process. Applying what she had learned from Golos, she concluded that the NKGB most likely had placed the FBI's New York City field office under surveillance or even planted a source among its agents. She looked for a more remote office and chose the bureau's much smaller New Haven field office, the same one that Katharine Nangle, the Lees' former landlady, had visited in 1940 to warn the FBI about Duncan and Ishbel.[8]

On August 23, 1945, Bentley entered a nondescript building in New Haven's downtown, took its elevator three stories above the FBI's office, and then walked down the building's fire stairs to the bureau's doorway. Once inside, she faced a small, dark man who sat at a metal desk. He offered her a cigarette, leaned back in his chair, and asked why she had come to see the FBI. Special Agent Edward Coady listened patiently for two hours as she theorized that Peter Heller was impersonating a federal agent. During their conversation, she told Coady that Heller had told her to collect intelligence on the Soviets who did business with USSSC. But first, Bentley said, she wanted the bureau to assure her that Heller was an actual FBI agent.[9]

Coady, sensing that Bentley was after more than just information on Heller, was perplexed by her but could not draw her out. Finally, he told her that he could neither confirm nor deny the identity of federal agents. He also jotted down her address and phone number. After she left, he typed a memorandum to his supervisor, recommending that the bureau consider using her as a source inside USSSC.[10]

Coady's supervisor forwarded the memorandum, titled "Peter Heller; Impersonation; Espionage," to the FBI's New York City field office on August 29. After it arrived, agents there quickly discerned that Peter Heller was not spying for anyone. He was a former investigator for the New York State Division of Parole and a lieutenant in the US Army reserves. He was also married with three children. He had deceived Bentley to impress her and had used his bogus spy story to justify their time apart. Intrigued by Bentley, however, the FBI opted not to tell her then that Heller was no more than a liar and a cad.[11]

Meanwhile, Bentley continued her relationship with the NKGB after she returned from Old Lyme. She had dinner in a restaurant with Gorsky during the third week of September in New York City. Before their meal, she had downed several dry martinis at a late afternoon luncheon. The alcohol killed any lingering inhibitions, and she blurted out that she had resumed her old job at USSSC. Visibly displeased, he offered to set her up in a travel agency or in a hat or dress shop. Bentley lost what little control she had left and lashed out, calling the Soviets gangsters. She raised her voice at the shocked spymaster and, in an odd burst of patriotism, shouted that she was an American and could not be kicked around. She also hinted that Golos had been on the brink of defecting just before he died because of Vassily Zarubin's callous treatment of him. In a final flourish, she claimed that Heller was trying to convince her to become his informant inside USSSC.[12]

Angered by Bentley's drunken behavior and alarmed by her not-so-subtle threats, Gorsky cabled Moscow Center and recommended killing her. Instead, the center urged him to placate her—to give her up to $3,000, let her return to USSSC, and remind her that her betrayal would ruin the lives of her American sources. Undoubtedly, Gorsky's Moscow masters realized that murdering an American agent, even a very difficult one, was a poor way to attract more recruits to the Soviets' cause.[13]

It was now Bentley's turn to be shocked. The New York City newspapers reported on October 11, 1945, that Louis Budenz, former editor of the CPUSA's *Daily Worker*, had renounced communism and converted to Catholicism under the approving gaze of radio priest Fulton Sheen. Although Budenz had actually abandoned communism in August, Bentley first learned about it by reading the newspaper accounts. The news stunned her because Budenz knew who she really was.[14]

Budenz had known Golos since the 1920s and Bentley since 1943. They initially met after Golos had told him about his heart problems. After this, Budenz had passed information to her at least thirty times. Budenz also knew her true name. While he had yet to reveal to the

FBI the names of those he knew to be spies, he had announced that he was embarking on a nationwide lecture tour to awaken Americans to communism's dangers.[15]

Five days after Bentley read about Budenz, an agent in the bureau's New York City field office asked her to come in to discuss Heller's impersonation of an FBI agent. Special Agent Frank Aldrich reached out to Bentley because she had written a letter to the field office in October, complaining again about Heller and his fantastic claims.[16]

When they met at the FBI's New York field office on October 16, she told Aldrich that Heller actually might be a Soviet spy and that FBI agents were following her. She further reported that she was closely tied to other people who might also be Soviet spies, including Louis Budenz. Aldrich, who was about to retire, wrote a report three weeks later describing his interview with Bentley. He raised concerns about her mental stability—he knew that no FBI agents were following her—but suggested to another agent that the bureau might be able to use her as an informant inside USSSC.[17]

Although she had gotten closer to admitting her own involvement with the NKGB, Bentley did not tell Aldrich that she would be meeting with Gorsky the very next evening at a restaurant less than four miles away. When she saw the portly Russian, Bentley apologized for her drunken outbursts in September. Pleased, Gorsky followed Moscow Center's instructions and told her that she could return to USSSC. He also gave her $2,000 in $20 bills to spend as she liked. Staring at the money, she now regretted meeting with Aldrich the day before. She and Gorsky agreed to meet again on November 21.[18]

Her remorse was short-lived. Lement Upham Harris, the Harvard-educated treasurer of the CPUSA's Secret Funds and the son of a Wall Street financier, barged into USSSC's office on October 24 and demanded that Bentley repay the $15,000 the party had originally invested in the company when Golos established it in 1941. She refused and told him to get this money from the Soviets. Harris, choking with rage, threatened to "blow her to hell" if she did not come up with the $15,000.[19]

Two days later, badly shaken, Bentley went to see Earl Browder, now the former general secretary of the CPUSA. Browder had run afoul of Moscow in 1944 when he renamed the CPUSA the Communist Political Association. He erred in believing his own rhetoric, naively planning to make the association the left wing of the Democratic Party. The Kremlin's hardliners had other ideas and ousted him for his apostasy in June 1945. Browder, still dazed by his abrupt fall from power, warned Bentley that Harris's threat might be real but said he could do nothing to help her. Any loyalty Bentley still felt for the CPUSA vanished that afternoon.[20]

Bentley started answering the FBI's telephone calls and laying the groundwork for her defection. On November 6, she picked up her telephone when Edward Buckley called. He was in charge of the bureau's investigations into the Soviets' use of front companies as cover for their espionage activities. Buckley asked her to meet with him the next afternoon. Bentley initially balked at returning to the FBI's office for another interview. She had played a key role in the NKGB's spying operations and had helped nearly forty other Americans betray their country. She realized that aiding and abetting espionage in wartime was a capital offense.[21]

But Bentley was a master at surviving and calculating risks. Her leverage was having the knowledge and the means the FBI needed to shut down most of the NKGB's American spy networks. Perhaps she could trade such priceless information for her freedom. Although a high-stakes gamble, this maneuver gave her better odds than the likely death sentence the NKGB was offering her in Moscow. She had no doubt that Lement Harris wanted to kill her and that, even if he failed, she would still have to contend with Gorsky's endless schemes to lure her to Moscow and the same fate.

Buckley persisted. The FBI had opened another investigation in November 1944 into World Tourists, which they knew was closely linked to the United States Service and Shipping Corporation. Bentley might be the wedge into USSSC they had been looking for. He appealed to her patriotism. Bentley, however, was more interested in saving her life than waving the American flag. Convinced that she had more chance of surviving with the FBI than with the NKGB, she agreed to see him late the next afternoon.[22]

Following Buckley's instructions, Bentley carried a magazine in her hand as she stepped off the subway. In an instant, Buckley materialized beside her and led her to his small, plain office in the federal building that overlooked Foley Square. Don Jardine, one of the New York field office's few resident experts on the NKGB, was waiting there for them. He was investigating a *Daily Worker* writer whom he suspected of spying for the Soviets.[23]

As the two agents furiously scribbled notes on their lined legal pads, Bentley methodically led them through her past lives. Remarkably, she did this without exacting a promise of immunity or requesting a lawyer. She and the two agents seemed to have reached an unspoken understanding that the FBI would somehow protect her.[24]

Jardine, in particular, was transfixed by her story. As Bentley talked, he became convinced "that we had hit gold on this one. We had files here and there and everywhere, and she kind of sewed it all together."[25]

Her first interview with Buckley and Jardine was a marathon, lasting eight hours. Sometime in the early-morning hours of November 8, 1945, she signed a single-spaced, thirty-one-page statement that spelled out the essentials of her espionage career. In it, she briefly discussed Lee but admitted that he had never liked giving her classified information from the OSS's files. The FBI scoured its indices for any hint of him. Its clerks uncovered only a fleeting mention of him as a onetime officer on the boards of the China Aid Council and Russian War Relief and a copy of his fingerprints submitted by the US Army when he had registered for the draft in 1940. Lee's name would soon no longer be a stranger to the bureau's files.[26]

Bentley's story broke like thunder over the FBI's Washington headquarters as its Teletypes rattled into action with the shocking news from New York. By the time he sat down for his usual breakfast of a poached egg on toast, J. Edgar Hoover, the FBI's bulldog-faced director, knew that the NKGB had infiltrated the US government on a massive scale. Stunned, he must have wondered how much longer he would be at the bureau's helm. Hoover had recovered enough by that afternoon to send the White House the names of fourteen persons

Bentley alleged were Soviet spies. One was Duncan Lee. Hoover told William Stephenson, chief of British Security Coordination and FBI liaison officer for the Secret Intelligence Service (MI6), about Bentley's defection the next day. Their conversation would shortly have devastating consequences for Hoover's investigation of Lee and the others Bentley named.[27]

Although she had no documents to support her extraordinary allegations, many of them based on mere hearsay and generalities, Hoover was inclined to trust her from the start. After all, Whittaker Chambers had already given FBI agents the names of several of the same people in May and July 1945. Some of the same men Chambers said were communists—Charles Kramer, Lauchlin Currie, Sol Adler, and Frank Coe—Bentley now fingered as spies.[28]

Hoover also thought she was probably telling the truth because of what the FBI had found five months before during its June 6, 1945, raid of the offices of *Amerasia*, a semischolarly, anti–Chiang Kai-shek, small-circulation magazine that dealt with East Asian matters. In the office shared by *Amerasia*'s two coeditors, the bureau found 591 documents, several of them highly classified, that belonged to the OSS, the War Department, the State Department, the Office of Naval Intelligence, and the Office of Postal and Telegraph Censorship; OSS and FBI agents had found scores more during secret and illegal searches conducted before the raid. The bureau arrested the magazine's editors, two State Department employees, one US Navy Reserve officer who worked for ONI, and a journalist whose articles appeared regularly in *Time* and *Collier's*. A grand jury indicted only three of the six persons the FBI arrested. None was convicted of espionage; two pled guilty to unlawfully possessing government documents and paid fines. Hoover and his top deputies were convinced that a major spy ring had been allowed to slip through their fingers because the Truman administration feared a trial would degenerate into a debate about its China policies.[29]

The events of September 5, 1945, in Ottawa, Canada, persuaded Hoover even more of Bentley's veracity. On that night, Igor Gouzenko, a GRU cipher clerk working in the Soviet embassy's code room, stuffed over one hundred secret documents inside his shirt and walked through the embassy's gates. Awaiting recall to Moscow for a security violation and wanting to stay in Canada, he narrowly escaped capture by a squad of GRU security officers who kicked in the door to his apartment. Gouzenko eventually made his way to Canadian authorities. His documents proved that the GRU and NKGB had targeted the Canadian and American governments and penetrated the Manhattan Project, the Anglo-American collaborative effort to build an atomic bomb. When FBI agents debriefed him that same month, he mentioned several high-ranking American officials, including an assistant to Secretary of State Edward R. Stettinius. Neither Gouzenko nor the FBI knew that this assistant was Alger Hiss.[30]

On November 15, 1945, President Truman called Hoover and asked him to meet with James Byrnes, his secretary of state, to discuss Soviet espionage. Hoover told Byrnes that while his agents had not had time to prove or disprove Bentley's allegations, he was inclined to believe her because his agents already knew about some of those she named. At least ten had been subjects of Hatch Act or other federal loyalty investigations.[31]

By the time he met with Byrnes, Hoover and his chief lieutenants had mapped out how they were going to prove or disprove Bentley's sweeping claims. They made the FBI's first priority identifying the high-ranking NKGB agent she knew only as "Al." After that, the bureau would focus on her most important sources and determine whether they were still spying for the Soviets. The bureau selected them based on their government positions and their "comparative usefulness as reflected in Bentley's statement." Lee was among those included.[32]

The FBI decided that doubling Bentley was the most effective way to investigate her claims. Hoover's G-men had used this tactic with great success against the German and Japanese intelligence services during World War II. If they could place a double agent inside the NKGB, they could beat the Soviets at their own game. Accordingly, they instructed her to keep her plans to meet with Al on November 21. In the meantime, the head of the New York City field office sought Hoover's permission to break into and search her hotel room while she was being interviewed. The FBI wanted to make sure she was not hiding any documents as a life insurance policy.[33]

At 4:20 p.m. on November 21, Bentley joined Gorsky in front of a Bickford's restaurant. They walked to another nearby restaurant for a light dinner. From the first moment, Gorsky felt something was off and cagily rebuffed her attempts to resume her espionage career. He questioned her about Peter Heller—she said she would stick a knife in him if she saw him again because she had found out about his wife and three children—and about the future of USSSC. After she claimed that she was restless and bored, Gorsky commented that she had wanted a normal, peaceful life, and she now had it. He also instructed her not to rejoin the CPUSA. They agreed to meet again on January 21, 1946.[34]

As he was departing the restaurant, Gorsky noticed three men following him in a car. He quickly vanished down the stairs of a subway station and returned to Washington. The next morning he learned why he had felt so uneasy the night before: Bentley had defected. On November 20, 1945, the NKGB's London station had cabled this staggering news to Moscow Center. Kim Philby, a prized member of the Soviets' Magnificent Five spy ring, was then a senior MI6 officer working in London. He had seen a summary of J. Edgar Hoover's conversation with William Stephenson and immediately passed it to Moscow.[35]

Moscow Center instantly acted on Philby's news, ordering Gorsky and Iskhak Akhmerov to break off all contact with their sources and return to the Soviet Union. The center also told them to instruct their sources in how to handle themselves during FBI questioning. Gorsky and Akhmerov coached them not to deny meeting with Bentley—the Soviets did not know when the FBI had started watching her—but to say that any contacts with her were purely social. They also told them to destroy any potentially damaging documents and gave them passwords for use once the crisis had passed. They did not warn Lee, perhaps fearing that he would panic, but Mary Price probably did later.[36]

Gorsky's instincts and training had saved him. Bentley's eagerness to resume her work for the NKGB had set off his highly sensitive internal alarm bells. His decision to heed them thwarted the FBI's best chance of doubling Elizabeth Bentley and breaking their case against Lee wide open.

Before he left for Moscow on December 7, Gorsky again recommended to Moscow Center that he liquidate Bentley. His specific techniques were eclectic, ranging from dousing her pillow or food with a slow-acting poison to pushing her under a speeding New York City subway train. He also pointed out that although Joseph Katz, one of the NKGB's most experienced officers, could break into her hotel room and stage her suicide, Bentley was a very strong, tall, healthy woman and not easily overpowered. Gorsky ruefully noted that Katz was not in peak health and might not be up to the job. Lavrenty Beria, the overall head of the Soviet intelligence services and Stalin's chief henchman, vetoed Gorsky's ideas for the moment.[37]

Gorsky's thirst for revenge was understandable. Bentley had single-handedly wrecked the NKGB's principal American spy networks. The Soviets were able to resume some intelligence operations in the United States by September 1947, but their American stations were still in disarray a year beyond that. They would never be completely rebuilt on such a vast scale inside the US government. Bentley's betrayal devastated the Soviets' ability to collect intelligence in the United States and was the worst setback their secret services experienced in their long history operating inside the country.[38]

The FBI knew none of this in late 1945. Hoover did know that his agency had a lot of catching up to do. The bureau's Washington field office, assigned to cover the Soviet embassy, did not even have a dedicated squad of agents to keep tabs on embassy employees. Instead, one of its squads tracked suspected American communists.[39]

On November 19, the FBI's Washington field office got Gorsky's photograph from the State Department and forwarded it to New York City, where Bentley positively identified Al as Gorsky. Two days later, the bureau's surveillance of their meeting on November 21 confirmed her identification, validating very strong suspicions that he had succeeded Zarubin as the NKGB's top officer in the United States. Galvanized by this, the bureau launched the largest espionage investigation in its then thirty-seven-year history. Hoover immediately ordered his other field offices to send agents to augment the 115 agents working out of his Washington field office. By December 12, 1945, 227 of the bureau's 4,370 agents were investigating Bentley's allegations.[40]

On December 10, 1945, Hoover spoke publicly at the annual convention of the International Association of Chiefs of Police in Miami, Florida. His speech, a blend of self-congratulation and self-delusion, assured his receptive audience that his G-men had once again triumphed during World War II: "We knew from the very outbreak of the war that espionage was under control. . . . The counter-espionage program which we developed did more than encircle spies and render them harmless, it enabled us to learn their weaknesses and their aims."[41] He did not tell his friendly audience about Elizabeth Bentley's claims or that the FBI actually had been asleep while the Soviets had stolen many of America's most precious secrets during the war.

While Hoover was revising history, Bentley signed a 107-page statement on November 30, 1945. She gave the bureau over 150 names. Hoover tapped Thomas Donegan, the elfin, tightly wound assistant special agent in charge of his New York field office, to spearhead the FBI's probe into those she had listed. After sifting through all the names, he selected fifty-one individuals to focus on. Twenty-seven of them, including Lee, still worked for the federal government in late 1945.[42]

Donegan, called "the Hat" by his fellow agents because he insisted on wearing his snap-brimmed fedora even while sitting at his desk, grouped all these investigations under the case name "Nathan Gregory Silvermaster, et al." The FBI gave Bentley the code name Gregory to mask her identity.[43]

Bentley had told Buckley and Jardine on November 7 that Lee had stopped spying for the NKGB, but only the bureau's investigation could confirm this. On November 21, Hoover wrote a memorandum to Attorney General Tom Clark, asking him to approve a wiretap on the Lees' home telephone "for the purpose of determining the extent of his espionage activities and for the additional purpose of identifying other espionage agents."[44]

That same afternoon, two agents secretly began shadowing Lee, monitoring and recording his every move. Most of what they observed was painfully ordinary. On November 29, the two agents dutifully logged what they saw most nights: "Surveillance of Lee's home was taken up at 5:00pm. . . . At 6:02pm Agents observed Lee walking north on 31st Street and entering his home. No one was observed to enter or leave his home during the remainder of the evening, and at 8:30pm, Lee was observed in the living room of his home wearing an old sweater. The surveillance was discontinued at 9:30pm because it appeared Lee had no intention of going out that evening."[45]

On December 4, however, the FBI followed Lee to New York City. He had gone on government business and to see Mary Price. The surveillance team saw him enter the Stonewall Inn Bar at 7:55 p.m. and meet a woman it described as "over average height, attractive, and having brunette hair, which she wore in an upsweep style." The agents recorded in their surveillance log that Lee and Price left the bar at 8:30 p.m. and climbed into a cab. Lee returned to his hotel at 12:25 a.m.[46]

Like Lee, Price had stopped spying long before. In late June 1944, she had collapsed again under the strain of working for the NKGB and told Earl Browder that she wanted out. He agreed to free her, but not out of compassion. He most likely realized that failing the OSS's background check had compromised her usefulness. But in December 1945, the FBI did not know that Price was no longer an NKGB courier. She too became a target of its massive investigation. By then, she had been living in New York City full-time since the end of 1943 or the beginning of 1944.[47]

Hoover approved a request from the FBI's Washington field office to secretly break into the Lees' Georgetown home and plant microphones. But that was not all. On November 27, the FBI placed a cover on the Lees' mail—meaning that it copied the information on the outside of the envelopes—and began intercepting and reading every telegram the family sent or received. Western Union also gave the FBI copies of telegrams Lee had sent and received before the bureau began investigating him.[48]

Less than a month later, the FBI uncovered what it considered derogatory information about Edmund. On December 21, its field office in Richmond, Virginia, sent a Teletype to Washington stating that a "highly confidential and reliable source" had discovered Edmund's name in the black notebook of Alice Burke, secretary of the Communist Party of the United States of America for District 16, which included Virginia and North Carolina. Her notebook contained the names of persons she believed sympathized with some of the CPUSA's goals. The Teletype also noted, "He is an advocate of racial equality, which has resulted in his not being popular in Chatham, Virginia."[49]

Despite all these efforts, the FBI had uncovered no evidence that Lee was or had been an NKGB spy. The Soviets' quick countermeasures played a decisive role in thwarting the FBI, but Kim Philby's treachery was not the only reason why Hoover had failed to arrest Lee for committing espionage.

Aside from the Soviets' huge head start in setting up their American spy networks, several other fundamental factors contributed to Lee's continued freedom—namely, the potent witch's brew of the myths Hoover fostered about his agents' competence, unprecedented demands on the FBI's resources, his misunderstanding of the threat communism presented, bureaucratic bungling, human error, and Franklin Roosevelt's cold-blooded calculations about what it would take to win World War II. Hoover's own deeply problematic personality also badly crippled the FBI's chances of bringing Lee to justice.

John Edgar Hoover was born on January 1, 1895, in Washington, DC, the son and grandson of federal civil servants. Despite being the nation's capital, the Washington of Hoover's youth had the sensibilities of a provincial, small southern town. He never questioned the sense of order, place, and hierarchy he developed while growing up there. He also never doubted the conservative strain of Progressivism that he absorbed as a child of the federal bureaucracy. This ideology taught him that government had a duty to regulate morality.[50]

His devotion to this uniquely American creed never wavered. Hoover's xenophobia—two very brief day trips to Juárez, Mexico, in the spring of 1939 are his only known excursions outside the United States—and no-holds-barred defense of a Norman Rockwell–like vision of America led him to champion middle-class, small-town values such as a devotion to God, country, and duty. It made no difference to his many admirers that he lived with his mother until she died when he was forty-three years old or that he had no other woman in his life.[51]

Hoover appointed himself guardian of these values and the standard bearer of a crusade to prevent their subversion, especially from within and by communists. To that end, he was willing to violate the Constitution. This did not mean that he did not believe in its Bill of Rights; he did—as long as its protections did not extend to communists, socialists, labor organizers, and others he wanted to purge from the American scene. Hoover's beliefs, while extreme, were not unique to him. Part of his widespread popularity rested on his being one of the most visible symbols of the country's long antisubversive history.[52]

Hoover had prepared himself for a career in the federal government by completing two law degrees at George Washington University in the late afternoon and at night while working full-time as a clerk at the Library of Congress. Family connections landed him a job in the Department of Justice in 1917. He steadily climbed its ranks because of his hard work, unquestioning willingness to take on any task, complaisant demeanor that pleased his supervisors, and preternatural attention to detail. He also brimmed with self-confidence.[53]

In January 1920, he had helped plan and execute the largest of the so-called Palmer raids, which targeted American citizens and resident aliens whom federal and local law enforcement officials believed were committed to bringing a Bolshevik revolution to the United States. These mass roundups detained somewhere between 6,000 and 10,000 persons. They also helped drive the American communist movement underground, providing the Soviet intelligence service with a ready base of willing future spies. On May 10, 1924, Hoover became the acting director of the Bureau of Investigation (BOI), the Department of Justice's investigative arm. That December, Attorney General Harlan F. Stone made this appointment permanent; Hoover would hold the post until his death on May 2, 1972.[54]

The Great Depression was as much a godsend for J. Edgar Hoover as it had been for the CPUSA. The economic devastation brought a sharp spike in crime and gave rise to the gangster. Americans, eager to escape their economic woes, developed an almost sporting interest in the much reported exploits of the likes of Charles Arthur "Pretty Boy" Floyd and John Herbert Dillinger as they raced across state lines robbing banks and shooting local lawmen with their smoking tommy guns.

Dramatic images in the nation's newspapers and on the screens of its movie houses highlighted that local law enforcement was either too inept or too corrupt to handle this crime wave. President Roosevelt, in a burst of New Deal fervor, seized upon this in his annual message to Congress on January 3, 1934, announcing that crime was a national security threat and requesting an expanded role for the federal government in combatting offenses traditionally policed by the states. By that summer, Congress had federalized the crimes of kidnapping across state lines, extortion, and bank robbery. It also authorized the bureau's agents to carry weapons and to execute search and arrest warrants.

Armed with new laws and real guns, Hoover's agents had killed or captured the most notorious gangsters by 1935. That same year, the BOI became the Federal Bureau of Investigation, the name change reflecting that the US government was now waging a federal war on crime. Hoover also began stocking the FBI with agents cast from his own mold. Almost all were white, came from small towns, had attended parochial schools, and held conservative beliefs. They also possessed his Manichaean worldview.[55]

Hollywood studios began to glorify the FBI's exploits, bringing to the silver screen the mythic G-man with his square jaw, cool efficiency, magnificent bravery, and absolute incorruptibility. Hoover's agents became the country's new white knights and loyal samurai. He promoted this image at every turn; the FBI's slain agents were even dubbed "martyrs."[56]

The legends Hoover fostered and conjured about the FBI's competence inflated the country's sense of what the bureau could actually do. Chasing and gunning down gangsters had nothing to do with understanding and combatting the subtle and nuanced threat Soviet espionage posed to the United States. The Soviets presented unprecedented challenges, and the bureau had virtually no experience in facing them. Reflecting this, the FBI opened just one espionage investigation between 1924 and 1936.[57]

The modern NKVD had a head start of almost two decades on Hoover's amateurs. And even with Stalin's ungrateful purges of those doing his bidding, the NKVD remained the world's best secret service, with a willing, able, and well-funded partner in the CPUSA. At the same time, the FBI still had no counterintelligence service. Several more years passed before tracking spies became an acceptable career path for agents. Even by the early 1940s, most of the bureau's agents still considered counterintelligence a professional backwater. The Byzantine work of monitoring suspected spies lacked the romanticism and career enhancement of handcuffing vicious and colorful criminals.[58]

The coming of World War II forced the FBI to learn about spies on the job. Although the Soviets, and communists in general, were never far from J. Edgar Hoover's thoughts, his first priority was protecting the country from the Japanese and Germans, a task he performed admirably. In the fall of 1940, Hoover assured FDR in a detailed report that the FBI had the threat posed by foreign espionage services well in hand: "Special Agents of the Federal Bureau of Investigation have under constant observation and surveillance a number of known and suspected Agents of the German, Russian, French, and Italian Secret Services. The FBI is able through its counter espionage efforts to maintain careful check upon the channels of communication, the sources of information, the methods of finance, and other data relative to these agents."[59]

Hoover's memorandum also revealed other demands on his agents' time. They were working undercover in national defense plants and conducting security surveys, gathering information from informants in "more than twelve hundred key industrial facilities," investigating complaints and tips from the public—over 2,985 were received on a single day—and establishing a special unit to enforce the Selective Service Act of 1940 by arresting draft dodgers.[60]

These were not the only drains on FBI resources. Hoover's G-men were also responsible for enforcing Section 9A of the 1939 Hatch Act, which stated that no one belonging to an organization or party that advocated the overthrow of the US government could be a federal employee. Between 1942 and 1945, the FBI investigated 6,193 Hatch Act cases. And over two hundred agents, as part of the bureau's Special Intelligence Service (SIS), investigated and countered German subversion outside the United States. Agents assigned to the SIS operated from Canada to South America.[61]

Even though the FBI increased in size from 713 agents in 1939 to 4,370 in 1945, these myriad responsibilities stretched its resources to the breaking point. By 1942, its Washington headquarters was already operating twenty-four hours a day, seven days a week. The bureau's personnel carried heavy caseloads on what Hoover called the war's "FBI front." The average agent handled twenty-three cases at a time.[62]

Even after Hitler had gobbled up most of Europe, Hoover remained adamant that communism was an even greater threat to the United States than fascism. He never wavered in his belief that communists planned to subvert his country's way of life. Illustrations of this abound in the letters, memoranda, and reports he sent to the White House.

Beginning in 1942, Hoover prepared a monthly General Intelligence Survey that he forwarded to Major General Edwin "Pa" Watson, the president's chief of staff. The largest sections of these reports dealt with "communist activities." His October 1942 survey contained twelve pages on this theme, including a subsection titled "Agitation Among the Negroes." This same survey devoted only eight pages to "German activities." Hoover's November 1942 survey spent eleven pages discussing the communists, including their relationship with the National Emergency Committee to Stop Lynching, while German activities merited only nine pages. His August 1944 survey was one of the most perversely apportioned, totaling eighteen pages on German activities, ten on the Japanese, five on the Italians, and sixty-two on the communists. A subsection on the communists included a lengthy discussion of the Southern Negro Youth Congress and the Southern Conference for Human Welfare.[63]

Hoover's growing obsession with what he believed was communism's malignant influence on African Americans stands out in his August 3, 1943, letter to the White House, which he filled with unsubstantiated rumors about racial unrest in the nation's capital. Quoting several confidential informants, Hoover warned of a marked uptick in communist-inspired agitation among Washington's "less desirable colored element." These included, one informant claimed, "younger negroes between the ages of 16 and 18 years old who are not in the Army and who have shown an insolent attitude that they will take nothing from anyone." In the meantime, while Hoover and his agents fixated on race, the Soviets continued to steal America's secrets in the same city on an industrial scale.[64]

Although none of Hoover's surveys discussed the Soviet Union's espionage efforts, the FBI was closely monitoring Soviet embassy and consular officials. This began around the time of Stalin's August 1939 nonaggression pact with Hitler. Hoover's agents bugged the Soviet embassy, Soviet consulates, the CPUSA's headquarters, and scores of leftist labor unions and political organizations. (Roosevelt secretly approved wiretapping in national security matters on May 21, 1940, despite bans from Congress and the Supreme Court on all electronic eavesdropping.) The FBI also broke into the offices and houses of prominent American communists, planted microphones, and intercepted their mail.

Despite such widespread illegalities, the bureau failed during World War II to uncover any American communists who were spying for the Soviet Union. As late as December 1944, an FBI summary on "espionage and counter-espionage operations inside the United States" discussed only the activities of German agents. That same year, though, Hoover reported to the Senate that the FBI had identified 1 million persons "associated" with communist front organizations, including the National Association for the Advancement of Colored People.[65]

Almost three and a half years before Hoover's report to the Senate, the FBI had nearly dealt the NKVD a major blow, one that could have led G-men to Lee's front door, but the bureau failed to connect the dots. On May 5, 1941, following a lead from the British and the Canadians, agents arrested Gaik Ovakimian, then the NKVD's most senior officer in the United States. American prosecutors charged him with violating the Foreign Agents Registration Act. Ovakimian, an engineer and chemist, led the NKVD's efforts in the United States to steal technology. He entered the country in 1933 and had been able to stay because the State Department extended his visa thirteen times. He worked undercover as an engineer at the Amtorg Trading

Corporation without diplomatic immunity. The State Department, in exchange for the emigration of several Russian-born wives of Americans, allowed him to leave the United States and return to the Soviet Union on July 23, 1941. The thaw in American-Soviet relations brought about by Hitler's invasion of the Soviet Union a month earlier had facilitated these negotiations.[66]

Before the FBI arrested Ovakimian, agents had seen Jacob Golos hand him a package on a New York City street corner. This was the first of seven meetings the FBI witnessed between the two men. Joseph Volodarsky, an NKVD defector, told the FBI in late 1940 that Golos gave intelligence reports to Ovakimian. Although the FBI followed Golos, it could not directly connect him to the NKVD until Bentley's defection. By then, he had been dead for nearly two years.[67]

The FBI's physical surveillance of Golos did, however, lead its agents to Elizabeth Bentley. She eluded them by entering one of Penn Station's ladies' room and leaving through a rear exit. Although the agents did not catch up with Bentley that time, they identified her through watching Golos. They continued following her until August 20, 1941, but dropped their physical surveillance because of a lack of manpower and their concentration on the demands of other, higher-profile cases.[68]

The FBI did place a mail cover on Bentley until sometime in 1942. In 1946, the FBI discovered, belatedly, that one of the intercepted letters they saw bore a March 6, 1941, postmark and had a return address of 2921 Olive Street, NW, Washington, DC. That address happened to belong to Mary Price. Bentley later told the FBI that the letter most likely concerned Price's next trip to New York City. In a surprisingly candid 1955 report, the FBI admitted a colossal blunder in not having connected Golos and Bentley to the NKVD, ruefully observing, "In light of what we know, we certainly should have."[69]

Almost as disastrously, the FBI drew a flawed conclusion from its investigation of Ovakimian: it reasoned that because none of the paid agents of the Russian espionage system were American Communists, no members of the CPUSA could be spies. Instead, the bureau convinced itself that the Soviets had instructed their spies not to take part in any party activities. It did not deduce that Stalin's purges had forced the NKGB to rely on the CPUSA for agents or that the Soviets used the party's underground to move agents from open work into espionage.

Similarly, the FBI had not managed to capitalize on a series of knowledgeable defectors. Walter Krivitsky, a former GRU and NKVD senior officer with encyclopedic knowledge of both services' operations, was one of the most important. Krivitsky came to the United States in late 1938, in the midst of Stalin's massacre of the Soviet intelligence services. When the FBI interviewed him on July 27, 1939, some of the information he provided contradicted what was already in its files. But instead of correcting the files, the FBI erroneously concluded that he was lying. Although his revelations were sometimes muddled and guarded, Krivitsky was not a liar. Without experience or training in handling nervous and suspicious defectors, FBI agents, in effect, signed his death warrant. He was found dead, with a gunshot wound to his temple, in a Washington, DC, hotel on February 10, 1941. The District of Columbia police department ruled his death a suicide.[70]

The FBI also failed to take advantage of the 1944 defection of Victor Kravchenko, an official with the Soviet Purchasing Commission, who offered to betray the Soviets' espionage rings in exchange for money and protection. Hoover suspected he might be a double agent and investigated him unsuccessfully.[71]

The bureau missed yet another opportunity in 1944, this time to identify Joseph Katz as a Soviet agent. On May 27, 1944, FBI agents had observed a secret meeting between a man who walked with a limp and Mikhail Chaliapin, a known NKGB agent who worked at the Soviets' New York consulate. Afterward, the agents trailed the unknown man to a Greenwich Village brownstone, which he entered with a key. The superintendent claimed not to know the man, but the bureau inexplicably failed to interview anyone else in the building. It took the FBI until the fall of 1948 to ask other residents about who he was and to learn that his name was Joseph Katz. In January 1949, Hoover's agents finally connected him with the gray-faced, limping handler Bentley described to them on her defection.[72]

Likewise, the bureau did not understand the crucial importance of a letter it received from the White House on July 5, 1944. Postmarked

April 14, 1944, and addressed to Franklin Roosevelt, it contained, surprisingly, a partial list of the communist underground in Washington, DC. Several of its members were part of the Perlo spy ring that Elizabeth Bentley managed after Jacob Golos's death. The FBI traced the unsigned letter to Katherine Wills Perlo, the estranged wife of Victor Perlo, a Soviet spy and economist who worked at the War Production Board. She had written the damaging letter on the stationery of WTSN, a Fort Worth, Texas, radio station. Agents interviewed her on October 13, 1944, and learned that she and Perlo were locked in a bitter divorce and custody battle. They also discovered that a psychiatrist had diagnosed her with paranoid schizophrenia. The FBI never followed up on her claims until after Bentley defected.[73]

Despite these staggering mistakes, the FBI was improving its game. A gradual but steady sea change had been taking place since 1943. In April of that year, agents saw Zarubin meet with a CPUSA official to discuss penetrating the University of California at Berkeley's Radiation Laboratory. Their surveillance, which included wiretaps and microphones, triggered two massive bureau investigations into the connections between Soviets operating under diplomatic cover and suspected American sources.[74]

The FBI got another break on August 7, 1943, when Hoover received an anonymous letter written in Russian claiming that Zarubin was the NKVD's chief in the United States. Its author named eleven other Soviet agents in New York, San Francisco, Buffalo, Washington, Mexico City, and Ottawa who worked closely with Zarubin. This letter forced Moscow Center to recall Zarubin and most of those named back to the Soviet Union in 1944.[75]

These breaks generated a dramatic surge in the bureau's efforts to monitor the Soviets. Its increased surveillance made meeting with sources much harder and sometimes impossible. The monitoring also interrupted the spying of at least four Americans stealing military and industrial secrets for the Soviets. Nonetheless, the FBI lagged far behind its Soviet adversaries.[76]

These missteps help explain why the FBI failed to counter the Soviets' espionage and detect Lee, but perhaps an even bigger reason—the drive to defeat Hitler—loomed larger than Hoover's pet obsessions and his agency's mammoth failures.

Almost from the moment the first German bombs hit the Soviet Union, Franklin Roosevelt perceived that the key to winning World War II lay on the eastern front. Soviet endurance, Roosevelt wrote on June 26, 1941, "[would] mean the liberation of Europe from Nazi domination—and at the same time I do not think we need to fear any possibility of Russian domination." Almost a year later, he told Treasury Secretary Henry Morgenthau, "The whole question of whether we win or lose the war depends upon the Russians." The unsettling fact that Stalin had already slaughtered millions of his own citizens paled next to his ability to annihilate Hitler's soldiers.[77]

Viewed through the lens of the Cold War, darkened by the events of the late 1940s and early 1950s, Roosevelt's words appear hopelessly shortsighted. Some then, rather recklessly, even called them treasonous. Trenchantly, FDR grasped that the United States was not ready to fight a two-front war and that Britain, the gateway to an American-led invasion of the Continent, was nearly on her knees. Only rivers of Soviet blood could stop Hitler and buy the United States enough time to mobilize for war and harness her enormous industrial might in the Allies' cause. Roosevelt grasped the supreme irony that only the Soviets could save the very Western democracies they vowed to overthrow.[78]

Cold mathematics proves FDR correct. By the late spring of 1941, Hitler's army consisted of 208 divisions. His generals considered 167 of these fully ready for combat. On June 22, 1941, Hitler unleashed 146 of them against the Soviet Union. From then until the end of the war, Germany committed two-thirds of its armed forces to fighting and dying on the eastern front. And as late as June 6, 1944—D-Day—70 percent of German divisions were tied down fighting the Red Army.[79]

All told, 27 million Soviet citizens perished in World War II, a loss of life unparalleled in modern history. Roughly 11 million of those killed fought in the Red Army. By contrast, the United States lost 407,316 soldiers, airmen, and sailors. The Soviets lost more soldiers at Stalingrad during the winter of 1942–1943 than either the British or the Americans did in all the battles of the war. That many of the

Soviet Union's soldiers died because of their generals' poor tactics does not erase this staggering sacrifice.[80]

At the same time, the Soviets inflicted somewhere between 80 and 90 percent of the estimated 5.5 million casualties Hitler's troops suffered in the war. Between June 1941 and May 1944, Stalin's soldiers killed 60,000 German soldiers a month, breaking the back of Hitler's war machine and destroying its offensive power. And by 1943, the Red Army's victories against the retreating Germans on the plains of southern Russia allowed the Americans to begin shifting more troops to the Pacific theater to fight the Japanese.[81]

These brutal, unsentimental facts had an enormous impact on Roosevelt's wartime planning and policies. To keep Stalin in the war and prevent him from negotiating a separate peace with Hitler, he made every gesture he could. Even as late as the fall of 1943, FDR's fears about Stalin's cutting a deal with the Nazi leader, just as Lenin had done with the Kaiser at the very end of 1917, were real.[82]

To feed Stalin's war machine, Roosevelt and Churchill extended Lend-Lease to the Soviet Union. The United States sent more than $5 billion in war supplies and equipment to Stalin, including 363,000 trucks, 6,000 tanks, 5,000 miles of telephone line, 58 percent of the Soviet air force's fuel, and 53 percent of its army's explosives. This, of course, did not satisfy Stalin, a functioning paranoid. Only a second front in France—which did not come until June 6, 1944—would appease him. In the meantime, Roosevelt realized that the United States could not afford to upset the deeply suspicious Soviets.[83]

Soviet foreign minister Vyacheslav Molotov arrived in Washington on May 29, 1942, packing a pistol and carrying a suitcase full of brown bread and thick sausages. He feared being assassinated or poisoned. As a welcoming gesture, Roosevelt commuted CPUSA general secretary Earl Browder's prison sentence and released him. The State Department also suppressed publication of the assassinated Leon Trotsky's scathing biography of Joseph Stalin. The Soviets reciprocated by abolishing the Comintern in 1943.[84]

As part of the Roosevelt administration's strategy to keep Stalin focused on Hitler and to unleash him on the Japanese after the Germans were beaten, Attorney General Francis Biddle promised Secretary of

State Cordell Hull on April 1, 1944, that he would "take no criminal action against any Russian connected with the Russian government without first obtaining [Hull's] approval." This never meant, of course, that Soviet spies such as Lee could not be forced out of their government positions or that the FBI could not have sent back to Moscow any NKVD and GRU officers it caught. It did mean that Franklin Roosevelt's Department of Justice was not going to arrest and prosecute Soviet spies while the Red Army's soldiers were dying in droves and the Americans were still planning their cross-channel invasion of France.[85]

Collecting intelligence on the Soviets and their sources was one thing. Sending them to jail was quite another. Lee realized this in March 1945 when he told Joseph Katz that the FBI knew all about CPUSA members passing information to the Soviets but that its agents were waiting for Germany's defeat before actually arresting anyone. Though wrong about what the FBI knew, he was spot-on about the US government's restraint.[86]

But the war was now over. Roosevelt lay in his Hyde Park grave, his diplomatic and strategic worries put to rest. The political context had changed profoundly. All that remained was to root out any current or former Soviet spies. The gnawing problem that kept Hoover awake at night was how to gather the clinching evidence and prove their guilt in the courts of law and public opinion.

SEVEN

ON THE OUTSIDE LOOKING IN

J. Edgar Hoover did not lack faith in Elizabeth Bentley. His ordered mind saw too many consistent patterns in her statements to his agents to doubt she was telling the truth. The problem was proving what she claimed. His G-men still had not found a way to make her allegations against Lee or any of the others she had accused stick. Over the next two years, scores of FBI agents would work tirelessly to corroborate her allegations and ensure that Lee would never again be able to steal his country's secrets.

On February 21, 1946, Hoover sent the White House a 194-page report summarizing the FBI's key findings since Bentley's first meeting with agents Buckley and Jardine more than three months before. Hoover underscored his confidence in his prized informant by titling his digest "Underground Soviet Espionage Organization (NKVD) in Agencies of the United States Government." Its preamble explained why he was so certain Bentley was telling the truth: "In no instance has Gregory—the FBI's code name for her—supplied information which could not either directly or circumstantially be verified."[1]

Bentley had given the FBI the names of over 150 people who actually existed. She had also described espionage methods practiced by every secret service in the world, identified Anatoly Gorsky, the NKGB's chief of American operations, and recited policies and positions that only those inside the US government could have known. As importantly, the bureau had confirmed that the Silvermasters—Gregory Silvermaster co-led the largest ring of Soviet spies inside the US government—had a photographic dark room in their basement. Nearly three months earlier, an agent had used a ruse on Helen Silvermaster to enter the couple's basement. There he found a dark room that contained developing fluids, drying frames, and paper. This crucial breakthrough provided the first physical corroboration of Bentley's information.[2]

But not a single revelation had led the FBI any closer to the legal proof it needed to arrest, prosecute, and convict Duncan Lee or any of the others on whom she had snitched. Even the agent's search of the Silvermasters' dark room had failed to uncover any incriminating evidence. Despite this, Hoover and his top lieutenants still clung to the fading hope that they could double Bentley and use her to coax her former sources back into spying.

On March 12, 1946, she came to Washington on a business trip. Following the FBI's guidance, she called the Silvermasters, who invited her to their home. Although civil, they were not warm. Neither Gregory nor Helen mentioned her past visits. Nor did they let on that they knew she had defected.[3]

The next day, Bentley had lunch at a Washington restaurant with Helen Tenney, one of her sources inside the OSS. By then, Tenney was convinced that the FBI was following her. She was right. Agents had already questioned her family's chauffeur. Now, two agents watched her from a nearby table. Sensing her paranoia and agitation, Bentley did not press her for any information. One night in late August 1946, after muttering to a friend that she was a Soviet spy, Tenney cracked and overdosed on a mix of phenobarbital and alcohol, leaving her unconscious for five days. After doctors revived her, she reacted violently to even the mention of the word "Russian." Five months later, Tenney was a mental patient at the Payne Whitney Clinic in Manhattan, where her psychiatrist diagnosed her as a psychotic hallucinating about being a Soviet spy. When agents finally interviewed her in 1947, they recorded that Tenney appeared "somewhat dazed and stated that the whole matter was beyond her comprehension."[4]

The Silvermaster and Tenney disappointments did not exhaust the FBI's hopes. On March 23, 1946, Bentley received a coded telephone message to meet Gorsky at a Bickford's restaurant in Manhattan. She promptly alerted the FBI. Although several agents eagerly waited inside and outside the restaurant, he never came because he was in Moscow. The NKGB had recalled him on December 7, 1945, in the wake of Bentley's defection. The coded message may have been an NKGB ruse to lure Bentley to a restaurant in order to kidnap her or to gauge what kind of FBI security she had.[5]

In fact, this was Bentley's last communication from the Soviets and the FBI's last chance to turn her into a double agent. On November 25, 1946, Edward A. Tamm, one of Hoover's top assistants, admitted in a memorandum what many agents assigned to the investigation already knew: "There does not appear to be any possibility of a reestablishment [of contact between the NKGB and] the informant."[6]

In the meantime, the FBI closed in on Lee from other directions. On February 26 and March 7, 1946, the bureau sent two reports on Bentley's allegations about him to G-2, the army's military intelligence branch, where the FBI had discovered he held a reserve commission as a lieutenant colonel. Lee had gotten it the same day he resigned from the OSS. Remarkably, it would take the army until March 1949 to transfer Lee from its active to its inactive reserve.[7]

A month later, in April 1946, the FBI delivered a similar summary to Admiral Sidney W. Souers, the first director of the newly created Central Intelligence Group (CIG), which had absorbed some of OSS's functions that January and would become the Central Intelligence Agency in 1947. Scores of former OSS officers, who had waited anxiously for President Truman to realize that Donovan was right about the country's need for a permanent external intelligence service, had begun streaming into the CIG. Lee's exemplary record as one of Donovan's top aides made him an ideal candidate for a high post in the new agency. The FBI's report to Souers ensured that CIG would never hire Lee.[8]

The FBI closed one door while building a hidden trapdoor. On July 2, 1946, the bureau placed Lee on its Security Index, a secret list of political subversives the FBI planned to detain and hold during a national emergency. Hoover started the list on September 2, 1939, one day after the Germans invaded Poland. By 1952, the Security Index contained 19,577 names. Two year later, it had swelled to over 26,000 names. The FBI planned to arrest what it characterized as the "most potentially dangerous" subversives, including Lee, within an hour after Hoover gave the order.[9]

While the FBI was blocking Lee's renewed access to America's secrets and making plans to detain him in a national emergency, Lee concentrated on his postwar life. He left the government officially on January 30, 1946.

At first, Lee planned to return to New York City and Donovan's law firm. He had deep personal ties to Donovan, Leisure—Otto Doering had returned there after resigning from the OSS when Donovan left—and he liked the money. Doering hoped that his brilliant erstwhile associate and trusted aide would rejoin him in their Wall Street practice. On February 4, 1946, he wrote Lee, praising his personal devotion and wartime service: "I shall remember most vividly not your intelligent, resourceful, and energetic handling of problems which took such a load off my shoulders but the unbounded measure of selfless loyalty and cooperation which you showed to me as your chief." When he penned these words, Doering had never heard of Elizabeth Bentley or her charges.[10]

But Lee did not like the firm's long hours and the drudgery of its corporate practice. He had also begun to think of Washington as his home. He and Ishbel considered it a better place than New York City to raise their growing family. The Lees had three children and would soon have another. Katherine Maxwell Lee was born on February 23, 1947.[11]

Briefly, Lee considered following his brother Armistead into the Foreign Service. Being a diplomat would satisfy his own interest in American foreign policy and could lead to an ambassadorship or even serve as a launching pad into politics. But a career in the Foreign Service would also mean constantly uprooting his family and living again on a federal paycheck.[12]

Instead, he decided to pursue his lifelong fascination with China, a sprawling country that needed to rebuild itself after the war. Lee relied on his OSS connections to find the job he wanted. While in the OSS he had become reacquainted with Michael Quinn Shaughnessy, a Harvard Law School graduate who had worked for the Securities and Exchange Commission until 1941. While there, he had reviewed the securities registration statements Lee filed for Donovan, Leisure's clients. The two men soon became friends.

After Pearl Harbor, Shaughnessy joined China Defense Supplies (CDS) and served in India and China. CDS was the private corporation that coordinated and administered the US Lend-Lease program in China during World War II. It was the brainchild of Tommy "the Cork" Corcoran, a brilliant Washington insider who, with Franklin Roosevelt's full backing, had incorporated CDS in the spring of 1941 in Delaware. Roosevelt judged this an easier way to get economic aid to China than going to a Congress increasingly nervous about the expanding US role in a war it hadn't officially joined. Corcoran established CDS as an arm of the Chinese Nationalist government, staffing it with Americans and setting up its headquarters in Washington.[13]

Shaughnessy joined the Marine Corps in January 1944 and was commissioned a first lieutenant. When assigned to the OSS that April, he renewed his friendship with Lee. Shaughnessy served mostly in China until he resigned from Donovan's agency in September 1945. After the war, he rejoined the newly named China Supply Commission (the successor to CDS, which liquidated itself on July 1, 1944), whose main purpose had shifted from fighting the Japanese to rebuilding China's devastated economy.[14]

Shaughnessy most likely introduced Lee to William S. Youngman Jr., a partner in the Washington law firm of Corcoran, Clark, and Youngman, in late 1945. Youngman was also a director, the general counsel, and the president of the China Supply Commission. Lee and Youngman, with their shared Ivy League educations and love for China, soon struck up a friendship and a business relationship that would span more than four decades. Youngman was also impressed with Lee's war service and his meteoric rise from first lieutenant to lieutenant colonel.[15]

Youngman introduced Lee to Corcoran sometime before the end of 1945. The savvy Washington lawyer liked what he saw. When he learned that Lee was looking for a job in Washington, he hired him as a lawyer principally for the China Supply Commission, by then a major client of Corcoran's law firm. If Lee saw the irony of working for Chiang Kai-shek, the man who had driven his father, Edmund, out of China, he never discussed it. When he told Donovan that he planned to accept Corcoran's offer, the retired general gave his one-time protégé his blessing.[16]

Shortly after joining Corcoran's law firm in January 1946, Lee learned, probably from Mary Price, about Bentley's defection and Hoover's investigation. After weighing his options, he decided to focus on his new job and wait for the FBI to knock on his door.[17]

Lee's initial job was to negotiate and prepare the contracts the Nationalist Chinese government needed to rebuild the country's war-torn infrastructure. His work included drafting railway repair contracts and purchase agreements that allowed the Nationalists to buy a fleet of cargo ships from the US Maritime Commission.[18]

Inexorably, Lee was drawn into Corcoran's efforts to prevent Mao Zedong's communist armies from driving Chiang's government into the sea. He later wrote that his work for Corcoran from 1946 centered on halting communism's advance in the Far East. Only two years before, Lee had been one of the NKGB's most highly placed spies. Gut-wrenching fear and badly frayed nerves had forced him to make an abrupt 180-degree turn.[19]

Perhaps something beyond self-preservation triggered his astonishing about-face. Even though he had rebelled against Edmund's teachings when a young man, he had absorbed more from his father, the Christian mystic, than he ever admitted. As a fervent believer in God's grace, Edmund had preached to his son that sin and guilt could be forgiven and erased with confession and atonement. In March 1945, Lee had confessed his guilt about betraying the United States to the NKGB's Joseph Katz. While Lee's writings are silent about any remorse he might have felt for his treachery—he went to his grave denying that he had ever spied for the Soviets—such feelings preyed on his conscience and most likely spurred him to atone by fighting communism in China. Opposing Mao Zedong, he hoped, would exorcise the demons haunting his conscience and build what he later called "a useful record of having struck a significant blow against international communism" that he could use against his accusers.[20]

J. Edgar Hoover, however, was no believer in forgiveness. His God dwelled in the pages of the Old Testament. He and his agents were determined to punish Lee for his crimes by sending him to the electric chair and an Episcopalian cemetery. Their confidence in Elizabeth Bentley, along with rapidly changing domestic and international political climates, urged them on.

Hoover, sensing these seismic shifts, moved to take full advantage of them to push his case against Lee. He realized that America's early enthusiasm for Harry Truman had all but vanished by the fall of 1946 as the country struggled to convert, socially and economically, from war to peace. Truman's own party underscored his unpopularity by playing Franklin Roosevelt's radio speeches during its congressional candidates' campaigns instead of inviting a sitting president to speak at their rallies.[21]

In November 1946, the Republicans won control of both houses of Congress for the first time since 1928. Their simple and direct campaign slogans of "Had enough?" and "Communism Versus Republicanism" captured the country's weariness with the long reign of the Democrats and their New Deal programs. Red baiters Joseph McCarthy and Richard Nixon arrived in Washington that winter. The Eightieth Congress would pack twenty-two probes of communism into its two-year life.[22]

Hoover added to Truman's woes by announcing a month before the elections that there were 100,000 communists in the United States—the CPUSA had roughly 50,000 members in 1946—and ten fellow travelers for each one. He insisted that this fifth column was poised to take advantage of any chaos.[23]

Deteriorating relations between the United States and the Soviet Union stoked these public fears. Stalin's unwavering determination to hold on to the Soviet Union's 1941 borders, his intention to dominate eastern Europe, his disagreements with America, Britain, and France over Germany's future, and his delay in removing his soldiers from the Iranian province of Azerbaijan in the spring of 1946 heightened

America's mounting suspicions of its onetime ally. Winston Churchill deepened this distrust on March 5, 1946, when he warned during a speech at Westminster College in Fulton, Missouri, that an iron curtain was descending across Europe, "from Stettin in the Baltic to Trieste in the Adriatic." His message was unmistakably clear: the Soviets could not be trusted, and worse, they were on the move.

Hoover was certain the Soviets were planning a Pearl Harbor–like attack on the United States that internal subversives would aid and abet. To shield himself and the FBI from any blame, he flooded the White House with rumors of spy rings and their Hydra-headed plots. He also believed that Harry Truman was too naïve and too focused on foreign affairs to understand how dangerous this internal threat was.[24]

Hoover was correct about Truman's focus on foreign affairs. It was the one arena his political foes had left him. The Republican-controlled Eightieth Congress blocked his domestic programs for full employment, farm price supports, small-business assistance, and an expansion of Social Security. Truman responded by exercising his veto power 250 times during his nearly eight years in the White House.[25]

The Soviets were also on the march. By 1947, Stalin had set up puppet governments in most of eastern Europe. More chillingly, he seemed to have set his sights on Turkey and Greece. On February 21, 1947, an exhausted and almost bankrupt Britain told the Truman administration that she could no longer afford to send money and matériel to Greece's anticommunist government.[26]

Harry Truman wanted to contain communism's spread, but first, in the words of Republican senator Arthur Vandenberg, he had to "scare the hell out of the American people." Vandenberg, who represented the internationalist wing of the Republican Party, understood that most Americans, after their sacrifices in World War II, wanted to repeat what they had done after World War I and retreat behind their two vast oceans. He also recognized that his fellow Republicans wanted to cut federal taxes by 20 percent and slash Truman's already tight budget by another $6 billion. The only way to mobilize the country for a crusade against communism was to frighten it.[27]

On March 12, 1947, Truman rose before a packed special session of Congress and shocked its members with the news that the United

States was now locked in a kill-or-be-killed battle with communism: "It must be the policy of the United States to support free peoples who are resisting attempted subjugation by armed minorities or by outside pressures." Shell-shocked, Congress gave him the $400 million he requested for Turkey and Greece. Nine days later, he inaugurated a loyalty program for federal employees. By overly dramatizing the dangers of internal subversion, Truman played into J. Edgar Hoover's hands and encouraged those who believed that the Soviet Union's postwar gains were not the outcome of military realities in eastern Europe but the work of Moscow's agents inside the US government.[28]

The two men's hatred for one another only added to this fear-polluted atmosphere. In 1939, the FBI had investigated then Senator Truman's ties to Tom Pendergast, the corrupt Kansas City, Missouri, political boss who had just been convicted of income tax evasion. Three years later, Truman questioned the FBI's competence in the wake of Japan's surprise attack on Pearl Harbor. He carried his doubts about the FBI with him into the White House. From his first days as president, he told his aides that he was "very much against building up a Gestapo" with Hoover at its head. Truman believed that the bureau threatened Americans' civil liberties and that Hoover held on to power by intimidating members of Congress with his thick files documenting and cataloging their sex lives.[29]

Despite the increasingly anticommunist climate forming in America in 1946, the FBI's investigation of Lee remained stalled. On October 21, Hoover sent a 335-page report to Attorney General Tom Clark that admitted as much. For the first time, he complained that the late date of Bentley's defection had hampered the bureau's investigation into her sources.[30]

With no new breaks on the horizon, the bureau's high command reluctantly decided to allow Department of Justice prosecutors to interview their prized informant. Edward Tamm, one of Hoover's top lieutenants and most astute advisers, shared his boss's low opinion of the department's lawyers. He also worried about leaks to the press. That Attorney General Tom Clark's Criminal Division was already "trying," in Tamm's words, "to squirm out of a decision as to prosecution" bothered him even more. He believed the attorney general's overriding concern was to protect the Truman administration from political embarrassment. Tamm did not want the FBI to give Clark an excuse to claim that the bureau was delaying the Department of Justice's investigation into Bentley's allegations by not making her available for an interview. Hoover's lieutenant echoed the frustration of hundreds of FBI agents when he prodded the director, saying, "It is essential that some decision be made in the Department about the case because we cannot go on and on in the present manner."[31]

Two days later, Clark confessed to Hoover that one of Tamm's fears had materialized: there had been a leak. Some facts of the case had fallen into the hands of the United Press International News Service. Hoover immediately blamed the Department of Justice and warned Clark that the leaks would trigger a congressional investigation "with all its undesirable results." That same day, James McInerney, a former FBI agent and a veteran Department of Justice lawyer, met with Hoover's star witness in New York.[32]

Although the FBI did not tell McInerney Bentley's true name, its agents handling her in New York shared their opinions about her strengths as a potential witness. They highlighted her intelligence and reliability but added that "she is rather a plain looking person" who might not make the best impression before a jury because "she is not particularly meticulous in her dress or appearance."[33]

While Bentley impressed McInerney favorably when he questioned her, he still waffled about what to do with her allegations. Briefly, he considered prosecuting Lee and the others for the fraud he believed they had committed against the federal government. He thought he could base his fraud charges on the services and time the government's agencies had lost while their employees were spying for the Soviets.[34]

The FBI had no confidence in McInerney's lame legal theory. That same week, Tamm asked Edward Pierpont Morgan, one of the bureau's most respected chief inspectors, to analyze the Gregory case under the existing espionage laws. Morgan, an excellent lawyer, pulled no punches in a tightly worded five-page memorandum dated January 14, 1947: "What we know to be true in this case is a far cry from what we are in a position to prove beyond a reasonable doubt." He realized full well that the FBI had Bentley's claims and little else. He also pointed out that many of her former sources, such as Lee, would be especially difficult to corner because they were "extraordinarily intelligent" and "unusually well-educated."[35]

Morgan methodically picked apart the bureau's case. He highlighted that its agents still had not identified "Bill" or "Jack" (Iskhak Akhmerov and Joseph Katz), that Gorsky had fled to Moscow, and that Bentley did not know to whom, besides Earl Browder, Jacob Golos had passed her information. He had intentionally kept her away from his own NKGB handlers.

Similarly, the bureau lacked evidence that Bentley's sources had intended to harm the United States for the benefit of a foreign country or that they had unlawfully passed government documents to anyone not supposed to receive them. One or the other was required if a charge under the existing espionage statutes was to have any hope of resulting in a conviction. Although Bentley recalled the contents of some of the documents she had seen, she had not kept copies of any of them. Morgan pointedly spelled out what all this meant: "Coming in after the event as the Bureau did, we are now on the outside looking in, with the rather embarrassing responsibility of having a most serious case of Soviet espionage laid in our laps without a decent opportunity to make it stick."[36]

Morgan branded McInerney's fraud theory "ridiculous," convinced that this was a case of Soviet espionage and nothing else. The daunting problem was how to prove the spying had taken place. He agreed with Tamm that the FBI had to change its tactics. It had to interview Bentley's sources and try to turn or break one. If, as he expected, that failed, Morgan recommended, as a last resort, publicly exposing what he labeled "this lousy outfit."[37]

The next day, Tamm seconded Morgan's proposal to conduct interviews. He too was skeptical of their success but advised Hoover again that the FBI could not investigate Bentley's allegations forever, adding that the interviews would, if nothing else, allow the bureau to save face: "The principal advantage, of course, of these interviews would be that at least it would put these people on notice of the fact

that the Bureau has known for a long time what they have been doing, and at least we would have the satisfaction of letting them know
that they haven't fooled us."[38]

Floyd L. Jones, an FBI supervisor in Washington, DC, joined the
internal debate and expressed an anxiety about the case shared by
many in the bureau's high command: it could turn into, as he phrased
it, a "political football." He worried especially that the Truman administration might maneuver the FBI into a failed prosecution and
then claim in the 1948 presidential election that the Republicans'
charges that communists had infiltrated the government had been
baseless. To prevent this, Jones argued the bureau should hand Bentley's claims over to a congressional committee.[39]

D. M. "Mickey" Ladd, the savvy head of the FBI's Domestic Intelligence Division, agreed with Jones but presciently opposed his recommendation to send the case to Congress: "I doubt it could be handled
without them playing a great deal of politics and resulting in its being
grief for everybody involved and in not resulting in a thing." Hoover
disagreed. To shield himself and the FBI from any possible congressional criticisms that the bureau had been sleeping while at least two
major Soviet spy rings operated in wartime Washington, and to ingratiate himself with the Republicans, Hoover secretly ordered the
bureau's Crime Records Division, headed by Louis Burrous Nichols,
who was also his liaison to Congress, to send choice bits of its Gregory case files to the House Un-American Activities Committee. The
FBI sent its first derogatory information on Lee to the HUAC on January 20, 1947.[40]

In the meantime, Tamm told Attorney General Tom Clark that
Hoover was "very, very reluctant" to prosecute any of Bentley's sources
because the chances for success were poor. Tamm also lectured Clark
on how the Justice Department's leaks had damaged the FBI's case.
Hoover agreed. In his characteristic blue ink, he scrawled the following note at the end of Tamm's report on his meeting with Clark: "Of
course, in view of all the gabbing done by the Dept [sic] to the press
there is little which can be expected from *any* action now."[41]

In late January 1947, Hoover informed Clark that his department's
leaks had undermined the bureau's ability to collect any more useful

intelligence. This seemed even more evident six days later. On the night of February 2, newspaper columnist Drew Pearson alerted the nation during his weekly radio program that a former University of Oklahoma professor, who had also worked for the State Department, faced indictment for communist activities. Although wrong about the pending indictment, he was referring to Maurice Halperin, one of Bentley's spies inside the OSS who had migrated to the State Department after Donovan's agency dissolved.[42]

True, all these leaks were damaging, but Hoover never suspected in 1947 that British turncoat Kim Philby had already derailed the FBI investigation almost before it started. Leakage, though, had some positive effects. By March, only seven people Bentley had named were still federal employees.[43]

The Department of Justice and the FBI seemed to be running out of options. On February 21, 1947, Attorney General Clark asked T. Vincent Quinn, head of the department's Criminal Division, and Tom Donegan, who had left the FBI and rejoined the department as a special assistant to the attorney general, to review all the Bentley case files and recommend a final course of action. As the two men pored over the files, Clark also ordered Hoover to interview fifteen of her sources. Most belonged to the Silvermaster or Perlo spy rings. Because two were outside the United States, the bureau decided to interview only thirteen.[44]

Twelve interviews took place on April 15. They went exactly as Morgan and Tamm had predicted. Gregory Silvermaster, who would eventually be enshrined in the KGB's Hall of Fame, called Bentley's allegations "preposterous" and insisted on his loyalty to the United States. He denied being a member of the CPUSA but admitted meeting Golos one time. According to Silvermaster, he had asked Golos about booking a trip to the Soviet Union. Helen Silvermaster also lied, telling the FBI that she first met Bentley at a Spanish Aid ball in 1937 in New York City. She acknowledged seeing her frequently during the war but claimed never to have asked why she came to Washington so often. Incredibly, Helen Silvermaster said she had believed Bentley worked for the OSS and that she had not wanted to pry into her secret work. She too denied being a member of the CPUSA, calling such allegations "ridiculous."[45]

The bureau's interview of William Ullmann, who worked at the Pentagon and co-led the Silvermaster spy ring, went similarly. He said he first met Bentley in 1939 or 1940 at the Silvermasters' home. At the outset, he admitted that she had visited the Silvermasters every two weeks between 1939 and 1944 or 1945. Several minutes later, he specified fifteen to forty visits. He denied knowing anything about her business, her past, or why she had come to Washington so many times. Bentley, he confided, was a "hysterical, highly emotional nuisance," and neither he nor the Silvermasters liked her.[46]

The FBI had planned to interview Mary Price on April 15 but could not because she was en route from Greensboro, North Carolina, to Birmingham, Alabama, to attend a meeting of the Southern Conference for Human Welfare (SCHW). She had joined that civil rights organization in September 1945 and risen to become the secretary of its organizing committee. In 1947, the HUAC branded the SCHW as a communist front "which seeks to attract southern liberals on the basis of seeming interest in the problems of the South, although its professed interest in southern welfare is simply an expedient for larger aims serving the Soviet Union and its subservient Communist Party in the United States."[47]

The FBI followed Price to Birmingham and dispatched two of its New York field office agents to interview her there. Price met with them at the bureau's Birmingham office at 12:30 p.m. on April 17. Her answers proved as useless as those the FBI had gotten during its other interviews. The only difference was that she was more combative. She demanded to know what the two agents wanted and asked them if she needed a lawyer. They assured her that they only wanted to ask her about some events in Washington. After hesitating, Price looked at photographs of Maurice Halperin, Jacob Golos, and Earl Browder. She denied knowing them, just as she did Donald Wheeler, Lee's fellow Rhodes scholar and another Soviet spy inside the OSS. In a memorandum to Hoover the next day, the special agent in charge of the FBI's Birmingham office wrote, "At numerous intervals, she became recalcitrant. It was very apparent that she would not volunteer any information."

Like the others, Price admitted that she knew Bentley, identifying her as a "Vassar gal" who worked for a travel bureau in New York City. She also conceded that she knew the Lees, telling the agents that her sister had introduced her to Duncan Lee. Price said that she had seen him on "numerous occasions" in New York City and Washington. She admitted as well that he had stayed at her apartment for a "week or two" in August 1942 while looking for an apartment for his family after he joined the OSS.

Price told the agents that she had been aware of his holding an important post in the OSS and that he had frequently visited her at her apartment while wearing his army uniform. But she denied ever receiving any secret information from him. Price volunteered that she was very fond of Lee and Ishbel but insisted that any dealings with them were purely social. Sloppily, the FBI agents never cross-examined Price about whether the Lees had first met Bentley at one of Price's cocktail parties.[48]

The bureau's other interviews yielded the same arid results. All Bentley's former sources followed the NKGB's script and replied to the FBI's questions exactly as Gorsky and Akhmerov had instructed back in late 1945.

The failure of these interviews left Tom Clark with only one choice: a grand jury. On March 10, Quinn met with Domestic Intelligence Division head Mickey Ladd at the FBI's headquarters and admitted that neither he nor Donegan thought they had the evidence to prosecute anyone Bentley had named. All the same, Quinn argued, a grand jury could serve an important political purpose: it could deflect charges from the Republican-dominated HUAC that the Democrats had done nothing with her shocking allegations.[49]

The FBI was about to knock on Lee's front door.

In June 1947, a little over three months after Quinn's meeting with Ladd, Attorney General Clark placed the case in the hands of a Manhattan grand jury. Meanwhile, Quinn and Donegan asked the FBI to interview "the remaining subjects and principals in the case." As early as February, the bureau had been mulling over whether to confront Lee. Could he be the weak sister Edward Pierpont Morgan, the bureau's savvy chief inspector, sought? Mickey Ladd thought so. He spelled out his reasons to Hoover on February 7. After pointing out that Lee came from a proud family with an old Virginia background that he would not want to tarnish, Ladd underscored Bentley's observation that at times he appeared unusually nervous and excited. He told Hoover that FBI agents should be able to exploit these traits to break him.[50]

On May 29, at exactly 10:30 a.m., two FBI agents walked into the Tower Building at 1401 K Street, the address of scores of Washington's most powerful lobbyists. As they rode in one of the art deco building's elevators, Special Agents Charles G. Cleveland and W. Raymond Wannall looked as if they had just stepped off the set of one of Hollywood's FBI movies. Dressed in the bureau's trademark starched white shirts, dark suits, and snap-brimmed fedoras, they personified Hoover's no-nonsense G-men. Lee's secretary led them to his office.[51]

After they sat down, Cleveland and Wannall immediately appealed to Lee's patriotism. They reminded him of his deep American roots and pointed out that he and they shared the same interest in the welfare of the country. Both agents noticed his visible agitation and recognized the same physical reactions to stress that Joseph Katz had seen in early March 1945. They recorded what they saw in their report: "At the outset of the interview, Lee appeared to be visibly shaken and extremely nervous. After talking for approximately an hour he became calm and stopped trembling. His shaking was so noticeable at the outset of the interview that it was noted he had difficulty in lighting a cigarette. After he became calm, Lee was asked why he had been so nervous and shaken. He replied that he believed that anyone would be excited when questioned by FBI agents."[52]

Lee attributed his anxiety to the rising anticommunism and antiprogressivism that had followed the end of the war. Although he lied about having been a member of the CPUSA, he did admit to being a "left-winger." Gradually, he pulled himself together and adjusted to the questions' dangerous pitch and roll.

When Cleveland and Wannall asked whether he had been expecting a visit from the FBI, Lee admitted that he had. He said that he had heard a year before that the bureau was interested in his relationship with Mildred and Mary Price. When the agents pressed him about who had told him that, he refused to answer.

After questioning Lee about his background and education, the agents showed him Bentley's photograph. He identified her as "Helen" and said that he did not know her last name or where she worked. He was not lying because Bentley had never told him either her true name or what she did for a living. Most NKVD sources knew nothing about their Soviet handlers beyond their fictitious first names. Lee said that he first met her in late 1942 at a party at Mary Price's apartment and that he had last seen her in late 1944 or early 1945 in New York City or Washington. He could not remember which.

When the agents quizzed him about why he knew so little about Helen, Lee replied weakly that he had a bad memory for names and that "most of his contacts with her were at social functions and that he did not recall any incident arising when he could have discussed her occupation with her." He said that she did not appear to be overly curious about his work in the OSS and had never asked him for any classified information; nor had he given her any. At most, he allowed he might have casually discussed some unclassified aspects of his work with her. Although Lee said that he had met Bentley twice in New York City, he denied ever meeting her in Georgetown's pharmacies. He did admit to running into her accidentally once or twice on the street in Washington.

Cleveland and Wannall also brought up Mary Price. Lee described her as "tall, brunette, and rather attractive." He claimed that he had first met her in 1941 and stayed at her apartment with Ishbel when they were looking for an apartment in Washington. He said he still saw her often in New York City for a drink. He denied telling her anything about the OSS that she couldn't read in the newspapers.

Lee also told the agents that he had had dinner with Bentley and a man she called John—John was Jacob Golos's cover name—once in New York in early 1943 and again that fall in Washington. Both dates matched those Bentley had given the FBI in November 1945. She had explained to the bureau then that Golos had used the first meeting in New York to assess Lee's potential as a spy and the second in Washington to calm Ishbel down after she had discovered her husband's affair with Mary Price. Lee claimed ignorance about John's background, yet said he liked him and thought he was a "very interesting guy." John's politics were, in his estimation, "very progressive." Lee denied, though, discussing anything about the OSS with him that was not already public.[53]

When Cleveland and Wannall questioned him again about giving secret information to Helen, John, or Price, Lee turned indignant. Although he admitted to perhaps discussing with them unclassified and publicly known aspects of his work and acknowledged having had access to everything Donovan saw, he claimed that his own pressing duties in the OSS did not leave him enough time even to read the daily summaries flowing into the Secretariat.

The two agents finished with Lee at 12:10 p.m. Thirty minutes later they were sitting in his Georgetown living room interrogating Ishbel. Like her husband, she appeared to the two agents to be "quite nervous and emotionally upset." She claimed that she was extremely surprised by their visit because no one was more loyal to the United States than she and Lee.

As Ishbel's maid, Lee's visiting sister Priscilla, and her mother Katherine Gibb watched her four children, Ishbel led the agents through her past in India and Britain. She dissembled about joining the CPUSA but owned up to membership in the British Labour Party while a student at Oxford.

Ishbel's answers about Bentley differed subtly from her husband's. When the agents showed her Bentley's photograph, she said that she knew her only as Helen. After thinking about the photograph some more, she ventured that Helen's last name might have been Grant. Ishbel also claimed that she first met Helen at a party at Mary Price's apartment sometime before October 1943. She remembered the date because she met Bentley's friend John at a Washington restaurant that month. She particularly recalled that meeting because she was then only a month away from giving birth to her second child.

Ishbel characterized her and Lee's meetings with Bentley as purely social. She recounted meeting Helen "about five times and possibly a few more times which she could not recall." She said that Bentley visited them because she was fond of the Lees and their children.

At no time did she hear Bentley ask her husband for any classified information.

The agents met with Ishbel for only a half hour. Their report reflected their total failure to pry any damaging admissions from her: "Mrs. Lee categorically denied having furnished any information to any individual, which might work against the interests of the United States. She denied further having any knowledge of the fact that her husband had furnished such information to anyone."[54]

Neither of the Lees had cracked. That same night, they held what the FBI described as a "beer party" at their Georgetown home. They had planned their party several days earlier. They were not going to let the FBI spoil their fun; nor were they prepared to remove their masks.[55]

EIGHT

THE TERRIBLE
SUMMER OF 1948

Hoover was bothered less by the Lees' effusive celebration than by fact that the FBI now had to rely on Department of Justice lawyers and a grand jury sitting in the Southern District of New York to turn Elizabeth Bentley's unproven allegations into prosecutable charges. It would take legal alchemy to make that happen. Although Hoover knew that any witnesses called before the grand jury could panic and confess or commit perjury and be indicted for lying, he did not believe these outcomes were likely. He was an experienced oddsmaker, and not only at the racetrack.

Lee probably testified before the grand jury sometime during the summer of 1947. While the exact date of his appearance has yet to be publicly disclosed, Mary Price called him four times between June 11 and July 13. She also met him twice at Parchey's Restaurant on 19th and K streets in Washington. Both meetings were hastily arranged, taking place within minutes of her phone calls.[1]

When Lee testified, he stood before the grand jury and took an oath to tell the truth. He did not exercise his Fifth Amendment right not to answer any questions that might incriminate him; nor did he deviate from what he had told Special Agents Charles G. Cleveland and W. Raymond Wannall. He stuck to his story and asserted his innocence. Mary Price testified before the grand jury on December 3, 1947. She took the Fifth when asked if she knew Lee, Golos, or Bentley. She took it again when asked if she was a member of the CPUSA.[2]

Perjury and the Fifth Amendment were not the grand jury's only problems. By the late fall of 1947, a series of sensational reports about its investigation began dripping steadily into the newspapers. On October 16, the *New York Sun* reported on a spy ring of "gigantic proportions" that had penetrated "at least six government agencies and paid or persuaded at least fifty Americans to serve as espionage agents." This article named Vincent Quinn and Thomas Donegan as the prosecutors and assured its readers that the ring would "be cracked wide-open soon." The next day, the *Washington Times-Herald*, an ardent foe of the Truman administration, published a front-page story that was captioned with the headline "Jury Expected to Indict 60 as Red Spies." These spies, the article grimly declared, had left the United States all but defenseless. Almost a month later, a *Washington Post* columnist revealed that a "woman of education" had triggered the grand jury's investigation. More than one observer traced these leaks to the Department of Justice, judging them as calculated to put maximum pressure on the grand jury to indict at least some of those Bentley had named.[3]

But the grand jury could not. Between June 16, 1947, and April 7, 1948, forty-seven witnesses testified before it. Nothing new emerged. The testimony of those the FBI had interviewed closely tracked with what they had already said. The grand jury's failure to indict Lee for espionage or perjury spared him from facing formal charges in a federal courtroom, but it did not take him out of harm's way. Lee had too many powerful enemies for that, and he was now caught in swift international and domestic political currents that would not have allowed him to escape unscathed. The grand jury's failure would also heighten Elizabeth Bentley's feelings of desperation and drive her into the eager arms of politicians falling over themselves to derail Harry Truman's 1948 campaign to remain in the White House. With a strong push from Hoover, Lee would soon find himself squarely before the most dangerous and volatile committee in Congress.[4]

Six days before the grand jury heard its last witness, Vincent Quinn faced an irate Hoover. Attempting to soften the coming blow, he assured the director that Bentley's charges had enraged the grand jury; nonetheless, the lack of concrete evidence had tied its hands. Hoover fired back, reminding Quinn that he had strongly opposed sending the case to the grand jury in the first place, a course advocated by Quinn. He ended with a dire warning: "I stated that it seemed to me that there would be a most vigorous condemnation of the Department and particularly of the FBI when this Grand Jury ended its proceedings and brought in no indictments."[5]

Quinn had anticipated Hoover's reaction. To assuage him and to muffle Congress's expected outrage over the case's collapse, Quinn had already discussed with Attorney General Tom Clark using the same grand jury and the Smith Act to go after the high command of the CPUSA. The Smith Act prohibited organizing or belonging to a political party that advocated the violent overthrow of the US government.[6]

Quinn's idea appealed to Hoover. A successful Smith Act prosecution against the CPUSA's leaders would decapitate the party and severely hamper its ability to attract new recruits. GRU defector Igor Gouzenko had warned the FBI in 1945 that only the destruction of the CPUSA could stamp out Soviet espionage in the United States. Smith Act convictions would also make the FBI's planned mass arrests of communists and their sympathizers in a national emergency more palatable to the American people.[7]

The FBI had already assembled a bulky brief against the CPUSA that numbered 1,350 pages and contained 546 exhibits, but Hoover distrusted the Criminal Division's judgment about its legal merits. He snidely told Quinn that he wanted "several *real* lawyers" to read and analyze it first. John F. X. McGohey, the US attorney for the Southern District of New York, sifted through the eight heavy, black cardboard folders that housed the bureau's brief and agreed to present the case to the grand jury.[8]

By the time McGohey reached his decision, Quinn and Donegan had already begun readying the grand jury for its new case. On March 30, 1948, they recalled Bentley to the stand and asked her about the CPUSA's plans to overthrow the US government. She balked, telling the jurors that she had never heard anyone in the CPUSA talk about fomenting a violent revolution. Her sources, she claimed, had wanted only to defeat the fascists.[9]

Despite Bentley's resistance, Quinn and Donegan's case against the CPUSA was much stronger than that against her sources. For one thing, 61 percent of Americans now favored outlawing the CPUSA. Rising tensions with Stalin also strengthened the Department of Justice's hand. In February 1948, Soviet-backed communists had staged a successful coup d'état in Czechoslovakia and seized control of the government. This triggered a war scare in the United States and forced Harry Truman to ask Congress in March for permission to resume the draft. On June 24, the Soviets imposed a full military blockade on the western sectors of Berlin, occupied by the United States, Britain, and France. War seemed inevitable.[10]

Bentley did not care about the Justice Department's case against the CPUSA. Her life was again in ruins. Worsening US-Soviet relations and the NKGB's refusal to pour any more money into the United States Service and Shipping Corporation, the business cover for espionage that Jacob Golos had set up in 1941 and for which she had served as vice president, had compelled the company to close its doors in October 1946. She had been forced to take a job as a secretary for the Pacific Molasses Company, a British enterprise with an office in New York City. Now, the grand jury had refused to indict any of her former sources. She had to salvage something.[11]

On April 1, 1948, Bentley dialed Frederick Woltman, a reporter for the *New York World-Telegram*. She told him that she had some information about the grand jury. This was not the first time that she had thought about going public. In December 1947, she had written Louis Budenz, her former source who was now making a handsome living as a lecturer and writer on the evils of communism, to seek his advice on writing a book about her own experiences. Budenz, who understood where his own interests lay, promptly turned her letter over to the FBI.[12]

Woltman was different. He and Nelson Frank, another reporter, agreed to meet with her. Both men were themselves former communists. Their first meeting with Bentley on April 2 lasted three hours. Even though she told them all about her life as an NKGB courier and handler, the two reporters made it clear that they could write nothing until the grand jury had finished its work. They also told her that they were going to tell the FBI about the meeting.[13]

When Hoover heard about it, he erupted. He ordered the bureau's New York City field office to rein in Bentley and stop her unauthorized contacts with the press. Chastened, she explained that she had been distraught and worried about her future. She promised not to meet with Woltman and Frank again until she had the FBI's permission.[14]

Her promise proved worthless. She had dinner with Frank on April 16 and April 25. Shortly after that, she and Frank agreed to write and market her story. On May 7, Frank told the FBI what he and Bentley planned. Frank warned the bureau that he was writing Bentley's autobiography and working on a series for his newspaper on her espionage career. The FBI was finding her as difficult to control as the NKGB had.[15]

Lee, in the meantime, had been lucky. He had beaten back the FBI and the grand jury. Perhaps, he prayed, the investigation had run its stomach-churning course, and his heart could stop racing every time his phone rang or someone knocked on his door. Although he did not know it, the FBI had stopped wiretapping his telephone on March 28, 1948, because of "nonproductivity." Then, his worst fear materialized like a stray bolt of lightning out of the blue sky.[16]

Just before noon on July 20, 1948, the grand jury indicted the CPUSA's twelve highest leaders, including longtime Stalinists William Foster, Gus Hall, and Eugene Dennis, for conspiring to overthrow the US government. The next morning, the *New York Sun* ran a story on the background of the grand jury's proceedings and its links to a mysterious blonde woman's claims of espionage in the federal government.[17]

Only a few hours later, the *New York World-Telegram* began running a series of front-page stories that would rock Lee's life for years to come. Sandwiched directly between the bone-chilling banner about Secretary of State George C. Marshall's efforts to "Avert a Third World War" over Berlin and another screaming, "Prison Farm Head Family Murdered," another smaller, but equally head-snapping, headline announced, "Red Ring Bared by Blond Queen."

Nelson Frank and Norton Mockridge, a rewrite man and another reporter for the *World-Telegram,* did not name Bentley in this story but described her fancifully as a "svelte and striking blonde" driven to defect by "gnawing pangs of conscience." Although Lee would hardly have recognized her in this sexed-up portrait, he was undoubtedly stricken by what he read on the story's second page: "Working for this woman was a man high in the councils of the Office of Strategic Services (supposedly the most secret of all of America's cloak and dagger agencies). This man, wearing his Army uniform, would meet the woman on a Washington street corner and turn over secret information to her."[18]

The next afternoon, another story appeared in the same newspaper, expanding on this shadowy partnership: "The government itself, the blond queen declared, was not unaware that some Communists were engaged in espionage. Proof of this came one day when a member of the ring, working for the OSS, stole a copy of a document prepared by that agency. It listed Communist members of the staff believed to be very dangerous, dangerous, or unreliable."[19]

This explosive paragraph contained inaccuracies, but it was clear enough to Lee. He knew it referred to the list of suspected communists and their sympathizers inside the OSS that he had given to Bentley in September 1944. He also knew that now everybody would learn of the allegations against him: his colleagues, his mentors, his friends, and his parents. Even worse, the HUAC planned to hold hearings on all of Bentley's charges. On July 21, the date of Frank and Mockridge's first story, the HUAC issued a subpoena for her to testify. The Republican-dominated committee, most likely aided by the FBI in discovering the blond spy queen's identity, wanted to tar the Truman administration with charges of handing the government over to communists, and Lee realized that he would be caught in the middle of this political warfare. He also understood that he would be facing Congress's most dangerous and vicious interrogators.[20]

The HUAC was fresh from investigating communist infiltration of Hollywood. The nation had watched transfixed during the last two weeks of October 1947 as the committee sought to expose Karl Marx's influence on the silver screen. In nine days of internecine bloodletting, the movie industry turned on itself and devoured its own. By the end of the hearings, ten screenwriters, producers, and playwrights, nine of them CPUSA members, had been jailed for contempt and blacklisted. A bad odor now hung over the committee because of its no-holds-barred, headhunting style of questioning. Even in a scared country, bullying did not go over well.[21]

The HUAC's many enemies howled for its abolition. But in one of the greatest miscalculations of his presidency, Harry Truman breathed new life into the committee and brought its anticommunist crusade against the Democrats to the front pages of every major newspaper in the United States.

By the summer of 1948, the Democratic Party was financially broke and splintered into warring political factions. Truman needed to shift the public's attention away from his own party's divisions onto what he derisively called the "no account, doing-nothing 80th Congress" that had excelled in blocking his legislative programs and little else. Clark Clifford, one of Truman's top advisers and his special counsel, had warned in late June 1948 that he could win the upcoming presidential election only by taking daring, but hazardous, steps. Clifford counseled Truman that the boldest move would be to call the recessed legislators back into a special session that August. He argued that this would magnify the "rotten record of the 80th Congress" and "keep the steady glare of publicity on the Neanderthal men of the Republican Party."[22]

Flushed with adrenaline from his party's nomination during the very early morning hours of July 15, Truman followed his special counsel's advice and stunned his Philadelphia audience by announcing that he planned to call Congress back into session on July 26, "Turnip Day" in his native state of Missouri. When that day came, he told his shocked audience, he would send to the Capitol a legislative package that would include national health insurance, a higher minimum wage, liberalized immigration, and aid for public education. The Republicans had lukewarmly endorsed all these initiatives at their own convention six weeks before, and Harry Truman intended to call their bluff. His political foes, especially the HUAC, jumped at the chance to tear him apart.[23]

J. Parnell Thomas, the HUAC's moonfaced chairman from New Jersey, led its members into battle. He was a veteran of World War I and an insurance broker. Noisy, arrogant, and opinionated, Thomas despised leftists and anything that smacked of communism.[24]

The HUAC's four Democrats, who hated communists and liberals equally, were all from the Deep South. Their membership on the HUAC reflected that region's growing alienation from the Democratic Party. Since at least the late 1930s, its people had little, if anything, in common with the urban liberals, blacks, Jews, eastern and southern European Catholics, and union members who comprised the rest of the New Deal's ruling coalition. Harry Truman had infuriated them further on June 29, 1948, when he appeared before the National Association for the Advancement of Colored People and declared that the federal government must take the lead in guaranteeing that all the country's citizens enjoyed civil rights. Four months later, the President's Civil Rights Commission would urge him to desegregate the armed forces. Truman's support for Senator Hubert Humphrey's civil rights platform during the party's July 1948 convention was the last straw, especially for HUAC members John Rankin and F. Edward Hébert. Both men became breakaway Dixiecrats, supporting South Carolina governor Strom Thurmond for president in 1948.[25]

Besides J. Parnell Thomas, the HUAC's Republican members included a onetime newspaperman, a steel manufacturer who worried about communism's thought control over America's youth, a former teacher, and a future president of the United States. The latter, Richard M. Nixon, was the HUAC's most talented member. He had been elected to the House from California in 1946 when he defeated five-time incumbent Democrat Jerry Voorhis by portraying him as a tool of what Nixon claimed was the communist-backed political action committee of the Congress of Industrial Organizations. A graduate of Duke University's law school, Nixon prepared carefully and methodically for each hearing. He was a feared and skilled cross-examiner, especially adept at pointing out the inconsistencies in witnesses' answers.[26]

The real brains of the HUAC, though, was Robert E. Stripling, its chief investigator. The son of a druggist from San Augustine, Texas, Stripling was rail thin and deathly pale. Eighteen months of military service during the war had cost him forty pounds that he never re-gained. His shellacked coal black hair, thin lips, and dark suits gave him all the appeal of a small-town undertaker. Martin Dies, the HUAC's first chairman, had recognized Stripling's potential in 1938 and taken him to Washington. Although he had attended the George Washington and American universities' schools of law, he graduated from neither. Still, the East Texan masterfully skewered witnesses. In his ten years with the committee, he developed a lethal style of questioning that combined a near photographic memory with sarcastic outrage.[27]

Although the "Turnip Session" lasted only twelve days, six of them consumed by a Southern-led filibuster of an anti–poll tax bill, that was enough to put Harry Truman on the defensive. The Republican National Committee immediately understood that he had blundered by calling Congress back into session. Representative Hugh Scott, the Republican's chief strategist, ordered Thomas to "stay in Washington to keep the political heat on Harry Truman."[28]

More than one congressional committee was eager to get in on the action. Nelson Frank, carefully orchestrating Bentley's first public appearance and hoping to avoid the notorious HUAC, negotiated her debut with Senator Homer Ferguson's Investigations Subcommittee of the Committee on Expenditures in the Executive Departments. Ferguson, with his shock of white hair and double-breasted suits, was a former prosecutor from Michigan. He had rocketed to national prominence by blaming Franklin Roosevelt for Pearl Harbor and calling for President Truman's impeachment for refusing to give Congress the loyalty files of executive branch employees.[29]

At 2:20 p.m. on July 30, Bentley appeared in a small, crowded room in what is now the Senate's Russell Building, raised her right hand, and swore to tell the truth, the whole truth, and nothing but the truth.

From the start, it was obvious that the FBI had slipped Ferguson's subcommittee bits and pieces of its secret files on Bentley's claims. *Washington Post* columnist Drew Pearson wrote that the bureau's Lou Nichols, head of its Crime Records Division and its liaison with Congress, was responsible for passing this information. Attorney General Tom Clark certainly thought so, concluding that Ferguson "was getting reports before I got them" through "a direct pipeline to the FBI."[30]

Ferguson knew the FBI's code name for Bentley, Gregory—
something she herself did not know—and asked her pointed and informed questions about William Remington, one of her Commerce
Department sources still working in the government, and about Mary
Price. Bentley, who wore a short-sleeved black dress, large earrings, and
a flowered hat, stared straight ahead into the blazing lights that stood
behind Ferguson. Coolly, she fielded the subcommittee's questions.[31]

Bentley did not defend her sources, but she did not attack them
either. This would change over time, especially after they started fighting back with allegations about her mental health and emotional stability. For now, she told the subcommittee that they had helped the
Soviets because "they were a bunch of misguided idealists. They were
doing it for something they believed was right." When the bewildered
senators pressed her, she cogently explained what had motivated
many of the Americans, including Lee (whom she did not name), who
had spied for the Soviets: "They felt very strongly that we were allies
with the Russians; that Russia was bearing the brunt of the war; that
she must have every assistance because the people from within the
Government, from what they had been able to dig up, were not giving
her things that we should give her, things that we were giving to Britain and not to her. And they felt that it was their duty, actually, to get
this stuff to Russia because she was hard-pressed and weakening, and
someone must help her." Ferguson and his fellow senators were unmoved by her attempt to justify and humanize her sources' motives.[32]

The Senators also quizzed Bentley about her reasons for defecting to the FBI. Her answer blended fiction and fact. Instead of describing the fear and anger that had driven her into the bureau's arms,
she claimed her motivation had been the wearing off of Golos's drug-
like effect and the realization that Earl Browder and the rest of the
CPUSA's high command were "cheap little men pulled by strings from
Moscow." Stunned by this discovery, she told Ferguson, she had abandoned communism and "[gone] back to being a good American."[33]

Declaring herself redeemed, Bentley clarified that she did not hate
her former sources because they "were roped into Soviet espionage
and did not know what they were doing." She also claimed that some
had believed she was passing their information to Browder to use in

his books. No committee member questioned why Browder needed classified intelligence to write arid polemics such as *Victory and After* and *Production for Victory*.[34]

Similarly, no one on the committee challenged Bentley when she claimed to have told the FBI everything about her espionage career during her visit to the New Haven field office on August 23, 1945, or when she testified that she had personally met only twenty of her roughly fifty sources and subsources. The subcommittee's lack of concern about her flimsy evidence and the FBI's failure to discover her espionage on its own underscored that these hearings were more about embarrassing Harry Truman than investigating and proving Bentley's charges.[35]

Bentley had mentioned the OSS only once in her nearly three hours of testimony. And when she did, she had merely listed it along with a string of other federal agencies. But this would change the next day when she appeared before the HUAC.

As Bentley took her seat at the HUAC's witness table on the hot last day of July 1948, she faced a committee that had long abandoned any sense of fairness. J. Parnell Thomas set the tone for this rare Saturday hearing in his opening statement, declaring that the HUAC's job was to root out spies. All those that the committee unmasked, he assured his audience, would get what they deserved.[36]

When she was at last allowed to testify, Robert Stripling patiently led the forty-year-old Bentley through her background, her CPUSA history, and her sources. Much of what she said rehashed her statements to Homer Ferguson's Senate subcommittee the day before.

Then it happened. Just before lunch, he asked her about Duncan Lee. She told the committee that he was a communist and that he had given her "highly secret information" about the OSS's operations in the Balkans, Hungary, and Turkey and about Donovan's plans to establish an open OSS presence in Moscow in exchange for an open NKGB one in Washington. Bentley also explained how she had taken Lee over from Mary Price, how she had first met him at his apartment, and how they later met in Georgetown drugstores after he became increasingly neurotic about getting caught by the FBI.[37]

In fewer than ten minutes, Bentley had accused Lee of betraying his country, destroyed all his hopes for a brilliant future in postwar Washington, and forced him into a fight for his very life. The only saving grace, if there was one, was that Bentley had provided more than thirty names to the HUAC by the time she finished testifying late that afternoon. This gave the committee multiple targets and rendered Lee's just another name in a long series.

Still, Lee issued a very short statement to the local newspapers that night, heatedly denying all her allegations. Curiously, he did not demand the opportunity to testify and clear his name. Most likely, he recognized that any appearance before the highly prejudiced HUAC would be exceptionally risky. Far better, he calculated, to give the Washington papers a short denial and hope his name blended and then blurred with all the others she had mentioned.[38]

J. Parnell Thomas, however, decided otherwise. On August 2, he told the *Washington Post* that all the people Bentley had named would be summoned before the HUAC and publicly questioned. That same day, Thomas subpoenaed Lee to appear before the HUAC on August 5.[39]

Lee did not fully understand it at the time, but he was greatly helped by something that happened before the HUAC on August 3. That day, an overweight, rumpled man whose shirt collars curled up like fried bacon took his seat at the witness table and, in a flat tone, told Stripling that his name was David Whittaker Chambers. The committee had subpoenaed him to bolster Bentley's testimony and credibility. Stripling later reflected that summoning Chambers was "a forlorn shot in the dark."[40]

Chambers, a former courier for the GRU, the Soviet military intelligence service, was known in publishing circles as the translator of *Bambi* from German into English. He was now a senior editor of Henry Luce's *Time* magazine. Badly shaken by Stalin's savage purges, he had left the CPUSA in 1938. Testifying before the HUAC ten years later, Chambers saw himself as a messiah who had stepped forward to save the republic from communism's evils.[41]

Instead of playing a supporting role, Chambers quickly emerged as the HUAC's star witness. His sensational accusations that Alger Hiss, a patrician-looking Harvard Law School graduate and former State Department official who had accompanied President Roosevelt to Yalta, had been a member of the communist underground in Washington became the committee's chief focus and caused it to lose sight of Lee. Hiss and Chambers testified or were recalled to testify fourteen times before the HUAC that August. Hiss first appeared on August 5, when the committee had originally scheduled Lee's hearing.[42]

Pushed aside by Hiss, Lee did not testify that day, but the HUAC did hear from Otto Doering, Lee's old mentor and commanding officer in the OSS. Doering cabled an offer to come to Washington to support his erstwhile assistant: "I knew his work during the war and I completely believe in his loyalty to the OSS and to his country. I have absolute faith in his innocence of the charges made against him by Elizabeth Bentley."[43]

The next day, Lee went on the attack. He complained in a letter to Thomas about the "exceedingly vague" nature of Bentley's allegations. He wanted the committee to provide more specific details about her charges. Lee also requested that its investigators notify Doering at least forty-eight hours before the hearing so that he could travel from his vacation in Wisconsin to Washington. Thomas nixed both requests. On August 9, Stripling called Lee and told him to appear before the committee the next morning.[44]

August 10 broke warm and humid over the Capitol's gleaming white dome. By afternoon, the temperature had climbed to a sticky eighty-one degrees. Lee rose in an empty house. On June 17, Ishbel had boarded the RMS *Queen Elizabeth* and accompanied her mother back to Oxford. This was Ishbel's first trip to Britain since coming to America in 1939. Over the last year, she had divided her time between teaching English at the Potomac School in Washington—she had taken over some of Alger Hiss's wife's teaching duties—and raising the Lee's four children. With their mother gone, the children were with Lucy and Edmund at Chatham Hall and at summer camp. Lee did not expect his family back until the end of August.[45]

That morning he dressed in a lightweight gray suit to fend off the stickiness and heat typical of August in a city that had sprung from a drained swamp. With his neatly pressed white shirt, dark tie, OSS veteran's lapel pin, and gold-rimmed glasses, he looked exactly like the thirty-four-year-old Yale- and Oxford-educated lawyer he was.

Lee was about to face the most perilous day of his life since that August morning five years earlier when he had jumped from the smoking army plane over Japanese-infested jungles while on the secret OSS mission to China. Had he been killed then, he would have been honored as a martyred war hero. Or, had his life run a different course, he might have used his time in the jungles as John F. Kennedy had used his as commander of PT-109, a patrol torpedo boat sliced in two by a Japanese destroyer, to propel his career to Washington's highest reaches. Instead, he now stood accused as a traitor and Soviet spy. Everything was at stake. One slip before the HUAC could mean his prosecution for perjury or far worse. A conviction for espionage during wartime, which had no statute of limitations, could lead to his execution.[46]

As he left his quiet home and made his way to Capitol Hill, Lee knew that no matter what questions the HUAC rained down on him, he could not retreat and take the Fifth Amendment. Taking the Fifth would ensure his professional death and permanently stain his family's name. No one in Washington would hire a lawyer who had taken the Fifth, despite what the Constitution said about fundamental rights, and he had four children to clothe and educate. Richard Nixon had once spelled out the hazards of taking the Fifth to another squirming witness before the HUAC: "It is pretty clear, I think, that you are not using the defense of the Fifth Amendment because you are innocent."[47]

Lee also sported one of the most famous names in American history. Anything but directness would sully it. Edmund and Lucy had been running Chatham Hall since 1928. The Lee name and their missionary zeal had raised the school to one of the finest of its kind in the United States. The institution depended heavily on donations. He could not admit anything that would harm his parents or tarnish their reputation.

Lee also recognized that the HUAC had picked up a full head of steam since Bentley and Chambers had first testified. The nation's newspapers, far more plentiful and robust than today, printed every charge and countercharge. By that evening, his photograph would be splashed across the front pages of newspapers from Washington to Los Angeles. It would also enliven the *Danville Bee*, the *Danville Register*, and the *Pittsylvania Tribune*, the three local papers that Edmund and Lucy read.

No matter. He had to pull himself together. After all, he knew he had not given Bentley any actual OSS documents. It was his word, that of an Ivy League Rhodes scholar, a decorated war veteran, and a member of a very distinguished family, against that of an admitted traitor and longtime communist whose stories had failed, so far, to convict anyone. He had survived an FBI interview and a federal grand jury. Now he had to survive this hearing and even turn things back on his accusers.

By the time Lee climbed the steps of the Old House Office Building and pushed through a waiting throng of reporters and onlookers, Gregory Silvermaster and Victor Perlo, two of Bentley's major sources and spy ringleaders, had already testified. Both had taken the Fifth when Stripling asked if they knew Bentley. In their prepared statements, however, they had attacked her as "a neurotic liar" and part of a "diabolical conspiracy," dismissing her and Whittaker Chambers's claims as "inventions of irresponsible sensation seekers." They had also branded her accusations against them as "false and fantastic," even "lurid." Lee followed them halfway. Although he could not fall back on the Fifth Amendment, he could attack Bentley's mental stability.[48]

Lee was unaware that the FBI had placed another wiretap on his telephone. On August 1 and 2, Hoover's agents recorded his two conversations with Michael Quinn Shaughnessy, the Washington lawyer who had served with Lee in the OSS and worked with him at China Defense Supplies. In these recorded telephone calls, the two men had discussed Lee's strategy before the HUAC. Although Lee told Shaughnessy that Bentley's testimony about her coming to his apartment and introducing herself as Helen was a "god damn lie," Shaughnessy warned him that he had to explain why he never learned her last name or asked any questions about her background.[49]

The HUAC summoned Lee to appear at 10 a.m. in Room 345, the House of Representatives' cavernous Caucus Room. After Chambers's explosive testimony on August 3, Thomas and his fellow committee members instantly recognized the public relations bonanza he had handed them. They now needed a room as massive and ostentatious as the heroic cause and sacred mission they had set for themselves. They also wanted a setting that would awe and overwhelm any witness unlucky enough to be brought before them.

Room 345 met both these requirements. Two architects who had studied in a France that hungered for its past glories had designed it. When finished in 1908, the Caucus Room measured seventy-four feet long and fifty-four feet wide and could easily seat four hundred people. With six towering windows, four crystal chandeliers that hung like three-tiered icicles, and a ceiling awash in classical motifs and detailed entablatures in rich reds, browns, and greens, the room belonged in Versailles, fit for Louis XIV, the Sun King himself. Instead, it now served as the HUAC's grand stage.[50]

As one of J. Edgar Hoover's agents sat quietly in the back of the massive room taking detailed notes, Lee stepped forward and took a seat near the witness table. He spotted Bentley, wearing a green flower-print dress, at the front of the room and eyed her like a wary prizefighter circling a very dangerous and skilled opponent. He knew he was going to get hit. The only questions were how hard and how many times.[51]

At exactly 10 a.m., Thomas motioned for Lee to take his seat at the witness table. Looking up at the mahogany dais, he faced a special subcommittee of only four HUAC members: J. Parnell Thomas, F. Edward Hébert from Louisiana, Karl Mundt from South Dakota, and John McDowell from Pennsylvania—all united in their hatred of communism and Harry Truman. Lee was lucky, though. Richard Nixon, the committee's most formidable cross-examiner, was absent.

Unsure about the veracity of Chambers's testimony but sensing its limitless possibilities, Nixon had driven alone the night before to Westminster, Maryland. There he met with this strangely introverted man who was determined to change the course of history. Nixon had been greatly relieved by this get-together at Chambers's isolated farm. He spent the following morning discussing Chambers's August 7 testimony with William P. Rogers, counsel to Ferguson's committee. Rogers, who eventually became President Nixon's secretary of state, agreed with the California congressman that Chambers's testimony was convincing.[52]

While Nixon wrestled with Chambers's credibility, Lee, appearing "boyish and tense," according to the *Washington Times-Herald*, drew a deep breath and settled into his chair. With rows of microphones in front of him, eager reporters behind him, and Stripling, sheet white and stooped with his signature pomaded hair, to his right, he raised his right hand, swore to tell the truth, and then brazenly lied.[53]

As the news cameras silently rolled, he stuck to much the same story he had spun for the FBI on May 29, 1947. Still, there were some stark differences. To minimize the duration of his friendship with Bentley, Lee told Stripling that he had first met Bentley in October 1943, at a cocktail party at Mary Price's apartment. But by doing this, Lee contradicted his own statement to the bureau. He had told agents Wannall and Cleveland that he first met Bentley at the end of 1942.[54]

He also amended his earlier statements about not knowing Bentley's last name and profession. Following Shaughnessy's advice, he now recalled both. She was Helen Grant, a business executive, most probably in sales and in the leather business. Previously unsure whether the FBI had him under physical surveillance, he now testified that he had met with her approximately fifteen times, including in "one or two pharmacies in Georgetown," thus retreating from his earlier denial to Hoover's agents of having met her in drugstores. "John something or other" (Jacob Golos), instead of being a "really interesting guy," became a colorless refugee writer who had spoken little and made no impression on him. Lee had previously told the FBI that he first met John in early 1943 in New York City. Now he said he first met him in Washington in the fall of 1943 and again in New York in the spring of 1944.[55]

After Stripling pressed him on why Bentley would lie about him, Lee outlined their relationship. He testified that he and Ishbel initially found her to be "attractive, well informed, and well educated." When Bentley asked if she could call them on her next visit to Washington, they readily agreed to see her. Gradually, their feelings began to change after they got to know her. They concluded that "she was a very lonely and neurotic woman, that she was a frustrated woman, that her liking and apparent ardent liking for us was unnaturally intense." She had become a "personal nuisance" and "an emotional weight around our necks." Eventually they tried to end the friendship over the phone when she called one evening, but she reacted violently and sobbed. As a result, Lee told her she could no longer come to their Georgetown home. He did agree, reluctantly, to see her occasionally in local drugstores and at Martin's Tavern, a longtime neighborhood restaurant where Jack Kennedy, according to legend, proposed to Jacqueline Bouvier. This break had unhinged Bentley emotionally and set her on a destructive course of spiteful revenge. Alger Hiss's criminal defense team later explained Whittaker Chambers's motives in much the same way.[56]

Lee added that Bentley's transformation from a seemingly moderate liberal to a pro-Soviet acolyte had also made him uneasy; he had worried that her outspoken opinions might damage his reputation if they became known. He told the committee that he ended his relationship with her in December 1944.[57]

Lee expressed outrage and hurt over Bentley's charges in his prepared statement, which Stripling, after firing questions at him all morning, finally allowed him to read. After reminding the committee of his distinguished war record, of which "I can feel justly proud," Lee launched into an unrestrained attack on Bentley's personality and motives: "I know that I have served my country with complete loyalty and to the best of my ability, and it is a profound shock to find my name and war record attacked by the irresponsible charges of this woman. It is hard for me to believe that Miss Bentley's statements are those of a rational person. I am tempted to believe that [she] used her social relationship with me merely to help her misrepresent to her employers for her own personal build-up that she had access through me to someone of the importance of General Donovan."[58]

When Stripling called Bentley to the witness table, she mostly repeated what she had told the FBI in November 1945 with very slight changes. She testified now that she had first met Lee in January or February 1943, instead of late 1942, at his apartment after Mary Price fell ill; she later became his temporary handler. Although she did not remember that he had met with Golos in New York City in January 1943, she did recall their meeting in Washington in October 1943.[59]

She also repeated her July 31 claims that Lee had given her valuable intelligence on such topics as internal OSS security investigations, Donovan's plans to exchange information with the NKGB, and the OSS's operations in China and the Balkans. For the first time, she mentioned that he had told her that "something very secret was going on at Oak Ridge," before that site's role in developing the atomic bomb had become publicly known.[60]

In a final attempt to undermine his credibility, Bentley testified that Lee had lied about why he and Ishbel had broken off their relationship with her; she also stated that he had suspected her of being a Soviet agent at least by the spring of 1944.

> Mr. Mundt: You recall his statement of your calling him at his home one night and he [sic] telling you that because of your Communistic views they were going to break off this acquaintanceship. Was that part of his statement correct? Can you corroborate that part of his statement?
>
> Miss Bentley: I am sorry, that did not happen. That never happened.
>
> Mr. Mundt: That never happened?
>
> Miss Bentley: No; it never happened.
>
> Mr. Mundt: You don't recall any stage of acquaintanceship with Mr. Lee where he made known to you that he may have suspected you were a Communist?
>
> Miss Bentley: He knew all along I was a Communist. There was a stage when he suspected I was a Soviet agent, if that is what you mean.
>
> Mr. Mundt: From the spring of 1944 on he knew you were both a Communist and a Russian agent?
>
> Miss Bentley: I imagine so because that was apropos of that proposed transfer between the NKVD and the OSS, and I remember he was quite frightened because he said "if they come over here, they will come to my house, knock on the door, shake my hand, and say 'Comrade, well done.'"[61]

F. Edward Hébert, no longer able to restrain himself, expressed the frustration of many in the hearing room:

Mr. Hébert: So, we get down to it, either you or Mr. Lee is lying today.

Miss Bentley: I guess that is the only conclusion you can draw.[62]

Throughout her testimony, Lee listened intently. His face betrayed no hint of fear or worry. The newspaper he had brought lay casually folded on the corner of the table in front of him. It gave him the appearance of a man attending a minor traffic court hearing instead of one that could send him to a federal prison or a Virginia graveyard. It was an extraordinary display of sangfroid, far different from the shaking nervousness he had displayed in front of the NKGB's Joseph Katz and the FBI.

Visibly frustrated, Stripling recalled Lee to the witness table:

Mr. Stripling: Mr. Lee, you have heard the testimony of Miss Bentley.

Mr. Lee: I certainly have, sir.

Mr. Stripling: Do you deny or affirm it?

Mr. Lee: I deny it; and in every respect in which it is contrary to the testimony I have previously given.[63]

Karl Mundt then pounced on Lee and ridiculed him for not reporting Bentley to the OSS's Security Office. Lee pushed back with the skill of the champion Yale debater he had once been.

Mr. Lee: Mr. Mundt, I must respectfully disagree that there was anything that happened in our relationship with Miss Bentley that led me to believe that I should report it to anyone. We considered this to be entirely, if not primarily, a personal matter.

Mr. Mundt: But surely a man who had the capacity in OSS to rise to the rank of lieutenant colonel had the capacity to figure out something was unusual: that this woman over a period of time had pursued you, either as an individual or an officer of the OSS, and gradually it dawned upon you that this woman was a Communist, so, "My wife and I should have no more to do with her." But then you do not tell a superior officer.

Mr. Lee: No, sir.

Mr. Mundt: All I can say is that whatever comes from this testimony, that I am bitterly disappointed to find out that this is how the OSS operated under Mr. Donovan.[64]

When Mundt dug deeper, asking him how Bentley had become a personal nuisance, Lee replied that she actually was "somewhat dull" and her affections for him and Ishbel were "unnatural and unhealthy."[65]

Stripling then mined Lee's meeting with Golos in New York City. Lee remembered meeting him there in the early spring of 1944. When Stripling pointed out that Golos died in November 1943, Lee replied dismissively, "Well, then, it must have been earlier."[66]

Hébert, picking up on Lee's combative tone, jumped back into the fray, questioning him about his claim that he had first met Bentley at a cocktail party at Mary Price's apartment sometime in October 1943.

Mr. Hébert: What was the occasion of your meeting with Miss Bentley?

Mr. Lee: We were asked to drop in for drinks.

Mr. Hébert: Miss Price asked you and your wife to drop in for some drinks?

Mr. Lee: Yes, sir. I believe there were several people present.

Mr. Hébert: Name some of the people present.

Mr. Lee: I do not recall who they were.

Mr. Hébert: You realize that it is important?

Mr. Lee: Yes, sir; but it was five years ago.

Mr. Hébert: But you do realize it is important for the sake of veracity right now.

Mr. Lee: Yes, sir. If I knew I was going to be questioned about it five years later, I would probably have made a memorandum, but there was no reason to think so.

When Hébert wondered why Bentley had latched on to the Lees at the cocktail party, Lee ducked the question but expressed his own bewilderment: "I know one thing from her testimony today. She has a very vivid imagination."[67]

Lee then emphatically denied passing any classified information to Bentley. About the OSS's Balkan and Turkish operations, he told the committee that, except in the most general way, he knew nothing. This was not true. As chief of the Secretariat, Lee had processed several detailed sets of the OSS's operational plans for both areas—a fact no one on the HUAC raised.[68]

One of the great riddles of Lee's testimony was why he felt so comfortable uttering such false statements about his OSS service and his unconditional loyalty to William Donovan. In his written statement, he underscored his fidelity to both: "I want to say categorically that I am not and have never been a Communist and that I have never divulged classified information to any unauthorized person. I had been an assistant in the legal offices of General Donovan before the war: I was therefore particularly aware of a requirement of personal loyalty to him in such matters along with my loyalty to the service of the United States."[69]

Probably Lee counted on Donovan's full support—he informed Stripling that the general wanted to testify on his behalf. Donovan's backing was grounded in emotion and self-interest. The old warrior looked after and was intensely loyal to his men. David Bruce, the OSS's London station chief and later US ambassador to France and Britain, summed up Donovan's commitment in a letter to the *New York Times*: "His country right or wrong was his primary impulse, but his boys right or wrong came a close second."[70]

That protection extended to Duncan Lee. Publicly, Donovan linked arms with his onetime protégé. During August 1948 when he was in Greece, investigating the murder of American journalist George Polk, he followed Bentley's allegations closely. When Donovan sailed into New York Harbor on August 30 aboard the RMS *Queen Mary*, he told a waiting gaggle of reporters what he thought about Lee: "I know Lee well. And it would be a shock and surprise to me, in view of his background, tradition and character, to learn that he had been in any way disloyal. He was a Rhodes scholar and a very high-principled boy. I believe he would be very loyal and would not disclose any classified material."[71]

Donovan's true beliefs about Duncan's guilt or innocence remain a mystery. Richard Dunlop, a former OSS officer and one of Donovan's biographers, confided to a CIA counterintelligence officer in 1986 that the general knew all about Lee but did not want to ruin his life. According to Dunlop, Donovan also doubted that any of the information Lee passed, which had gone to an ally, had damaged the OSS's wartime operations. But Walter Pforzheimer, one of Donovan's confidants, told the same officer that Donovan remarked several times that Lee had not been disloyal.[72]

Whatever the truth, Donovan realized that more than Lee's fate was at stake. The general's own reputation was on the line as well. For Donovan, Lee's HUAC appearance was as much about the OSS and his leadership of it as it was about Lee himself. He was extremely proud of his organization's World War II achievements and of his reputation as America's top spymaster. HUAC's proving that one of his most trusted aides had been a Soviet spy would tarnish both badly. As a consequence, Donovan secretly hired Frank Bielaski, a former OSS security officer, to dig into Bentley's past and find anything he could to discredit her.[73]

Donovan also did not want to give Hoover any advantage in what was shaping up to be a battle of titans. Donovan appreciated that Hoover and the HUAC were allies and that the FBI's director wanted to destroy him personally. They had disliked each other since 1924, when Donovan had headed the Department of Justice's Criminal Division and overseen the Bureau of Investigation and its new chief, J. Edgar Hoover. Their different backgrounds contributed to their mutual animosity: Donovan was a suave Ivy League graduate, a war hero, and a consummate ladies' man; Hoover had attended night law school at George Washington University, seen no fighting in World War I, and lived with his mother into his mid-forties.

Since their initial clash at the Department of Justice, the two titans had come to see in each other a dangerous and cunning foe to be watched and thwarted. They had jockeyed for decades, especially in the 1940s, to become czar of the American intelligence community. Each maintained thick investigative files on the other that contained every unsavory tidbit and seamy piece of gossip he could gather. Donovan, for example, ordered his OSS operatives to prove the persistent rumors that swirled around Washington that Hoover was a "fairy," while Hoover's G-men kept close tabs on Donovan's many extramarital affairs. They even spread the vicious lie that Donovan had slept with his son's wife. Seemingly nothing was out of bounds, and neither could rest until the other was ruined or dead.[74]

Despite Lee's vigorous denials, none of the HUAC's members bought his innocence. John McDowell, who had stayed largely silent during the hearing, strongly hinted that he believed the worst—that Lee's testimony had been a lie and his actions treasonous. Looking down at Lee, he grimly observed, "I believe for the first time since the conspiracy of Aaron Burr, a high officer of the Army has been accused publicly of a violation of the Articles of War, [for] which he must certainly realize the punishment." McDowell was not alone. CIA counterintelligence officers sitting in the audience did not believe him either.[75]

Chairman Thomas excused Lee at 12:05 p.m. after Hébert, completely disgusted by what he had heard, demanded that the Department of Justice investigate Lee and Bentley for perjury.[76]

The next morning, Guy Hottel, the special agent in charge of the bureau's Washington field office, wrote Hoover about Lee's HUAC appearance, highlighting that "Lee did not make any admissions that were pertinent and denied all allegations of espionage." As if to soothe Hoover's deepest fear, Hottel noted that "during the proceedings before the House Committee, there was no derogatory reference whatsoever to the FBI." Hoover must have been greatly relieved. No one on the HUAC had asked why the FBI had failed to uncover Bentley's spies during the war. Hoover's ties with the committee had helped expose Lee publicly and had shielded the director and his agency from withering criticism.[77]

Lee had worried about the newspapers' reaction to his testimony, and what he read that evening while sitting in his living room did little to comfort him. Washington's *Evening Star* set the tone: under a half-inch banner that screamed, "Ex-Army Officers Deny Bentley Charges," appeared the headline "Lee Swears He Never Was a Red." Worse, the *New York World-Telegram* ran the sensational headline "Spy Says OSS Aide Hinted Atom Plant Supersecret." In Chatham, Virginia, the *Danville Bee's* headline shouted, "Lee Denies Giving Reds Secrets."

From coast to coast, newspapers ran wire service photographs of him confronting the "blonde spy queen." A full-blown media circus had commenced.[78]

The next day's coverage was no better. The *New York Herald-Tribune*, for example, focused on the sharp differences in Lee's and Bentley's testimony and wryly commented that "the committee members were just downright yearning for a lie detector." The *Danville Register*, however, in an editorial praised Lee's directness and showed its loyalty to the Lees of neighboring Chatham Hall: "Few of those named by the confessed Russian spy, or by Whittaker Chambers, an avowed Communist, have, as did Duncan Lee, sworn they are not, and never had been, a Communist."[79]

The *Washington Post*, among other newspapers, sharply attacked the HUAC for demonstrating "the worst in congressional investigative procedure." Herblock, its chief editorial cartoonist, caricatured Thomas and Bentley as blatant publicity seekers. The editorial page also criticized the HUAC for violating the civil rights of its witnesses and hungering for headlines. Still, the *Post* conceded that the hearings "[had] left many Americans in a state of profound and confused disquiet."[80]

Lee joined in his own coverage. On August 10, the same day he testified, he wrote a letter to the *Pittsylvania Tribune*, one of the local newspapers his parents read. He lambasted the paper for its coverage of Bentley's charges. In particular, he was upset that the *Tribune* had omitted to mention that "Miss Bentley's story had been investigated in every detail by a Grand Jury which sat in New York for over a year and which found her charges so unsubstantial and uncorroborated that it had refused to take action against any Government official whom she had accused." The newspaper printed his letter on its front page under the banner "Duncan Lee Denies All Charges Before Congress and in Letter."[81]

Edmund wanted to write Governor Thomas Dewey, the Republican's nominee for the presidency in 1948, to complain about the HUAC, but Lee asked him not to because of the "extremely delicate situation." Edmund did send his son several letters of support he and Lucy had received. These condemned the HUAC and Bentley and expressed shock and disgust at the "ridiculous," "unfair," "unsubstantiated," and "unjustified" attacks. One relative summarized these sentiments in his letter to Edmund: "Since it is inconceivable that any Lee of Virginia and especially one raised by you and Aunt Lucy could be guilty of such charges, I am sure the whole dirty mess will be cleared up and that Duncan will emerge with his reputation not only untarnished but enhanced."[82]

Lee was also helped by the Truman administration's all-out assault on Chambers and Bentley. With November's presidential election looming, Harry Truman could not afford the political fallout and acute embarrassment from charges that he had been soft on communists inside his own government. On August 5, the day that Alger Hiss testified before the HUAC, Truman ignited a firestorm by agreeing with a reporter's suggestion that the hearings were a "red herring," a sideshow orchestrated by Republicans to distract the public's attention from their failure to pass any meaningful legislation.[83]

George Elsey, a Truman aide, spelled out to Clark Clifford how the administration planned to deal with the HUAC's two star witnesses: "[The Department of] Justice should make every effort to ascertain if Whittaker Chambers is guilty of perjury" and conduct "an investigation of Chambers's confinement in a mental institution." It should also "make clear that Miss Bentley was not successful in transmitting secret material to the Russians which they did not already have." Attorney General Tom Clark went a step farther: he tried to discredit her by planting stories that she was crazy.[84]

Truman also instructed his attorney general to get a statement from Hoover that the HUAC's "meddling had dried up sources" that the FBI could have used to prosecute suspected spies and communists. Following Truman's wishes, Clark called Mickey Ladd, the head of the bureau's Domestic Intelligence Division, but got nowhere. Ladd told Hoover about his conversation with the attorney general: "I very carefully made no commitment or acknowledgement so that [my] statement could not be attributed to me or the Bureau as being critical of the Committee." Angered by this and by Karl Mundt's claim that he was receiving intelligence reports from the FBI under the table, Clark called Ladd again and shouted, "Any S.O.B. that gives Congressman Mundt any information gets his ass kicked out of this

building. I want you to get the word around that anyone giving information to the Committee is out—O.U.T."[85]

Hoover scoffed at Clark's hollow threats. In a staggering act of
insubordination, he secretly ordered the bureau to cooperate with
Thomas Dewey's campaign to unseat Truman in that November's
presidential election. The FBI provided the Republican candidate
with position papers on the emerging Communist threat and Truman's failure to understand it. Despite this, Truman upset Dewey
in the election by running on the New Deal's record and smearing
Henry Wallace, the Progressive Party's candidate, as too sympathetic
to the Soviet Union. Distraught, Hoover, feigning a bout of pneumonia, did not return to work until twelve days after Harry Truman's
January 20 inauguration.[86]

President Truman was not the only one eager to discredit Elizabeth Bentley by fair means or foul. On July 31, a reporter tracked
down Mary Price in North Carolina and asked if she was a communist. Price, now the Progressive Party's candidate for governor of
North Carolina, tersely answered, "Let's not go into that. I have contacted my lawyer." Several days later, though, she gave a detailed statement to the press: "Miss Bentley's charges against me are absurd. My
indignant rejections of her [homosexual] advances and my refusal
to take part in her endless cocktail parties apparently caused resentment." Still later, Price characterized Bentley's allegations as a "put up
job to discredit" her gubernatorial run. If so, it would have been over-
kill: Price received only 2,231 votes.[87]

The nation's political pundits and public intellectuals also had
a field day with Bentley. A. J. Liebling, playing on her Connecticut
roots, mocked her in the *New Yorker* as "the Nutmeg Mata Hari." And
Archibald MacLeish penned a poem that appeared in the *New York
Herald-Tribune* and summed up the feelings of many of her critics
among the literati: "God help that country where informers thrive,
Where slander flourishes and lies contrive."[88]

Lee had battled the dreaded HUAC to a draw. He had given the performance of his life. Fortunately for him, he had faced a HUAC more
interested in scoring political points than uncovering the disturbing

truth. He had also been helped enormously by the committee's powerful foes, themselves more intent on discrediting Elizabeth Bentley than pursuing justice, and by the self-interest of Washington's politicians and power players.

Still, the hearing was physically and emotionally punishing. He always referred to the summer of 1948 as that "terrible summer" and later admitted to his children that his appearance before the HUAC had shattered him. He was especially upset, he later confessed, by all the devastating publicity, which cast him in the demeaning role of the baby-faced OSS colonel confronting the blonde spy queen.[89]

Lee collapsed physically after he testified. He developed a severe case of phlebitis in his right leg and began suffering from chronic hypertension. His heavy drinking also worsened. He remained addicted to alcohol for the next twenty-five years. He found refuge where he could. Close friends took him in and shielded him from the press. When Ishbel returned from Britain at the end of August, Lee immediately sent her to be with their children at Chatham Hall to keep them out of the uproar in Washington.[90]

But there would be no time to recover and take stock. Although he had survived the HUAC, he knew that J. Edgar Hoover was coming for him. Luckily, Tommy Corcoran had other plans for Lee.

Members of the Student Volunteer Movement at the Virginia Theological Seminary in 1897, with Edmund Jennings Lee IV standing in the center rear. Galvanized by their pre-millennialist battle cry to bring about "the evangelization of the world in this generation," members of the Student Volunteer Movement, such as Edmund, were determined to bring God's message to foreign lands at any cost (LEE PERSONAL PAPERS).

Edmund Jennings Lee IV in 1901. An unflinching and uncompromising man who believed himself God's instrument, Lee's missionary father served for him as both a paragon and a source of crippling insecurity and lingering guilt (LEE PERSONAL PAPERS).

Lucy Chaplin Lee in Anqing, China, circa 1915. The daughter of a wealthy wool merchant and an ardent follower of the Social Gospel movement, Lucy Lee was a powerful role model for her impressionable son (LEE PERSONAL PAPERS).

Armistead, Lucy, and Duncan Lee in Anqing, China, circa 1918. Both Lucy Lee's sons were profoundly affected by her deep religious convictions and Social Gospel philosophy, which they were exposed to as young boys growing up in Anqing's missionary compound (LEE PERSONAL PAPERS).

Duncan Lee in Anqing, China, circa 1922. Lee's immediate postwar career was inextricably tied to the fate of the land of his birth (LEE PERSONAL PAPERS).

Duncan Lee in 1935, while a senior at Yale University. Lee's four years at Yale taught him to think for himself and prepared him to win a Rhodes scholarship to Oxford (LEE PERSONAL PAPERS).

Lee's Rhodes Scholar Class of 1935 aboard the *SS Washington*; Lee is fifth from the left, second row. As one of Cecil Rhodes's best men for "the world's fight," Lee was about to enter a highly politicized Oxford that was waking up to the horrors of fascism and the collapse of capitalism (Lee's Personal Papers).

Ishbel Gibb Lee, early 1940s. Lee's Scottish wife, who played a pivotal role in steering him toward communism and radicalizing him while he was a Rhodes scholar at Oxford in the mid-1930s (Lee Personal Papers).

Katharine Robb Rawles Nangle. The daughter of an Indiana University business school professor and, during 1938–1939, the Lees' landlord in New Haven, Connecticut, Nangle told the FBI in May 1940 that her former tenants were communists (KAREN AND ROBERT NANGLE).

Jacob Golos, circa 1940. Recruited by the OGPU by 1930, Golos was a highly skilled but sometimes careless spy handler who ordered Mary Price to recruit Lee as a Soviet agent in 1942 (NATIONAL ARCHIVES AND RECORDS ADMINISTRATION).

Mary Price, 1946. A native of North Carolina, Lee's first NKVD handler, and his lover, Price began working for the Soviets in the late 1930s after a trip to Russia (Associated Press).

Brigadier General William J. Donovan in March 1943. A war hero who intuitively understood the country's need for a centralized, strategic intelligence service, Donovan was a mediocre administrator whose ecumenical personnel policies made the Office of Strategic Services the most penetrated intelligence service in American history (Lee Personal Papers).

Duncan Lee with a headhunter in northern Burma, August 1943. Forced to jump from a smoking airplane over the jungles of northern Burma while on a secret OSS mission to China, Lee lived for over twenty days with headhunters who helped him and his fellow Americans evade Japanese army patrols (LEE PERSONAL PAPERS).

Major Duncan Lee in 1944. By this time, Lee had become chief of the Secretariat, the nerve center of the Office of Strategic Services, and the transmitter of its most secret reports to William J. Donovan, the spy service's head (NATIONAL ARCHIVES AND RECORDS ADMINISTRATION).

Georgetown Pharmacy, Wisconsin Avenue and O Street, NW. One of two neighborhood drugstores where Lee met Elizabeth Bentley during the spring of 1944 after he became convinced that the FBI was tapping his telephone and watching his house (NATIONAL ARCHIVES AND RECORDS ADMINISTRATION).

J. Edgar Hoover at his desk in March 1940. Seven months after this photograph was taken, the bulldog-faced FBI director confidently but falsely assured President Franklin Roosevelt that his G-men had Soviet espionage inside the United States under control (LIBRARY OF CONGRESS).

The terrible summer of 1948: John Lee, Ishbel (holding Kathy Lee), Katherine Gibb, Duncan Lee, and Edmund Lee VI at Chatham Hall. Two months before Lee testified before the HUAC, he accompanied Ishbel, her mother, and three of his children to visit his parents in southern Virginia (LEE'S PERSONAL PAPERS).

Elizabeth Bentley testifies before HUAC on August 10, 1948, while Lee, in the background, listens to her allegations about him. Although many observers did not believe his rebuttal to her testimony, no one who watched Lee's performance that morning questioned his coolness and aplomb while under fire from the most dangerous committee in Congress (ASSOCIATED PRESS).

"Have A Good Time, Dear—Get Lots Of Publicity"

Herblock cartoon, August 12, 1948. Drawn two days after Lee's appearance before the HUAC, Herblock's cartoon captures the sentiment of those who believed that J. Parnell Thomas, the committee's moonfaced chairman, and Elizabeth Bentley were more interested in embarrassing President Harry Truman than in exposing Soviet spies (HERBLOCK FOUNDATION).

Thomas Gardiner Corcoran in his law office during the late 1940s. Perhaps the greatest "fixer" in Washington's history, Tommy "the Cork" Corcoran defended Lee in public but privately harbored doubts about his young associate's truthfulness (LEE'S PERSONAL PAPERS).

Major General Claire Lee Chennault in Kunming, China, in 1944. A gifted air tactician who was also a born rebel, Chennault linked arms after World War II with Chiang Kai-shek in his struggle with Mao Zedong, plunging Civil Air Transport and Lee into China's civil war (ASSOCIATED PRESS).

Duncan Lee with Louise and Whiting Willauer in 1950. The cofounder of Civil Air Transport, "Whitey" Willauer joined forces with Lee in late 1949 to give the United States its first Cold War victory in East Asia (LEE PERSONAL PAPERS).

A Civil Air Transport cargo plane refueling for a mission in China's civil war sometime in 1948. Founded in 1946 by Claire Chennault and Whiting Willauer, two capitalist freebooters, Civil Air Transport gave Lee the chance to redeem himself and become a Cold Warrior in East Asia (LEE PERSONAL PAPERS).

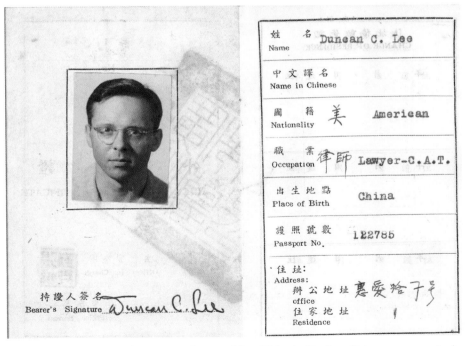

Duncan Lee's 1948 identity card issued by China's Nationalist government. A Soviet agent only four years before, Lee had transformed himself into a Cold Warrior on the front lines of America's struggle against Mao Zedong's communists (LEE PERSONAL PAPERS).

Duncan Lee in Bermuda, December 1953. Deep in thought after the governor of Bermuda had ordered his deportation, Lee knew that he was being sent back to the United States, where the Rosenbergs had been executed that June and McCarthyism was now at high tide (LEE PERSONAL PAPERS).

Secretary of State John Foster Dulles presents Ruth B. Shipley with the Distinguished Service Medal, April 28, 1955. In Ruth Shipley, the head of the State Department's notorious "Queendom of Passports," Lee found an enemy as cunning and menacing as J. Edgar Hoover (NATIONAL ARCHIVES AND RECORDS ADMINISTRATION).

Duncan Lee in Bermuda in 1957. Having been allowed to return to Bermuda by the then–British colony's governor in 1955, Lee looks more relaxed, but still pensive, as he enjoys his return (LEE PERSONAL PAPERS).

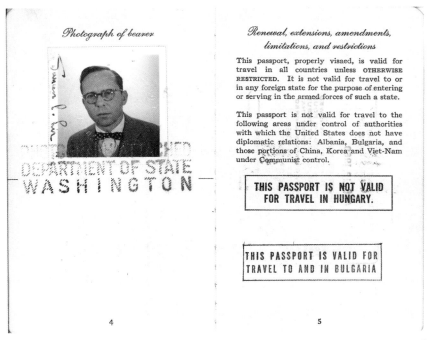

Photograph of bearer

Renewal, extensions, amendments, limitations, and restrictions

This passport, properly visaed, is valid for travel in all countries unless OTHERWISE RESTRICTED. It is not valid for travel to or in any foreign state for the purpose of entering or serving in the armed forces of such a state.

This passport is not valid for travel to the following areas under control of authorities with which the United States does not have diplomatic relations: Albania, Bulgaria, and those portions of China, Korea and Viet-Nam under Communist control.

THIS PASSPORT IS NOT VALID FOR TRAVEL IN HUNGARY.

THIS PASSPORT IS VALID FOR TRAVEL TO AND IN BULGARIA

DEPARTMENT OF STATE
WASHINGTON

4

5

Duncan Lee's 1958 passport photograph. Before this passport was issued to Lee in 1958, he had not had a valid one for six years, thanks to the determined efforts of Ruth Shipley, the violently anticommunist chief of the State Department's passport office (LEE PERSONAL PAPERS).

Duncan Lee in the 1960s. Although only middle-aged and having successfully eluded J. Edgar Hoover, Lee's face reflects the steep toll that heavy drinking, smoking, and worrying have taken on him (Lee Personal Papers).

NINE

THE WORLD'S MOST
SHOT-AT AIRLINE

By the time Bentley's allegations surfaced publicly in the summer of 1948, Lee had transformed himself from a Soviet spy into an American Cold Warrior. His job with Tommy "the Cork" Corcoran bound him not only to one of the capital city's most sought-after lawyers but also to one of its most vehement anticommunists. His relationship with Corcoran altered the course of Lee's life as much as his earlier one with Donovan. It provided him with essential cover and gave him the means to make amends for his treachery with the Soviets.

Short and square, with large ears, a ruddy face, and a quick stride, Tommy Corcoran was a man of enormous talent and grand ambitions. Born on December 29, 1900, in Pawtucket, Rhode Island, he was the oldest son of Irish Catholics determined to see their children succeed.[1]

He graduated first in his class at Brown University and starred as a running back on its football team. After earning a master's degree in classics and narrowly missing a Rhodes scholarship to Oxford, he enrolled at Harvard Law School. There, Corcoran repeated his academic success and won a reputation as the most brilliant member of his class. His ice-blue clarity of intellect and Irish charm caught the attention of Professor Felix Frankfurter, who became his mentor and gateway to Washington's corridors of power.

After stints as US Supreme Court associate justice Oliver Wendell Holmes's secretary and as a Wall Street lawyer, Corcoran migrated to Washington in 1932 to work at the Reconstruction Finance Corporation. While there, he answered Frankfurter's call to help him overhaul the nation's inadequate securities laws as part of President Franklin Roosevelt's efforts to shore up the country's crumbling finances. Frankfurter also recruited Ben Cohen, a cerebral young lawyer from the University of Chicago and a master legal draftsman. Touted in the newspapers as the "Gold Dust Twins" or as Frankfurter's "Hot Dog Boys," Corcoran and Cohen collaborated in fashioning some of the early New Deal's most important and revolutionary pieces of legislation, including the Securities and Exchange Act of 1933 and the Federal Housing Administration Act of 1934.[2]

Corcoran summed up how he got things done this way: "I don't get away with anything that isn't right. I just have more imagination than most." Fueled by large cups of black coffee and dextrose tablets, he rapidly rose to become one of the White House's most energetic and tireless troubleshooters and fixers. He also ranked among its most feared. Even powerful congressmen trembled upon receiving a phone call that began, "This is Tommy Corcoran calling from the White House."[3]

After Roosevelt declined to appoint him solicitor general at the Department of Justice or undersecretary of the Navy, he decided to leave the government in 1941. To his credit, FDR knew Corcoran had too many foes in the Senate to be confirmed. But Corcoran also left because he wanted to make more money. To that end, he created a new kind of law practice, one that specialized in steering clients through the very federal bureaucracy he had midwifed. By 1941, he was well on his way to becoming one of Washington's most powerful lawyer lobbyists. Soon, he was able to boast, "I know the corners of this town in the dark."[4]

Tommy Corcoran performed miracles circumventing the federal laws and regulations he had earlier written. In a telephone call recorded by the FBI in 1946, he explained his amoral business philosophy: "You can't luxuriate yourself in your personal friendships and your likes and dislikes and your senses of justice and injustice when you are playing in this racket." In his first few months of practice, he earned $100,000, a huge sum in 1941 ($1.5 million now). Although he made a lot of money representing companies like Lever Brothers and Sterling Products, Corcoran always considered himself more an entrepreneur than a lawyer. He once famously quipped that "the law [is] where all good men are wasted."[5]

Corcoran did not intend to squander his chance to make a pile of money after World War II ended. In September 1945, the same month that Japan formally surrendered to the Allies, he formed Rio Cathay, a corporation that pursued business ventures in China and South America. David Corcoran, his brother, and William Young-man, his law partner, rounded out its board.[6]

Corcoran was especially interested in China because of his wartime service as the founder of China Defense Supplies. This experience had opened his eyes wide to the extraordinary economic opportunities that beckoned, given China's seemingly limitless reserves of tin, coal, iron ore, and tungsten. Nearly eight years of constant fighting with the Japanese, though, had severely damaged much of the country's road system, its riverboats, and 90 percent of its railroads. Only air transportation offered the Chinese an immediate way to get back on their economic feet.[7]

Corcoran and his partners believed that a civilian air cargo line flying between China's seaports and her far-flung interior could generate vast profits. But first, Rio Cathay needed to hire the right men to send to China. Corcoran invested his trust in Claire Chennault and Whiting Willauer, a pair of nonconformist adrenaline junkies and ardent anticommunists.[8]

When the Japanese formally surrendered on the deck of the USS *Missouri* on September 2, 1945, Claire Lee Chennault was just four days short of his forty-eighth birthday. He had hoped to still be in uniform on that day, standing aboard the battleship with his fellow officers and watching the war that he had been fighting since 1937 finally end. Repeated rows with the US Army Air Corps' high command over doctrine and strategy, however, had shattered that dream a month before, when he was sent home from China. Short-tempered,

chronically out of step, but brilliant at close-formation flying and aerial acrobatics, he had been forced out of the army for the second
time. Although his Flying Tigers and Fourteenth Air Force had performed heroically against the Japanese in China, downing nearly
3,000 of their planes and destroying 2.23 million tons of their supplies, Chennault's unconventional methods and an ingrained dislike
of authority had made him a senior commander's nightmare.[9]

When Chennault returned to Washington in the summer of 1945,
he immediately went to see Tommy Corcoran. The two men had first
met in March 1941 when Roosevelt sent Corcoran to evaluate Chennault's scheme to recruit volunteer American pilots to fight in China.
Corcoran, a lifelong talent scout, reported to FDR that they were
"dealing with something original, whether it is genius or madness."
Chennault and Corcoran became close friends.[10]

Now, in the summer of 1945, the two men talked about the newly
retired general's next step. Chennault displayed all the bitterness
of a man whose life had not turned out as expected, grumbling to
Corcoran that the military establishment had blackballed him. This
meant that no one in the Pentagon was likely to help him gain a foot-
hold in the lucrative military supply business. He even talked about
returning to Louisiana, entering politics, and running for a seat in
the US Senate. Chennault also had one other idea. He told Corcoran
he thought an American-run airline in China could make money.[11]

Whiting "Whitey" Willauer, soon to be Chennault's partner, believed the same thing. A romantic throwback to another era, he feared
only fear. He belonged in an earlier age, fighting with the great English privateer Sir Francis Drake for the Queen, glory, and profit. Born
into an upper-middle-class family in New York City on November
30, 1906, Willauer graduated from the elite Phillips Exeter Academy
in 1924 and from Princeton University four years later. At Princeton, he was a superb athlete and a gifted scholar, playing fullback on
the varsity football team and graduating with honors in English. At
both schools, he roomed with Howard Corcoran, Tommy's youngest brother. In fact, Willauer knew all three Corcoran bothers well—
David also attended Princeton—and Tommy encouraged the star
athlete to go to Harvard Law School. There, he roomed once more
with Howard Corcoran.[12]

Predictably, the burly Willauer did well academically, finishing thirty-sixth in a class of five hundred. After an early law career marked by restlessness, he became a troubleshooter for China Defense Supplies after failing his navy induction physical because of an old football injury. Willauer helped organize Chennault's Flying Tigers before spending most of the war consumed with solving the Fourteenth Air Force's mammoth logistical problems. While in China, he discreetly commissioned a study to examine that country's need for air transport facilities. In a letter to his wife, Willauer later confessed loving his wartime duties and the emotional satisfaction they gave him: "Indeed, I shall have a hell of a time going back to anything less exciting than a war job." He did not have to.[13]

In the fall of 1945, Willauer shopped the idea of establishing an airline in China to Tommy Corcoran and his Rio Cathay partners. Sure that an airline would be a moneymaker, Rio Cathay persuaded Pennsylvania Central Airlines to give Willauer the $50,000 he needed to pay for the preliminary work on his scheme.[14]

Before he left for Shanghai in December 1945, Willauer asked Chennault to join him. With nothing holding him in the United States, Chennault agreed to go after Pennsylvania Central Airlines paid him $35,000. Corcoran was overjoyed. Chennault was a national hero in China. His close ties with Chiang Kai-shek, coupled with Willauer's administrative abilities, could open up unlimited business opportunities.[15]

At first, making a fortune seemed credible. On October 25, 1946, the two Americans signed a contract with the Nationalists' Chinese National Relief and Rehabilitation Administration (CNRRA), forming a franchise airline called CNRRA Air Transport (CAT) to carry badly needed medical supplies and food from the country's ports into its interior. Although relief supplies got first priority, the Chinese government allowed CAT to sell unused cargo space to the public on all return flights. As part of the contract, the United Nations agreed to spend $2 million to buy the necessary airplanes and equipment. Chennault, Willauer, and their Washington backers had to put up another $1 million. They also received an option to buy the airplanes.[16]

To finance their end, Chennault and Willauer had no alternative but to borrow money from a group of Chinese businessmen who demanded an exorbitant rate of interest and 42 percent of the airline.

With their backs to the wall, they swallowed hard and accepted these stiff terms. On January 31, 1947, CAT's first flight took off from Shanghai and flew to Guangzhou. Three days later, another of CAT's six original planes, a tiger boldly painted on its nose, left Guangzhou for Liuchow, stuffed with 9,000 pounds of medical supplies that had been sitting in crates for three months.[17]

This was just the beginning. In March, CAT staged Operation Little Bo Peep, ferrying hundreds of sheep and rams deep into the countryside to restock depleted village herds. In April, its planes delivered 40,000 pounds of cotton and vegetable seeds for spring planting in Hunan province. A profitable contract with Standard Oil to carry petroleum products followed. By the end of the year, the airline was fairly prosperous and looking forward to expanding its operations.[18]

Before CAT's first plane had left the tarmac, Lee was involved in establishing and running the airline from Corcoran's Washington law office. He operated as its principal attorney, handling day-to-day legal problems. CAT offered him a chance to redefine himself just as much as it did Chennault and Willauer. While they hoped to find mere fortune and glory, Lee most likely sought a way to atone for his wrongdoing, insulate himself from the FBI, and build a new life.[19]

Although Lee could not foresee all that was in store for him when he joined Tommy Corcoran's law firm in 1946, he could make out the future's distant outlines. Corcoran, a champion of the Catholic Church and capitalism, was strongly anticommunist, as were Chennault and Willauer. Communism's basic tenets clashed with their prized values of Christian faith, economic freedom, and personal independence. Lee had already met Willauer on his aborted trip to China in 1943, and Corcoran had introduced him to Chennault in early 1946.[20]

When he cast his lot with these Cold War crusaders, Lee embraced three of the country's most fervent foes of Joseph Stalin and Mao Zedong. He also linked arms with men who, like himself, made their own rules and lived by their own codes of conduct, whatever the costs.

CAT was a stable, growing airline by the summer of 1947 with more cargo than it could fly. Willauer grew optimistic. To his wife, he bragged, "The General and I are both getting to the point when at least once a week we are inclined to be proud of our progeny." Lee was now the principal lawyer for an airline that included eighteen airplanes and eight hundred employees. But in December 1947, the CNRRA, facing severe money problems, closed its doors. With its parent organization gone, CAT scrambled for new patrons. It found one in Chiang Kai-shek himself. On January 2, 1948, he granted CAT—now renamed Civil Air Transport—a one-year extension, but this support came at a steep price. Chiang's armies were losing their war against Mao's communists. When he extended CAT's life, Chiang, who was known in China as the "Generalissimo," made it clear that he expected the airline to support his military operations by transporting supplies and personnel. Before the year was out, he had plunged CAT and Lee into China's raging civil war. By then, his control of the mainland had entered its final phase.[21]

After the Japanese surrendered on September 2, 1945, Mao Zedong had moved quickly to occupy Manchuria. The Soviets, who had invaded this huge region on May 8, 1945, following Stalin's February promise at Yalta—a meeting at which Roosevelt, Churchill, and Stalin had discussed postwar Europe's reorganization and the Soviet Union's declaring war on Japan after Hitler's defeat—aided Mao's forces by giving them huge stockpiles of captured Japanese weapons.[22]

Unwilling to cede this mineral-rich area to the communists, Chiang concentrated the flower of his army in Manchuria. Although the Nationalists captured and occupied the province's major cities, they soon realized that these were no more than well-constructed traps. In December 1947, Mao's forces surrounded Shenyang and its 200,000 Nationalist defenders. Desperate for food and medicine, they called on CAT to save them. Before Shenyang fell to the communists in October 1948, the airline had evacuated 7,000 noncombatants and delivered 17,208 tons of supplies to the besieged city. This was the first of CAT's seventy-two evacuation missions.[23]

The Shenyang operation opened the curtain for CAT's new role as Chiang's paramilitary air force. By the end of 1947, CAT had engaged in the battles of Xuzhou and Pengpu. Its planes, under heavy ground fire, brought out scores of wounded troops and flew in tons of ammunition and medicine. It was well on its way to earning its sobriquet as "the World's Most Shot-At Airline." It also collected military intelligence on the movements and tactics of Mao's troops. The fighting made it the world's largest freight-carrying airline.[24]

CAT still carried lucrative cargos of raw cotton, salt, and tobacco when it could, but it functioned increasingly as the backbone of the Nationalists' resistance and retreat. At the start of 1948, Willauer, who escorted Chennault on several of CAT's most dangerous missions, congratulated himself that he was "number three on the list of assassination by the Communists, a singular honor."[25]

Assassins were only one of CAT's mounting worries. Its planes were nearly grounded in mid-June 1948 by runaway inflation as the Chinese economy teetered on the edge of collapse. One American dollar now equaled 4 million Chinese dollars. The airline's fuel and maintenance costs soared as Mao's forces continued pushing Chiang's armies south.[26]

In the meantime, Chennault started returning periodically to the United States, trying to rally wider support for Chiang's faltering regime and sounding the alarm about the implications of a communist victory in China for the United States. To achieve this goal, he turned to Duncan Lee, an ex-communist in search of redemption and still being hunted by the FBI.

When Chennault arrived in Washington in early 1948 to wage his anticommunist crusade, Lee, as his personal lawyer and editor, helped draft the general's congressional testimony, hawkish speeches, and newspaper and magazine articles.[27]

One of Chennault's earliest salvos probably ghosted by Lee appeared in the *Washington Daily News* on February 2, 1948. In an article titled "United States Can Stamp Out the Threat of War," Chennault insisted that Mao Zedong was Joseph Stalin's proxy and that the Soviets would not start a war in Western Europe until they had dominated the Far East. Only a free China, he preached, could prevent this. A month later, Chennault testified before the House Committee on Foreign Affairs and reiterated the importance of a free China to US security. In April, he warned in a national radio address that the United States must prepare for a war against the Soviet Union because Stalin planned to conquer the free world.[28]

Lee even helped Chennault publish his memoir, *Way of a Fighter*, in January 1949. A month before, he had negotiated the book's release date, costs, and press release with G. P. Putnam, Chennault's publisher. The agreed-on press release set the tone for what the book was really about: "Claire Lee Chennault's story is a scathing exposé of ineptitude in high places," something about which Lee had firsthand experience. Corcoran, who worried that Chennault's manuscript was too incendiary, had argued in vain against its publication.[29]

The memoir's first sentence captured Chennault's apocalyptic view of events in China: "The United States is losing the Pacific War." His book forecast "a ring of Soviet Red Bases" stretching "from Siberia to Saigon." With those, Stalin could eventually destroy the United States. Chennault claimed he could "hear the time fuse of a third world war sputtering in China as it burns toward the final powder keg, and I cannot stand idly by without making every effort to snuff it out." Duncan Lee, of all people, made sure that copies of the scaremongering *Way of a Fighter* blanketed Congress and the press.[30]

On May 3, 1949, Chennault expanded on these themes before the Senate's Armed Services Committee. Leaning forward and speaking calmly and deliberately, he shocked the committee's members with his domino theory. Mao's takeover of China, he grimly predicted, would result in massive communist aid to Ho Chi Minh's guerrillas in Indochina and a French defeat there. The communists would target Thailand, Burma, Malaya, Japan, and the Philippines next. With the Pacific a Russian lake, the United States would be forced to rely on nuclear weapons to defend itself.

To preempt this, Chennault argued, the United States had to send arms, military advisers, and large numbers of airplanes to establish what he called "a sanitary zone" stretching from the Islamic- and warlord-dominated provinces of Northwest China, through Szechwan and Hunan, to Yunnan in the southwest. These provinces were strongly anticommunist and historically autonomous. "With the proper kind of aid and support from the United States," Chennault argued, "these peripheral areas could be welded into an effective union of Chinese resistance"—in effect, a second Great Wall of China. This would not be the last time American policymakers heard talk of using Islamic warriors to roll back communism's threat.[31]

Unwilling to wait for a dithering Congress to act, Chennault and Willauer plunged into the shadowy world of gun trafficking in order to supply the black-bearded Ma Pu-fang, the Islamic leader of China's northwestern provinces, with weapons. Ma had scored a major victory against Mao's forces in mid-May and wanted to restock his depleted stores of guns and ammunition. He was quickly becoming Nationalist China's only hope. Mao's troops had already crossed the Yangtze River without a shot being fired. Nanjing had fallen on April 24 and Shanghai on May 25.[32]

On June 6, 1949, Willauer sent Lee and a Washington associate a list of everything Ma needed, including 10,000 rifles, 2,000 light machine guns, 400 heavy machine guns, 12 flamethrowers, 50 light portable field guns, and over 30,000 rounds of ammunition. Willauer instructed them to buy these from a French arms dealer whose company had the suitably vague name of Import Export Industries Inc.[33]

Chennault tried to marshal additional support for Ma in a July 11, 1949, article titled "Last Call for China" that appeared in *Life*, Henry Luce's pro–Chiang Kai-shek magazine. In stark terms, he told the magazine's nearly 4 million readers that "the best part of China was already lost because of a policy of American passivity."[34]

Eleven days later, Lee flew to Guangzhou for a firsthand look at how CAT was faring in the midst of China's civil war. This was the first of at least two lengthy trips he would take to East Asia in 1949 and 1950. With Willauer physically exhausted, Lee assumed much of the daily burden of keeping CAT's planes in the air. Although he continued to drink and collect lovers while his wife and children were in Washington, he also immersed himself in CAT's daily operations. On July 27, James Brennan, the airline's executive vice president, wrote Tommy Corcoran and William Youngman to thank them for sending Lee to China: "WW [Whiting Willauer] is very tired [and] should get out for a spell. I do *not* believe the General should replace him. I feel especially with Duncan here, that we can run the show."[35]

Lee followed this vote of confidence with his own letter to Corcoran and Youngman on August 14. His news was grim. The communists had counterattacked Ma's forces in early August, and the warlord had met with Willauer and Lee to talk about the war supplies he needed.

None were forthcoming. The communists defeated Ma in late August, but CAT rescued him and his $1.5 million in gold bars, flying him to Guangzhou. With all hope quickly fading, Lee predicted the imminent fall of Guangzhou and western China.[36]

With Mao's troops hot on its heels and about to capture Guangzhou, CAT was on the run. By September 4, the airline had moved its people, planes, and maintenance shops from Kunming, its hub in neighboring Yunnan province, to Hainan Island: "We could not afford to have American personnel of any importance caught," Lee wrote Corcoran. "Some of them are on the Commie blacklist. The Reds have made such a point of their determination to get CAT that this much was obvious."[37]

By the time Lee wrote his letter, the State Department had already released its 1,054-page *United States Relations with China, with Special Reference to the Period 1944–1949.* This scholarly but sterile white paper concluded that the political and military events in China were beyond US control. Willauer exploded when he read the State Department's apologia and condemned it, as did most ardent anticommunists, as a cowardly exercise in hand washing: "The God damned State Department ought to be taken out one by one and hung [*sic*]. The White Paper is a disgrace."[38]

The State Department's position should not have surprised Willauer. Since mid-1947, the Truman administration had quietly written off Chiang Kai-shek's chances of survival.[39]

Dean Acheson, Truman's secretary of state in 1949, was an Atlanticist preoccupied with Europe, not Asia. He also found the Nationalist government's venality and corruption repellant. Though increasingly concerned about the spread of communism in Asia, he questioned America's resolve and power to prevent the Nationalists' defeat. Acheson realized that the American military's rapid demobilization immediately after World War II meant that the United States no longer had the manpower to fight a ground war in China. In any event, Harry Truman knew better than to try: in his memoirs, he wrote that the American people would never have stood for such a war.[40]

Acheson also lacked faith in Chennault's wistful plan to use China's Islamists to contain Mao. On June 23, 1949, he told a closed session of the House Committee on Foreign Affairs what he thought of Chennault's idea: "We are of course familiar with General Chennault's views. Military authorities do not consider them to be soundly taken. I am not in a position to come to Congress and ask Congress for money at this time to do something which we do not believe can possibly be effective."[41]

Others believed that Chennault was right and that the Truman administration was willfully abandoning China to the communists. This conviction was especially strong among those who comprised the powerful and vocal China Lobby, a group of mostly conservative, Protestant, wealthy Americans with a missionary, paternalistic attachment to the country. Its members argued that more American aid could save China and that Truman was applying his containment doctrine unequally. They also pointed to alleged traitors in the State Department who, they claimed, had undermined support for Chiang in Washington. The lobby's supporters included *Time* publisher Henry Luce, Congressman Walter Judd of Minnesota, and Senator William Knowland of California.[42]

Despite the China Lobby's relentless political pressure, President Truman announced during a press conference on January 5, 1950, that the "United States Government will not pursue a course which will lead to involvement in the civil conflict in China." The statement was false. His CIA was already secretly supporting Chiang's cause, and it was using CAT to do it.[43]

When Harry Truman abolished the OSS on October 1, 1945, he all but erased the country's ability to carry out covert intelligence operations overseas. Continued Soviet aggression compelled him to reverse that state of affairs. In December 1947, the newly created CIA launched its first secret operations. Most were limited and amateurish, consisting of transmitting radio programs critical of communism and using balloons to drop pro-democracy leaflets in central and eastern Europe.

But balloons and radio broadcasts were pathetically inadequate to counter what many in Washington saw as repeated acts of Soviet aggression. On February 25, 1948, Kremlin-backed communists seized power in Czechoslovakia. At the same time, communist-inspired labor strikes wracked France and Italy. Over 6,000 miles to the east, the Hukbalahaps, the militant arm of the Communist Party of the Philippines, were fighting a guerrilla war against the corrupt but pro-Western government in Manila. And in March 1948, a cable from Germany threw the US government into a state of near hysteria. On March 5, General Lucius Clay, the army's commander in Europe and the military governor of Berlin, sent a memorandum to the Joint Chiefs of Staff in Washington that contained a chilling premonition: "I have felt a subtle change in Soviet attitude which I cannot define but which now gives me a feeling that [war] may come with dramatic suddenness."[44]

Clay's warning, combined with the worsening events in Europe and Asia, galvanized George F. Kennan, director of the State Department's Policy Planning Staff, to push for an expansion of the CIA's covert operations. Kennan, the architect of Harry Truman's containment policy, argued that the United States should employ all available means, short of nuclear war, to stop the Soviets. Two methods proposed were massive economic aid to Western Europe under the Marshall Plan and a broad array of clandestine psychological and political operations to reinforce the benefits this money brought to Western Europe. Kennan argued that the United States needed an organization that could "do things that very much needed to be done, but for which the government could not take official responsibility." The CIA's success in funding the centrist Christian Democrats in the Italian national elections of April 18–19, 1948, captivated him especially. This funding, together with the Vatican's strongly anticommunist policies and the aftershocks of the Soviet-engineered coup in Czechoslovakia, had led to the defeat of the Italian Communist Party. Kennan believed that the CIA could replicate its accomplishments in Italy in other countries threatened by communism.[45]

Dean Rusk, later secretary of state for John Kennedy and Lyndon Johnson, captured the gloves-off mood in the American capital's more shadowed hallways: "The feeling in Washington" was that "the Soviet Union was already operating with such methods. It was a mean, dirty, back-alley struggle, and if the U.S. had stayed out it would have found out what Leo Durocher [the manager of baseball's Brooklyn Dodgers] meant when he said 'nice guys finish last.'"[46]

In response to Kennan's advocacy, the National Security Council adopted directive 10/2 on June 18, 1948, authorizing a dramatic increase in covert action, as well as the use of political warfare, psychological warfare, and paramilitary activities, against the Soviet Union. The long and dangerous US love affair with "plausible deniability" and off-the-books clandestine operations had begun.

To carry these out, directive 10/2 established the Office of Special Projects, which the CIA quickly renamed the even more anodyne Office of Policy Coordination (OPC). Although the OPC's budget and personnel came from the CIA, its policy direction came from the State and Defense departments. On September 1, 1948, Frank Gardiner Wisner, an OSS veteran from Laurel, Mississippi, became its first head. A Wall Street lawyer with degrees from Woodberry Forest and the University of Virginia, the compactly built Wisner throbbed with pent-up energy. He had been a near-Olympic-class sprinter and hurdler in college and would always approach life that way: on the balls of his feet, darting around or over obstacles. He had also been a top student and a member of his university's leading honor societies.[47]

Kennan encouraged the tightly wound Wisner to think big. By 1952, his OPC had forty-seven stations overseas, reflecting Washington's growing addiction to covert action and countering the Soviets on the cheap. Wisner had transformed his agency into a modern version of the Knights Templar, crusading to save the West from the horrors of communism. At first, Wisner confined the OPC's operations to Western Europe. Its operatives—roughly one-third of them had served in the OSS—channeled funds to pro-American political parties and newspapers. They also trained refugees to foment anticommunist unrest in their native countries and worked with labor unions to blunt Moscow's influence on their workers.[48]

When Chennault arrived in Washington during the spring of 1949, Wisner was already planning to unleash his OPC in East Asia. His designs would aid Lee's bid for redemption.

On March 3, President Truman approved NSC 34/2, his administration's latest policy statement on China. Although he ruled out further overt military aid to Chiang, Truman did not completely abandon China to Mao. Paragraph 18 made this clear: "Our principle [sic] reliance in combatting Kremlin influence in China should, however, be on the activities of indigenous Chinese elements. Our official interest in any support of these elements should not be apparent and should be implemented through apparent clandestine channels."[49]

Sometime during the first week of May 1949, Corcoran arranged a meeting between Chennault and Rear Admiral Roscoe H. Hillenkoetter, the CIA's director. Hillenkoetter, a man more at ease with ships than planes, did not react to Chennault's plan. But Paul Helliwell, a CIA officer, close friend of Duncan Lee, and former chief of the OSS's intelligence operations in China, immediately grasped what Chennault could offer Wisner's OPC. He had known Chennault in China and admired him. Helliwell encouraged Wisner to meet with him.[50]

Wisner and several OPC officers met with Chennault on May 9 at the Hotel Washington. His plan to keep anticommunist forces in Northwest and Southwest China in the field impressed them. Chennault talked frankly, however, about CAT's deteriorating finances and its need for an immediate cash infusion. Chiang Kai-shek, who would flee to Taiwan by the end of that same month, had not paid the airline since the beginning of the year.[51]

After the meeting, Wisner sent a memorandum to the State Department that outlined his interest in CAT and the airline's near bankruptcy. The State Department declined to broker a grant for the airline from the Economic Cooperation Administration. Unfazed, Wisner asked Helliwell to find another way to fund CAT because he wanted the OPC to use the airline in China.[52]

On June 29 Helliwell met with Corcoran, who bluntly admitted that CAT was in severe financial trouble. In a memorandum to Wisner, Helliwell diagnosed the airline as suffering from "acute dollaritis." The prognosis, however, was good. Despite its affliction, Helliwell believed the airline could be saved: "If at all possible action must be taken to hold CAT intact. The 'face' of the CAT operation, coupled with its communications operation, cannot be established by a new operation without the expenditure of many millions of dollars."[53]

While the State Department and the CIA debated Helliwell's rescue plan, Mao announced that China under his leadership would "lean" toward the Soviet Union. In late August, the Soviets successfully detonated their first atomic bomb. Harry Truman somberly shared this stunning news with the American people on September 24. A week later, Mao stood in Beijing's Tiananmen Square and announced the birth of the People's Republic of China.[54]

CAT began flying for the OPC on October 10, 1949. Although no one in the State Department or the CIA felt that American intervention could now turn the tide in China, the airline could make life difficult for Mao's new regime. It also might be of future use in Southeast Asia, which increasingly vexed Foggy Bottom's foreign policy experts and the White House by 1949.[55]

On November 1, Corcoran, acting for CAT, signed a formal contract with the OPC. The CIA agreed to pay the airline $500,000. In exchange, CAT promised to give priority to the OPC's cargo and personnel for one year. To help keep the airline aloft, OPC immediately paid CAT $200,000. The CIA had saved CAT, but it could not save China. The fall of Guilin on November 22, 1949, ended the Nationalists' Pollyannaish hopes of holding onto the mainland.[56]

CAT, its fortunes inextricably bound with Chiang Kai-shek's, followed him into exile on Taiwan. As the end neared, the beleaguered airline flew at least 100,000 of China's best-trained technicians to Taiwan. Many of these university-educated technocrats spawned the island's rapid industrialization and became the heart of its anti-Maoist resistance. According to Corcoran, Chiang's armies would have crumbled at least a year earlier without CAT's herculean efforts. He also thought the airline had enabled the Generalissimo to consolidate his defenses on Taiwan. Willauer even claimed that CAT had bought time for the United States, giving the country a breathing spell during which to rethink its foreign policy toward China and East Asia.[57]

Through all this, Lee had stood shoulder to shoulder with Corcoran, Chennault, Willauer, and CAT in their quixotic quest to stop Mao Zedong. His fortitude and loyalty particularly impressed Willauer: "Mr. Lee was with us in the dangerous period of evacuation of our airline from Canton [Guangzhou] whereby we avoided seizure of our planes and equipment by the Communists. At this time, Mr. Lee showed considerable personal courage under very trying circumstances, and I should like to state that any impartial witness who had observed Mr. Lee's conduct in these circumstances could only have had the most favorable opinion of Mr. Lee's personal integrity and anti-Communist views."[58]

But Willauer found much more than Lee's courageous actions in Guangzhou impressive. In December 1949 in Hong Kong, he and Lee set into motion what William J. Donovan jubilantly described as America's "first Cold War victory in the Far East."[59]

Seven months before, Chiang had ordered what was left of his country's two national airlines to fly their planes and equipment to Hong Kong. Knowing Mao lacked air power, the Generalissimo did not want the communist leader to capture and use the Nationalists' own airlines against him. The Chinese National Aviation Corporation (CNAC) and the Central Air Transport Corporation (CATC) obeyed Chiang's command and flew eighty-three airplanes and spare parts to Hong Kong after Shanghai fell on May 25, 1949.[60]

From the outset, Mao's agents targeted the airlines' employees, using bribes and threats against family members still on the mainland to engineer the defection of CNAC's and CATC's general managers with twelve airplanes on November 9, 1949. After these desertions, Mao demanded the return of the remaining seventy-one aircraft as the sacred property of the People's Republic of China.[61]

The news of these defections shocked Chennault and Willauer. Chennault contacted newspaper columnist Joseph Alsop and told him how important the remaining planes were: "This air force constitutes the balance of power in Asia because its possession gives complete mobility to its owners." He later informed another newspaperman that the seventy-one planes would more than quadruple Mao's transport fleet and allow him to carry 10,000 troops to Taiwan within six hours of an invasion. By mid-November, the two Americans had intelligence that Mao was training paratroopers for an assault on Taiwan. Chennault and Willauer believed that Mao planned to use the seventy-one transport planes to launch this assault.[62]

Chiang had the same intelligence. He again asked Chennault and Willauer for help. On November 10, 1949, they agreed to act as his agents and to keep Mao's government from getting its hands on the remaining airplanes. In the meantime, Willauer personally led a midnight raid on the Hong Kong airfield where the planes were parked, flattening their tires and stationing trucks across the runways to prevent disloyal employees from absconding with any more aircraft. The British authorities governing Hong Kong, however, seemed inclined to hand the planes over to Mao once the Foreign Office in London had formally recognized his government in January 1950.[63]

Lee played a pivotal role in ensuring this did not happen. His colleagues in Hong Kong cabled Tommy Corcoran in Washington that only buying the planes would prevent them from falling into Mao's hands. Corcoran wanted to test the political waters in Washington first. He was impressed. He reported back that "responsible US government officials" had decided that it was in the "national interest" to buy the airplanes.[64]

Corcoran hastily formed two corporations to undertake this purchase and enforce it in Hong Kong's courts. Fortified with the necessary official support from Washington, Chennault and Willauer approached Chiang's government and offered to buy CNAC's and CATC's airplanes. By December 5, 1949, Willauer had roughed out an agreement with the Nationalists. Lee, then in Hong Kong, took Willauer's barebones agreement and transformed it into a binding contract. He also drafted the airplanes' sales and transfer documents. As Willauer recalled, "A very intricate legal situation was presented in the process of making this purchase. I personally handled the policy aspects of negotiations with the Nationalist government; and since Mr. Lee was then with us in Hong Kong I turned over the entire problem of drafting the necessary legal documents to accomplish this purchase. The importance to the Communist cause of obtaining these airlines cannot be over-exaggerated."[65]

The Nationalists, who ratified the deal on December 12, forced Willauer and Chennault to sign promissory notes for $4.75 million for the airlines and their assets. The Americans also agreed to "use their best efforts" to ensure that the Chinese communists would not get the airplanes. On December 18, Corcoran wrote to Willauer, assuring him that "you now have a solid basis of appreciation all through the top levels, straight up to H. T. [Harry Truman]. And I personally am very proud of my association with such thoroughly adequate and effective 'war criminals.'"[66]

The CIA's official role in this seems to have been confined to advancing money to CAT to defray litigation expenses and other costs, but Corcoran later maintained that Chennault and Willauer were working as "individuals" for the agency when they bought the airplanes. He also said in a taped interview that he was "very marginally CIA" during this same time.[67]

Whatever the truth, Lee returned to Washington in late December and registered the airplanes with the Civil Aeronautics Administration. Corcoran also hired William J. Donovan to get the planes out of Hong Kong. Donovan, who had lost none of his fire since leaving the OSS, flew to the British Crown colony on January 4, 1950, and demanded that the colony's governor turn the planes over to him. He undiplomatically reminded the governor that if not for the United States, Britain would have lost World War II.[68]

From 1949 until 1952, Lee worked almost exclusively on recovering the airplanes. As the chief architect of Chennault and Willauer's legal strategy, he worked closely in Washington and London with Donovan and barrister Sir Hartley Shawcross, a former British attorney general, to implement it. After losing nine times in Hong Kong's courts, Chennault and Willauer eventually prevailed on appeal in 1952 when the Privy Council in London, Britain's highest court, upheld as legal Lee's contract.[69]

By then, Harry Truman had hardened his position against the People's Republic of China. Although Secretary of State Dean Acheson had declared on January 12, 1950, that the United States had no plans to defend Taiwan, the administration's policy shifted over the next six months, influenced by a tidal wave of events that included Alger Hiss's conviction for perjury on January 25; the Sino-Soviet Treaty of Friendship, Alliance, and Mutual Assistance on February 14; Mao's matériel support to Ho Chi Minh's revolutionaries against the French in Indochina; and the outbreak of the Korean War on June 25.[70]

After North Korean troops streamed across the 38th parallel that day, Truman ordered the US Navy's Seventh Fleet to sail through the Taiwan Strait to defend Chiang's government from any possible attack from China. Chennault's domino theory had now become gospel in Washington's foreign policy circles. In April 1951, Chennault urged the United States to carry the fighting in Korea into China. With thousands of Americans dying in Korea and the State Department under fire for harboring communists and Maoists, no one in official Washington or London wanted to boost Mao's military capabilities by giving him the Hong Kong–based airplanes.[71]

The Korean War also saved CAT. The CIA bought it on August 23, 1950. The airline was soon flying missions for the agency in Korea, Indochina, Indonesia, and Laos. In March 1959, the CIA would change its name to Air America.[72]

After the Privy Council's favorable decision, Harry Truman sent the USS *Cape Esperance*, a light escort carrier, to ferry twenty-three of the larger aircraft now owned by Chennault and Willauer to the United States. When Chennault walked down the carrier's gangway in Hong Kong, he crowed to a throng of waiting reporters that CAT's victory in London was "the first defeat the Communists had suffered in the Far East." All the while, the FBI and the army, still trying to prove Elizabeth Bentley's claims about him, had monitored Lee's trips to Hong Kong and Britain.[73]

Lee next worked on selling the airplanes and tying up the loose ends of CAT's sale to the CIA. Although gradually eased out of CAT's operations, Chennault and Willauer remained proud of their airline's feats and especially of the role they and Lee had played in keeping the seventy-one airplanes out of Mao's hands. Willauer celebrated this hard-won victory in a 1954 letter to Chennault: "Despite the hell we went through, I know you will agree with me that what we did very probably saved Formosa [Taiwan], if not from a takeover by parachuters [sic], [then] from a very nasty situation which would have prevailed in 1950 had the Communists been in possession of the assets."[74]

Willauer did not exaggerate. In the spring of 1950, the CIA estimated that Mao had nearly 1 million troops in place to invade Taiwan. He had assembled a fleet of 5,000 junks to carry them across the Taiwan Strait. Mao worried, though, about the risk of moving large numbers of men across the eighty to one hundred miles of open water and assaulting well-fortified positions once they made it ashore. The Nationalists' victory over the communist leader's amphibious invaders in October 1949 on Kinmen Island had highlighted these dangers.[75]

Mao coveted a larger air force, especially more jet fighters that could protect his invading forces. He also needed more transport planes to support them and to drop 15,000 paratroopers on Taiwan's defenses. But these airplanes took time to acquire. His generals hoped to begin large-scale maneuvers for their amphibious assault forces by the spring of 1951 as a prelude to their actual invasion of Taiwan. If Mao had gotten the seventy-one airplanes, he could have accelerated his timetable for the attack. Instead, Kim Il-sung's invasion of South Korea overtook the Chinese leader's plans.[76]

Lee had performed brilliantly in the Chinese civil war. He successfully remade himself from one of the Kremlin's best-placed spies inside US intelligence into a Cold Warrior who enjoyed the gratitude of Harry Truman's White House, although it had not been easy. While fighting Mao's communists in China, at home he still faced Elizabeth Bentley's accusations that he had betrayed his country during World War II. Neither the FBI nor the HUAC had gone away, and either could pounce again at any moment. To keep J. Edgar Hoover's agents from knocking on his front door or the HUAC's investigators from slapping another subpoena into his hands, Lee had cloaked himself in the mantle of anticommunism and surrounded himself with men with unassailable anticommunist credentials.

In 1983, he wrote in a memoir about his time with Corcoran, Chennault, and Willauer, observing that this period had allowed him to establish "a useful record of having struck a significant blow against international communism." As importantly, it had allowed him to dry-clean his conscience. If his father was right about a forgiving God, Lee may have believed that he had finally broken even. He had also won the confidence of Corcoran, Chennault, and Willauer, despite the public allegations against him in the summer of 1948, though at least one of them had serious doubts as to whether he was telling the truth about his relationship with Bentley.[77]

Tommy Corcoran's support for Lee stemmed from a complex mixture of empathy and self-interest. For one thing, they shared a common enemy. J. Edgar Hoover hated Corcoran, and Corcoran knew it. Their bad relations started while Corcoran was still working for Franklin

Roosevelt. On November 14, 1940, the *Chicago Herald-American* ran an article headlined "New Deal Purge Planned," claiming that Corcoran was the ringleader of a plot hatched by "a group of inside New Dealers" to drive Hoover out of the FBI and into private life. Hoover immediately opened a file on Corcoran.[78]

When Harry Truman asked the FBI to tap Corcoran's telephones in June 1945 because he believed the lawyer was engaged in what the White House called "questionable activities," Hoover eagerly complied. This wiretap lasted until April 1947. In one recorded phone call, Corcoran had questioned Truman's intelligence because he thought he could "surround himself almost entirely with dumb Missourians and run the greatest country in the world." A second wiretap ran from mid-April 1948 to mid-May 1948. Corcoran enraged Truman in that year when he backed US Supreme Court associate justice William O. Douglas to be the Democrats' presidential nominee. When Truman offered the vice presidency to Douglas, Corcoran reportedly remarked to him, "Why be a number-two man to a number-two man?" These wiretaps generated 6,250 pages of transcriptions in 175 summary logbooks.[79]

Corcoran, through his web of Department of Justice and FBI contacts, knew all about the wiretaps. To thwart them, he regularly took handfuls of nickels to drugstores and hotels near his office to make his more sensitive phone calls. He even deducted this money from his income taxes and regularly joked that all the nickels J. Edgar Hoover forced him to carry had ruined the pockets of more than one good pair of dress pants.[80]

On July 25, 1951, the Department of Justice's Criminal Division and the FBI started investigating Corcoran to determine whether he was acting in the United States as an unregistered agent of the Nationalist Chinese government. Among the FBI reports in Corcoran's private papers was one on Bentley's allegations against Duncan Lee. As a target of the FBI himself, Corcoran well appreciated the lengths that Hoover would go to. All the same, he never wholly trusted Lee, whose story, especially his statements to the HUAC, he thought, contained too many inconsistencies. For the moment, though, Corcoran kept his doubts to himself. He personally liked Lee and, if nothing else, did not want his many anticommunist clients believing his firm had hired a former Soviet spy and taking their lucrative fees elsewhere.[81]

Chennault, who shared distant blood ties with Lee and trusted him enough to make him his personal attorney, also stood by him in the wake of Bentley's sensational testimony. He had experienced character assassination firsthand: he believed that vicious personal attacks had cut short his military career and that they had not ended when he retired. Chennault was the kind of man who relied on what he saw, not what he heard secondhand, and in his view, Bentley had presented no proof against Lee. Lee, on the other hand, had performed superbly in East Asia and in Washington, and Chennault felt duty bound to back him.[82]

Willauer was more circumspect. Bentley's allegations worried him, and he admitted to keeping an eye on Lee. Despite this, Lee had proved himself a trusted colleague and courageous patriot in China: "I naturally was much concerned by [Bentley's] accusation and attack, and I have on many occasions since that time made it my business to observe Mr. Lee closely. I can only say that in this connection, actions speak louder than words. I have never hesitated, despite this accusation, to entrust the legal affairs of the airline's legal business to Mr. Lee."[83]

James Rowe Jr., one of Corcoran's law partners and a member of a State Department board that had looked into espionage there, was even more effusive about Lee's anticommunism. He commended Lee's actions in Hong Kong as "the single most concrete performance by any American individual against World communism. Most Americans talk against it but few do anything about it. Mr. Lee is a shining exception."[84]

To J. Edgar Hoover and the FBI, however, Lee remained a traitor. He may have helped save Taiwan from Mao Zedong, but none of his actions in East Asia erased his service to Joseph Stalin. And thanks to a huge break in their investigation, Hoover and his agents now had the evidence they needed to back up Elizabeth Bentley's charges.

TEN

A LOYAL AMERICAN

The big break that J. Edgar Hoover and the FBI had been praying for occurred at an unlikely time and in an even unlikelier place. It came as Lee played a leading role in US efforts to roll back communism in East Asia. Even stranger, it had originated almost nine years before at a finishing school in a Washington suburb.

From their first days in the United States, the Soviet Union's intelligence services had faced the very real difficulty of communicating secretly with their masters in Moscow. In 1927, three years after establishing the Amtorg Trading Corporation in New York City, the Soviets developed, in their view, an unbreakable communications network between Moscow and the United States. The system, which relied on codebooks and ciphers, allowed their espionage services to send and receive secret messages over cables and circuits owned by commercial companies such as Western Union.[1]

The US Army's Signal Intelligence Service (SIS) began collecting the Soviets' communications in January 1939 as Europe lurched toward war. The SIS operated seven monitoring stations across the United States, from Fort Monmouth in New Jersey to Fort Shafter in Hawaii. Even though modestly staffed, the listening posts managed to intercept small numbers of encrypted Soviet messages as part of a general monitoring of most foreign diplomatic communications flowing into and out of the United States.[2]

The army accelerated its collection of these secret exchanges after the Japanese attacked Pearl Harbor in December 1941. Under Executive Order 8895, President Franklin Roosevelt created an Office of Censorship that monitored "mail, cable, radio, and other means of transmission between the United States and any foreign country." As required, RCA Global, ITT World Communications, and Western Union gave the army copies of all international messages they carried. The SIS set the Soviets' messages aside, however, and concentrated its cryptanalytic and translation resources on breaking and reading in plain text the German, Japanese, and Italian codes.[3]

Although the Americans and Soviets were allies after Pearl Harbor, rumors of secret German-Soviet peace negotiations shook the US War Department in early 1943. On February 1, Colonel Carter W. Clarke, chief of the army's Special Branch, ordered the SIS to establish a small program to work on cracking the thousands of coded and encrypted Soviet messages it had collected. By 1944, the army had eighteen wooden cabinets stuffed with 150,000 seemingly impenetrable Soviet messages.[4]

Clarke, whom a fellow officer once described as a "very unconventional man of considerable moral courage," believed that the United States needed a code-breaking program to keep its leaders informed of its friends' and foes' intentions. By the time Clarke focused on the Soviets' communications, the newly renamed Signal Security Service was operating out of Arlington Hall, a former all-female junior college in Arlington, Virginia. In June 1942, the army had taken over the financially strapped school across the Potomac River from Washington and made it the locus of its efforts to break German and Japanese codes.[5]

World War II revolutionized the army's code-breaking program, forcing it to recruit and develop a new generation of exceptionally gifted and skilled cryptanalysts. With British collaboration, they penetrated both Japanese and German ciphers of all grades and complexities, making an invaluable contribution to the war effort. By 1943, with profound postwar implications for Duncan Lee, they had discovered a recurring flaw in the Soviet system for encrypting messages.[6]

While one subgroup of American code breakers stripped away the Soviet ciphers, another reconstructed the Kremlin's codebooks.

Meredith Gardner, a reclusive linguist from Texas, spearheaded this latter effort. The SIS had hired him in 1942 because of his uncanny aptitude for learning foreign languages. A former instructor of German at the University of Akron, he quickly switched from working on German to Japanese codes after having taught himself that extraordinarily complex language in three months. After the war ended, he learned Russian and switched to the "Soviet problem." In December 1946, he unbuttoned part of an NKGB message that listed American scientists who were building the atomic bomb.[7]

Despite this remarkable breakthrough, the army's cryptanalysts labored alone and in a tightly compartmented vacuum. An obsessive secrecy limited their understanding of what they were reading. Although the identities behind some of the cover names they had unmasked were transparent, many others remained obscure. Carter Clarke, now a brigadier general in G-2, the army's intelligence corps, asked the FBI for help.

On September 1, 1947, Clarke briefed Special Agent S. Wesley Reynolds, the bureau's liaison to Arlington Hall, about the treasure trove of Soviet messages. Soon thereafter, Reynolds gave Clarke a list of over two hundred cover names, including those that Igor Gouzenko and Elizabeth Bentley had provided the FBI. In exchange, Clarke entrusted Reynolds with his cryptanalysts' fragmentary decrypts. In turn, Reynolds passed these pieces of the puzzle to the FBI's spy catchers, who did the unthinkable: they tossed them into a safe and ignored them.[8]

Bored by his work on the espionage services of eastern European countries operating in the United States, Special Agent Robert J. Lamphere asked for permission to take on these fragments. Lamphere, who joined the FBI in 1941 after graduating from George Washington University's law school, had spent his entire career at the bureau working on counterintelligence cases. The bespectacled, scholarly Idaho native was a rarity in an agency that viewed counterintelligence as a backwater and an unsuitable avenue for promotion.[9]

Lamphere's quiet and reflective nature made him the perfect partner for the shy and brilliant Meredith Gardner. Lamphere brought his encyclopedic knowledge of the NKGB's operations and personalities to their collaboration, while Gardner contributed his extraordinary linguistic talents and uncommon ability to translate extremely difficult material. Between 1948 and 1951, their close partnership played a pivotal role in helping unmask the Comstock Lode of traitors: Klaus Fuchs, Harry Gold, David Greenglass, Theodore Hall, the Rosenbergs, and Donald Maclean. It also delivered proof that Bentley had told the FBI the truth in November 1945.[10]

Much later, in 1995, the National Security Agency, which took over this effort in 1952 after Harry Truman created it that same year, declassified slices of its official history of "Venona," the final code name for this wizardry. NSA's history assessed Bentley's credibility: "We can state quite confidently that the controversial information she provided, first to the FBI and later to a grand jury, to Congress and to the public, was accurate." Twenty-nine Americans she named as Soviet spies and sources appeared in the NKGB's intercepted traffic. One of them was Duncan Lee.[11]

They did not know it at the time, but the cryptanalysts' first glimpse of Lee surfaced in a message from the NKGB's New York City station to its headquarters in Moscow on September 15, 1944. On June 23, 1950, the FBI issued a lengthy study summarizing what the army's code breakers and the bureau knew about the identities behind the cover names that the NKGB had used in its secret traffic. It focused on the messages the Soviets transmitted between April 28, 1944, and June 26, 1945, from New York to Moscow because they were the easiest to break.[12]

The study revealed that the army and FBI had positively or tentatively identified sixty-four people discussed in the NKGB's cables. These included Jacob Golos, Joseph Katz, and Gregory and Helen Silvermaster. At the same time, the bureau admitted that it had not identified another 215 cover names. Among these, according to one decoded Soviet message, was "Koh" or "Koch," who had told the Soviets in September 1944 that the OSS had compiled a list of two types of reds within its organization: (1) open Communist Party members, and (2) sympathizers, leftists, and strong liberals. The decoded message also said that Koh was trying to obtain the list. Bentley had told the HUAC virtually the same thing on August 10, 1948, when she testified against Lee.[13]

As the FBI rifled through its own files for clues as to who "Koh" or "Koch" was, it turned its attention to arresting Joseph Katz. Bentley had identified him as her handler "Jack" when agents showed her his photograph in January 1949, but her identification remained uncorroborated. His unmasking in the Venona traffic in the spring of 1950 confirmed what she had said about him.[14]

Katz, though, had already left the United States and was living in Paris, France. In the meantime, the failure of the grand jury and the HUAC to uncover any new facts had brought the FBI's investigation of Lee and the others Bentley had accused to a standstill. On March 11, 1949, Hoover had instructed his field offices to break down the Gregory case into separate case files and review each to ascertain if "it appears additional investigation is necessary to determine whether the subject is presently engaged in Soviet espionage or other activity against the best interests of the country." With no new leads and Lee fighting communists in China, the bureau's Washington field office closed his case on September 26, 1949.[15]

Less than a year later, Congress, badly shaken by the outbreak of the Korean War in June, decisively overrode Harry Truman's veto of the Internal Security Act of 1950. Senator Pat McCarran of Nevada and HUAC alumni Richard Nixon and Karl Mundt, now US senators, fathered this highly charged legislation. Its guts required all members of the Communist Party of the United States of America and its front groups to register with a newly created Subversive Activities Control Board.[16]

The act's passage slowly breathed new life into the case against Lee. On September 26, 1950, the Department of Justice's Criminal Division asked the FBI to review Bentley's charges to determine if anyone she had accused should be required to register. This request triggered an internal debate within the bureau about the best way to proceed. Almost a month later, A. S. Brent, an FBI official, spelled out his agency's options in a memorandum. After discussing the possibilities that Katz might cooperate with the FBI, one of Bentley's sources might unexpectedly come forward, or Venona might yield more clues, Brent argued, just as Chief Inspector Edward Pierpont Morgan had three years earlier, that the bureau stood the best chance of breaking the case wide open by "concentrate[ing] our investigative efforts at this time on trying to find a weak spot in the armors of these people, which will allow us to obtain successful interviews with them."[17]

After highlighting that Lee had been nervous and upset during his May 29, 1947, interview and pointing to the seven discrepancies in his testimony before the HUAC, Brent laid out a plan to interview Lucy and Edmund: "Lee comes from an old prominent Virginia family and it is possible that if we start with his parents and relatives he may become cooperative. If these interviews draw complaints from him, then it is felt that we would be in a position to interview him thoroughly concerning the noted discrepancies."[18]

Arlington Hall's code breakers preempted Brent's hardball plan. Sometime in late October or early November 1950, they broke an NKGB cable from the New York station to Moscow headquarters dated October 10, 1944. It reported that "Koh" or "Koch" had told Elizabeth Bentley about an OSS officer in China working with a group of communists who planned to use Korean communists to infiltrate Japan. The bureau recorded this break in a letter dated November 14, 1950. This was the second of nine NKGB cables broken by Arlington Hall between 1950 and 1974 that would confirm Lee had worked for the Soviets.[19]

Strongly suspecting by then, after reexamining all that Bentley had said about him, that Koh or Koch was Lee, the FBI reopened his case on March 10, 1951. Fortified by Arlington Hall's breakthroughs and with renewed faith in his star witness, Hoover came at him from all sides. A month later, he ordered the head of the Washington field office to locate any OSS reports that supported Bentley's claims. The FBI now had to ask the CIA for help because it had inherited most of the OSS's files.[20]

Hoover did not trust the agency. He worried that the Soviets had penetrated it, just as they had the OSS, and believed that it contained what he called "questionable personnel." In 1947, about one-third of the CIA's senior officers had served with Donovan. Although not ready to tell the CIA about Arlington Hall's successes, Hoover reluctantly conceded that he had to work with the agency to arrest Lee. On April 11, 1951, the FBI asked the CIA to find any OSS files that supported Bentley's November 30, 1945, statement and her congressional testimony. These included files on OSS agents parachuting into Hungary, Yugoslavia, and Turkey, the OSS's investigation into communists and Soviet sympathizers, and its dealings with Tai Li, the head of Chiang Kai-shek's secret service.[21]

While the CIA raked through its OSS files, two FBI agents reinterviewed Bentley on April 24, 1951, at the bureau's New York field office. The bureau had not questioned her extensively about Lee since November 1945. Absolutely sure now that she had told the truth about their relationship, the two agents pressed her for precise details. They were especially interested in what he had told her about the OSS's operations and if she had passed any of this classified information to Joseph Katz.[22]

Her answers confirmed what Arlington Hall had already reported. Bentley told the agents about the plan to infiltrate communists into Japan. When they asked whether Lee had told her that the OSS had compiled a list of reds, Bentley immediately answered yes, adding that the list had been divided into three categories. The September 14, 1944, cable that Arlington Hall's cryptanalysts had broken mentioned only two categories of suspects, but the NKGB's files in Moscow show that Koch provided a "list [that] indicates three categories of people whom the security division considers to be particularly dangerous reds."[23]

Bentley also correctly recalled that two individuals on the list had the last name Jiminez. Manuel and Michael Jiminez were on the list forwarded to Moscow. Despite their communist backgrounds, Donovan had recruited both men because they had guerrilla warfare experience from fighting with the Abraham Lincoln Battalion during the Spanish Civil War. Bentley told the FBI agents that she had passed Lee's list to the Soviet agent she knew only as "Bill." The bureau did not know then that Bill was Iskhak Akhmerov, chief of the NKGB illegals station in the United States.[24]

Although it had been nearly seven years since Lee had given her any classified information and almost five and half years since the FBI had questioned her about him, Bentley was able to recall specifics about intelligence he had passed to her that she had not reported earlier to the bureau. Whittaker Chambers discussed his own experience with long-delayed recollections in his autobiography, *Witness*: "Even today [1952], after exhaustive recollection, I sometimes remember fresh details that had slipped my mind."[25]

The agents' questions released a flood of memories about Lee's confidences, including that Ambassador Carlton Hayes had complained about how the OSS operated in Spain, Mary Price's attempt to obtain a job inside Donovan's organization, and the OSS's effort to parachute agents into Hungary. Her recollections prompted another request to the CIA for any OSS files that discussed these specific subjects.[26]

At the same time, the army was moving to revoke Lee's commission as a reserve officer in its intelligence arm. Since January 13, 1946, he had been a lieutenant colonel in G-2. Although the army had transferred him to the inactive reserves on March 31, 1949, it now wanted to purge him completely from its ranks.[27]

The FBI had first raised the question of Lee's commission on August 16, 1949, in an internal memorandum. On September 26, the same day it closed its espionage case on him, the bureau sent a detailed report on Lee to G-2. On April 23, 1951, almost ten months after the start of the Korean War, the army's adjutant general asked him to respond to nineteen charges stemming from what the FBI had sent. The grounds ranged from former landlady Katharine Nangle's 1940 statement to the bureau's New Haven office about him and Ishbel being "decidedly Communistic" to his admitted association with "John," or Jacob Golos. There is no evidence, though, that the adjutant general knew anything about the service's top-secret, highly compartmented Venona program.[28]

With Corcoran's help, Lee assembled a detailed "Reply to Allegations," rebutting each of the charges against him. He also rewrote history. Lee now conjured up a new past in which he and Ishbel had always been liberal democrats and supporters of Franklin Roosevelt. Similarly, they had consistently opposed communism and all it stood for: "We have always disagreed emphatically with the Communist outlook. We have always considered Russian Communism as vicious and oppressive tyranny by which its ruthless disregard for human rights and liberties destroys the very values in human welfare which the Communists profess to seek and promote."[29]

Ignoring his letters to his mother, Lucy, gushing about the Soviet utopia after he and Ishbel had visited Leningrad and Moscow in August 1937, Lee recast the visit and painted a sinister and Kafkaesque portrait for the adjutant general: "My strongest impression from this trip was of the pervading atmosphere of fear which gripped everyone in Russia, and I returned with the conviction that nothing which Communism could possibly promise to anyone was worth the price that was being paid in Russia in the crushing of the individual and the suppression of human freedom."[30]

Lee targeted more than communism. On Corcoran's advice, he continued to attack Bentley's character and motives. In nine and a half tightly worded pages, Lee traced his first meeting with her from the "spring of 1943" until her final descent into "bitter and vindictive hatred." He thereby changed for the third time the date of their initial encounter but otherwise stuck close to the rest of his HUAC testimony.[31]

He repeated that he and Ishbel had first met Bentley at a cocktail party hosted by Mary Price. During the party, Bentley had singled out the Lees and spent most of the evening talking with them. Lee described his first impressions of Bentley: "She seemed to be an unusually well integrated, intelligent and cultured woman with a wide range of interests. Her New England background was very apparent. She was obviously from old American stock. She dressed in good taste and in all respects appeared to be the typical Vassar alumna that in fact she was. She had a flattering way of appearing to be completely absorbed and interested in what anyone was saying to her."[32]

Some weeks later Bentley started visiting the Lees "fairly regularly" at their home. Lee admitted dining out with her twice in Washington and twice in New York City. A refugee writer or scholar Bentley introduced as "John" (Jacob Golos) had joined them at one dinner in Washington and at another in New York City, but he made no impression: he looked very ill and did not speak much. Their dinner conversations revolved around the war, movies, children, the weather, and "events of the day and all the innumerable subjects which make up the casual conversation over drinks of friends everywhere." Neither Bentley nor John asked him about his OSS work or seemed interested in it.[33]

Lee then claimed that he gradually noticed a marked change in his relationship with Bentley. This happened after John's death: "Thereafter her attitude became increasingly what I can only describe as an urgent dependence upon me and my wife. As all this became more apparent we began to feel that we were being made the objects of an unwholesome and exaggerated affection and were being used to compensate for what had recently been an emotionally barren existence." Her unhealthy emotional demands, coupled with her outspoken support for the Soviet Union, forced the Lees to sever their ties. This rupture, he explained, triggered feelings of rejection and gave rise to her "bitter vindictive hatred of my wife and me which was one of the principal motivations for the false charges which she later brought against me."[34]

Bentley was not Lee's sole villain. He also threw a punch at the FBI, comparing his own failing to realize that she had worked for the Soviets with the bureau's failure to catch her: "Miss Bentley was never detected until she made her voluntary confession. In all the circumstances I do not feel that I should be condemned for not having seen through Miss Bentley and for feeling that she was a personal, not a security problem—when all the counter-espionage forces in this country also failed to see through her."[35]

He wrapped up his formal response with a complete denial and an all-out attack on Bentley's character. After excoriating her failure to provide a motive for "why I should have betrayed my country, my uniform, my friends and my oath, to engage with her or anyone else in a conspiracy to give the Communists or the Russians classified information" and claiming there was "nothing in my background, education, beliefs or character that would have led me to such a course," he savaged her as a "pathological liar, whose whole record shows her to be innately treacherous and false."[36]

Lee submitted eleven affidavits to support his self-characterization as a devoted patriot and staunch anticommunist. These came from William Donovan, Claire Chennault, Whiting Willauer, and other men who had known him at Yale, in the OSS, and at the New York Bar. Otto "Ole" Doering, his mentor at Donovan's law firm and his boss for his first two years in the OSS, directly attacked Bentley's claims that Lee had betrayed his country: "In his wartime service Mr. Lee displayed exceptional loyalty, courage and selfless devotion to his country." Doering, who felt personally assaulted by her accusations that the Soviets had infiltrated the OSS, picked her specific charges apart in a lawyerly fashion. For example, he criticized her for testifying before the HUAC about the proposed exchange of "agents" instead of "missions" between the OSS and NKGB.[37]

Doering did more than just split hairs. He unknowingly turned Lee's decision to give Bentley only what he chose to his erstwhile protégé's advantage: "It is wholly incredible that Mr. Lee would have given to Miss Bentley [that which] she claims he gave her and at the same time withheld from her information which would have been of much more interest and importance to the Communist cause." Doering would not have known about Lee's refusal to take orders from the Soviets and their intense frustration with him.[38]

Lee also attached an affidavit from Archbold Van Beuren. Now the head of Cue Publishing, Van Beuren had served during the war as the head of the OSS's Personnel Security Division and as assistant chief and then chief of its Security Office. He endorsed Lee emphatically: "There was never at any time during the entire period I served in the Security Office of the OSS any information received by me which would in any way indicate that either Mr. Lee or his wife was sympathetic to Communism, or a member of the Communist Party, or sympathized with the government of the USSR. Mr. Lee's reputation among his associates as to his character, ability and security was excellent."[39]

Lee attached a "Personal History Statement of Duncan Chaplin Lee as a Loyal American" to his rebuttal and affidavits. To showcase his patriotism and his illustrious roots, he discussed his blood ties to the two Lees who had signed the Declaration of Independence, to Robert E. Lee, and to the Mayflower's John and Priscilla Alden. For the very first time, he invoked the bald-faced lie that he had developed a lasting hatred for and distrust of communism while fleeing China as a young boy in 1927. He also discussed his grueling time among the headhunters in the Naga Hills, his decorated OSS service, his anti-communist work for Chennault, and his wife, Ishbel, who was not a dangerous radical but an all-American mom, a stalwart member of her Georgetown Episcopal Christ Church's Christian education committee, and the den mother of a Cub Scout pack. Lastly, Lee assured the adjutant general that he was ready to help the United States in any way he could: "My greatest hope and desire is to remain in Washington, continue to practice law here, and to serve my community and my country in whatever way and in whatever capacity I can."[40]

As Lee waited for the army's decision about his commission, Corcoran appealed to Bishop Fulton Sheen, now a Catholic televangelist, for help. He asked the wildly popular clergyman, whose weekly television program drew almost 30 million viewers, to support Lee publicly. Sheen, who had converted Bentley to Catholicism on November 5, 1948, and hated communism as much as J. Edgar Hoover, declined. He believed it his God-given mission to save ex-communists' souls, not to defend those who had not openly confessed their sins.[41]

Despite all this effort, on September 12, 1951, G-2's assistant chief of staff formally recommended that Lee be ousted from the Reserve. With American soldiers dying in Korea, the adjutant general agreed and discharged Lee from the army on April 15, 1952, under regulations that governed disloyal or subversive officers.[42]

Arlington Hall, Elizabeth Bentley, and the army were not the only banes of Lee's existence. In the spring of 1951, the US Immigration and Naturalization Service (INS) began investigating whether it could deport Ishbel to Britain under the provisions of the Subversive Control Act of October 16, 1918. This law permitted the federal government to detain and deport resident aliens found to be anarchists or threats to national security. In the midst of this investigation Alexander Scott Lee, the couple's fifth and last child, was born on March 18, 1951.[43]

While the INS moved against Ishbel, the Senate's Internal Security Subcommittee began probing into the affairs of the Institute of Pacific Relations (IPR), a think tank devoted to studying East Asia. In 1950, Senator Joseph McCarthy had accused Owen Lattimore, the longtime editor of *Pacific Affairs*, the IPR's journal, of being the most important Soviet espionage agent in the United States.[44]

The Internal Security Subcommittee picked up the threads of McCarthy's charges about IPR's alleged malignant influence on the country's China policies. Senator Pat McCarran, the subcommittee's chairman, was determined to play his part in saving what he described as "our way of life from subversion and erosion" and uncovering "who lost China." McCarran called his first witness on July 25, 1951. Bentley testified three weeks later on August 14. Lee, who had joined the IPR in 1946, figured strongly in her testimony.[45]

Although Bentley confused the IPR with the China Aid Council, the organization on whose executive committee Lee had served before joining the OSS, she did publicly repeat that he had been a member of the CPUSA: "Yes, he had been a Communist Party member. He paid his dues to me, I brought him his literature, and he was under Communist discipline. He was quite definitely a member." She also testified that he was "our most valuable source in the OSS."[46]

A little over two months after Bentley testified, the FBI's Washington field office categorized Lee as among the most dangerous men in its files. On November 6, 1951, it placed him on its Comsab (communist sabotage) and Detcom (detention communists) lists. Hoover had created these two highly secret rosters in 1949 to refine his Security Index, which already included Lee's name. Comsab concentrated on identifying communists whom the FBI deemed potential saboteurs. The bureau automatically placed Lee on this list because of his OSS service and tabbed him as among the very first to round up in a national emergency. Hoover's Detcom program created a priority list of communists supposed to present the greatest threats to national security.[47]

In September 1951, Bentley's autobiography about her years as a Soviet courier and spy handler appeared. Lee had read parts of Bentley's *Out of Bondage* when *McCall's* serialized it that spring. Reviewers roundly savaged its content and style. Columnist Joseph Alsop noted, "A deep strain of phoniness runs through her whole story"; the *New Yorker* derisively observed that it read as if Bentley "had almost as grievous a tussle with Freshman English at Vassar as she had later with her New England conscience." Alsop did concede that he did not believe that "the whole fabric is phony."[48]

Bentley's highly dramatized account featured Lee prominently. He later wrote of wanting to sue Bentley for libel, but Tommy Corcoran and William Youngman, another of the senior partners in the law firm where Lee worked, had talked him out of it: "They pointed out that all libel suits are risky at best. And that in the then prevailing climate a libel suit against a darling of the FBI and the Republican Party would be flying in the face of all odds." Corcoran and Youngman were more right than they realized.[49]

On September 12, 1948, Bentley had appeared on NBC's *Meet the Press* and declared that William Remington, a Dartmouth College– and Columbia University–educated economist who had worked for the War Production Board, was a communist. In July 1948, Bentley had told Homer Ferguson's Senate Subcommittee of the Committee on Expenditures in the Executive Departments that Remington had given her information on airplane production figures and a new method for producing rubber. She also testified that he had known her only as "Helen" and Golos as "John."[50]

Remington sued NBC for broadcasting these allegedly libelous statements and asked for $100,000 in damages. Although neither Bentley nor NBC retracted anything she said on the program, the company settled for $9,000. Remington's lawsuit, combined with his decision to appeal a loyalty board's determination that he should be fired from his job in the Commerce Department, enraged the FBI and the Department of Justice. They launched a massive investigation into his past. A federal grand jury finally indicted him after his ex-wife testified against him.[51]

On January 28, 1953, after a second trial—his first trial was rife with ethical and legal problems for the government—a jury convicted Remington of lying about having given sensitive information to Bentley and denying that he knew anything about the Young Communist League while he was at Dartmouth. A month later, a judge sentenced him to three years in the federal penitentiary at Lewisburg, Pennsylvania. Two fellow prisoners beat him to death with a brick wrapped in a sock on November 22, 1954.[52]

Corcoran and Youngman could control Lee, but they could not rein in the FBI. In the early fall of 1951, the bureau tasked its liaison agent in London to ask Britain's Security Service (MI5), whether it had any information that either of the Lees had joined the British Communist

Party when they were at Oxford. The bureau was especially interested in gathering information that the INS could use to deport Ishbel.[53]

While the FBI waited to hear from the British, Hoover asked the head of his Washington field office whether he thought his agents should reinterview Lee. Before making a recommendation, the special agent in charge reread the transcript of Lee's May 29, 1947, interview; his August 10, 1948, HUAC testimony; and the June 21, 1951, "Rebuttal of Allegations" that he had submitted to the army's adjutant general. On June 2, 1952, the special agent in charge told Hoover what he thought.[54]

He admitted that all three statements contained inconsistencies but argued that Lee, with his agile intellect and solid legal background, could explain them away as differences in recollection. Instead, the FBI had to find a way to apply "sufficient leverage to dislodge his present way of thinking concerning this matter." The lever it needed to upend him was Ishbel: "In as much as Ishbel Lee is an alien, if Bentley's allegations of her interest in Communist matters could be corroborated, since this would make her subject to deportation, it is believed that perhaps Lee would be more willing to assist in developing the facts concerning himself and her."[55]

The special agent in charge also told Hoover that his office had already taken the next steps in its investigation: "The [Washington field office] report of May 6, 1952, concerning Lee has set [sic] out leads for interviews of 17 individuals who attended Harvard University [sic] in England during the time that Lee was in attendance for the purpose of determining if there is any knowledge of him and Ishbel Lee having engaged in any Communist activities in England." The FBI had acquired a list of Rhodes scholars who had attended Oxford with Lee from the Thames Valley Police. It also tracked down a copy of a 1950 edition of Oxford University Press's *Register of Rhodes Scholars, 1903–1945*. This register, when merged with the police's roster, allowed the bureau to identify and locate Lee's Oxford classmates.[56]

In the early spring of 1952, the bureau interviewed dozens of Americans who had been with Lee at Oxford. Most of his fellow Rhodes scholars rallied around him and dismissed Elizabeth Bentley's allegations as fantastic or malicious. Their recollections of Lee were almost entirely at odds with what the bureau knew about him.[57]

John Espey, a member of Lee's class of Rhodes scholars who was also the son of a missionary and who had roomed briefly with him at the American School in Lushan, told the bureau in 1952, "It is inconceivable that anyone could accuse or consider Lee to be a Communist or pro-Soviet." Espey reported that his classmate had always been politically and socially conservative and only interested in his personal advancement as a lawyer. He also recounted Lee's drunken declaration one night in Oxford that if the United States had a royal family, it would be the Lees of Virginia.[58]

Other Rhodes scholars remembered Lee as a "stuffed shirt" who was "somewhat standoffish," a "conservative Southern gentleman" who was "on the other side of the fence from communism," and a "loyal patriot." One declared his amazement at Bentley's charges because he had always tagged Lee as politically conservative. He added that if Lee was left-wing or pro-Soviet, he kept it "a deep dark secret from the people who knew him." None of Lee's classmates seemed aware of his uncanny ability to compartmentalize and hide his thoughts and actions.[59]

Elvis Stahr, a member of the Rhodes Scholar Class of 1936 who was then dean of the University of Kentucky's law school and later secretary of the army, told the FBI that Lee "maintained the air of a 'super Virginian,' and was somewhat pompous and snobbish." He added that Lee was still "somewhat that way but much improved." Stahr also said that Bentley's charges seemed "fantastic and incomprehensible" because Lee "did not seem to be the type who would fall into the activities in which Miss Bentley claimed [he] would have engaged." He cited Lee's work for Claire Chennault as proof of his fellow Rhodes scholar's anticommunism.[60]

Murat Williams, another member of the Rhodes Scholar Class of 1936, a former roommate of Lee at Woodberry Forest, and later a US ambassador to El Salvador, painted a more nuanced portrait for the FBI. Williams traced Lee's interest in the Soviet Union back to their days at Woodberry Forest. He admitted that he and Lee had supported the Spanish loyalists against Franco. Williams also volunteered that the Lees had traveled to the Soviet Union in 1937 and confessed that he regretted not going with them. While he openly discussed Lee's interest in the Soviet Union, Williams made it clear that he believed his former roommate was not a communist and could not have been a Soviet spy. Williams, who attended the Lees' wedding, also said he knew nothing about Ishbel's activities at Oxford.[61]

Another Rhodes scholar told the FBI an altogether different story about Lee in early 1953. Daniel Joseph Boorstin, who then taught American history at the University of Chicago and became the Librarian of Congress in 1975, attended Oxford's Balliol College as a Rhodes scholar from 1934 until 1937 after graduating from Harvard University. He, like Lee, read jurisprudence and later sat for the examinations for the bachelor of arts and bachelor of civil law degrees, earning rare first-class honors in both. In August 1937 he had accompanied the Lees to the Soviet Union. After Boorstin returned to Harvard, he joined the CPUSA in 1938.[62]

The FBI interviewed Boorstin for the first time in 1947, although Lee did not come up then. Boorstin's name had appeared in the address book of Israel Halperin, who had taught mathematics briefly at Harvard in the late 1930s. After Canadian authorities began investigating Halperin as part of their probe into GRU code clerk Igor Gouzenko's espionage allegations, they turned Boorstin's name over to the bureau. He admitted to the interviewing agents that he had joined the CPUSA in 1938 but said that he had left the party in 1939 after the Soviet Union and Germany signed their nonaggression pact. He also claimed that he now had nothing but contempt for the CPUSA and no longer viewed history through the lenses of a Marxist but as a religious believer.[63]

On July 14, 1952, Boorstin, who had no reservations about giving the HUAC the names of his former classmates, testified in an executive session about Lee: "Another fellow is a fellow by the name of Duncan Lee. I would not swear to his membership in the group at Oxford, but I know he was awfully close to it, and he may have been in the group or on the verge."[64]

The FBI interviewed Daniel Boorstin about Lee on January 12, 1953, in his office at the University of Chicago. He repeated what he had told the HUAC six months before, declaring that Lee had "strong pro-Communist leanings while at Oxford" and "was a student of

Marxist theory." Although he had lost contact with Lee after Oxford, Boorstin declared adamantly that he "would find it hard to believe that Lee had not joined some organization affiliated with the Communist Party in the United States if not the Communist Party itself when Lee returned to the United States from Oxford." He based this on what he called Lee's "strong pro-Communist leanings while at Oxford." For good measure, Boorstin added that Lee had appeared "vastly interested" in Soviet affairs when they had visited the Soviet Union.[65]

The FBI also interviewed an employee of Donovan's law firm in early 1953. She described Lee as "an extremely nervous and timid individual" who, she believed, "lacked the personal courage to have been a Communist or to have engaged in espionage." She also admitted that when Lee visited Donovan and Doering, she and others had teased him about Bentley's charges because they thought they were "preposterous," but they stopped after he became "quite upset and uncomfortable."[66]

The bureau interviewed other people from Lee's past besides Rhodes scholars and a former colleague. In early 1952, Hoover ordered his New Haven field office to find people who had known the couple in 1938 and 1939 while Lee attended Yale Law School. In late February, the FBI interviewed James Osborn. A Yale literature professor, Osborn had employed Ishbel to do research for him on eighteenth-century periodicals. He was dismissive of both. Although he declared that he knew nothing about their politics, Osborn dismissed the Lees as "mousey persons who never impressed him as having any particular aggressiveness or ability."[67]

The FBI also talked to Katharine and Benjamin Christie Nangle, the Lees' New Haven landlords. The Nangles repeated that the Lees had been "decidedly Communistic." Yet two informants who were former members of the CPUSA in New Haven when the Lees lived there said that they did not remember them.[68]

The Senate's Internal Security Subcommittee, however, did remember Duncan Lee. Robert Morris, its chief counsel, was trying to locate him in May 1952 at Corcoran's law firm. The firm found these telephone calls highly disturbing. More testimony and more bad publicity were the last things Tommy Corcoran wanted. He liked the shadows and preferred to manipulate and channel power and influence while operating in them.[69]

Though not directly tarred by Lee's August 1948 appearance before the HUAC, because of the adverse publicity his testimony had generated, Corcoran's law firm had not emerged unscathed. George Dixon, who wrote a nationally syndicated column called "Washington Scene," had underscored Lee's ties to Corcoran in a piece he wrote in August 1948 shortly after Lee's HUAC testimony: "Well, what do you suppose Duncan Lee does for a living now? He's with the law firm of the ubiquitous gentleman once supposed to be the second closest to the late F.D.R., the fellow credited with the ability to get more profitable favors out of the White House than any other operator—Thomas G. (Tommy the Cork) Corcoran."[70]

By 1952 Corcoran, who always knew which way the political winds were blowing in Washington, had calculated that Dwight Eisenhower would become the next president of the United States and that the Republican Party would win control of the Congress in that fall's elections. Their victory would ensure that the anticommunist fever gripping the country increased in intensity before burning itself out. It would also mean that Corcoran, a Democrat who made his living chiefly through lobbying, would have to ingratiate himself with a Republican-dominated government.[71]

Against this political backdrop, Corcoran had already decided that Lee could no longer work for him. On March 14, 1952, the US Bureau of Customs had questioned Lee at New York City's Idlewild—later John F. Kennedy—Airport. During this interview, he admitted that although he still had a desk there, he was no longer a member of Corcoran's law firm.[72]

Corcoran had not thrown Lee to the wolves, though. Donovan, who refused to admit publicly that his trusted aide had betrayed him and who badly wanted to become the next director of the CIA, had pressured Corcoran to find Lee another job. After months of trying, he found him a position as a lawyer with the American International Underwriters Corporation in New York City, which in 1967 became known as the American International Group (AIG). William

Youngman had left Corcoran's law firm in the fall of 1950 to become the president of C. V. Starr and Company, the parent company for the Starr insurance companies, including American International. Youngman, always fond of Lee, agreed to hire him.[73]

Corcoran and Donovan did not want Lee in the United States, however. They wanted him far away and out of sight. By early 1953, Joseph McCarthy had taken over as the chairman of the Senate's Permanent Investigating Subcommittee of the Government Operations Committee. McCarthyism was about to reach its boiling point.[74]

Ironically, Lee's espionage, together with the FBI's and the HUAC's failure to bring him and the others Bentley accused of spying to justice, had helped lay the groundwork for McCarthy's rise. Many who paid attention to Lee's and the others' testimony before the HUAC in August 1948 believed that they had not only lied about being Soviet spies but gotten away with it. The collective perjury and almost complete escape of the accused had left deep bitterness and lingering suspicion in their wake.

By the time McCarthy stepped forward at the 1950 Lincoln Day dinner in Wheeling, West Virginia, with the astonishing claim that he held in his hand a list of 205 known communists inside the State Department, Americans were inclined to believe him. By then, the Soviets had exploded their first atomic bomb on August 28, 1949, and Mao Zedong, standing on the great Tiananmen gate, had announced the formation of the People's Republic of China on October 1. These events seemed to confirm to many Americans that traitors had undermined their country's security from within, just as Elizabeth Bentley had said.[75]

McCarthy, in search of a cause that would impress his Wisconsin constituents and bring him to the attention of the media, decided to capitalize on this belief, especially in the aftermath of Alger Hiss's conviction on two counts of perjury in January 1950, the arrests of a ring of atomic spies that included Harry Gold and Klaus Fuchs, and the outbreak of the Korean War that same year.[76]

By 1953, this fear had created an extremely dangerous environment for anyone accused of espionage. On June 19, Julius and Ethel Rosenberg died in the electric chair after their conviction for spying for the Soviet Union two years earlier. On July 30, 1953, although they had recently bought a new home in Washington, Lee and his family arrived abruptly in Hamilton, Bermuda, to start a new life. Lee had accepted Youngman's offer to become an attorney in American International's Hamilton office.[77]

He was now safe and employed. In no time, he found a house, enrolled his children in the local schools, and settled down to a quiet life as a lawyer for one of the British colony's biggest insurance companies. He needed a new life, one not constantly haunted by nightmares of arrest and execution. These nightly visitations, mixed with the alcohol he now relied on and the two packs of L&M cigarettes he smoked each day, kept him emotionally on a razor's edge. To his children, whom he loved, he often seemed remote and unpredictable. It was time to turn the page on all that.[78]

By Christmas, however, he found himself in greater danger than before he moved to Bermuda.

ELEVEN

ISHMAEL

The Lees' new life in Bermuda seemed idyllic. For the first two months, they lived on Spice Hill, near the island's spectacular South Shore beaches. With his family safely settled, Lee bought a motorcycle, joined the Coral Beach and Tennis Club, and immersed himself in his new work as the vice president, general counsel, and secretary for American International Underwriters Overseas Inc. On August 13, 1953, he described for Tommy Corcoran his new life: "We are on a hilltop overlooking the South Shore and open to the prevailing South wind. Behind us is a tropical garden (bananas, papayas and the like). We have a Morris station wagon, drivers' licenses, and nicely developing tans. The principal vileness consists of the fiercely biting land ants and the cockroach, a brute much larger than anything in Washington, which flies! . . . I feel more relaxed and unworried than I have in fifteen years."[1]

Two months later, he and Ishbel rented "Clermont," a large, rambling eighteenth-century house. Although something of a wreck, it offered spectacular views of Hamilton's harbor and oozed old-world charm. In no time, the Lee children realized they were living in a paradise. Their parents agreed. Lee had a well-paying job, and the British colony offered nonstop socializing and overflowing alcohol. It also put 825 miles between them and J. Edgar Hoover.[2]

That was all about to change. Contacts inside the Immigration and Naturalization Service had tipped the FBI off as early as July 2,

1953, that the Lees were thinking about leaving the United States for Bermuda. The bureau knew the couple faced two steep hurdles: his passport had expired, and Ishbel had been unable to get a permit to reenter the United States. Lee did not need a valid passport to travel to Bermuda if he stayed there fewer than six months, but Ishbel, as a resident alien and a British national, needed a reentry permit to return to the United States. The Internal Security Act of 1950 had given the INS the power to bar aliens who were suspected communists from coming into the country. It also prohibited American members of the Communist Party of the United States of America from applying for passports.[3]

On July 8, R. B. Hood, head of the FBI's Washington field office, had asked the State Department's Passport Office to notify him immediately if Lee applied for a new passport or inquired about any travel restrictions to Bermuda. Hood knew that Lee had asked the INS about what penalties Ishbel would face if she left the United States without a valid reentry permit, but he did not know that the Lees had decided to go to Bermuda anyway. They left for Hamilton after consulting with an immigration attorney who warned them that the INS would never give Ishbel a reentry permit. She could, though, as a British citizen, enter and stay in Bermuda, then one of Queen Elizabeth II's colonies.[4]

Almost two weeks after the Lees landed in Bermuda, the FBI learned that they had left Washington. An agent making a routine inspection of Lee's passport file discovered a notation that he was in Bermuda.[5]

Lee already had a bad history with Ruth Shipley, the long-serving chief of the State Department's Passport Office. Shipley was a titanic creature of the Washington bureaucracy, a new breed of administrator/empire builder who wielded an astonishing amount of unfettered power. On July 22, 1949, she had given him a new passport to travel to China. Five months later, Donald L. Nicholson, chief of the State Department's Security Division, acting on information supplied by the FBI, pointed out to her that Elizabeth Bentley had testified before Congress a year earlier that Lee had been a communist and a Soviet spy. Hearing this, Shipley vowed that he would never get another passport.[6]

In Ruth Bielaski Shipley, Lee found an enemy as dangerous, cunning, and relentless as J. Edgar Hoover. A daughter of a Methodist minister, she grew up with strong convictions about her faith and her country. She passed the civil service examination at eighteen and became a clerk in the US Patent Office. In 1914, she joined the State Department, just as World War I was erupting in Europe. The fighting brought limitations on Americans' rights to travel overseas. Although these restrictions ended in 1921, the government had firmly set the precedent that it could curb Americans' right to travel abroad if doing so was in the best interests of the country. While Americans did not need a passport to leave the United States between 1921 and 1942, other countries required them to have one to enter. In 1926, Congress passed the Passport Act, giving the State Department exclusive authority to issue these documents. It also limited their validity to two years.[7]

These rules gave an enormous amount of power to the individual who controlled access to passports. That person was Ruth Shipley, who, as Hoover had done at the Department of Justice, steadily climbed the State Department's career ladder by attending personally to every detail, working untold hours, and making herself seem indispensable, especially to her supervisors. Promoted to chief of the Passport Division in 1927, a position she held for the next twenty-eight years, Shipley was another self-appointed guardian of an America that needed salvation from God-denying radicals and their dangerous influences.[8]

The coming of the Cold War only augmented her power, self-importance, and stature. In its October 1951 issue, *Reader's Digest* emphasized the key role she played in deciding who could leave the country: "No American can go abroad without her authorization. She decides whether an applicant is entitled to a passport and also whether he would be a hazard to Uncle Sam's security or create prejudice against the United States by unbecoming conduct." A month later, *Time* declared her "the most invulnerable, most unfirable, most feared and most admired career woman in Government." Dean Acheson, acknowledging her power and independence, called Shipley's division the "Queendom of Passports."[9]

By 1953, she presided over an office that occupied six floors of Washington's Winder Building and numbered over two hundred employees. Shipley also oversaw the workings of satellite passport offices in New York, Boston, Chicago, New Orleans, and San Francisco and in three hundred posts overseas. Known as "Ma" inside the State Department, she kept files on more than 12 million people.[10]

Shipley preferred to work inside the bureaucracy and said very little publicly, but she was absolutely certain about her mission: "One thing I believe in is refusing passports to Communists. They have been working against us for a long time." To keep them from getting these documents, she worked very closely with the FBI, though she concealed her office's relationship with the bureau from the rest of the State Department. Her terms were clear: she would not allow the FBI to quote from any of her passport files in its memoranda to other offices in the State Department.[11]

Lee had managed to avoid her until February 1952, when he applied to renew his passport. As Corcoran explained in a letter to Shipley on February 18, Lee needed to travel to London and Paris to represent CAT in its appeal before the British Privy Council. A week later, Corcoran sent Shipley copies of several of the character affidavits that Lee had filed with the army's adjutant general in 1951 in his unsuccessful battle over his Reserve commission.[12]

Lee's anticommunist work in China and sterling character testimonials meant absolutely nothing to Shipley. Caring only about Bentley's claims that he had been a communist and spied for the Soviet Union, she planned to deny Lee's application. Shipley relented only under pressure from the department's assistant secretary for administration, who feared that the State Department would take the fall if CAT lost its appeal and Mao Zedong got his hands on the contested airplanes. She agreed to give Lee a tightly restricted passport but placed a memorandum in his file that made it clear his case was far from over: "Inasmuch as Lee has filed a complete affidavit with us as part of his request for a renewal of his passport, and could be held for perjury if it later developed that his statements were false, I saw no reason why we should not issue the passport for a limited period."[13]

On February 25, 1952, she gave him a passport that expired on March 25, 1952. Before he got it, Shipley made him hand-write on his application that he was not, and had never been, a member of the CPUSA or Earl Browder's Communist Political Association. The next day, she asked the HUAC to send her Lee's August 10, 1948, testimony. Shipley was preparing to block his next move.[14]

In the meantime, the FBI had continued to feed the State Department's Office of Security, which acted as the department's liaison to the bureau, a steady diet of negative information about Lee—his file there contained at least thirteen bureau reports on him—and asked that office's acting director to "advise this Bureau in the event that Lee files an application for a passport or makes inquiry about his status." While Shipley watched and waited in Washington, the American consulate in Hamilton kept close tabs on Lee through a source inside American International.[15]

On December 21, 1953, Shipley finally got the news she had been waiting for. That same day, the chief of Bermuda's Criminal Investigative Division served Lee with a deportation order that gave him only ten days to leave the island. The colony's Governor's Council had decided that he was an undesirable alien. Although he could not see it, Lee could feel the hidden hand of J. Edgar Hoover guiding him to the airport.

Lee immediately appealed the deportation order and asked the American consulate for help. He was not aware that the consulate had been monitoring him since he arrived on the island. When it received his appeal, the Bermuda government queried the consulate about "whether Lee is still considered [a] security risk by [the] FBI and [the] Department."[16]

The State Department's answer arrived the next evening: "Dept still considers security risk. Ppt [passport] not needed for return [to] US and not repeat not authorized for travel elsewhere." Although the telegram was signed "Dulles," the initials "RS" appeared underneath that name. John Foster Dulles, who had replaced Dean Acheson when Dwight Eisenhower became the president, was the secretary of state, but Ruth Shipley was the queen of passports.[17]

Lee would always claim that the Bermuda government had knuckled under FBI pressure. The truth was far more complicated and nuanced.

Between December 4 and 8, 1953, President Eisenhower, British prime minister Winston Churchill, and French president Joseph Laniel met in Bermuda to discuss, among other pressing international issues, meeting with the new leaders of the Soviet Union after Joseph Stalin's death that March. Before the summit, the British Security Service had visited the colony to ensure that it was safe, and it took a special interest in any aliens living on the island. While there, one of its officers passed on information to the Bermuda police about Lee's past ties to the Soviets. The FBI had sent this information to MI5 when the bureau's liaison agent stationed in London had asked the Security Service for any information it had about the Lees' involvement with communism during their student days at Oxford.[18]

At first, American International thought that because of its size, influence, and importance to the local economy—in January 1954, its Hamilton office employed 140 people—it could pressure the Bermuda government to rescind the deportation order. Its intervention failed, but in a surprising bureaucratic twist, the American consulate decided to support Lee's appeal for a delay based on the general principle that he was an American citizen and deserved due process. The Bermuda authorities agreed to delay his deportation for thirty days while the company tried to clear him. In the meantime, William Youngman, president of American International, turned to Tommy Corcoran, his old friend and former law partner, for help in Washington.[19]

On January 26, 1954, Corcoran had a tête-à-tête with Ruth Shipley. She recorded their conversation the next day in a memorandum to Scott MacLeod, a former FBI agent and disciple of Joseph McCarthy, who headed the State Department's Bureau of Inspection, Security, and Consular Affairs. MacLeod kept McCarthy's signed photograph on his desk and hated communists and radicals almost as much as his Wisconsin mentor.[20]

Shipley lied to Corcoran when she denied knowing anything about Lee's threatened deportation, but she admitted her certainty that Lee was a security risk. Corcoran, in a burst of candor—and probably a calculated move to curry favor with one of the State Department's most powerful officials—wavered and told Shipley that his own feelings about Lee were conflicted. According to the memorandum she sent to MacLeod,

> [Corcoran] said that he had never written a letter of endorsement for Lee, although many of his close associates had, and he never had been quite sure about him. In recounting the various efforts to have Lee placed where he could earn a living for himself and his family, he said that he had had Ernest Cuneo [a well-known New York City attorney and former OSS officer] read the published [HUAC] testimony of Lee and evaluate it for him. He said Cuneo was unable to give him a real clearance of Lee from his testimony, as he saw in it traces of Communist-disciplined conduct—drug store meetings, etc.[21]

Corcoran also explained to her that attorneys had advised Ishbel not to apply for American citizenship while she lived in the United States. Shipley snidely suggested that the Lees could move to Britain. The British, she claimed, seemed to have no objections to communists. She ended her memorandum by noting, "Mr. Corcoran insisted several times that our conversation was confidential, which, from my point of view, means that such information as he gave me is usable to the government's interest."[22]

While Corcoran was meeting with Shipley, William Youngman was meeting with State Department officials in Washington. They explained that the Bermuda government wanted to deport Lee because of Bentley's allegations. Youngman scoffed, pointing out that all her claims about Lee had been refuted before a federal grand jury and Congress. Unlike Corcoran, Youngman displayed no outward reservations about Lee. Although not convinced, the State Department did agree to ask the Bermuda government to give Lee a second thirty-day extension on the island.[23]

On February 1, 1954, Youngman flew to Bermuda and met with Robert Streeper, the American consul general. Paul McNutt, the former governor of Indiana and American International's corporate-wide general counsel, and Clayton Seitz, the president of the company, accompanied him to this meeting. Youngman assured Streeper that before hiring Lee, the insurance giant had been well aware of Bentley's claims, all of which had been disproved. He also cited Lee's outstanding anticommunist work for Claire Chennault and Whiting Willauer.[24]

The next morning, the delegation met with Oswald Raynor Arthur, Bermuda's colonial secretary. Arthur blamed the United States for Lee's predicament. According to Streeper, "The Colonial Secretary stated that the local government had based its decision solely on information received from agencies of the United States Government. [He] closed the interview by stating that he would be glad to cancel the deportation order on assurances from the United States that Mr. Lee was no longer a security risk." Arthur, observing diplomatic niceties, did not tell Youngman and the others about the State Department's telegram confirming that Lee was a security threat.[25]

Streeper, a career diplomat, sympathized with Lee's plight. On February 5 he sent a dispatch to the State Department that said as much. In it he underscored the hardship Lee's family would suffer if he were deported and ventured that Lee was a victim of McCarthyism.[26]

Shipley refused to budge. On February 27, 1954, the Bermuda police escorted Lee to the airport and watched him board a flight to New York City. As his plane lifted off, Lee reflected on how deluded he had been to believe that Bermuda would offer him a peaceful safe haven.[27]

That night, he found himself exiled to Room 1301 in the Parkside Hotel, his new home. Unwilling to cut him loose or back away from his statements about Lee during his talks with Streeper and Arthur, Youngman granted him an unlimited leave of absence from the Hamilton office and let him work out of the insurance company's New York City offices. His responsibilities there, as Lee later described them, consisted of routine and unchallenging "made work." Still, it paid the bills at Clermont and kept him and his family afloat.[28]

On March 4, Corcoran met with Shipley again in her office. He had called the day before to request an appointment before he left for New Orleans to handle some business for the United Fruit Company. He wanted to bring her an update on Lee's case. Their conversation was wide-ranging. Corcoran began by theorizing that Lee's troubles had grown out of the bitter rivalry between J. Edgar Hoover and William Donovan, which Shipley instantly dismissed. He then repeated his doubts about Lee. Shipley captured his reservations in another memorandum for the record:

> Mr. Corcoran said, in considering Lee's case from the position of Mr. Youngman, who was a client of his, that it was becoming apparent that it was more difficult to believe, without question and wholeheartedly, Mr. Lee's story about the matters charged against him by Miss Bentley. Corcoran felt that he himself and others could not be quite satisfied that everything was all right. I gathered that Mr. Corcoran had a pretty frank talk with Mr. Lee and indicated that he should examine his position with a very critical eye and see whether he was putting the company in a position of employing someone who might be a serious risk.[29]

Corcoran also hinted that Lee might apply for a passport and then appeal Shipley's inevitable denial to the newly created Passport Board of Appeals. She brushed this possibility aside, saying that Lee would first have to swear that he had never been a member of the CPUSA. If he lied, Shipley warned, she would then be forced to refer his case to the Department of Justice's Criminal Division and ask that it prosecute him for perjury. She saw no need to tell Corcoran that the board of appeals existed only on paper. It had been established to deflect maverick senator Wayne Morse's criticisms about Shipley, but its procedures made it little more than a kangaroo court.[30]

After listening to Corcoran, Shipley, always a minister's daughter, spoke from her own pulpit and lectured him that the FBI felt Lee had been dishonest and that "if he felt completely innocent, it would be well to go down there and talk with them and that, if he was not, it was about time he did make up his mind to come clean." She concluded her memorandum by observing, "I gathered that no one of the persons now concerned with Duncan Lee's employment are too sure of the truth of his story, which seems to get a great deal of its strength from the fact that General Donovan still believes absolutely in this man. I believe that if Mr. Corcoran told Mr. Lee what he tells me he said to Mr. Lee that the latter must be having a very uneasy time making up his mind what his next step is to be."[31]

That same day, the FBI, worried that Ishbel might somehow slip back into the United States, asked the INS to post a lookout notice for her at all its offices.[32]

If Corcoran had a conversation with Lee about confessing, it had no effect. Lee stuck to his claims of innocence, and Corcoran, with mere suspicions that Lee had lied about the true nature of his relationship with Bentley, had no concrete evidence to impeach him. There was nothing left to do but fight on and try to disentangle Lee from Shipley's web. He and Lee were too closely identified with one another to do anything less.

On July 12, 1954, William Youngman informed Shipley that Lee was going to apply for a passport. American International needed to send him to London to work on some pressing legal questions. Youngman reported that Paul McNutt, the insurance company's general counsel, had met with J. Edgar Hoover about Lee and offered to bring him in for questioning if the FBI wanted to meet with them. Youngman also promised to make Lee available to Shipley if she wanted to quiz him.[33]

Shipley remained unmoved. In another for-the-record memorandum, she noted that Hoover had refused McNutt's request to meet with Lee. She also made it clear that she deeply resented American International's attempts to use her office as a courtroom to clear Lee and enlist others in the government to help him. Corcoran had informed her that he planned to discuss Lee's case with William Rogers, the deputy attorney general of the United States. In a flash of anger, Shipley recorded her reactions to what she deemed McNutt's and Corcoran's endless meddling: "I am of the view that we shall have to move along carefully to insure [sic] that this case be determined on the real merits and not on some biased and restricted presentation by either Mr. McNutt or Mr. Corcoran to high officials who will not be acquainted with the many ramifications of this case."[34]

Shipley decided to teach those "high officials" a lesson. She sat down and wrote a letter to the Department of Justice, asking it to prosecute Lee for lying to her, a federal official, and on his expected passport renewal application about not being, or ever having been, a member of the CPUSA. At the time, each offense then carried up to five years in federal prison. She then placed the letter in her desk and waited.[35]

On July 19, Lee applied for a passport to travel to London. Shipley made him attach to his application an affidavit stating, "I am not, and have never been, a member of the Communist Party."[36]

Youngman and McNutt were not the only ones pressuring Ruth Shipley to relent and grant Lee a passport. Edmund, by then retired from Chatham Hall since 1949 and living in Washington, tried to enlist the help of a US senator on his son's behalf. During the second week of July, he visited Harry F. Byrd of Virginia, the powerful chairman of the Senate's Finance Committee, and briefed him on his son's application for a passport. Shipley, a master at fighting back, called to remind one of Harry Byrd's aides about Elizabeth Bentley's claims. Afterward, the aide assured Shipley that the conservative senator had no interest in forcing her hand.[37]

Tired of the pressure and believing she had Lee trapped, Shipley decided to strike. She opened her desk, removed the letter she had written almost two months earlier, and had it hand-delivered on September 10, 1954, to Warren Olney III, the assistant attorney general in charge of the Department of Justice's Criminal Division. She asked him to prosecute Lee for lying to obtain a passport.[38]

Shipley still had to contend with Edmund. Now seventy-seven years old, he was not done arguing his son's case. On September 14, he came face-to-face with Shipley in her office. Both, reflecting their unwavering faiths, were wholly convinced of the righteousness of their causes. Although Edmund agreed that Bentley had told the truth about a number of people she had accused of working for the Soviets, he claimed that his son's case was different. He repeated this in a sermonizing letter he sent to Shipley the next day: "There was no evidence in any other case that Miss Bentley was actually motivated by revenge in making the charge. In Duncan's case, he and his wife at first met her advances with kindness, but as soon as they came to know what kind of person she was, though not suspecting her of Communism, they broke off the relationship, and in so doing, made her a revengeful enemy."[39]

In the meantime, Shipley's request that Lee be prosecuted had landed in the Department of Justice's Internal Security Division. On October 19, she got the answer she did not want: the chief of the Subversive Activities Section wrote to her, "Prosecution of the subject is not possible at the present time." Still, the letter assured her that "the investigation will continue in an active status in an effort to develop the necessary evidence." Neither Shipley nor the Department of Justice's lawyers knew about the highly classified evidence of Lee's spying for the Soviet Union uncovered by the Venona program. And without that proof, it remained a case of his word against Bentley's. The National Security Agency and the FBI were not willing to acknowledge the top-secret program's existence, much less its extraordinarily sensitive methods, which were still very much in use when Shipley sent her letter to the Department of Justice in 1954.[40]

More bad news for Shipley came a month later and for the same reason—lack of concrete evidence. On November 17, William F. Tompkins, assistant attorney general for the Internal Security Division, told Hoover that based solely on Bentley's claims, Lee could not be prosecuted for failing to register with the Subversive Activities Control Board as a spy for the Soviet Union or for violating the country's espionage laws.[41]

Elizabeth Bentley was not going to give Hoover and Shipley what they needed. She was falling apart emotionally. Her swift descent had begun shortly after her public coming out in 1948. Although her many critics always claimed otherwise, she had not fallen easily into her public role as a communist apostate. Her zenith had come when she served as Jacob Golos's right hand. Since those halcyon days, Bentley had struggled to remake herself and come to terms with widespread ridicule and denunciation as a psychopathic liar. Under tremendous stress, she had followed Whittaker Chambers and Louis Budenz in making that short leap from communism to Christianity. With Monsignor Fulton Sheen approvingly looking on, she had converted to Catholicism on November 5, 1948.[42]

After trying unsuccessfully to earn her living on the lecture circuit, Bentley accepted a job in September 1949 as a political science and sociology instructor at Mundelein College in Chicago. Her stay at the all-women's Catholic school on Lake Michigan was predictably short and stormy. The college administration accused her of practicing "loose morals." Bentley, who liked calling herself a devout Catholic more than living like one, abused alcohol and lived with a man who was not her husband. After barely one semester, the college fired her.[43]

Bentley spent the next year absorbed with testifying in court against William Remington and completing her autobiography. When *Out of Bondage* failed to sell, Bentley needed money. She turned to the FBI for help. On July 15, 1952, the bureau began sending her $50 a week. Three months later, when she could no longer pay her bills, the bureau gave her a lump sum of $500. As Alan Belmont, head of the Domestic Intelligence Division, spelled out in a memorandum to D. Milton "Mickey" Ladd, Hoover's assistant, "Her current indebtedness is causing considerable worry and is jeopardizing our use of her as a source of information on a wide variety of matters."[44]

The FBI's worries about her multiplied. That spring, Bentley's married handyman and lover had beaten her senseless—he hit her so hard during a drunken argument that two of her teeth pierced the lower part of her face—and she had been in three car wrecks. On August 26, the head of the bureau's New York City field office told Hoover that Bentley was becoming increasingly neurotic and drinking heavily.[45]

At times her growing instability bordered on lunacy. In 1954, Bentley somehow landed another teaching job, this time at the College of the Sacred Heart in Grand Coteau, Louisiana. While there, she contacted the FBI's New Orleans office, demanding that its agents protect her from the Huey Long machine that still dominated Louisiana's politics nearly two decades after the "Kingfish's" assassination. The special agent in charge in New Orleans characterized her in a May memorandum to J. Edgar Hoover as "irrational and illogical and her talk impressed [the agent who took her call] as being that of a demented person."[46]

More trouble followed. In June 1955, the Internal Revenue Service (IRS) froze Bentley's bank account because she had not paid her federal income taxes. Bentley's misconduct and mental imbalance, the FBI candidly admitted, made her harder and harder to question. A field report from 1955 underscored this: "Bentley appeared somewhat hysterical, wept occasionally during conversation, and expressed herself incoherently when trying to relate circumstances of incidents in which she was involved."[47]

At about the same time as the IRS's investigation, Harvey Marshall Matusow—a former communist, FBI informant, and yet another of Bentley's lovers—testified before the Senate Internal Security Subcommittee that she had confessed to him that to keep herself in demand, she had to invent new revelations. Matusow later admitted to being a habitual liar, but the bureau, for a time, took his allegations against Bentley seriously. Since she had testified at Lee's HUAC hearing, FBI agents had watched her steadily embellish and exaggerate her stories in the courtroom, before Congress, and in her autobiography. Matusow's attack only added to her paranoia and convinced her that the communists, too, were out to destroy her. She may have been correct. Although neither she nor the FBI knew it, the Soviets monitored her whereabouts until at least 1955.[48]

Despite such mounting difficulties, the FBI had never doubted her basic claims. As early as November 1953, J. Edgar Hoover publicly underscored the bureau's faith in her when he told the Senate's Internal Security Subcommittee, "All [the] information furnished by Miss Bentley which was susceptible to check, has proven to be correct."[49]

Between April 24, 1951, and September 25, 1954, the FBI interviewed her six times about Lee. From the outset, its agents relied heavily on the CIA to find classified OSS documents that pertained to Bentley's claims against him. The CIA, though, warned the FBI that the general nature of her allegations and the challenge of piecing together the OSS's old files would likely hamper its search. This was especially true when the FBI asked the agency to find documents about such broad topics as "anti-Soviet work by [the] OSS in Europe" and "liberals in Rumania, Bulgaria, and other Balkan countries opposed to post-war Russian domination carrying on secret negotiations with OSS in Switzerland [and] OSS groups stationed in Istanbul ultimately intended for operations in the Balkans." These topics derived from the statements Bentley had made about Lee on November 30, 1945, at the FBI's New York City field office.[50]

Further complicating the CIA's task was the simple fact that Lee had never given her any OSS reports. His 1942 decision not to pass to Bentley any documents may have saved his life. A May 28, 1952, interview demonstrated this graphically when two FBI agents showed her an OSS report that discussed Donovan's plan to establish an open OSS presence in Moscow in exchange for an openly acknowledged NKVD office in Washington. Lee had first told her about Donovan's proposal in January 1944 and kept her updated about it throughout that winter, but he had always done so orally. When Bentley read one of the OSS's actual reports about the plan, the best she could muster was that it "was in substance similar to the information she had received from Julius Joseph, a deputy chief and economist in the OSS's Far Eastern Division, and Duncan Lee."[51]

Another example took place on July 24, 1953, when a CIA officer showed her an OSS document that discussed Operation Sparrow, the OSS's disastrous mission that air-dropped three of its men into Hungary on March 15, 1944. The Americans had hoped to detach that country from its military alliance with Germany. Instead, Hitler's Gestapo arrested all three agents shortly after they landed. The Germans invaded Hungary four days later. While in the Secretariat, Lee had access to the operation's plans as well as cables about its failure. Once again, Bentley conceded that she had never seen the document; she could only say "that sometime in 1944 Lee told her essentially the same story." Frustrated and confused, she then highlighted a basic weakness that Lee or anyone else who had served in the OSS and given her classified information could use against her in a courtroom: "She stated that she had heard so much about OSS operations during and after the war that it was difficult for her to recall just when she did hear about the incident or a version of it. Bentley was reasonably sure, however, that Lee told her about it and that she in turn told it to Joseph Katz." In fact, she was correct—Lee had told her about Operation Sparrow—but the only people who could prove it were in Moscow.[52]

The FBI understood that in an espionage trial, the Department of Justice's lawyers would have to prove Lee's guilt "beyond a reasonable doubt," a much higher standard of proof than Bentley's claim of being "reasonably sure." Any competent defense lawyer would shred her on the witness stand, and the bureau knew it. And unlike Whittaker Chambers, she had no secret cache of documents that she could produce to show that she had not been lying. She had only a memory ravaged by time and alcohol.[53]

The FBI's interview with James R. Murphy on September 28, 1954, badly crippled whatever hopes J. Edgar Hoover still harbored about using Bentley against Lee. Murphy had served in the OSS as a special assistant to Donovan and later as chief of X-2, its counterintelligence branch. Donovan had brought Murphy into his intelligence service in August 1941 for a specific purpose: to keep the knives out of his back. Murphy's British counterparts had rated him the best US intelligence officer they met during World War II.[54]

Murphy gave the FBI decidedly mixed information. He confirmed that Lee had access to most of the OSS's secrets but pointed out that the organization's leaders considered him completely trustworthy. Murphy both confirmed and dismissed what Bentley had alleged. On the one hand, he said she was right about the OSS's troubles with Ambassador Carlton Hayes in Spain, that the Sparrow mission to Hungary had been betrayed, possibly by a leak in Turkey, that Donovan might have been briefed on the atomic bomb project at Oak Ridge, and that Lee's aborted trip to China in 1943 had something to do with Tai Li, Chiang Kai-shek's chief of intelligence. On the other hand, Murphy said that he knew of no anti-Soviet operations undertaken by the OSS, that Donovan's plans for an exchange with the NKVD were well known, especially inside the US Army, and that the OSS operated openly in Turkey. After weighing his statements, the bureau rated Murphy as more a liability than an asset.[55]

Bentley's fading memory and Murphy's mixed recollections added to the FBI's predicament. The bureau's plans to arrest Joseph Katz had fared no better. In 1953, Katz left Paris and moved to Haifa, Israel. The FBI tracked him down by placing a mail cover on his brother, who lived in New York City. With the help of the CIA, the bureau planned to lure Katz aboard an American boat in international waters and bring him back to the United States. An enraged Hoover vetoed the joint operation after the CIA talked directly to the Department of Justice about the plan.[56]

While the FBI struggled to build a prosecutable case against him, Lee appeared before another federal grand jury. On September 23, 1954, he went to Camden, New Jersey, and repeated the same denials he had been making since the FBI interviewed him more than seven years before. Congress's passage of the Immunity Act of 1954 had led to the empaneling of grand juries in Camden and Washington, DC. The act gave federal prosecutors the option of immunizing grand jury witnesses testifying in espionage and subversion cases. But in exchange for their freedom, these witnesses could no longer assert their Fifth Amendment right not to incriminate themselves. Lee, who had never taken the Fifth, sailed through unharmed.[57]

In the wake of his successful appearance in Camden, Lee wrote to William Tompkins at the Internal Security Division on November 2, 1954, asking that he be allowed to return to Bermuda. He pointed out that he had not seen his family since late February and could not return to them until the US government assured the Bermuda authorities that he was not a security threat. A little over a month later, Tompkins replied that the department had no plans to recall him as a witness before the federal grand jury still sitting in Camden. Lee immediately turned Tompkins's reply over to Gordon B. Tweedy, vice president of C. V. Starr and Company, American International's parent company. Tweedy sent a copy of Tompkins's letter to Bermuda's colonial secretary and asked him to readmit Lee.[58]

That same day, December 10, 1954, an even more powerful supporter intervened on Lee's behalf. William J. Donovan, who had continued to monitor his wartime aide's troubles, asked the president of Bermuda's largest independent bank to pressure the local government. Donovan assured the banker that Sir William Stephenson, the famous "Intrepid" who had directed British intelligence in the United States during World War II and now lived in Bermuda, also backed Lee's return.[59]

Tompkins's letter, coupled with the pressure, worked. The Bermuda government relented after the State Department notified it that the "U.S. has no objection." On December 22, 1954, Lee left his job in New York City and arrived in Hamilton for a holiday visit. During his exile in New York City, Ruth Shipley had continued to receive updates on his whereabouts and his efforts to return to Bermuda. Although she still refused to give him a passport, he did not need one for such a brief stay.[60]

Sensing that Lee was about to slip through its fingers again, the FBI made another big push to prove Bentley's charges. In January 1955, the bureau's New Haven office tracked down Nathan Sherman and Lena Halpern, two self-admitted members of the CPUSA who had known the Lees there in 1938 and 1939. Sherman and Halpern were two of the fourteen "decidedly red" people whom Katharine Nangle named to the FBI in August 1940 as having visited the Lees at her house at 23 Livingston Street.[61]

Both Sherman and Halpern characterized the Lees, particularly Ishbel, as "leftist." Sherman described Lee as having a "mousey personality" and being "somewhat anemic" but as captivated by the Spanish Civil War. Although he had the "impression" that Lee may have been a member of the CPUSA, he could not recall his attending any party meetings. Halpern reported that Ishbel was "quite sold on Communism" but added that she would have been greatly surprised if Lee had agreed completely with Ishbel's views. When the agents pressed her about the Lees' memberships in the CPUSA, Halpern replied that she had not been in a position "to be looking at [party] cards." Two other CPUSA members who, according to Katharine Nangle, had frequently met with the Lees told the FBI that they did not remember them.[62]

While the FBI searched desperately for evidence other than the priceless Venona to back up Bentley's charges, Lee enjoyed his reunion with Ishbel and their five children. On March 14, 1955, he returned to his small room at the Parkside Hotel in New York City.[63]

Although the authorities had once again forced Lee to leave Bermuda, his visit had established an important precedent. His employer immediately seized upon this and bombarded Ruth Shipley with urgent requests that she give him a passport. William Youngman, American International's president, who admired Lee's legal skills, was especially eager to send him to work on some knotty problems that had arisen in the insurance conglomerate's London office.[64]

After Shipley balked, Youngman met with Bermuda governor Sir Alexander Hood on April 1, 1955. Sir Alexander, whom Winston

Churchill's personal physician described as "a full-blooded red-faced Scot, with no neck to speak of," was a graduate of the University of Edinburgh's medical school and the former director general of the British army's Medical Services. In the army, Hood had developed a keen dislike for rule-bound civil servants. In making difficult decisions, he preferred to rely on what he called his common sense.[65]

Sir Alexander expressed great sympathy for Lee and his family but said that the sole issue was Bermuda's security. Some American agency had to provide assurances that Lee was not a security threat to the colony.[66]

Ten days later, Tommy Corcoran hand-delivered a written summary of Youngman's meeting with Sir Alexander to a State Department security officer. He also passed on something that Youngman had confided to him privately: Lee was only part of the problem. The other part was Ishbel. The local authorities were upset because she was attending Bible meetings with the island's blacks. They wanted to force her to leave, but her British citizenship did not make that easy. Instead, they hoped she would go once it was clear her husband could not return.

Corcoran had come to the State Department to help Lee, and so, as his meeting drew to a close, he suggested to the security officer that the consul general in Hamilton explain to Sir Alexander that the Department of State had no power to "clear" Lee as a private citizen. It issued passports to American citizens, not security clearances.[67]

While the State Department's security experts were mulling over Corcoran's suggested reply to Sir Alexander, the roulette ball seemed to land briefly on Lee's number: Ruth Shipley retired on April 30, 1955. Like any queen abdicating her throne, she had already selected her successor. As she prepared to retire, she openly bragged to the press that she was leaving her realm in good hands: "Yes, my successor has been chosen—by me. We have a good ship. Don't you think that after 28 years, I should know what's needed?"[68]

In many ways, Frances Knight Parish, who used her maiden name while working at the State Department, was Ruth Shipley's mirror image. Reported to be part of what Senator Joseph McCarthy called his "loyal American underground," Knight believed she had a legal right and a moral responsibility to protect Americans from ideas and political philosophies she abhorred, especially communism. Joseph Rauh Jr., the chairman of Americans for Democratic Action, called her selection "shocking to all who wish to preserve American freedom."[69]

Knight shared Shipley's abiding hatred for all things on the political left. Over time—she finally took a forced retirement in 1977 after two extensions—she became known to her critics on Capitol Hill as "the ogress." But, like Shipley, she was a master at defending herself. When her foes in the State Department tried to oust her in 1966, she called a press conference and declared, "Some creeps are out to get me."[70]

Knight proved as ruthless as Shipley in policing her domain, but the Passport Office's glory days of unrestricted power were already fading by the time she settled behind Shipley's old desk. By then, it faced increasing congressional scrutiny, lawsuits that attacked the Internal Security Act of 1950, investigations launched by private bodies such as the Association of the Bar of New York City, and the emergence of a more liberal US Supreme Court led by Earl Warren.[71]

All this reflected an easing of the distemper called McCarthyism. Joseph McCarthy was right when he claimed that the Soviets had penetrated the US government and had used the CPUSA to do it, but his timing and targeting were off. When he launched his crusade, Stalin's spymasters in Moscow were complaining bitterly about their lack of sources inside Washington's federal agencies since Bentley's and Chambers's revelations: "The most serious drawback in organizing intelligence in the U.S. is the lack of agents in the State Department, intelligence service, counterintelligence service, and other most important U.S. governmental institutions." The heyday of Soviet spies inside the US government had already come and gone. Almost none of the people McCarthy accused surfaced in the Venona traffic.[72]

When sworn in as president in January 1953, Dwight Eisenhower shrewdly waited for McCarthy to overstep. While he bided his time, the Cold War's tensions subsided. Stalin died on March 5, 1953, and just over four months later, the Korean War ended in a bloody stalemate. A little more than a month before the war ended, the US

government executed the Rosenbergs. Fears of Soviet tanks roll-
ing down Main Street no longer terrorized Americans. A year later,
McCarthy himself finally self-destructed.[73]

"Tailgunner Joe's" witch hunt for communists inside the army in
late 1953 and early 1954, prompted by his failed attempt to force the
service to give one of his aides preferential treatment, backfired hor-
rifically and put him on the defensive. For the first time, because of
the miracle of television, millions of Americans were able to watch
McCarthy in action. They were stunned by what they saw. With his
chronic five o'clock shadow and incessant bullying of frightened witnesses, he seemed to belong with inquisitor Tomas de Torquemada
in fifteenth-century Spain rather than in twentieth-century Washington. His public support vanished as quickly as the whisky he had
come to rely on at night. McCarthy finally sputtered out on December 2, 1954, when his fellow senators censured him.[74]

With McCarthy in disgrace, Eisenhower moved rapidly to take the
country's domestic war against communism off the front pages of its
newspapers. He could afford to do so because any appeal communism still had for Americans was rapidly waning. By the end of 1955,
the CPUSA had dwindled to roughly 22,000 members. Soviet leader
Nikita Khrushchev's denunciation of Joseph Stalin's crimes at the Soviet Communist Party's Twentieth Congress in February 1956 and his
invasion of Hungary that October all but finished gutting the American party. At year's end, the CPUSA had shrunk to between 3,000 and
6,000 members. Even J. Edgar Hoover, who was plotting to destroy it
once and for all, no longer believed the party posed a serious espionage threat.[75]

President Eisenhower, personally close to Hoover, urged the American public to forget about communists and leave them to the bureau:
"Our great defense against those people is the FBI. The FBI has been
doing for years in this line of work a magnificent job."[76]

Lee, in particular, benefited enormously from McCarthyism's collapse and the bureau's continuing failure to corroborate Bentley's
claims with evidence unconnected to the highly classified Venona intercepts. On May 23, 1955, Frances Knight cabled Robert Streeper to

say that while she was not going to give Lee a passport, the Passport Office did not object to his presence in Bermuda. Two weeks later, Streeper informed the colonial secretary that the State Department did not oppose Lee's return to Hamilton "on the grounds of security or otherwise." Five days before that, Edmund had threatened the State Department again with congressional action.[77]

While the State Department waited for the Bermuda government to decide whether Lee could return, Corcoran continued to pull strings inside the State Department. After the American consulate learned that Corcoran had complained about the slow response, one of its officers sent a heated cable to Washington: "Reply will be forthcoming in due course and in my opinion if attorney [Tommy Corcoran] sticks his nose into things and tries to high pressure authorities here, such action will probably only delay decision and might even cause decision to be adverse to Lees [sic] desires."[78]

On July 8, 1955, Sir Alexander, weary of Lee's case, canceled his government's deportation order and allowed him to return, but not without conditions. Sir Alexander said he planned to revisit his decision to readmit Lee every three months and reserved the right to deport him at any time. Two days later, Lee boarded Pan American Flight 136 and flew to Bermuda. He was returning to his interrupted life, but his forced departure had cost him more than he could ever have imagined. The exorbitant price turned out to be Ishbel.[79]

TWELVE

THE IRONY OF MY LIFE

The aftershocks of Lee's service for the Soviets during World War II would periodically shake up his life until he died in 1988 at age seventy-four. These tremors would also roll through the lives of his family, his supporters, and his foes, sometimes with devastating consequences.

Until the governor of Bermuda deported him in December 1953, Lee had been able to spare his family the worst consequences of his espionage activities for the Soviets. That changed after he was forced to leave the British colony. At the top of the list of casualties, his marriage never recovered from this separation.

For nearly sixteen months, Ishbel was left on her own with the couple's five children. The stress and her sense of abandonment finally overwhelmed her. Lee had always played by his own sexual rules in their marriage. Like many women of her era with children, she had reluctantly tolerated her husband's extramarital affairs and remained faithful to him. That double standard ended in Bermuda.

While Lee was marooned in New York, Ishbel met Brian Berkeley Burland, who later became Bermuda's most famous novelist and her third husband. Seventeen years younger than Ishbel, Burland came from one of Bermuda's wealthiest and most prominent families. A born rebel, he played for an all-black cricket team and refused to turn a blind eye to Bermuda's racial inequalities. Burland's lack of patience for the colony's rigid social structure appealed to Ishbel's moral sensibilities as much as his ready smile eased her loneliness.[1]

Although it is not clear when their affair began, Ishbel and Burland had openly acknowledged it by the summer of 1958. By then, the Lees had concluded that their marriage was unsalvageable and decided to euthanize it. In her memoirs, Ishbel pinpointed the cause of its collapse: "We tried to resume our old life, but we had both formed new attachments. We were more interested in them than in each other, which meant that the marriage was soon on the rocks."[2]

In 1983, Lee reminisced about the end of his union with Ishbel. The primary blame, he charged, lay not with either of them but with Elizabeth Bentley. "Our marriage, which had from the outset been beset by many problems of mutual adjustment (especially Ishbel's lax house-keeping), could not survive the extra strain put on it by the Bentley affair and its consequences." On September 15, 1958, they formally separated. A little more than a year later, they divorced in Cortez, Mexico. Beyond recriminations, the Lees listed incompatibility as the official reason.[3]

Lee never broke under the strain of being torn from his family and the unraveling of his marriage, but he came close. On November 26, 1956, his doctor noted that he still smoked between two and three packs of cigarettes a day, suffered from chronic anxiety, tension, and hypertension, and "sigh[ed] deeply rather often." Two years later, the same doctor wrote that Lee "always [gave] the impression of some tension," "smoke[d] 40 cigarettes a day," and displayed "recurring tremors, interrupted sleep, [and] clammy hands."[4]

Lee's marriage was not the only casualty of the choices he had made nearly a decade and a half before. Armistead Mason Lee, his brother, had joined the Foreign Service in 1942. Before that, he had followed his brother to Yale and then Oxford as a Rhodes scholar. After assigning him to Dakar, Melbourne, Wellington, and Washington, DC, the State Department notified Armistead in 1954 that it was stationing him in Bonn. In the early 1950s, a posting to the capital of West Germany was frontline duty in the Cold War and a necessary step in promotion to the Foreign Service's highest echelons.[5]

But before Armistead could leave, the State Department canceled his assignment as too sensitive. Instead, the Foreign Service sent him to Jamaica, then a British colony, for two years. After that, he spent a year at Harvard. His next posting was to Iceland. Armistead had not helped his own career by speaking critically about Vice President Richard Nixon and supporting John Stewart Service, one of the Foreign Service officers serving in China during World War II whom Senator Joseph McCarthy blamed for "losing China." When the State Department fired Service in 1951, Armistead had circulated a petition protesting what he believed to be its unfair treatment of him.[6]

Armistead's anti-Nixon remarks and his petition caught the attention of the State Department's Bureau of Inspections, Security, and Consular Affairs, but his blood ties to Lee caused its investigators to question his loyalty to the United States. Believing in his brother's innocence, he pushed back and responded in what his wife described as a "haughty manner." Within no time, Armistead's FBI file, she said, "reached to the skies."[7]

He had also crossed Ruth Shipley. On February 2, 1955, Armistead had written to her from Jamaica to complain about her treatment of his brother. He closed his letter with a thinly veiled warning: "I could hardly blame Duncan if he should decide to make the whole affair public, and I feel sure that the results would hardly enhance the Department's stature." Shipley dismissed his letter with a flick of her pen: "As you know, passports are not required of American citizens traveling to Bermuda and your brother's request for one seems to arise from a need to show foreign authorities that the United States Government does not give credence to the accusations which have been made against him. This, as you know, is not the proper function of a passport."[8]

Lee's wartime actions also continued to bedevil his former mentor, William J. Donovan. When Dwight Eisenhower was sworn in as the country's thirty-fourth president in January 1953, Donovan hoped to be nominated as the director of the CIA. Instead, Eisenhower selected Allen Dulles, who had headed the OSS's station in Switzerland, to lead the agency and offered to appoint Donovan ambassador to Thailand. Donovan accepted. On June 12, 1953, Secretary of State John Foster

Dulles (Allen's brother) asked J. Edgar Hoover "to conduct a full field investigation of General Donovan."[9]

Dulles expected the FBI to finish its work on the Medal of Honor winner within ten days. Instead, the background check took until July 15. One reason for the delay was Duncan Lee. On July 7, the Washington field office explained its tardiness to D. Milton "Mickey" Ladd, the head of the FBI's counterintelligence investigations: "While the investigation has generally been highly favorable to General Donovan, there is considerable information regarding his soft policy towards pro-Communists in the Office of Strategic Services at the time he headed that Agency. There is also information as to pro-Communist employees in his law firm." At least one FBI summary in Donovan's file included a lengthy recitation of Elizabeth Bentley's allegations against Lee. Although the final report that Hoover submitted on Donovan underscored that he was a "bubblehead" who had allowed communists into the OSS, the Senate confirmed him anyway.[10]

Meanwhile, J. Edgar Hoover was weathering his own storm. On October 17, 1955, the US Supreme Court had agreed to hear a case challenging the Smith Act, the cornerstone of the FBI's successful prosecutions against the Communist Party of the United States of America. That same day, an agent in the FBI's counterespionage division analyzed Lee's case and recommended that the bureau close it "in view of the inability to establish espionage violations or CP membership on the part of Lee at this time."[11]

Hoover refused to shelve the case, but the FBI's chances of arresting Lee all but ended after it decided that Venona's decrypted intercepts could not serve as direct evidence in espionage trials. The codebreaking program had been enormously successful in producing leads and corroborating facts—it had helped the FBI gather other evidence that convicted the Rosenbergs and at least ten other people—but in several cases, including Lee's, it supplied the bureau's only concrete proof of spying.[12]

On February 1, 1956, Alan Belmont, Mickey Ladd's successor as the assistant director of the FBI's Domestic Intelligence Division, drafted a top-secret memorandum that weighed the advantages and disadvantages of using the Venona intercepts in espionage prosecutions. After observing that publicly using Venona information "would corroborate Elizabeth Bentley and enable the government to convict a number of subjects whose continued freedom is a sin against justice" and "vindicate the Bureau in the matter of the confidence we placed in Elizabeth Bentley's testimony," Belmont regretted that the drawbacks of doing this were "overwhelming." He argued that defense lawyers would seek to discover and challenge the highly secret techniques that Arlington Hall had used to unbutton the communications. He also doubted that the deciphered intercepts could survive any of the defense's inevitable hearsay challenges and be admitted into evidence during an actual espionage trial. Even more importantly, Belmont did not want the Soviets to learn the full extent of what Arlington Hall had been able to do with their messages.[13]

Venona, which ultimately revealed that more than 350 American citizens, permanent residents aliens, and immigrants had aided the Soviet intelligence services against the United States in World War II, was very much an ongoing counterintelligence program in early 1956. This was true even though the National Security Agency and the FBI knew or strongly suspected that the Soviets had successfully penetrated the project. Kim Philby, stationed in Washington as Britain's MI6 liaison to the US intelligence community between 1949 and 1951, and William Weisband, a mole the NKGB had planted inside Arlington Hall in 1945, had outlined the program's major successes to their Moscow masters. Despite this, the Soviets did not know everything about Venona, and the NSA wanted to keep it that way.[14]

Belmont also worried about politicizing the highly classified program. He pointed out that 1956 was an election year and that the Republicans would use Venona's revelations to embarrass the Democrats by emphasizing the scale of the Soviets' penetration of the American government during World War II. At the same time, he fretted that the Democrats would blame the FBI while taking credit for sponsoring the code-breaking program in the first place. "The Bureau," Belmont lamented, "would be right in the middle."[15]

Lastly, he predicted the Soviets would kick their propaganda machine into overdrive if Venona were made public and "scream that the U.S. had never acted in good faith during the war." Hoover agreed with all of Belmont's arguments and decided, in partnership with the NSA, that the program should remain top secret.[16]

More trouble followed. On March 15, 1956, the Department of Justice, following the Supreme Court's lead, informed Hoover that all the FBI's future Smith Act cases had to include evidence of an actual plan for violent revolution. The bureau had relied on the Smith Act's broad prohibitions against advocating the violent overthrow of the US government to decapitate the CPUSA's leadership, but the department's instructions required a much higher standard of legal proof, all but eliminating the act as a viable prosecution tool.[17]

Deprived of the extremely potent weapons of the Smith Act and Venona in the courtroom, J. Edgar Hoover remained determined to destroy the threat that he believed communism posed to the American people. He had almost succeeded after World War I, but, he had convinced himself, those who failed to grasp the true magnitude of the menace had reined him in before he could complete his mission. Their reservations about his "anything-goes" tactics and their obsession with legal niceties had kept the communists off the mat and even strengthened them.[18]

Incapable of self-criticism, Hoover never admitted that his own actions between 1919 and 1922 had contributed to driving the American communist movement underground. To survive, it had made secrecy and conspiracy its lifeblood. The Kremlin was able to turn to the CPUSA's secret cells and networks after Stalin, out of pure paranoia, had killed off his most experienced intelligence officers. The CPUSA's espionage during World War II had made a fool of Hoover, who had grossly overestimated the party's ideological appeal to the overwhelming majority of Americans while underestimating its ability to attract a small fraction prepared to steal their country's secrets.

Harry Truman should have fired Hoover after the full scope of Bentley's revelations became clear. But the Republicans, who captured both houses of Congress in 1946, had been more interested in discrediting the Democrats than investigating the FBI's failures and had forced the president to defend his administration's handling of the espionage threat posed by communism. Hoover, a master at survival, had quickly and nimbly allied himself with the Republicans and successfully argued that the Democrats had tied his hands.

Self-interest and politics had saved J. Edgar Hoover, but he did not expect to be spared again if he left himself exposed to his enemies. To shield himself, as well as to replace the Smith Act and compensate for his inability to rely on Venona in court, he decided to fight fire with fire and annihilate the communists, using their own methods against them. He knew that Lee and most of the other communists Bentley had named were guilty of espionage but had gotten away. He vowed that this would never happen again.

On August 28, 1956, Hoover authorized the FBI's highly secret Counter Intelligence Program (COINTELPRO) "to disrupt, disorganize, and neutralize" those organizations and individuals he deemed dangerous to the "American way of life." To destroy these threats, he gave his agents free rein to use bags full of dirty tricks. Hardball methods included planting false stories with "friendly" newspapermen who claimed that their subjects had engaged in embezzlement, fraud, or bigamy and spreading derogatory information or outright lies through anonymous letters and phone calls alleging a person was a homosexual, adulterer, or FBI informant.[19]

Hoover's first COINTELPRO target was the CPUSA. The party's total destruction became his driving obsession. Three years later, the FBI's New York City field office had four hundred agents assigned to investigating the moth-eaten CPUSA; it had only four agents looking into organized crime. That the Soviets no longer used the informant-riddled CPUSA for espionage mattered not at all to a modern-day Ahab—Hoover still believed that it intended to undermine the middle-class America that he championed.[20]

By the 1960s, Hoover had deployed this no-holds-barred campaign of informants and dirty tricks against the civil rights and antiwar movements because he saw international communism's hidden puppet strings everywhere and was determined to cut them. But just as Joseph McCarthy had done, J. Edgar Hoover had set into motion the destruction of his own reputation.

While Hoover plotted to gut American communism, the head of his New York City field office wrote to him on March 26, 1957, renewing the request to close Lee's case "inasmuch as all logical leads have been covered and the subject is currently outside the United States." Four months earlier, agents from the same field office had monitored Lee while he was in New York City, Delaware, and Connecticut on a business trip. An informant inside American International had given them his itinerary, and another at his hotel had passed on information about whom he telephoned. Despite this blanket coverage, they had seen and heard nothing but routine business meetings and discussions.[21]

As Hoover mulled over the field office's request, C. V. Starr and Company, American International's parent company, renewed its quest for Lee's passport. The company needed him to travel abroad to oversee its far-flung legal matters. Frances Knight, now head of the Passport Office, resisted but suggested that Lee file a new passport application. As part of it, she made him sign another affidavit stating that he had never been a member of the CPUSA. Armed with the affidavit, Knight asked the State Department's security experts to analyze his file again. On April 1, 1958, they handed her a four-page summary of their findings that echoed the HUAC's conclusion of ten years earlier: "Either Miss Bentley is telling the truth and Lee is lying or vice versa." Realizing that his case was at an impasse, they recommended that Knight give him a passport.[22]

After the Department of Justice's Internal Security Division admitted that its investigation of Lee was all but dead, Knight finally relented and issued him a passport on May 16, 1958. That same day, she told J. Edgar Hoover about his new passport and his plans to use it to travel to the United Kingdom, France, and Italy. A month later, the US Supreme Court decided *Kent v. Dulles*, ruling that Congress did not intend to give the secretary of state "unbridled discretion to grant or withhold a passport to a citizen for any substantive reason he may chose." The "Queendom of Passports," built by Ruth Shipley and perpetuated by Frances Knight, was finished.[23]

By then, Hoover had run out of options. On June 24, 1958, he gave in and granted the New York City field office's request to bring the curtain down on Lee's case. The bureau's Washington field office followed suit and asked the Passport Office to stop sending it information on

Lee. Frances Knight, adamant that Lee was a threat to national security and that she knew best, ignored that request. She continued sending the FBI regular updates on Lee's travel plans and passport renewals for almost another decade.[24]

If he sensed that the bureau had finally ended its thirteen-year investigation of him, Lee never showed it. This time, there were no beer parties or boasts about being beyond the FBI's reach. His wife was gone, and his family was scattered. In 1959, Ishbel left Bermuda with their youngest child for Britain. The four other Lee children, using money their father provided, visited their mother periodically. She settled in Oxford, where she became a part-time lecturer at the College of Further Education and a landlady for Oxford students.[25]

On April 15, 1989, a retired CIA counterintelligence officer interviewed Ishbel. She remained adamant that neither she nor her husband had been communists or had ever betrayed the United States. She admitted, however, that Lee never got over being labeled a traitor. The Immigration and Naturalization Service did not give her an unrestricted visa to visit the United States until 1977. She died on May 19, 2005, in Edinburgh.[26]

In January 1960, Lee transferred from American International to C. V. Starr and Company, becoming an assistant vice president and a member of its New York City legal department. He continued to enroll his remaining four children in expensive preparatory schools. Hardly an easy parent, he loved them deeply and took his obligations to them very seriously. He sent them to the Taft, Groton, Chatham Hall, and Forman schools. He also sent money to Ishbel every month in England and later in Scotland—a practice he continued until he died—and paid for the education of their youngest child, Scott.[27]

During his first two years in New York City, Lee lived in a small apartment in Brooklyn and in a tiny "railroad" apartment in Manhattan. He struggled both with depression and financial worries. He also continued to wrestle with alcoholism. In a rare moment of candor, he told his oldest son, "Once you kids are educated, I don't care what happens to me."[28]

There were other sides to his extraordinarily complex personality. Lee could be warm and charming one moment and distant and curt the next. He remained a raconteur, with a razor-sharp sense of humor. To his niece, he was a romantic figure, urbane and sophisticated, but gave off strong whiffs of cynicism and disappointment with how his life had turned out.[29]

Things improved for him in 1964. On July 31, he married Frances Adoue Bull, who had grown up in Toronto, Canada, as a member of that city's upper crust. An excellent cook and highly organized, she was everything Ishbel was not. Ten months later, C. V. Starr, recognizing his exceptional legal skills, promoted Lee to be one of its two vice presidents and its general counsel. His financial worries ceased, especially after the company gave him shares of American International Underwriters stock.[30]

Lee and his new wife moved to 1111 Park Avenue on New York City's affluent Upper East Side. Lunching at the Wall Street Club and belonging to the Yale Club, the Democratic Party, the American Bar Association, and the vestry at the Episcopal Church of the Heavenly Rest, he epitomized the comfortable capitalist and solid member of the Establishment that he had so detested as a radical student at Oxford.[31]

Still, Lee never freed himself totally from his past. On March 25, 1968, John R. Rarick, a congressman from Louisiana, denounced him as a Soviet spy in one of his periodic rants against communists on the floor of the House of Representatives. The FBI, even though it had officially closed its case on him, periodically questioned C. V. Starr's personnel department about his work and travel. Similarly, Frances Knight, still convinced of his guilt, continued to delay his passport renewals.[32]

But these were mere skirmishes in a war that was long over. On March 6, 1970, the special agent in charge of the bureau's Washington field office asked Hoover for permission to destroy some of the case logs his office still had on the people Elizabeth Bentley had accused. His reason for wanting to shred these records was straightforward but rueful: "Since the grand jury and the House [Committee] of

Un-American Activity [*sic*] proceedings, this case has been analyzed over and over again in an effort to corroborate the allegations of Bentley. To date, we have not been able to develop a source who is in a position to corroborate Bentley. Corroboration of her allegations has been obtained through Bureau source 5 [Venona] but this information cannot be used for evidentiary purposes. All efforts have failed to break this conspiracy of silence." Hoover denied his request.[33]

In 1973, Lee retired as C. V. Starr's general counsel, secretary, and vice president. The company may have forced him to leave early because of his drinking. Lee regularly downed two to three martinis at lunch. He continued as a consultant until February 1975, but the insurance giant never asked him to work on any of its special projects as it did some of his peers.[34]

With little holding him in New York, and with his new wife's children living in Toronto, he decided to emigrate there. "Toronto," Lee explained to Arnold Smith, his closest friend at Oxford, was a "big city but not too big, with the amenities of a lively metropolis with few of the horrors of New York." He first explored moving there on November 28, 1972, when he wrote the Canadian consulate general in New York City to inquire about that country's admission requirements for permanent residents.[35]

Emigration meant dredging up his past and possibly reigniting Bentley's charges. On September 15, 1973, he contacted one of Toronto's most respected law firms about how deeply the Canadian authorities would probe into his background. He was especially concerned about Question 31(2)(d) of his application for permanent residency, which asked whether he had ever been deported from Canada or any other country. His lawyer's answer was not reassuring: "We are informed that inquiries are made of the R.C.M.P. [Royal Canadian Mounted Police] and the F.B.I. if the applicant had been a resident of the United States. We could not ascertain precisely what inquiries are made but are informed they are very thorough."[36]

Lee had no stomach for new investigations or the damage they might inflict on his carefully crafted image as a victim of Bentley's madness and the political bloodletting that had wracked the United States in the late 1940s and early 1950s. Still, he decided that the best defense was an aggressive offense. He attacked Question 31(2)(d) head on: "The Bermuda government's action was taken at the height of the McCarthy anti-Communist hysteria. It resulted, I believe, from some publicity I received in the late 1940s from charges made by Elizabeth Bentley, a self-confessed Communist agent whom I had known in the early days of World War II. Specifically, she accused me and others of being Communist Party members and sources of information to her. In my case the charges were totally untrue and I categorically denied them under oath on several occasions."[37]

Lee ended a follow-up letter to his lawyer with a plea: "I hope that the present concern will be limited to whether my admission to Canada at this date represents any present threat to the security of your country." It was. He was admitted as a permanent resident on January 17, 1974. He brought with him securities and assets worth over $8 million in 2014 dollars and an annual pension of nearly $80,000.[38]

Living at 5 Castle Frank Road in Toronto, Lee mulled over what he wanted to do next. Now sixty years old, he told Arnold Smith that he would like to perform some public service. He never found the right cause but did join the University Club, a Toronto hub for lawyers, judges, doctors, academics, and businessmen, as well as the Association of Canadian Rhodes Scholars and the Veterans of the OSS. He also traveled, wrote about his family's distinguished history, and drafted a long essay on his wish that his grandchildren be exposed to the teachings of the Episcopal Church. Occasionally, he wrote letters to the Toronto *Globe and Mail*'s editorial page. On May 29, 1977, he criticized the newspaper for "an intemperate and irrelevant anti-American diatribe" against Charles Lindbergh and his solo 1927 flight across the Atlantic Ocean.[39]

The focus of Lee's life changed with a diagnosis of emphysema in 1982. His two-plus-packs-a-day smoking habit had finally run him to ground. His drinking, though, was mostly under control. A true alcoholic after he retired in 1974, he had spent time drying out in several different clinics. It had not been easy. Once, at a final lunch before heading off to a treatment center, he deliberately drank himself into a stupor. While he relapsed occasionally, he was no longer a heavy drinker by the time his doctors told him that he had emphysema.[40]

Lee's addiction to cigarettes was a different story. After his diagnosis, he made it clear that he could never quit smoking. He insisted on smoking even after he started using oxygen tanks to stay alive. He simply pulled the tubes from his nose and continued to smoke. Accelerating his physical decline with nicotine, he sensed the shadows lengthening. Their coming forced him to think about his past.[41]

Most of those who had played a meaningful role in it were gone. Edmund, after moving back to his birthplace in Shepherdstown, West Virginia, died of leukemia on May 24, 1962. While battling this disease, he sent Lee a copy of Edward W. Bauman's *The Life and Teachings of Jesus.* Lucy outlived Edmund by almost nine years, dying on February 25, 1971. *The Chat*, Chatham Hall's alumnae magazine, ran an "appreciation" of her after she died, reporting that "she [had] awaited death eagerly, not resentfully or fearfully. She said that she had no proof, but she knew she would join Dr. Lee and the others she loved, and she was looking forward to that." Lucy and Edmund rest side by side in a Shepherdstown cemetery.[42]

Mary Price was also dead. Struck by a hit-and-run driver while crossing a street on December 6, 1949, she sustained a triple basal skull fracture and suffered total amnesia for nearly a month. At the time, she was working as a clerk and stenographer for Czechoslovakia, then a Soviet-dominated satellite, at its embassy in Washington. While recovering from her injuries in France, Price met and married Charlie Adamson, then an American expatriate. In 1957, she went to work for the National Council of Churches and then moved to Oakland, California. On April 19, 1976, the University of North Carolina at Chapel Hill's Southern Oral History Project interviewed her. During this interview, Price summed up her life's philosophy: "I can't regret the trials and tribulations and so forth, because I feel that my life has been a lot more interesting for me and worth a little bit. I am glad to have participated. I had made up my mind that in the class struggle that goes on, I was on the side of the working class. I am glad to do what I can to make this a better [place] and I'm a patriot." Price died in 1980. She never admitted her unpatriotic work for the Soviets.[43]

Neither did several of the others Bentley had accused. Maurice Halperin, an OSS colleague of Lee and another of her sources, refused to answer the Senate Internal Security Subcommittee's questions in

1953 about his relationship with Bentley. Blacklisted at Boston University where he was teaching, he decamped to Mexico, the Soviet Union, and then Cuba after receiving an invitation from Che Guevara himself to move there. He, too, finally emigrated to Canada and died in 1995 in Vancouver.[44]

Donald Wheeler, Lee's friend and fellow Rhodes scholar, became an oil burner mechanic and dairy farmer after Bentley's allegations surfaced. Although he took the Fifth when the HUAC asked him about his membership in the CPUSA, he spoke on March 10, 1955, at Reed College in Oregon, his alma mater, and dismissed the FBI's charges against him "as completely false." Wheeler obtained his DPhil from Oxford in 1973 and taught at Brandon University in Manitoba, Canada, until 1980. He died on November 8, 2002. His obituary in the *People's World* noted that he was a "longtime member of the CPUSA" who remained active in the party until he died.[45]

William J. Donovan—who brought Lee into his law firm in 1939 and the OSS in 1942, defended him in August 1948 after his appearance before the HUAC, and then persuaded Tommy Corcoran to get him out of the United States in 1953—died of arteriosclerotic atrophy of the brain on February 8, 1959. Lawrence Houston, the CIA's first general counsel and a frequent visitor to the old hero's bedside, later recalled that communists had plagued Donovan until the very end: "Lying in his bed, he could look out over the Queensborough Bridge. His clouded mind imagined Russian tanks were advancing over the bridge to take Manhattan."[46]

Claire Chennault and Whiting Willauer were also long in their graves. Chennault died of lung cancer on July 27, 1958—two days after President Eisenhower announced that he had finally been awarded the third star of a lieutenant general. Chennault remarked bitterly that it had come ten years too late.[47]

Willauer, after serving as the US ambassador to Honduras and Costa Rica, died of an embolism on August 6, 1962. Until the end, he remained a Cold Warrior. While serving in Honduras, he had taken part in the CIA's 1954 overthrow of Jacobo Arbenz in neighboring Guatemala. He later bragged, "I received a telegram from [CIA Director] Allen Dulles in which he stated in effect that the revolution could not have succeeded but for what I did. I am very proud of that telegram." In his last assignment for the Eisenhower administration, Willauer reviewed the CIA's plans for what later became known as the Bay of Pigs disaster. The incoming John F. Kennedy administration ignored his complaints about the lack of air cover for the doomed anti-Castro invaders.[48]

Tommy Corcoran died of a pulmonary blood clot on December 6, 1981. The *New York Times* eulogized him as a "lawyer of undisputed brilliance and wit," who "was the personification of the Washington insider." The *Washington Post* was equally complimentary: "If critics had problems with Mr. Corcoran's later transition to private practice in government circles, neither he nor his clients did. Many of the very people who had damned him as a policy-maker were to find him a useful colleague and attorney in those later years, and he found these marriages of mutual interest rewarding in the fullest senses." Lee served as an honorary pallbearer at his funeral.[49]

Lee's foes were also gone. Elizabeth Bentley, the FBI's deeply troubled linchpin, had all but vanished from its operational files by the early 1960s. After consulting and lecturing on communism, she taught briefly at an Episcopal school on Long Island, clerked for a Connecticut construction company, and took evening classes at Trinity College in Hartford. After she suffered another emotional collapse, Bentley's psychiatrist told her that she needed to forget her past and build a new life.

When she became very nervous and nonresponsive at an April 1959 meeting, FBI agents decided not to push her and ended their interview. By that fall, Bentley was teaching at the Long Lane School, an institution for wayward girls in Middletown, Connecticut. She hoped, she told J. Edgar Hoover in a letter, to "build up good citizens," defeat communism, and "contribute to a better America." She continued to meet occasionally with agents to discuss their cases involving communism. These consultations lasted until December 2, 1963, when Bentley succumbed to stomach cancer, no doubt accelerated by the gallons of alcohol she drank. She was not quite fifty-five years old. After she died, the head of the FBI's New Haven field office cabled Hoover that Bentley had "demonstrated warm regard and affection toward [the] Bureau to the end."[50]

J. Edgar Hoover was also in the ground. His nearly forty-eight-year reign as the nation's top law enforcement officer ended suddenly with a massive heart attack sometime in the early morning hours of May 2, 1972. Hoover was buried on May 4 in Washington's Congressional Cemetery, but more than his body descended into his grave. The spades and shovels also buried his iconic reputation as the incorruptible guardian of the country's security and morals.[51]

Within a year, the first revelations about COINTELPRO seeped into the press. More followed. Against the dark backdrop of the Watergate scandal, Congress launched sweeping hearings that forced the bureau to admit that Hoover and its agents had often operated outside the law in their crusade to protect the country.

On April 28, 1976, the Senate's so-called Church Committee released its massive report on the FBI's illegal activities under Hoover. Its verdict was devastating: the domestic war that Hoover and his agents had waged in the name of national security had created "a pattern of reckless disregard that threatened our constitutional system." In the end, Hoover had become as much a menace to the American way of life as the CPUSA he so hated. With his reputation vanished the recognition that he and the FBI had been right about Lee and many of the other spies that Bentley had exposed.[52]

Another casualty of the times was the HUAC. Never widely embraced by Americans because of its unsportsmanlike methods, the committee had fallen further in the public's estimation after J. Parnell Thomas, its chairman when Lee testified before it, was convicted of accepting kickbacks from his office staff on their federal government salaries. On November 4, 1948, he appeared before a grand jury investigating the charges against him and took the Fifth. His many foes did not miss the striking hypocrisy of Thomas's cloaking himself in the civil liberties protections of the US Constitution, a practice he roundly condemned and mocked while the HUAC's chairman.[53]

Although the HUAC had been a standing committee for almost thirty years, the House of Representatives voted to abolish it on January 14, 1975. It finally fell victim to some of the same forces, especially its investigations of domestic dissent and social protest movements, that had demolished J. Edgar Hoover's reputation. The Senate followed, abolishing its Internal Security Subcommittee in 1979.[54]

With his main opponents dead or discredited, Lee decided to write his memoirs for his family. The only question was how much of his past he would omit or obscure with lies. On December 23, 1977, he asked Armistead and his wife to safeguard the letters he and Ishbel had written from Oxford to Lucy and Edmund. Lucy still had them when she died in 1971: "I am writing to ask you not to release or show that correspondence to *anyone*, including my children, until I have had a chance to review it. Sorry to bother you with this, but I want to make my wishes concerning this matter quite clear."[55]

These letters, he knew, contained his highly romantic impressions of the Soviet Union; they also disclosed his intention to join the CPUSA's underground once he and Ishbel were financially independent. They were smoking guns the FBI could never find. Armistead assured him that "nobody but Ishbel has seen the box—nor will." Lee's reasons for never destroying the letters, once he got possession, remain a mystery, but they may have had to do with his declining health.[56]

On June 30, 1979, he sat down in his Toronto home and sketched out in pencil two outlines of seventeen chapters that covered his life from his birth in China to his retirement in Canada. His first outline omitted Elizabeth Bentley completely. The second included a chapter called "Elizabeth Bentley's Accusations." He then set aside both outlines until February 1982, when he scrapped what he had written and began a new version. This time, Lee cut out his proposed chapter on Bentley and instead discussed her in a brief introduction.[57]

After admitting that his account would be highly selective and confessing that he had tried for years to forget about her charges, he repeated the same claims he had made since she first accused him publicly in the summer of 1948: "To save her own skin, she became a professional anti-communist informer. As such, the more people she could implicate the more her value to the FBI and she proceeded to level charges against everyone she knew. I don't know about the others, I do know that the charges against me were totally false. I have said so under oath before an open hearing of the Un-American Affairs [*sic*] Committee and before two grand juries and so have left myself open to perjury charges. I have never invoked the Fifth Amendment."[58]

That same month, he authored another draft that did not name Bentley but did refer to her obliquely: "Some experiences were so painful that I have tried for years to put them out of my mind. Certainly I shall not dwell on them here." Once again, Lee failed to move beyond a draft.[59]

Nineteen months later, now coughing and wheezing from emphysema, he jettisoned the whole notion of writing a memoir that stretched from his birth to his retirement. Instead, he focused solely on his relationship with his now dead nemesis and how she had sabotaged his life. On September 15, 1983, he finished "The Elizabeth Bentley Matter (A Memorandum to My Children)," marking it "confidential" and signing it simply "Duncan C. Lee." In it, he spoke directly to his children, although, at times, he seemed to address a much wider audience.

His account skillfully blended fact and fiction, veering back and forth, sometimes in the same sentence. As always, he portrayed himself as a victim of political hysteria and dark psychological forces beyond his control. The HUAC, a product of those constitutionally concussed times, had mounted a witch hunt that targeted him and the others Bentley had accused. He also astutely blamed the FBI's need to show competence after its World War II failure to root out Soviet spies came to light and claimed that Hoover's pathological need to embarrass and destroy Donovan had rendered Lee an ideal FBI target.[60]

He crossed over into pure fiction when he portrayed himself as a casualty of Bentley's mental instability: "Her demeanor towards me was so personally vindictive and spiteful that I haven't the slightest doubt that she was paying me back for what she considered our rejection of her as a person and a friend in 1944." He repeated his story that he and Ishbel had found her too emotionally suffocating after "John" (Jacob Golos) died and had stopped seeing her after she displayed increasingly pro-Soviet beliefs.[61]

Lee admitted that Bentley had been a Soviet courier but reiterated that she had never asked him for any OSS secrets. Rather, their common social background and liberal political beliefs had drawn her to him and Ishbel. He confessed that he and Ishbel had once held very favorable views of the Soviet Union, and even at one time some communist sympathies, but maintained, "We were never Communists in the technical sense." Instead, he said, they were committed firmly to the New Deal and its Keynesian underpinnings. He also claimed that the US Army Reserves had discharged him without any stigma, ignoring the reality that the adjutant general had done just the opposite.[62]

Lee did tell the truth about his family's remarkable heritage, particularly Edmund's deep faith, and how he had felt that he could never measure up. Searching for a way to live up to this lofty legacy and his father's expectations and to quell his feelings of inadequacy, he admitted, he had become radicalized at Oxford because he was "disillusioned to the point of despair with capitalism" and convinced that "Hitler was the Anti-Christ." Although he denied belonging to the CPUSA and spying for the Soviets, Lee acknowledged sorrowfully that his entanglement in leftist politics had derailed his once grand ambitions: "The irony of my life is that the Bentley affair, into which I was indirectly drawn by my political sympathies at a particular time in my life, would effectively bar me forever from any meaningful political participation or action whether in elective office or government service. I would always be proscribed as a security risk. Except for my contribution to the War effort, I have accomplished nothing with my life except to earn a living and help raise a family. Both are important but with the promise of my youth I had hoped to do much more." He ended his account with a lawyerly half-truth: "I will freely confess to naïveté and poor judgment. But I never knowingly betrayed my country, my highest principles or my friends."[63]

It was unthinkable for Lee to admit what he had actually done, and he never did. In his doctored approach to his past, Lee was not alone. The Rosenbergs and Alger Hiss went to their graves denying any disloyalty to their country.[64]

Lee died on April 15, 1988. He was cremated and buried in Toronto. Seven years later, the NSA declassified its Venona intercepts.

Their revelations stunned Lee's children. For John Lee, Duncan's second-oldest son and a graduate of Harvard Law School, they came as a "shocking bolt from the blue" that struck without warning. He had always believed his parents' declarations of his father's innocence. As John and his siblings understood it, Elizabeth Bentley had been deranged and had lashed out because their parents had severed ties with her. Her need for revenge had driven her into the waiting arms of the FBI, the HUAC, and Joseph McCarthy. Their father had never taken the Fifth; nor had he ever been arrested, indicted, or convicted as a Soviet spy. Rather, he had been a decorated officer who had served his country to the best of his ability during World War II. Venona and the eight notebooks of Alexander Vassiliev—which contain NKVD and NKGB archival records that Vassiliev hand-copied between 1994 and 1996 and describe, in part, the Soviets' covert relationship with Lee—told them a different story altogether.[65]

The NSA's declassification of Venona also ignited a firestorm among historians. Although more than one student of American communism questioned the broken cables' reliability and often fragmentary nature, most agreed that their revelations ended any serious debate as to whether scores of Americans had aided the Soviet Union's spy services during World War II.[66]

Lee never had to confront this evidence. To the end, he professed his innocence, expecting to be remembered as the victim of an insane woman and the vicious political witch hunts of the late 1940s and early 1950s.[67]

Believing his reputation to be safe behind this carefully crafted façade, he died knowing that his choices in the late 1930s and early 1940s had irrevocably redirected his life. Traumatized in the mid-1930s by the Great Depression's economic devastation and fascism's rabid appetite for violence, and cheered on by Ishbel, he joined the CPUSA for many of the same reasons that his father had enrolled in the Student Volunteer Movement in the late 1890s. Both dreamed of transforming humanity and preparing the way for the dawning of a new age, be it a kingdom on earth led by a returned Christ or a worker's paradise guided by the utopian teachings of Karl Marx. Just as Edmund entered the ranks of those determined to bring about "the evangelization of the world in this generation," his son had joined a new breed of crusaders loyal not to nations but to a powerful abstraction, mankind. The salvation and deliverance of both their worlds depended on nothing less than their high-mindedness.

Lee came of age at an exhilarating and romantic time when the complacency and drift of the "Lost Generation" of the 1920s gave way to the almost frantic urgency and sense of purpose of his "Crisis Generation" of the 1930s. He was not the only one to hear communism's dog whistle. Scores of his generation's well-meaning men and women believed that capitalism's collapse during the Great Depression had exposed its rotten moral foundations. These decayed underpinnings—and with them the poverty, inequality, despair, and spiritual breakdown they had so long supported—needed replacing.

This vision appealed greatly in that beyond being emotionally satisfying, it also had a seemingly firm empirical grounding in social reality. As the American novelist Upton Sinclair sermonized in 1937, the Soviets seemed to have established a genuine workers' government. They had also assumed the leadership of the world's life-or-death struggle against international fascism. The Soviet Union in the 1930s offered a shining alternative to the United States, with its Hoovervilles, park sleepers, demoralized farmers, and joyless youth, and its selfish decision not to supply the Republicans in Spain with rifles and grenades.[68]

Bentley called Lee and her other sources "a bunch of misguided idealists" upset with how the United States and Britain were letting the Soviet Union bear the brunt of the fighting against Hitler. They were determined, she told her congressional interrogators, to see that Joseph Stalin got what he needed to defeat the Nazis, even if this meant they had to violate their country's espionage laws and their countrymen's trust. They believed that higher causes—the survival of the Soviet experiment and of mankind itself—justified these betrayals. They either disbelieved or disregarded news that Stalin had systematically shot and starved millions of his own countrymen. Adolf Hitler simply had to be stopped.

President Franklin Roosevelt shared Lee's belief that the Allies must beat Hitler at any price. The cost included a shotgun marriage to Joseph Stalin's Soviet Union. Roosevelt nurtured his rocky alliance with Stalin because he understood that it was the key to defeating Adolf Hitler's war machine. His calculus, with its cold-blooded premise that only the Red Army's soldiers combined with America's machines could defeat Hitler, created an extraordinarily permissive environment for the Kremlin's spies inside the United States. Although Churchill's and Roosevelt's Lend-Lease programs greatly aided his war effort, Stalin relied on his spies to take what his allies would not give him—especially in the fields of atomic research and advanced industrial technology.

Roosevelt's administration, unwilling to cross Stalin while the Red Army was killing 60,000 German soldiers a month, made plain that it wanted no FBI arrests and Department of Justice prosecutions of suspected Soviet spies, even if they had caught any. No one in the White House could foresee that this brutally pragmatic policy would later be viewed through the dramatically refracting lenses of the Cold War instead of those of the desperate days of World War II, when the United States was on the ropes fighting Germany and Japan. The policy blew up on Harry Truman's watch.

That approach also guided William J. Donovan's helmsmanship of the OSS: Hitler's defeat came first, and he relied on the communists he knowingly recruited into the organization to help bring it about. He never expected them to choose the Soviet Union over their own country. His attitude and hiring practices made the OSS the most penetrated intelligence service in American history.[69]

Meanwhile, during most of World War II the FBI concentrated on rounding up Axis spies and neutralizing communism's perceived threat to America's way of life instead of ferreting out Stalin's agents. Bentley operated with impunity in Washington and never worried about the bureau while collecting classified intelligence from her networks and individual sources. By the time the FBI had set its sights on Lee, his spying career was over.

The political extremism of the late 1940s and the early 1950s also worked in Lee's favor. The HUAC and its Senate counterparts accused so many Americans of disloyalty that sorting the guilty from the innocent was nearly impossible. The HUAC, in particular, pandered to party politics and was more intent on shredding Harry Truman than on presiding over a meaningful inquiry into how the Soviets had managed to penetrate the US government with such ease. Politics, as so often in Washington, trumped love of country.

Tactics mattered too. Lee's calculated gamble to spar with the HUAC and not wrap himself in the protections of the Fifth Amendment made it much easier for him to maintain his innocence and claim to the end that he was just one more victim of a Washington run amok.

To counter this political insanity, he surrounded himself with very powerful men who rallied to his defense. Circling the wagons were William Donovan, Thomas Corcoran, Claire Chennault, and Whiting Willauer, each of whom mistakenly erred on the side of trust and self-interest. Just possibly John le Carré's observation of Kim Philby's easy acceptance by his British colleagues applied to Lee and his well-connected associates: he was of their blood and hunted with their pack. Robert Lamphere, the FBI agent who played such a critical role in breaking the Soviets' codes during World War II and who worked with Philby in Washington, theorized that Philby had gotten away with his treachery because of the British upper class's inability to believe ill of their own. MI6 had hired him not because he passed any rigorous background check but because he had gone to the right schools, joined the right clubs, and professed the right beliefs.[70]

The same might be said of Lee, although Corcoran seems to have had shallower faith in him than his other patrons. Lee, like Philby, rallied the Establishment to his side and maneuvered it into protecting him as one of its own. Ironically, this rendered him dependent on the very men he had deceived.[71]

Lee's chameleon-like personality also saved him, allowing him to spy for the communists before 1945 and become a Cold War warrior immediately afterward. He benefited enormously from his ability to mold his personality to the situation at hand. This talent and his ability to compartmentalize psychologically made it impossible for most of those who knew him before and after the war to believe Elizabeth Bentley's charges.

This was especially true after his brilliant postwar service in China against Mao Zedong's communists. His work there gave him a thick anticommunist veneer. Hard-right Cold War allies such as Claire Chennault and Whiting Willauer defended him in his time of greatest need. His ties to them also gave him a remarkable opportunity to compensate for his earlier treachery and to redeem himself. By the time he began working for Corcoran in early 1946, he was no more a communist or Soviet spy than J. Edgar Hoover, but the FBI never believed that. Lee's attempt to balance the scales by playing a key role in keeping Taiwan out of Mao Zedong's grasp meant nothing to his single-minded federal pursuers.

Less clear is how deeply Lee held any of his convictions. Edmund's were all-encompassing—his son's, decidedly less so. Although certainly no Julius Rosenberg, he had once believed in the communist cause firmly enough to justify passing classified information to the Soviets—but not enough to die for it. Lee was most comfortable helping the Soviets on his own terms, with managed risk. He preferred being in charge and became unnerved when he felt control slipping away. He also liked the ambiguity that Bentley's involvement offered at first. Her role as a middleman allowed him to pretend in his lawyerly way that he never "knowingly" betrayed the United States because he gave his information directly to her and Mary Price, not to the Soviets.

But even this self-deception was not enough to insulate him from his real fears of exposure. He cracked under the strain of his double life when he heard his own information parroted back to him by the Soviets and learned of Donovan's plans to work more closely with them. By then, any lingering illusions or delusions that his information was going only to the CPUSA had long fallen by the wayside.

If Lee was no Julius Rosenberg, he was also no Whittaker Chambers. His rejection of his past convictions was never powerful enough to convert him into a tormented apostate who professed a messianic mission to come forth and reveal communism's innate evils. Lee never considered confessing what he had done and seeking public absolution. It was much easier to double down on lies than to act the penitent.

It was also much safer. He knew that there was no statute of limitations on espionage committed during wartime. If convicted, he could face execution. He also knew that taking the Fifth Amendment, tantamount to a confession, would have ruined him professionally—Lee had children to clothe, feed, and educate—and tarnished his illustrious family name.

Although there is no evidence that the CIA's psychiatrists ever studied Lee's background, his personality reflected several of the basic traits that they have seen in others who have stolen their country's secrets. Most spies have the ability to exhibit a sham, superficial loyalty. As narcissists who believe themselves destined to play a special role in history, they have already led lives full of mini-defections before they finally cross over into full-blown betrayal. Perhaps most importantly, they are capable of ignoring the devil in themselves while condemning it in others. This permits them to deflect guilt, blame, and responsibility.[72]

Lee's multiple sexual affairs, or "mini-defections," his compartmented personality, his violation of his government's and mentors' trust, his prodigious ability to lie, his belief that his hour had come when Mary Price recruited him to spy for the Soviets, his wallowing in victimhood, and his cruel attacks on Bentley underscore how accurately the CIA's profile fits. To unleash these traits and commit espionage, Lee needed only a great cause, access to classified information, and a permissive environment.

In the end, however, guilt and remorse probably caught up with him. His father, Edmund, taught that a sinner could always atone and find redemption. If Lee ultimately came to believe this, J. Edgar Hoover never did.

The damage Lee did to the national security of the United States is harder to sum up than his battle with Hoover. Arthur M. Schlesinger Jr., one of America's foremost political historians and a veteran of the OSS, argued in his memoirs that the information the OSS moles transferred to the Soviets did little to harm the US war effort. Instead, Schlesinger ventured, their stolen intelligence may actually have helped the Americans by showing Joseph Stalin that Franklin Roosevelt was not plotting against him and thereby reducing the likelihood of Stalin's making a separate peace with Hitler, a more-than-possible prospect until the Red Army forced the Germans to surrender in early 1943 at Stalingrad.[73]

Schlesinger may be right, because the classified information that Lee passed to Mary Price and Elizabeth Bentley went to an ally, although a monstrous one. Nonetheless, his intelligence alerted the Soviets to British and American diplomatic strategy for negotiating with Stalin over postwar Poland's borders and US diplomatic activities in Romania and Bulgaria, especially with those nations' pro-Western politicians, who were in great danger once they found themselves behind the Iron Curtain.

At least one former OSS officer believed that Lee had severely damaged his country's long-term interests. Future US Supreme Court associate justice Arthur Goldberg, chief architect of the OSS's disastrous Sparrow mission into Hungary that sought to detach that country from its wartime alliance with Adolf Hitler, strongly suspected that the Soviets, tipped off by Lee, leaked the mission to the Germans to ensure the erasure of Hungary's pro-Western politicians, paving the way for Stalin's postwar domination. Information the Russians have released so far from their intelligence archives, however, provides no evidence to support Goldberg's suspicions.[74]

The most damaging intelligence that Lee passed to the Soviets may have been the information he gathered about the OSS's internal investigation of employees it suspected as security risks. His tip about this investigation allowed the Soviets to warn Donald Wheeler, their most prolific spy inside the OSS, and deactivate him for six months. Later, Wheeler exposed a number of OSS agents and their networks operating covertly in Soviet-controlled territory. In this sense, Lee inflicted an indirect yet profound—and, to some, probably fatal—injury.[75]

No matter what the assessment, Soviet penetration rendered the OSS an open book. It gave the Kremlin a clear look into the previously obscure activities of the foreign intelligence service of its most important wartime ally. As John le Carré observed, an intelligence service discloses its own ignorance when it reveals its targets. Thanks to its moles inside Donovan's organization, the NKGB came to understand the OSS's tradecraft, training, and personnel. This insiders' knowledge may have given Moscow's spymasters an early understanding of the CIA's sources, methods, and personnel after Harry Truman created the agency in 1947, because the new espionage service adopted many of the OSS's operational tactics and hired scores of Donovan's most experienced officers. Roughly one-third of the agency's senior officers in 1947 came from the OSS. Elizabeth Bentley's defection and the successes of Venona gave Hoover's agents the same sort of window into the inner workings of the NKGB.[76]

President Harry Truman may have temporarily blinded the United States when he shut down the OSS, but he also inadvertently neutralized a sizable security risk to his country. Lee had quit spying and ended his relationship with the Soviets by the early spring of 1945, but others in the OSS had not; the office's demise on October 1, 1945, followed by Bentley's defection, ended their opportunities to steal any more of its secrets. The postwar discovery of moles inside the OSS forced the CIA to tighten its background investigations and take counterintelligence seriously. No evidence has come to light that the Soviets penetrated the early CIA.[77]

The domestic fallout from Lee's and other Americans' spying for the Soviets was enormous, however. The press savaged Bentley, but others beyond the HUAC's members believed that she had told the truth. By the time Senator Joseph McCarthy stepped onto the national stage, Washington's atmosphere was already highly charged with bitterness and recrimination because so many suspected spies had escaped punishment.

These feelings help explain why so many Americans supported McCarthy until he self-destructed. The existence of real spies in the 1940s had created lifelike mirages of them by the early 1950s. The convictions of Alger Hiss, Harry Gold, and Klaus Fuchs in 1950 and of the Rosenbergs in 1951—all of whom had actually done their spying much earlier—only lent credence to his terrifying claim that scores of hidden spies remained at work.

McCarthy's allegations that the Democrats had presided over the biggest ever foreign penetration of the US government led to the Republicans' claim that the Democrats were weak on national security and could not be trusted to protect the country. To counter these allegations, the Democrats became even more militant and willing to show how tough they were. These scathing allegations that the Democrats were weak on national security and soft on communism helped push the United States into the Korean War, the Bay of Pigs, and the Cuban Missile Crisis, and its disastrous escalation in Vietnam. The Republicans' charges of weakness and the Democrats' countercharges remain very much alive today.

If Lee ever thought about the damage he had left in his wake, he never said so. Perhaps it was all too painful. He had hoped to see communism usher in a new kingdom on earth; instead, his commitment to the doctrine had irrevocably disfigured his life and set into motion events and forces that he could scarcely have imagined when he agreed to spy against his own country.

Lee never admitted it, but Bentley was right about him. He was a misguided idealist who chose his conscience over his country. He spied for the Soviets because he believed in a cause greater than his loyalty to his country and the government he worked for. He did not commit espionage for money, glory, ego, ethnic loyalty, or revenge—classic motives of post–World War II Americans who have stolen their country's secrets—but because he thought he was helping to save and reform mankind, the same grand mission his evangelical father and Social Gospel–minded mother had undertaken when they went to China to preach the Gospel. Although moral philosophers who study Hitler's atrocities might agree with Lee's choice to aid Stalin in his battle to the death with the Führer, the keepers of the country's secrets and the enforcers of its laws could not.

Lee got away with espionage, but not without paying the highest of prices. In the end, he deceived himself as much as anyone else.

Acknowledgments

Many people and institutions made this book possible.

Foremost, I could not have written it without the help of John Lee, Katherine Lee Cole, Gavin Lee, and Eleanore Lee, four of Duncan Lee's children and his niece, who allowed me to use his personal papers and answered countless questions about the man they knew. Although often pained and unsettled by my conclusions about their father and uncle, they were always remarkably helpful and open. Lee's children and niece represent all the best traditions of a great American family. John Lee, in particular, opened his home to me and read my draft chapters and final manuscript. His close reading of his family's history and of events he actually remembered saved me from making countless errors. I tried throughout to follow John's request for fairness and that I "let the chips fall where they may."

But even the extraordinary opportunity provided by Lee's family would have been wasted if not for the careful oversight and generous support of a small group of scholars I am fortunate enough to call mentors and friends. Dr. Barry F. Machado, who taught me American history at Washington and Lee University, read my proposal, draft chapters, and final proofs as if they were his own. His trenchant criticisms and much needed words of encouragement kept me from slipping off the tracks more than once. I could not have finished this book without Barry's backing. Dr. John Walsh and William Thomas, two of my modern history tutors at Oxford, continued to push me, as they had done decades before, to sharpen my arguments and presentation. I also took full advantage of the close editing of Dr. Nicholas Reynolds, a keen student of the history of the Office of Strategic

Services and a close friend since our student days at the University of Virginia School of Law.

While these four men bore the brunt of reading and commenting on my draft chapters, others stepped in at critical points to answer my questions and clarify my thinking. These included John Earl Haynes, this country's foremost historian, along with Harvey Klehr, on Soviet espionage inside the United States during World War II; Hayden Peake, a former CIA counterintelligence officer and curator of the CIA's Historical Intelligence Collection, who was the first to write about Duncan Lee, Elizabeth Bentley, and the Soviets' penetration of the Office of Strategic Services; Dr. Daniel Horowitz, Mary Huggins Gamble Professor Emeritus of American Studies at Smith College, who urged greater clarity in my writing and especially helped shape my views about Yale University during Lee's undergraduate years; David Garrow, Research Professor of Law and History at the University of Pittsburgh, whose scholarship on J. Edgar Hoover's Federal Bureau of Investigation remains seminal; Dr. Ken White, William P. Ames Professor Emeritus in Sociology and Anthropology at Washington and Lee, whose careful eye picked up errors in the manuscript that mine missed; and Eugene Fidell, the Florence Rogatz Visiting Lecturer at Yale Law School, for answering my questions on military law.

Several people who knew Duncan Lee kindly shared their insights into his personality and character: David Acheson, who was Lee's closest friend during the late 1940s and early 1950s; Elizabeth "Betty" McIntosh, who served with Lee in the Office of Strategic Services; Dr. John P. Scully, Lee's roommate at Yale University; Walter Pforzheimer, who also knew Lee as an undergraduate at Yale and later in Washington; Herbert Merillat, who knew Lee at Oxford and Yale Law School; and John Espey, another of Lee's Rhodes Scholar classmates.

Dr. William Black of Chatham Hall shared his scholarship on Edmund Jennings Lee IV, when this book was still little more than an idea.

Robert and Karen Nangle sent me the photograph of Katharine Robb Rawles Nangle that appears in this book. Bob gave me his reminiscences about his mother's interactions with Duncan and Ishbel Lee.

I would also like to thank Orianne Dutka, who helped shape my chapter on Lee's youth in China; Dr. Jerrold Post of George

Washington University, who very kindly sent me a typescript of his penetrating psychological study on traitors; Jim Semivan, who served with me in the CIA, who gave my final manuscript a very close read; and Ken Moody and James Ward, who retrieved much needed documents for me from the Franklin D. Roosevelt Presidential Library in Hyde Park and the Library of Virginia in Richmond, respectively.

A host of friends at the Department of Justice commented on my writing or acted as sounding boards as this book crept its way to its finish. These include Kevin Tiernan, Susan Kim, Lisa Farabee, Heidi Bauer, Michael Dick, Rosemary Hart, John Dion, and Jeff Boodman.

In addition to the persons above, I relied on a host of institutions to write this book. These included the Library of Congress; the Hoover Institution, where I spent a week as a William C. and Barbara H. Edwards Media Fellow, researching in the papers of Claire Lee Chennault and J. Russell Forgan; the National Archives and Records Administration, where my research benefited enormously from the labors of John Taylor, Larry McDonald, William Davis, David Langbart, and Robert Reed; the Franklin D. Roosevelt Presidential Library; the Harry S. Truman Presidential Library; Rhodes House, where I benefited from the help of Sir Anthony Kenney and Sir Colin Lucas; the library and archives of Christ Church, Oxford (a special thanks to Judith Curthoys); Princeton University's Seeley Mudd Library; the Albert and Shirley Small Special Collections Library at the University of Virginia; the Eugene McDermott Library at the University of Texas, Dallas; the Center for the Study of the American South at the University of North Carolina, Chapel Hill; Yale University's Sterling Memorial Library (special thanks to Judith Schiff, Rebecca Hatcher, and Kristen McDonald); the US Army Military History Institute at Carlisle Barracks, where I was ably assisted by the late Dr. Arthur Bergeron Jr.; the Wellcome Library, London; the Library of Congress; and, especially, the Education and Research Institute, which provides an outstanding collection of thousands of pages of declassified Federal Bureau of Investigation reports.

Likewise, I could not have written this book without reference to the work of other historians who have gone before me. In addition to the writings of John Earl Haynes and Hayden Peake, I found those of the following particularly useful: Alexander Vassiliev, Kathryn

Olmstead, Harvey Klehr, Maurice Issermann, Ellen Schrecker, Athan Theoharis, Curt Gentry, John Fox, Katherine Sibley, Jeffrey Kahn, Michael Warner, Richard Gid Powers, William Leary, and Douglas Waller.

Todd Schuster, my agent, and Jacob Moore, one of his editorial assistants, did yeoman's work on my proposal, helping me mold and refine my ideas. Luckily, Todd shopped it to Lara Heimert, now publisher of Basic Books. I benefited enormously from Lara's razor-sharp sense of how a book should flow. She rescued me from littering this book with too many extraneous details. Her team at Basic Books— Katharine O'Donnell, Michelle Welsh-Horst, and especially Roger Labrie and Jennifer Kelland—made this book much stronger than what I originally presented. None of the above should be incriminated for the shortcomings of the final product.

Lastly, I want to thank Liza, Anna, and Robin. Writing a book is necessarily a solitary and self-absorbed task. Your patience and love truly made this book possible.

Because I am a former Central Intelligence Agency officer, the CIA's Publications Review Board read this book before it was published to ensure that it contained no classified information. It does not, but the board requires that all CIA employees and former employees include the following disclaimer in nonfiction books:

> All statements of fact, opinion, or analysis expressed are those of the author and do not reflect the official positions or views of the CIA or any other U.S. government agency. Nothing in the contents should be construed as asserting or implying U.S. government authentication of information or agency endorsement of the author's views. This material has been reviewed by the CIA to prevent the disclosure of classified information.

I thank the board for its thorough review.

Notes

Abbreviations in Notes

AG	adjutant general of the US Army
AL	Armistead Lee
AmConsul	American Consulate General
COI	Coordinator of Information
CPGB	Communist Party of Great Britain
CPUSA	Communist Party of the United States of America
DCL	Duncan Chaplin Lee
DOA	Department of the Army
DOS	Department of State
EJL	Edmund Jennings Lee IV
ERI	Education and Research Institute
FBI	Federal Bureau of Investigation
FDR PL	Franklin D. Roosevelt Presidential Library
F&RS	File and Reference Section
HQ	Federal Bureau of Investigation Headquarters
HUAC	House Un-American Activities Committee
IF	investigative files
ISA	Internal Security Act of 1950
JEH	J. Edgar Hoover
LCL	Lucy Chaplin Lee
LOC, MD	Library of Congress, Manuscript Division
MHI	Military History Institute, Carlisle, Pennsylvania
NARA	National Archives and Records Administration
NF	name file
NKGB	People's Commissariat of State Security
NKVD	People's Commissariat for Internal Affairs
NSA	National Security Agency
NYFO	New York Field Office
OSS	Office of Strategic Services
PHS	personal history statement

PSF   president's secretary's files
RG   records group
RTA   reply to allegations
SAC   special agent in charge
SGMML   Seeley G. Mudd Manuscript Library, Princeton University
SOHPC   Southern Oral History Program Collection
TGC   Thomas Gardiner Corcoran
USA   US Army
WIROM   electronically dispatched State Department messages
WFO   Washington Field Office
WN   White Notebook
WW   Whiting Willauer

Prologue: Helen

1. FBI Report, September 26, 1949, WFO, DCL, 4. Lee lived from November 1942 until July 1944 at 3014 Dent Place, Apartment 18, Washington, DC, NW.

2. NARA, RG 233, IF, Series 1, NF, DCL, Box 193, Classification Questionnaire of Reserve Officers, DCL, July 6, 1942.

3. NARA, RG 226, M1642, Records of the Washington Office of the Director of Strategic Services, Roll 104, Frame 1227.

4. NARA, RG 226, Roll 104, Frames 1228–1229. According to SA 4489, "Eden's view of the situation is that while he is Foreign Minister, the British government must stand by the Polish Government in London. Churchill, on the other hand, is apparently more willing to bring pressure on the Poles than Eden. . . . The contemplated territorial announcement would give East Prussia to Poland to compensate for their losses in Russia." For an explanation of how Lee passed classified intelligence to Bentley, see Vassiliev, WN #3, 102. The complete collection of Vassiliev's notebooks can be found at Wilson Center Digital Archive, Vassiliev Notebooks.

5. Peake, "Afterword," 219. Director, FBI, from Guy Hottel, SAC, WFO, April 17, 1947, Subject: Gregory Espionage-R, Re: DCL, 1, Vol. 118, ERI. The ERI, located in Washington, DC, has collected over 160 volumes of FBI files that chronicle the bureau's investigation into Elizabeth Bentley's claims.

6. Bentley, *Out of Bondage*, 126–127. Office Memorandum to Director, FBI, from Guy Hottel, SAC, WFO, April 17, 1947, Subject: Gregory Espionage-R, Re: DCL, Silvermaster File, 2, Vol. 118, ERI.

7. Lee would have faced a range of punishments. As he was a US Army officer, the June 4, 1920, Articles of War governed his conduct. While the articles contemplated passing classified information to an enemy, they did not contemplate a service member passing it in an unauthorized way to an ally. Nothing, however, would have prevented the army from turning Lee over to the civilian authorities. If it had, he would have been prosecuted under 50 United States

Code, Section 32, the Espionage Act. Lee did not technically commit treason because he committed espionage on behalf of an ally, not an enemy. Article III, Section 2 of the Constitution specifically refers to "enemies."

8. Vassiliev, WN #3, 105. Peake, "Afterword," 223–225.

9. Venona 887, New York to Moscow, June 9, 1943. American code breakers also spelled Lee's cover name "Koch." The National Security Agency apparently did not break this message until October 31, 1968. All the Venona messages the Americans broke can be found at www.nsa.gov/public_info/declass/venona, at the Manuscript Division of the LOC, and at the NSA's National Cryptologic Museum, Fort Meade, Maryland.

10. Burns, *Roosevelt: The Soldier of Freedom*, 87, 413. Service, *Stalin: A Biography*, 463.

11. Vassiliev, WN #3, 102.

12. See Weinstein and Vassiliev, *The Haunted Wood*, xv–xix, for an explanation of how Vassiliev gained access to this material and why, and Haynes and Klehr, "Alexander Vassiliev's Notebooks." Lee's files are among those of hundreds of other Americans who spied for the Soviet Union. The notebooks span 1,115 pages and cover Soviet intelligence activities in the United States from the 1930s to the 1950s. There are eight notebooks and a ninth collection of loose pages.

Chapter 1 Born to Serve

1. Post, "The Anatomy of Treason," 1. Dr. Post kindly gave me a typescript of this article. It originally appeared in the spring 1975 issue of the CIA's *Studies in Intelligence*.

2. DCL, "The Elizabeth Bentley Matter," 1, 18.

3. "Lees of Virginia: An American Legacy," 1.

4. "Lees of Virginia: An American Legacy," 1.

5. Middlekauff, *The Glorious Cause*, 325. DCL, "My Family," 1.

6. Robert E. Lee was Duncan's great-grandfather's first cousin. See DCL, "My Family," 2.

7. LCL, *An American Sojourn*, 4.

8. Robert, *Occupy Until I Come*, 46. Phillips, "The Student Volunteer Movement," 92. DCL, "My Family," 14, 16. The SVM was both a pre- and postmillennial movement.

9. Brinkley, *The Publisher*, 5–6.

10. Fitzgerald, *Way Out There in the Blue*, 23–24. Swanberg, *Luce and His Empire*, 20–21.

11. LCL, *An American Sojourn*, 5. Spence, *The Search for Modern China*, 231–235. Swanberg, *Luce and His Empire*, 22–23.

12. LCL, *An American Sojourn*, 5.

13. Schlesinger, "The Missionary Enterprise," 356. Phillips, "The Student Volunteer Movement," 103. Bates, "The Theology of American Missionaries in China, 1900–1950," 158.

14. DCL, "My Family," 19, 25.

15. LCL, *An American Sojourn*, 13.

16. DCL, "My Family," 7–8.

17. LCL, *An American Sojourn*, 8.

18. LCL, *An American Sojourn*, 8. "Our History."

19. DCL, "My Family," 35–36. LCL, *An American Sojourn*, 9. Hopkins, "Christodora Settlement House," 1–7. H. May, *Protestant Churches and Industrial America*, 91–92, 108, 111, 170.

20. LCL, *An American Sojourn*, 25.

21. LCL, *An American Sojourn*, 25.

22. LCL, *An American Sojourn*, 21, 22, 25.

23. DCL, "My Family," 39.

24. LCL, *An American Sojourn*, 15, 21, 23, 27, 34, 41.

25. AL, "Reflections," 4.

26. LCL, *An American Sojourn*, 24. DCL, "My Family," 32.

27. LCL, *An American Sojourn*, 18, 22, 35.

28. DCL, "My Family," 26–27.

29. AL, "Reflections," 1–2.

30. LCL, *An American Sojourn*, 18, 25, 36–37, 42–51.

31. AL, "Reflections," 3. LCL, *An American Sojourn*, 28. AL, "Kinsmen in the Clergy," 3. DCL "My Family," 20.

32. DCL, "My Family," 20, 22. LCL, *An American Sojourn*, 14.

33. "DCL—Biographical Synopsis." Espey, *Tales out of School*, 29.

34. G. May, *China Scapegoat*, 31. LCL, *An American Sojourn*, 52.

35. LCL, *An American Sojourn*, 54.

36. Swanberg, *Luce and His Empire*, 19.

37. DCL, "My Family," 28.

38. *Yale Banner 1935*, 256–257. AL, "Some Reminiscences," 2. William Black, dean, Chatham Hall, telephone interview with author, April 22, 1999.

39. AL, "Some Reminiscences," 2, 4. Black, telephone interview with author, April 22, 1999.

40. Black, telephone interview with author, April 22, 1999.

41. AL, "Reflections," 5. E. Lee, "Notes on My Memories of Duncan."

42. AL, "Reflections," 5.

43. DCL, "My Family," 21.

44. Willey and Dry, *Woodberry Forest*, 10, 11, 43.

45. Woodberry Forest School Report of DCL for Scholastic Month Ending June 6, 1931. DCL's Rhodes scholarship file, Extracts from Letters of Recommendation, the Rhodes Scholarship Trust. DCL's letters to LCL: October 26, 1930, October 30, 1930, November 9, 1930, and May 10, 1931.

46. DCL to EJL, October 15, 1930.

47. DCL to LCL, October 20, 1930. DCL, undated notecard.

48. DCL to LCL, October 20, 1930.

49. DCL to Hugh Chaplin, January 6, 1928.

50. DCL to LCL, April 1, 1931. *A Register of Rhodes Scholars, 1903–1981*, 181. DCL to LCL, October 9, 1932. *Yale Banner 1935*, 256–257.

51. DCL, "My Family," 28.

52. Brinkley, *The Publisher*, 55. Dr. Daniel Horowitz, e-mail to author, March 30, 2013. Kelley, *Yale: A History*, 370, 387–388.

53. Pierson, *Yale Book of Numbers*, Section A. Enrollments and Degrees, 9. "Angell Welcomes Freshmen to Yale." G. Smith, "Life at Yale During the Great Depression," 2.

54. Kennedy, *Freedom from Fear*, 163–164. "Yale Lists Honors for 704 Students."

55. G. Smith, "Life at Yale During the Great Depression," 2.

56. DCL to LCL, August 2, 1935. G. Smith, "Life at Yale During the Great Depression," 4.

57. DCL to LCL, October 18, 1931.

58. *Yale Banner 1935*, 256–257.

59. DCL to LCL, March 17, 1933.

60. DCL to LCL, October 15, 1933. Schiff, "The Hoot Heard Round the World." *Yale Banner 1935*, 256–257.

61. "Seniors Elect 86 Juniors to Yale Societies." John Lee, e-mail to author, June 19, 2011.

62. *Yale Banner 1935*, 256–257.

63. Yale College-Scholarship Record, DCL, BA, June 1935. A scholar of the second rank was a student who graduated with a grade average between eighty-five and eighty-nine. Lee was a scholar of the first rank during his junior year because he had a grade average of ninety on a hundred-point scale.

64. DCL to LCL, November 30, 1931.

65. DCL to LCL, January 8, 1932.

66. DCL to LCL, October 9, 1932. Dr. John P. Scully, letter to author, June 8, 1999.

67. DCL, "The Elizabeth Bentley Matter," 19.

68. Hobsbawm, *The Age of Extremes*, 32, 35, 97.

69. Aydelotte, *The American Rhodes Scholarships*, 20. Ziegler, *Legacy*, 19, 129. DCL to LCL, January 4, 1934.

70. DCL's Rhodes scholarship file, Rhodes House, Oxford, Extracts from Lee's Essay and Letters of Recommendation.

71. "4 Yale Students Rhodes Scholars." EJL to DCL, January 11, 1935.

72. DCL, "The Elizabeth Bentley Matter," 19.

Chapter 2 "A Nursery of Somewhat Revolutionary Ideas"

1. DCL to LCL, October 12, 1935.

2. *A Register of Rhodes Scholars, 1903–1981*, 256–265. The Class of 1904 yielded the first American Rhodes scholars. No Americans were selected in 1906, 1909, 1912, and 1915. When the United States entered World War I in

1917, elections to the scholarships were postponed until 1919. Vassiliev, WN #3, Biography of Izra, 129.

3. Reverend Beverly D. Tucker to DCL, January 8, 1935.

4. Ybarra, *Washington Gone Crazy*, 384–385. "Arnold Cantwell Smith."

5. Michelmas 1935 Lectures, Tutors' Reports, Lee, D. C. DCL to LCL, October 12, 1935, and October 19, 1935.

6. Ziegler, *Legacy*, 128, 130.

7. Burleigh, *Moral Combat*, 36.

8. Gregory, *The Last Great War*, 290.

9. Winter, *The Great War and the British People*, 93. Morris, *Oxford*, 264.

10. Boyle, *The Climate of Treason*, 18. McElwee, *Britain's Locust Years*, 252.

11. Thomson, *England in the Twentieth Century*, 148.

12. Gardiner, *The Thirties*, 171, 185, 186, 498. This resolution became known as the "Oxford Pledge."

13. Overy, *The Morbid Age*, xx, 3.

14. Gardiner, *The Thirties*, 396.

15. Gardiner, *The Thirties*, 392–393. Hobsbawm, *The Age of Extremes*, 157–159.

16. Gardiner, *The Thirties*, 392. Burleigh, *Moral Combat*, 10.

17. Sinclair, *The Red and the Blue*, 63.

18. DCL to LCL, March 9, 1936.

19. Petrie, *Not a Bowl of Cherries*, 25.

20. Petrie, *Not a Bowl of Cherries*, 2–3, 7–8, 17.

21. Brendon, *The Decline and Fall of the British Empire*, 266–267, 269.

22. Petrie, *Not a Bowl of Cherries*, 15, 23–25. "Engagement Announced."

23. DCL to LCL, February 14, 1938.

24. Ishbel Scott Gibb to LCL, October 4, 1936.

25. Ishbel Scott Gibb to LCL, October 4, 1936.

26. Evans, *The Third Reich in Power*, 633. DCL to LCL, April 5, 1936.

27. Petrie, *Not a Bowl of Cherries*, 26.

28. DCL to LCL, undated letter, Kiefersfelden, Germany. DCL to LCL, September 5, 1936.

29. DCL to LCL, November 7, 1936. DCL to LCL, November 15, 1936. DCL to EJL, August 30, 1936. In at least one presidential election, Edmund and Lucy voted for Thomas. See AL, "Memories of My Parents, 3.

30. DCL to LCL, January 3, 1937. Schlatter, "On Being a Communist at Harvard."

31. DCL to LCL, May 10, 1937. DCL to LCL, July 10, 1937.

32. DCL to LCL, April 10, 1937. Pelling, *The British Communist Party*, 102. Collard, *Soviet Justice and the Trial of Radek and Others*, 82.

33. DCL's Rhodes scholarship file, Rhodes House, Oxford, Report to Selection Committee 1936–1937.

34. DCL to LCL, July 16, 1937. Crosby, Aydelotte, and Valentine, *Oxford of Today*, 111.

35. DCL to LCL, August 8, 1937.

36. DCL to LCL, August 15, 1937.

37. Burleigh, *Moral Combat*, 89, 92.

38. DCL to LCL, September 2, 1937.

39. DCL to LCL, September 2, 1937. Petrie, *Not a Bowl of Cherries*, 26.

40. Petrie, *Not a Bowl of Cherries*, 27.

41. Perry, *Last of the Cold War Spies*, 39–49, 67.

42. Conquest, *The Great Terror*, 180.

43. DCL to LCL, September 2, 1937.

44. DCL to LCL, September 11, 1937.

45. DCL to LCL, September 19, 1937.

46. Ishbel Scott Gibb to LCL, September 19, 1937.

47. DCL to EJL, September 26, 1937.

48. DCL to LCL, undated. DCL to LCL, October 18, 1937.

49. "Engagement Announced." DCL, "My Family," 44. DCL to LCL, April 20, 1938.

50. DCL to LCL, April 30, 1938. DCL to LCL, undated. DCL to AL, March 3, 1938.

51. Christopher Merillat, interview with author, June 20, 2005. DCL to LCL, May 9, 1938. Papers of the Williams Family, Box 16, Letters of Murat Williams to his Parents—Oxford University, Folder 1, 1937–1938, Special Collections, University of Virginia Library.

52. DCL to LCL, March 11, 1938. Kelley, *Yale: A History*, 384. EJL to DCL, March 9, 1938. Myres McDougal to DCL, March 11, 1938.

53. Myres McDougal to DCL, March 11, 1938. White, *Alger Hiss's Looking Glass Wars*, 27.

54. DCL to LCL, February 7, 1938. Ascherson, "What Sort of Traitors?" 6–7.

55. *A Register of Rhodes Scholars, 1903–1981*, 260. DCL to LCL, May 20, 1938. FBI Report, September 26, 1949, WFO, 14–15. EJL to DCL, May 5, 1938.

56. DCL to LCL, May 29, 1938.

57. DCL to LCL, May 20, 1938.

Chapter 3 The Party

1. FBI Report, May 29, 1952, New Haven, Connecticut, DCL, Espionage-R, ISA of 1950, 2. Robert Nangle, telephone interview with author, December 9, 2011. See also the nineteen-page summary of Katharine Nangle's interviews with the FBI in J. E. Franzmathes, August 27, 1954, DCL, 1–9, in NARA RG 59, General Records of the State Department, File Unit 130, Classified, A-Le, 1950–1959, Box 23 (DCL Passport file). Persico, *Roosevelt's Secret War*, 31. Haynes and Klehr, *Venona*, 104–105.

2. Haynes, *Red Scare or Red Menace?* 18.

3. Persico, *Roosevelt's Secret War*, 32. B. Smith, *The Shadow Warriors*, 21.

4. Robert Nangle, telephone interview with author, October 17, 2011. Katharine Nangle died on October 2, 1988.

5. Robert Nangle, telephone interview with author, December 9, 2011.

6. Franzmathes, August 27, 1954, DCL, 2, DCL Passport file.

7. FBI HQ file, Subject: Silvermaster, 69, Vol. 19, ERI. FBI Summary of File, References, Subject: DCL, June 3, 1953, 23.

8. FBI Report, May 29, 1952, Washington, DC, 1. NARA RG 233, IF, Series 1, NF, DCL, Box 193, August 5, 1948. Robert Nangle, telephone interview with author, December 9, 2011. Benjamin Christie Nangle, Yale University Manuscripts and Archives Historical Register Online, Nangle, Benjamin Christie. Benjamin died on June 20, 1972.

9. Robert Nangle, telephone interview with author, December 9, 2011.

10. Franzmathes, 2–3, DCL Passport file. Robert Nangle, telephone interview with author, December 9, 2011.

11. Franzmathes, 3, DCL Passport file. Goldstein, *American Blacklist*, 16, 105.

12. FBI Report, May 29, 1952, Washington, DC, 2–4, found in Franzmathes, DCL Passport file. FBI Report, May 29, 1952, New Haven, Connecticut, DCL, 2. Lee's law school professor is quoted in FBI Report, February 11, 1955, New Haven, Connecticut, DCL, Espionage-R, ISA of 1950, 3. Letter to Director, NY100-96630, undated.

13. Franzmathes, 3, DCL Passport file. Petrie, *Not a Bowl of Cherries*, 27.

14. Franzmathes, 8, DCL Passport file.

15. Franzmathes, 7–9, DCL Passport file.

16. Vassiliev, WN #3, 102. Klehr, Haynes, and Firsov, *The Secret World of American Communism*, 10. The static membership of the CPUSA is hard to gauge. Maurice Isserman estimates CPUSA membership in 1939 at between 50,000 and 75,000. Isserman, *Which Side Were You On?* 10. Ellen Schrecker states that the CPUSA had approximately 82,000 members at the end of 1938. Schrecker, *Many Are the Crimes*, 15.

17. Ackerman, *Young J. Edgar*, 23.

18. Klehr, Haynes, and Firsov, *The Secret World of American Communism*, 5. Romerstein and Breindel, *The Venona Secrets*, 96. Isserman, *Which Side Were You On?* 10.

19. Klehr, Haynes, and Firsov, *The Secret World of American Communism*, 6–7. Schrecker, *Many Are the Crimes*, 11.

20. Schrecker, *The Age of McCarthyism*, 7.

21. Schrecker, *Many Are the Crimes*, 7.

22. Klehr, Haynes, and Firsov, *The Secret World of American Communism*, 8.

23. Aaron, "A Decade of Convictions," 741. Schrecker, *Many Are the Crimes*, 14. Fried, *Communism in America*, 250. Browder's actual words, which were later altered, were "Communism is the Americanism of the twentieth century."

24. Andrew and Gordievsky, *KGB*, 147–148. Aaron, "A Decade of Convictions," 741, 743.

25. Hastings, *Inferno*, 4. Haynes, *Red Scare or Red Menace?* 4–5.

26. Schrecker, *Many Are the Crimes*, 16. Burleigh, *Moral Combat*, 110–114. Benson and Warner, *Venona*, ix.

27. Newton, *The Cambridge Spies*, 38.

28. US House of Representatives, Subcommittee on Un-American Activities, 84th Cong., 2d Sess., Communist Activities in New Haven, Connecticut, Area, September 24 and 25, 1956, New Haven, Connecticut, 5657. Communists were drawn to New Haven because of its brass industries and its manufacturing. Vassiliev, WN #3, 107. Peake to Benson, memorandum, October 22, 1996.

29. DCL, "The Elizabeth Bentley Matter," 25. Haynes and Klehr, "J. Robert Oppenheimer." DCL to the AG, DOA, Rebuttal of Allegations, PHS, June 21, 1951, 21.

30. Fox, "What the Spider Did," 206. Romerstein and Breindel, *The Venona Secrets*, 59.

31. Dallin, *Soviet Espionage*, 2, 401–402.

32. Chervonnaya, "Golos," 4. Cave-Brown and MacDonald, *On a Field of Red*, 341. Haynes, Klehr, and Vassiliev, *Spies*, 496.

33. Andrew and Gordievsky, *KGB*, 230. Dallin, *Soviet Espionage*, 14–15. Trotsky founded the GRU. It was originally known as the Fourth Department of the Army.

34. Sibley, *Red Spies in America*, 14, 24. Divine, *Roosevelt and World War II*, 75.

35. Romerstein and Breindel, *The Venona Secrets*, 4, 8.

36. Haynes, Klehr, and Vassiliev, *Spies*, 489, 501. Andrew and Mitrokhin, *The Sword and the Shield*, 107.

37. Conquest, *The Great Terror*, 180. Burleigh, *Moral Combat*, 109. Dallin, *Soviet Espionage*, 6–7. Ferguson, *The War of the World*, 210. Haynes and Klehr, *Venona*, 165. Walter Krivitsky and Aleksandr Orlov were two other major Soviet defectors.

38. Haynes, Klehr, and Vassiliev, *Spies*, 500–501.

39. Dallin, *Soviet Espionage*, 410. Report of the FBI NYFO, October 13, 1948, on the personnel effects of Jacob Golos, FBI HQ File, Subject: Silvermaster, Vol. 146, ERI.

40. Chervonnaya, "Golos," 1–2. Golos's 1923 US passport lists April 23, 1890, as his birth date.

41. Chervonnaya, "Golos," 2–3.

42. Chervonnaya, "Golos," 4. US Government, US Department of State, and Bureau of Diplomatic Security, "The Vital Function."

43. Haynes, Klehr, and Vassiliev, *Spies*, 498–500.

44. Fried, *Nightmare in Red*, 47, 52.

45. Haynes, Klehr, and Vassiliev, *Spies*, 499–500.

46. Vassiliev, WN #2, 15. Chervonnaya, "Golos," 5–6. Haynes, Klehr, and Vassiliev, *Spies*, 203. Abraham Glasser was the CPUSA's mole inside the Department of Justice.

47. Ryan, *Earl Browder*, 182, 192. Weinstein and Vassiliev, *The Haunted Wood*, 92.

48. SOHPC, Mary Price Adamson interview, April 19, 1976, 3–4.

49. SOHPC, Mary Price Adamson interview, April 19, 1976, 4, 21, 54. FBI, HQ File, Subject: Silvermaster, File No. 65-56402, Vol. 118, ERI, FBI Report, April 5, 1947, WFO, Director, FBI, Re: Gregory, Espionage-R, Mary Wolfe Price, 1, 4.

50. SOHPC, Mary Price Adamson interview, April 19, 1976, 30, 69–72. FBI Report, April 5, 1947, WFO, Mary Wolfe Price, 4, Vol. 118, ERI. See FBI Report, February 12, 1952, WFO, 1, for Price and the Young Communist League.

51. FBI Report, November 29, 1945, Washington, DC, Nathan Gregory Silvermaster, Espionage, 110, Vol. 5, ERI. FBI Report, November 16, 1945, Mary Wolfe Price, Personal History, 2, Vol. 1, ERI.

52. FBI Report, December 5, 1945, NYFO, Re: Signed Statement of Elizabeth Bentley, dated November 30, 1945, 71, Vol. 6, ERI.

53. FBI Report, April 27, 1952, NYFO, DCL, Espionage-R, ISA of 1950, 1. Andrew and Mitrokhin, *The Sword and the Shield*, 106, states that Price started working for Lippmann that June. Vassiliev, WN #2, 9. Haynes, Klehr, and Vassiliev, *Spies*, 174. FBI Report, February 13, 1947, Director, FBI, Confidential Letter, NY 65-14603, 14.

54. Christopher Merillat, interview with author, June 20, 2005.

55. Waller, *Wild Bill Donovan*, 39–42.

56. Application for Federal Employment, DCL, July 1, 1942. Lee's HUAC file states that he started with Donovan's firm on June 16, 1939. This is not correct. Christopher Merillat, interview with author, June 20, 2005. DCL, "The Elizabeth Bentley Matter," 22.

57. EJL to DCL, December 21, 1940.

58. DCL to the AG, 2. The FBI publicly released Osborn's name in FBI Report, August 4, 1952, NYFO, DCL, Espionage-R, ISA of 1950, 3. Osborn died on October 17, 1976.

59. FBI Report, January 14, 1955, NYFO, DCL, 12.

60. Fried, *Nightmare in Red*, 52–53. John Earle Haynes, e-mail to the author, September 21, 2010.

61. John Earle Haynes, e-mail to the author, September 21, 2010. FBI Report, April 9, 1951, Washington, DC, File No. 65-5688, Espionage-R, 5. FBI Report, October 21, 1946, Underground Soviet Espionage Organization (NKVD) in Agencies of the United States Government, 163, Vol. 82, ERI. In her February 16, 1949, federal grand jury appearance, Bentley testified that Ishbel never joined the CPUSA because she feared that her membership would be uncovered and prejudice Lee. This contradicts with what she said on p. 36 of the signed statement she gave the FBI on November 30, 1945.

62. DCL to EJL, September 29, 1940.

63. FBI Summary of File References, Subject: DCL, June 3, 1953, 32. DCL to EJL, March 9, 1941.

64. DCL to the AG, June 21, 1951, PHS of DCL as a Loyal American, 9.

65. DCL to the AG, June 21, 1951, 22–23. FBI Report, September 29, 1949, WFO, DCL, 24, 27. Haynes and Klehr, *Venona*, 105.

66. FBI Report, undated, WFO, 100-21412, 15. DCL to the AG, June 21, 1951, 8, 25–26. Hastings, *Inferno*, 137.

67. Vassiliev, WN #3, 102, 104. Lee told the army that he met Mary Price in 1941. He told the HUAC that he first met her in 1939. Bentley told the Soviets that Lee met Mary Price in the spring of 1942. Price corroborated the year in an April 17, 1947, interview with the FBI. She told the FBI that she met Lee while he was on CAC's Executive Committee. He was elevated to the committee in 1942. Official Memorandum, to Director, FBI, from SAC, Birmingham, April 18, 1947, Subject: Gregory, Espionage-R, Subject: Silvermaster, 3, Vol. 118, ERI.

68. Vassiliev, WN #3, 102. Isserman, "Disloyalty as a Principle," 5.

69. FBI Report, September 26, 1949, Washington, DC, DCL, 5. Haynes and Klehr, *Venona*, 105. Vassiliev, WN #3, 102. The COI was renamed the OSS and placed under the Joint Chiefs of Staff on June 13, 1942.

Chapter 4 My League of Gentlemen

1. DCL to EJL, March 9, 1941. Lee registered for the draft on October 16, 1940. See Application for Federal Employment, DCL, July 1, 1942. His draft board classified him 3A.

2. Divine, *Roosevelt and World War II*, 7.

3. Brands, *A Traitor to His Class*, 283, 480.

4. Divine, *Roosevelt and World War II*, 25, 30. Hastings, *Inferno*, 181–182. Persico, *Roosevelt's Secret War*, 82.

5. Heinrichs, "The United States Prepares for War," 10–11. Troy, *Donovan and the CIA*, 7. E. J. Kahn, *The China Hands*, 70–71.

6. Troy, *Donovan and the CIA*, 7–10.

7. Cameron-Watt, *How War Came*, 126.

8. Brands, *A Traitor to His Class*, 575–581. Divine, *Roosevelt and World War II*, 40.

9. Heinrichs, "The United States Prepares for War," 11–12. Burns, *Roosevelt: The Soldier of Freedom*, 100.

10. Troy, *Wild Bill and Intrepid*, 117. Warner, *The Office of Strategic Services*, 2.

11. Troy, *Donovan and the CIA*, 30. Waller, *Wild Bill Donovan*, 43–44.

12. Ranelagh, *The Agency*, 38.

13. Schlesinger, *A Life in the 20th Century*, 296.

14. Troy, *Donovan and the CIA*, 31. Cline, *Secrets, Spies, and Scholars*, 27–28. Brands, *A Traitor to His Class*, 526.

15. Warner, *The Office of Strategic Services*, 3. Waller, *Wild Bill Donovan*, 61.

16. Troy, *Donovan and the CIA*, 37–39. Waller, *Wild Bill Donovan*, 66.

17. Troy, *Donovan and the CIA*, 417–20; Donovan quote from p. 419.

18. Troy, *Donovan and the CIA*, 66–68, 421. McDonald, "The OSS and Its Records," 83. Cline, *Secrets, Spies, and Scholars*, 35–36. Waller, *Wild Bill Donovan*, 70–72.

19. Warner, *The Office of Strategic Services*, 4.

20. Cave-Brown, *Wild Bill Donovan*, 173.

21. Troy, *Donovan and the CIA*, 78. Donovan quoted in Cave-Brown, *Wild Bill Donovan*, 298.

22. Davies quoted in Carter, "Mission to Yenan," 307. Donovan quoted in Persico, *Roosevelt's Secret War*, 424. At the time Donovan said this, the US Army's policy on hiring known communists was far from clear. In the wake of Hitler and Stalin's 1939 nonaggression pact, it had excluded all communists from its ranks. The army modified this policy in 1941 and 1942, keeping suspected communists from serving in sensitive posts and as officers. This changed again in 1944 when it decided that "no action will be taken . . . that is predicated on membership in or adherence to the doctrines of the Communist Party unless there is a specific finding that the individual involved has a loyalty to the Communist Party as an organization that overrides his loyalty to the United States." See Rafalko, *Counterintelligence in World War II*, 2:3, 14, 20–22. For a list of Soviet spies inside the OSS, see John Earl Haynes, e-mail to author, May 14, 2012: "Akra" or "Akr" (unknown); Linn Farish; Jane Foster; Irving Goff; Stanley Graze; Maurice Halperin; Hans Hirschfield; Captain Hogman (?); Bella Joseph; Emma Harriet Joseph; Julius Joseph; Philip Keeney; Duncan Lee; Leonard Emil Mims; Franz Neuman; John Scott; Alfred Tanz; Helen Tenney; Dimitry Vladimrovich Varley; David Wahl; Donald Wheeler; and George Wuchinich. The GRU recruited four of the twenty-two. There may have been eight more Soviet agents inside the OSS. Most of these eight appear to have been secret communists, but it is not known if they were actually recruited as spies. For the assertion that as many as one hundred OSS employees were CPUSA members, see Tanenhaus, "Tangled Treason." Donovan quoted in "Donovan Backs Duncan Lee as Loyal in War."

23. Warner, *The Office of Strategic Services*, 9. Cline, *Secrets, Spies, and Scholars*, 39.

24. Troy, *Donovan and the CIA*, 80. Cave-Brown, *Wild Bill Donovan*, 172.

25. DCL to the AG, DOA, Rebuttal of Allegations, PHS, June 21, 1951, 10. DCL to Robin Winks, March 7, 1985. John J. McDonough, Memorandum on DCL, May 1, 1942,

26. NARA, RG No. 233, Records of the HUAC, IF, Series 1, NF, DCL, August 5, 1948. *A Register of Rhodes Scholars, 1903–1981*, 181. McDonough, Memorandum on DCL, May 8, 1942. Coffin, as a prominent leader of the Episcopal Church, knew Edmund well.

27. Memorandum for Mr. Hugh R. Wilson from Mr. Allen Dulles, May 21, 1942. Grose, *Gentlemen Spy*, 141. NARA, RG 226, Records of the OSS, COI/OSS Central Files/Entry 92, Box 55, Folder 58, John J. McDonough to Watts Hill, May 29, 1942.

28. Troy, *Donovan and the CIA*, 427. This was the military order of June 13, 1942. Warner, *The Office of Strategic Services*, 8.

29. Application for Federal Employment, DCL, July 1, 1942. Personal Affidavit, OSS, DCL, July 1, 1942. Oath of Office, OSS, DCL, July 1, 1942.

30. OSS, July 2, 1942, Director of Personnel. See also NARA, RG 233, IF, Series 1, NF, DCL, Box 193, Army Separation Qualification Record, May 4, 1946.

31. Peake, "Soviet Espionage and the Office of Strategic Services," 112–113. NARA, RG 233, IF, Series 1, NF, DCL, Box 193, August 5, 1948. On August 5, 1948, the HUAC noted, "His security approval was based on a brief unidentified investigation conducted in June 1942." On May 19, 1942, the OSS established its Office of Security, with the specific task of preventing the agency from employing "persons of dubious allegiances or affiliated with anti-American elements." While small, this office was able to weed out some applicants who were Nazi sympathizers or CPUSA members.

32. Franzmathes, August 26, 1954, Memorandum for the Files, 4, DCL Passport file. See also FBI Report, August 4, 1952, NYFO, DCL, Espionage-R, ISA 1950, 4–5. FBI Report, August 4, 1952, NYFO, 4–5. NARA, RG 233, IF, Series 1, NF, DCL, Box 193, "List of Residents of 531 East 84 Street, NY, NY." Seward died on February 15, 2012.

33. NARA, RG 233, IF, Series 1, NF, DCL, Box 193, Classification Questionnaire of Reserve Officers, DCL, July 6, 1942. Warner, *The Office of Strategic Services*, 9. About two-thirds of the OSS's personnel held a US Army or Army Air Forces rank. Army of the United States, Separation Qualification Record, DCL. The army made Lee a first lieutenant in its reserves on July 29, 1942, and called him to active duty on August 3, 1942. FBI Summary of File References, Subject: DCL, June 3, 1953, 91.

34. Vassiliev, WN #3, 102. This report highlights the hazards of relying on raw intelligence reports for completely accurate information. It wrongly states that Lee attended the universities of Virginia and Cambridge and graduated from Yale's law school. It also states that he worked for the COI in New York. On the other hand, it correctly notes that he married Ishbel, worked for RWR, and met Price through Mildred, her sister.

35. Vassiliev, WN #3, 104. Office Memorandum, Director of FBI from: SAC Birmingham, Subject: Gregory Espionage-R, April 18, 1947, Subject: Silvermaster, 3, Vol. 118, ERI.

36. Pincher, *Traitors*, 89. FBI Report, July 26, 1951, Washington, DC, DCL, Espionage-R, ISA of 1950, 3. OSS, Washington, DC, July 7, 1944, Memorandum for All Branch Chiefs and Strategic Services Officers, DCL. NARA, RG 233, IF, Series 1, NF, DCL, DOA, Separation Qualification Record. Report of Efficiency Rating, as of March 31, 1943, DCL.

37. NARA, RG 226, Records of the Office of the Director, Strategic Services, Roll 136, 590–591. Roll 18, 33–36.

38. Vassiliev, WN #3, 104. The Lees lived at 1820 Clydesdale Place, NW, in Washington, DC, and then moved to 3014 Dent Place, Apartment #18, in November 1942.

39. Vassiliev, WN #3, 103.

40. Vassiliev, WN #3, 103. NARA, RG 226, Entry 146, Box 183, Folder 2608. Feklisov and Kostin, *The Man Behind the Rosenbergs*, 17.

41. Vassiliev, WN #3, 103. Vassiliev, WN #1, 40. Vassiliev, WN #3, 103.

42. Weinstein and Vassiliev, *The Haunted Wood*, 249. Benson and Warner, *Venona*, x.

43. FBI Report, December 5, 1945, NYFO, Re: Signed Statement of Elizabeth Bentley, dated November 30, 1945, 33, Vol. 6, ERI. Vassiliev, WN #1, 50. FBI Report, April 27, 1952, NYFO, DCL, Espionage-R, ISA of 1950, 3.

Chapter 5 A Crisis of Conscience

1. FBI Report, November 13, 1945, to Director of FBI from E. E. Conroy, Re: Elizabeth Bentley, 1. Vassiliev, WN #2, 11. Olmstead, *Red Spy Queen*, 1–2. FBI Report, November 13 1945, 1. Kessler, *Clever Girl*, 15–16.

2. Olmstead, *Red Spy Queen*, 1–2. Vassiliev, WN #2, 11.

3. FBI Report, December 5, 1945, NYFO, Re: Signed Statement of Elizabeth Bentley, dated November 30, 1945, 5, 7, Vol. 6, ERI.

4. Olmstead, *Red Spy Queen*, 3, 5. Peake, "Afterword," 219. Vassiliev, WN #2, 12. Peake, "Afterword," 223.

5. Vassiliev, WN #2, 12.

6. Olmstead, *Red Spy Queen*, 5–9.

7. Vassiliev, WN #2, 13. FBI Report, December 5, 1945, NYFO, Re: Signed Statement of Elizabeth Bentley, dated November 30, 1945, 3, Vol. 6, ERI.

8. FBI Report, December 5, 1945, NYFO, Re: Signed Statement of Elizabeth Bentley, dated November 30, 1945, 3, Vol. 6, ERI. Dallin, *Soviet Espionage*, 515. Olmstead, *Red Spy Queen*, 16.

9. Olmstead, *Red Spy Queen*, 15–17. Peake, "Afterword," 228.

10. FBI Report, December 5, 1945, NYFO, Re: Signed Statement of Elizabeth Bentley, dated November 30, 1945, 3, 7–8, 10, Vol. 6, ERI. Bentley, *Out of Bondage*, 68.

11. Peake, "Afterword," 231–232. FBI Report, December 5, 1945, NYFO, Re: Signed Statement of Elizabeth Bentley, dated November 30, 1945, 10, Vol. 6, ERI.

12. Underground Soviet Espionage Organization in Agencies of the United States Government, August 24, 1948, 7, Vol. 144, ERI.

13. FBI Report, December 5, 1945, NYFO, Re: Signed Statement of Elizabeth Bentley, dated November 30, 1945, 56–57, 68–69, Vol. 6, ERI.

14. Peake, "Afterword," 232. Olmstead, *Red Spy Queen*, 41.

15. FBI Report, December 5, 1945, NYFO, Re: Signed Statement of Elizabeth Bentley, dated November 30, 1945, 15–16, Vol. 6, ERI.

16. FBI Report, December 5, 1945, NYFO, Re: Signed Statement of Elizabeth Bentley, dated November 30, 1945, 14–15, Vol. 6, ERI. Olmstead, *Red Spy Queen*, 37–38.

17. Vassiliev, WN #2, 16.

18. The FBI listed the following as members of the Silvermaster Group: Nathan Gregory Silvermaster, Helen White Silvermaster, William Ludwig Ullmann, George Silverman, Harry Dexter White, Lauchlin Currie, Sol Adler,

William Taylor, Irving Kaplan, Sonia Gold, and Bela Gold. FBI Report, December 7, 1945, NYFO, Director, FBI, Re: Nathan Gregory Silvermaster, Espionage, Subject: Silvermaster, Vol. 15, ERI. In October 1946, the FBI added Norman Bursler, Frank Coe, and Anatole Boris Volkov.

19. Weinstein and Vassiliev, *The Haunted Wood*, 158–159. Olmstead, *Red Spy Queen*, 48.

20. Weinstein and Vassiliev, *The Haunted Wood*, 161.

21. Vassiliev, WN #2, 1. Bentley told the FBI in November 1945 that her first contact with Helen and Gregory Silvermaster was in August 1941. FBI Report, December 5, 1945, NYFO, Re: Signed Statement of Elizabeth Bentley, dated November 30, 1945, 23, Vol. 6, ERI. Andrew and Gordievsky, *KGB*, 283. Kessler, *Clever Girl*, 81. FBI Report, October 21, 1946, Underground Soviet Espionage Organization (NKVD) in Agencies of the United States Government, Table of Contents, Vol. 82, ERI.

22. FBI Report, December 5, 1945, NYFO, Re: Signed Statement of Elizabeth Bentley, dated November 30, 1945, 34, Vol. 6, ERI. Bentley told the FBI that she met Lee in late 1942, but she told the HUAC that she first met him in late 1942 or early 1943. NARA RG 233, IF, Series 1, NF, 1, Mary Price, Box 37. See also F&RS, Price, Mary, Box 270 in the same RG. FBI Report, September 26, 1949, Washington, DC, DCL, 8.

23. Vassiliev, WN #1, 50. Price was also known to the NKVD as "Kid." Bentley may not have attended this meeting. Her reporting on this is contradictory. See FBI Report, April 27, 1952, NYFO, DCL, Espionage-R, ISA of 1950, 5–6.

24. Confidential Letter to the Director, NYFO, February 13, 1947, Subject: Silvermaster, 4–5, Vol. 118, ERI. Price contracted viral pneumonia in April 1943. She was absent from Washington in April and May 1943. Venona 782, May 26, 1943, from New York to Moscow. Vassiliev, WN #3, 103.

25. Vassiliev, WN #3, 131. FBI Report, November 9, 1954, Washington, DC, DCL, Espionage-R, ISA of 1950, 10. FBI Report, December 5, 1945, NYFO, Re: Elizabeth Bentley's Statement, dated November 30, 1945, 52, Vol. 6, ERI.

26. OSS Memorandum, June 16, 1943, Subject: Request for Transportation and Orders, William J. Donovan. OSS Letter, June 10, 1943, to Colonel Gustave Guenther, USA, from William J. Donovan. NARA, RG 226, Office of the Director of Strategic Services, Roll 67, 457.

27. Waller, *Wild Bill Donovan*, 207–208. FBI Report, January 4, 1952, Washington, DC, DCL, Espionage-R, ISA of 1950, 46. NARA, RG 226, Chronological Development of FE-4-CBI, Entry 210, Box 420. FBI Report, December 28, 1953, Washington, DC, DCL, Espionage-R, ISA of 1950, 15. Vassiliev, WN #3, 106.

28. Sevareid, *Not So Wild a Dream*, 245.

29. Ghio, "Lost in Head-Hunter Country," 6, 8.

30. Sevareid, *Not So Wild a Dream*, 251. Ghio, "Lost in Head-Hunter Country," 8.

31. Sevareid, "Our Good Friends, the Head-Hunters," 124.

32. DCL to the AG, DOA, Rebuttal of Allegations, PHS, June 21, 1951, 10.

33. Sevareid, *Not So Wild a Dream*, 245. Davies to Brigadier General William J. Donovan, November 1, 1943.

34. NARA RG 233, IF, Series 1, NF, DCL, Box 193, Army Separation Qualification Record, May 4, 1946. Vassiliev, WN #3, 104.

35. FBI Report, April 27, 1952, NYFO, DCL, Espionage-R, ISA of 1950, 5.

36. Bentley also told the FBI about Lee and Price's intimate relationship in 1955. See FBI Office Memorandum, July 25, 1955, Director, FBI, from SAC, New Haven, Connecticut, Subject: Nathan Gregory Silvermaster, et al., Espionage-R, Subject: Silvermaster, 4, Vol. 161, ERI.

37. Vassiliev, WN #3, 103–104.

38. Vassiliev, WN #3, 104–105. FBI Report, April 27, 1952, NYFO, DCL, Espionage-R, ISA of 1950, 2.

39. FBI Report, September 24, 1951, Washington, DC, DCL, Espionage-R, ISA of 1950, 2, 4. FBI Report, November 14, 1945, Mary Wolfe Price, with Alias, Mary Watkins Price, Personal History. Price applied to Arlington Hall on October 27, 1943, and to the OSS on November 9, 1943. Haynes, Klehr, and Vassiliev, *Spies*, 81. Benson and Warner, *Venona*, xxxviii. FBI Report, November 9, 1954, Washington, DC, DCL.

40. FBI Report, July 7, 1954, Washington, DC, DCL, Espionage-R, ISA of 1950, 11–12. FBI Report, August 8, 1953, to Director, FBI, 2.

41. Vassiliev, WN #3, 104. Undated FBI Letter to Director, NY 65-14913, 3. FDR PL Library, PSF OSS Reports, October 29, 1943, Box 153.

42. Lee became chief of the Secretariat on January 31, 1944. FBI Report, July 26, 1951, Washington, DC, DCL, Espionage-R, ISA of 1950, 4. OSS Memorandum, Major DCL, 0-912627, May 8, 1945. Lee requested a transfer to the OSS's Secret Intelligence Branch on October 1, 1944. His military file lists the November date as his official start date. David Acheson, interview with author, June 20, 2008.

43. Vassiliev, WN #3, 105.

44. FBI Report, September 26, 1949, Washington, DC, DCL, 5–6, Security Matter-C. Golos did give Browder selected items that covered political, economic, and social matters.

45. Vassiliev, WN #2, 16. Some of her sources had no doubt about where their information was going. Victor Perlo, the ringleader of the Perlo Group, asked her point blank if "Joe" (Stalin) was getting the information he was passing. FBI Report, April 27, 1952, NYFO, DCL, Espionage-R, ISA of 1950, 6. FBI Report, September 26, 1949, Washington, DC, 5. FBI Report, September 26, 1949, Washington, DC, 6.

46. NARA RG 226, Entry 146, Box 192, File 2712, DCL to Mr. Sulloway, November 21, 1943. Vassiliev, WN #3, 106.

47. Vassiliev, WN #3, 110. NARA RG 226, Office of the Director of Strategic Services, Roll 45, Frames 1320–1326. FBI Report, April 27, 1952, NYFO, DCL, Espionage-R, ISA of 1950, 6.

48. B. Smith, *Sharing Secrets with Stalin*, 186. "Milestones: 1937–1945: The Tehran Conference, 1943." Bentley told the FBI that she also got information on Overlord's date from Silvermaster's group.

49. Burns, *Roosevelt: The Soldier of Freedom*, 483. Vassiliev, WN #3, 106.

50. Waller, *Wild Bill Donovan*, 220–223.

51. Bentley, *Out of Bondage*, 259–260. FBI Report, July 7, 1954, Washington, DC, DCL, Espionage-R, ISA of 1950, 8. Bentley told the HUAC the same story on August 10, 1948.

52. Sibley, *Red Spies in America*, 107–108. Vassiliev, WN #1, 92–93.

53. FBI Report, February 13, 1947, NYFO, Director, FBI, Re: Gregory Espionage-R, Silvermaster, 5, Vol. 118, ERI. FBI Report, December 5, 1945, NYFO, Re: Elizabeth Bentley's Statement, dated November 30, 1945, 36, Vol. 6, ERI.

54. Waller, *Wild Bill Donovan*, 224–225. Vassiliev, WN #1, 92, 88. See NARA RG Group 226, Office of the Director of Strategic Services, Office, Roll 79, Frame 283–287, 295–298, 415–419, 430–433, and 437.

55. Vassiliev, WN #3, 110. Cave-Brown, *Wild Bill Donovan*, 394. Vassiliev, WN #3, 107. This cable, dated February 14, 1944, was from Major General John R. Dean to Donovan. NARA RG 226, Roll 88, Office of the Director of Strategic Services. On March 23, 1944, Donovan sent a report on Kouyoumdjisky to the White House. FDR PL, PSF, OSS, Box 4, March 1944.

56. FBI Report, February 13, 1947, NYFO, 6. Bentley told the FBI that Lee failed to meet with her in the fall. The NKGB files, however, indicate that this meeting happened in the spring. Vassiliev, WN #2, 5. Bentley told the FBI essentially the same story in 1947.

57. Venona 830, June 9, 1944. Vassiliev, WN #3, 104.

58. Petrie, *Not a Bowl of Cherries*, 29. FBI Report, September 26, 1949, Washington, DC, DCL, Security-Matter-C, 4. FBI Report, April 27, 1952, NYFO, DCL, Espionage-R, ISA of 1950, 7.

59. Vassiliev, WN #3, 105. FBI Report, February 13, 1947, NYFO, 5. Bentley grand jury testimony, February 16, 1949. This testimony was made public by order of a federal judge. The Harry S. Truman Library has all the transcripts that have been released. See Records of United States Attorneys and Marshals, Transcripts of Grand Jury Testimony in Alger Hiss, NARA RG 118, 1947–1949.

60. Security Office Memorandum to William J. Donovan and O. C. Doering, July 20, 1944, Box 137C, Donovan Papers, Military History Institute, Carlisle, Pennsylvania, July 20, 1944, Memorandum to Donovan and Doering. Rafalko, *Counterintelligence in World War II*, 2:20.

61. Security Office Memorandum, July 20, 1944. Haynes and Klehr, *Venona*, 192–193. Klehr, Haynes, and Firsov, *The Secret World of American Communism*, 277–278. The four men were Milton Wolff, Vincent Lossowski, Irving Fajans, and Irving Goff.

62. Nathan Gregory Silvermaster, with Aliases, et al., August 24, 1948, 67–68, 205, Vol. 145, ERI. FBI Report, undated, Washington, DC, 100-21412, 19. FBI

Report, November 29, 1945, Washington, DC, Nathan Gregory Silvermaster, et al., 64. NARA RG 233, IF, Series 1, NF, Donald Niven Wheeler, Box 50. See Wheeler's file in the same RG, F&RS, Box 368.

63. Vassiliev, WN #3, 107. FBI Report, July 7, 1954, Washington, DC, DCL, Espionage-R, ISA of 1950, 12. Venona 1325, 1326, September 15, 1944. FBI Report, July 7, 1954, Washington, DC, DCL, Espionage-R, ISA of 1950, 12. This list included those OSS employees accused of spying for the Soviets, open communists, and communist sympathizers. Venona 1354, September 22, 1944. Haynes, Klehr, and Vassiliev, *Spies*, 308–309. Halperin's name is not on the list found in Vassiliev, WN #3, 110. FBI Report, May 12, 1951, NYFO, DCL, 6. Haynes, Klehr, and Vassiliev, *Spies*, 309. FBI Report, July 7, 1954, Washington, DC, 12. Vassiliev, WN #3, 125. Incredibly, the OSS appointed Wheeler to investigate leak suspects in his division. See also FBI Report, February 13, 1947, NYFO, 7.

64. OSS Memorandum, October 9, 1944, DCL, Subject: Transfer, Through: Chief, SI. FBI Report, July 26, 1951, Washington, DC, DCL, Espionage-R, ISA of 1950, 4. EJL to DCL, August 25, 1944.

65. Venona 1353, September 23, 1944. Vassiliev, WN #3, 104. Vassiliev, WN #3, 105.

66. Kessler, *Clever Girl*, 90. Haynes, Klehr, and Vassiliev, *Spies*, 503. Vassiliev, WN #1, 10.

67. Chervonnaya, "Zarubin," 1–2. Conquest, *Inside Stalin's Secret Police*, 145.

68. Olmstead, *Red Spy Queen*, 60. Haynes, Klehr, and Vassiliev, *Spies*, 506.

69. Vassiliev, WN #1, 9; WN #2, 3.

70. FBI Report, November 13, 1945, NYFO, Signed Statement of Elizabeth Bentley, November 8, 1945, 15. Olmstead, *Red Spy Queen*, 64. Haynes, Klehr, and Vassiliev, *Spies*, 503.

71. Olmstead, *Red Spy Queen*, 64. Haynes, Klehr, and Vassiliev, *Spies*, 507. Vassiliev, WN #2, 3.

72. Vassiliev, WN #2, 1, 2, 5.

73. Haynes, Klehr, and Vassiliev, *Spies*, 307, 508. FBI Report, December 7, 1945, NYFO, Director, FBI, Re: Nathan Gregory Silvermaster with aliases, et al., Espionage-R, Chart.

74. Fox, "What the Spider Did," 220–221,

75. Vassiliev, WN #2, 6, 18. Haynes, Klehr, and Vassiliev, *Spies*, 512.

76. FBI Report, February 21, 1946, Underground Soviet Espionage Organization (NKVD) in Agencies of the United States Government, 189, Vol. 82, ERI. Andrew and Gordievsky, *KGB*, 320.

77. Bentley quoted in FBI Report, November 13, 1945, NYFO, Signed Statement of Elizabeth Bentley, November 8, 1945, 18–19. Underground Soviet Espionage Organization in Agencies of the United States Government, August 24, 1948, 379, Vol. 144, ERI.

78. Kessler, *Clever Girl*, 106. Olmstead, *Red Spy Queen*, 67, 76.

79. Haynes, Klehr, and Vassiliev, *Spies*, 513. FBI Report, September 26, 1949, Washington, DC, DCL, Security Matter-C, 7. Kessler, *Clever Girl*, 102. FBI Report, April 27, 1952, NYFO, DCL, Espionage-R, ISA of 1950, 4.

80. Vassiliev, WN #2, 8. Olmstead, *Red Spy Queen*, 70.

81. Chervonnaya, "Katz," 1. Hyde, "Bernard Schuster and Joseph Katz," 38.

82. FBI Report, November 13, 1945, NYFO. Bentley, November 8, 1945, 16–17.

83. Vassiliev, WN #3, 106.

84. Vassiliev, WN #3, 106–108.

85. FBI Report, December 5, 1945, NYFO, Re: Elizabeth Bentley's Statement, dated November 30, 1945, 36, Vol. 6, ERI.

86. FBI Report, December 5, 1945, NYFO, Re: Elizabeth Bentley's Statement, dated November 30, 1945, 45, Vol. 6, ERI.

87. Vassiliev, WN #3, 109.

88. DCL Military Record and Report of Separation, Certificate of Service. FBI Report, December 5, 1945, NYFO, Re: Elizabeth Bentley's Statement, dated November 30, 1945, 36, Vol. 6, ERI.

89. David Acheson, interview with author, June 20, 2008. Walter Pforzheimer, interview with author, June 17, 1999. Elizabeth "Betty" McIntosh, telephone interview with author, April 17, 2008. The woman was named Annabell Andies. McIntosh, telephone interview with author, May 14, 2008. Andies, according to McIntosh, killed herself in 1945 or 1946.

90. FBI Report, September 29, 1949, Washington, DC, DCL, Security Matter-C, 3. Strategic Services Unit, Washington, DC, December 6, 1945, SI Branch Order No. 82. Troy, *Donovan and the CIA*, 287. Warner, *The Office of Strategic Services*, 42.

91. Donovan to DCL, OSS, Washington, DC, September 28, 1945.

92. OSS Separation Process, January 24, 1946, DCL. FBI Report, November 9, 1954, Washington, DC, DCL, Espionage-R, ISA of 1950, 18. Murphy was the chief of X-2, the OSS's counterintelligence branch. DCL, Military Record and Report of Separation, Certificate of Service. War Department, Office of the Assistant Secretary of War, Strategic Services Unit, Commendation, Lieutenant Colonel DCL, AUS, ASN-0912627.

93. Mangold, *Cold Warrior*, 254–256. Karlow was later accused of being a Soviet spy while working for the CIA. He was not. Karlow, S. Peter, Lee, Duncan C. Index Card, November 5, 1945. Troy, *Donovan and the CIA*, 289–290.

94. Olmstead, *Red Spy Queen*, 99.

Chapter 6 Gregory

1. Underground Soviet Espionage Organization in Agencies of the United States Government, August 24, 1948, 389, Vol. 144, ERI.

2. D. M. Ladd to the Director, August 24, 1948, Nathan Gregory Silvermaster, et al., Espionage-R (the Gregory Case) 1, Vol. 145, ERI. Olmstead, *Red Spy Queen*, 76–77. Kessler, *Clever Girl*, 116.

3. Olmstead, *Red Spy Queen*, 77. Haynes, Klehr, and Vassiliev, *Spies*, 514–515. Kessler, *Clever Girl*, 116.

4. Underground Soviet Espionage Organization in Agencies of the United States Government, August 24, 1948, 379, Vol. 144, ERI.

5. Haynes, Klehr, and Vassiliev, *Spies*, 515.

6. Bentley, *Out of Bondage*, 194–195.

7. Bentley, *Out of Bondage*, 194–196.

8. FBI Report, July 25, 1955, SAC, New Haven, Connecticut, to Director, FBI, 9, Vol. 161, ERI.

9. Olmstead, *Red Spy Queen*, 90. Bentley, *Out of Bondage*, 199. Peake, "Afterword," 219–220.

10. Olmstead, *Red Spy Queen*, 90–91. FBI Memorandum to Director, FBI, from SAC, New Haven, Connecticut, July 30, 1955, 1–2, Vol. 161, ERI.

11. Olmstead, *Red Spy Queen*, 91, 104. Kessler, *Clever Girl*, 123.

12. FBI Report, December 5, 1945, NYFO, Re: Signed Statement of Elizabeth Bentley, dated November 30, 1945, 86, Vol. 6, ERI. Olmstead, *Red Spy Queen*, 94–95.

13. Haynes, Klehr, and Vassiliev, *Spies*, 519.

14. D. M. Ladd to the Director, August 24, 1948, Nathan Gregory Silvermaster, et al., Espionage-R (the Gregory Case) 101, Vol. 145, ERI. Sibley, *Red Spies in America*, 119. Olmstead, *Red Spy Queen*, 94–95.

15. Peake, "Afterword," 326–327. Olmstead, *Red Spy Queen*, 95.

16. Peake, "Afterword," 220.

17. Olmstead, *Red Spy Queen*, 96–97.

18. Underground Soviet Espionage Organization in Agencies of the United States Government, August 24, 1948, 380, Vol. 144, ERI. Olmstead, *Red Spy Queen*, 97.

19. Olmstead, *Red Spy Queen*, 98.

20. Klehr, Haynes, and Firsov, *The Secret World of American Communism*, 11. Olmstead, *Red Spy Queen*, 99.

21. Olmstead, *Red Spy Queen*, 103.

22. Sibley, *Red Spies in America*, 118. Olmstead, *Red Spy Queen*, 97, 99.

23. Kessler, *Clever Girl*, 126.

24. Peake, "Afterword," 220.

25. Olmstead, *Red Spy Queen*, 100.

26. FBI Report to Director, FBI from E. E. Conroy, SAC, NYFO, Re: Signed Statement of Elizabeth Bentley, dated November 8, 1945, 10. FBI Summary of File References, Subject: DCL, June 3, 1953, 6.

27. FBI Report to Director, FBI from E. E. Conroy, SAC, NYFO, Re: Signed Statement of Elizabeth Bentley, dated November 8, 1945. See Gentry, *J. Edgar Hoover*, 117, for Hoover's food preferences. JEH to Brigadier General Harry Haskins Vaughan, Military Aide to the President, November 8, 1945, Vol. 16, ERI. JEH to William Stephenson, November 14, 1945.

28. Haynes, "Adolph Berle's Notes on His Meeting with Whittaker Chambers." Tanenhaus, *Whittaker Chambers*, 203, 206. Chambers first met with the FBI in 1942.

29. Klehr and Radosh, *The Amerasia Spy Case*, 3, 9. FBI Report, November 27, 1945, 45. Ybarra, *Washington Gone Crazy*, 374–375. Haynes and Klehr, *Early Cold War Spies*, 26, 33. Haynes, *Red Scare or Red Menace?* 52–54. Several of the OSS's and FBI's searches and wiretaps of the magazine's offices and the homes of its employees were illegal. These constitutional violations forced the Department of Justice to negotiate the plea deals.

30. Ybarra, *Washington Gone Crazy*, 384–385. FBI Report, November 27, 1945, 48.

31. These included William Taylor, Harry Dexter White, Nathan Glasser, Alger Hiss, Henry Magdoff, Donald Wheeler, Maurice Halperin, Robert Miller, Willard Park, and William Remington.

32. FBI Report, November 27, 1945, 8, Nathan Gregory Silvermaster, with Aliases, et al.

33. Olmstead, *Red Spy Queen*, 103. D. M. Ladd to E. A. Tamm, November 19, 1945.

34. FBI Report, November 29, 1945, Washington, DC, Nathan Gregory Silvermaster, with Aliases, 8–9.

35. Weinstein and Vassiliev, *The Haunted Wood*, 103. Haynes, Klehr, and Vassiliev, *Spies*, 519. Other members of the Magnificent Five spy ring were Guy Burgess, Donald Maclean, Anthony Blunt, and John Cairncross.

36. Haynes, Klehr, and Vassiliev, *Spies*, 519. DCL, "The Elizabeth Bentley Matter," 2.

37. D. M. Ladd to the Director, August 24, 1948, Nathan Gregory Silvermaster, et al., Espionage-R (the Gregory Case) 5, Vol. 145, ERI. Haynes, Klehr, and Vassiliev, *Spies*, 520, 543.

38. Haynes, Klehr, and Vassiliev, *Spies*, 27, 29,

39. J. K. Mumford to D. M. Ladd, November 8, 1945, Vol. 1, ERI.

40. FBI Report, November 29, 1945, Washington, DC, Nathan Gregory Silvermaster, with Aliases, 6. D. M. Ladd to the Director, August 24, 1948, Nathan Gregory Silvermaster, et al., Espionage-R (the Gregory Case) 5, Vol. 145, ERI. B. C. Hendon to Mr. Tolson, November 19, 1945, Vol. 1, ERI. D. M. Ladd to the Director, December 12, 1945. Theoharis, *The FBI*, 4.

41. Hess, "Oral History Interview with Stephen J. Spingarn," 17.

42. FBI Report, December 5, 1945, NYFO, Re: Signed Statement of Elizabeth Bentley, dated November 30, 1945, Vol. 6, ERI. FBI Report, February 21, 1946, Underground Soviet Espionage Organization (NKVD) in Agencies of the United States Government, 5, Vol. 23, ERI. D. M. Ladd to the Director, August 24, 1948, Nathan Gregory Silvermaster, et al., Espionage-R (the Gregory Case) 3, Vol. 145, ERI.

43. Morgan, *Reds*, 250.

44. FBI Report to Director, FBI from E. E. Conroy, SAC, NYFO, Re: Signed Statement of Elizabeth Bentley, dated November 8, 1945, 10. Memorandum for the Attorney General from JEH, November 21, 1945. Clark signed Hoover's request on December 3. The first tap on Lee's phone lasted until March 28, 1948.

45. FBI Report, November 29, 1945, Washington, DC, Nathan Gregory Silvermaster, with Aliases, 71, Vol. 5, ERI. FBI Summary of File References, Subject: DCL, June 3, 1953, 14.

46. FBI Office Memorandum, April 17, 1947, from Guy Hottel to Director, FBI, 7, Vol. 118, ERI.

47. Underground Soviet Espionage Organization in Agencies of the United States Government, August 24, 1948, 256, Vol. 144, ERI. FBI Report, April 5, 1947, WFO, 2. Price left Washington in July 1943, returned that fall, and then submitted a change of address form to her New York address in February 1944.

48. FBI Report, February 13, 1947, NYFO, Director, FBI, Re: Gregory, Espionage-R, 15–16. Memorandum, November 26, 1945, JEH to SAC Carl Heinrich. FBI Report, December 13, 1945, Washington, DC, Nathan Gregory Silvermaster, with Aliases, et al., 84. FBI Coversheet, November 2, 1946, DCL, from Western Union.

49. FBI Summary of File References, Subject: DCL, June 3, 1953, 39.

50. Gentry, *J. Edgar Hoover*, 62–63.

51. Theoharis and Cox, *The Boss*, 37–38. Gentry, *J. Edgar Hoover*, 62–63, 215.

52. Powers, *Secrecy and Power*, 279. Schrecker, *The Age of McCarthyism*, 12.

53. Gentry, *J. Edgar Hoover*, 68–69.

54. Theoharis, "Successes and Failures," 54. Gage, *The Day Wall Street Exploded*, 264–265. Theoharis, *The FBI*, 11, 374.

55. Theoharis, *The FBI*, 11–14, 363. Garrow, *The FBI and Martin Luther King*, 225.

56. Powers, *Broken*, 160–162.

57. Fox, "What the Spider Did," 207.

58. Batvinis, *The Origins of FBI Counterintelligence*, 51. Fox, "What the Spider Did," 219.

59. JEH to Major General Edwin M. Watson, October 25, 1940, White House Official Files, Justice Department—FBI Reports, Box 12, FDR PL.

60. JEH to Major General Edwin M. Watson, October 25, 1940, White House Official Files, Justice Department—FBI Reports, Box 12, FDR PL.

61. Bernstein, "The Loyalty of Federal Employees," 254–255. Batvinis, *The Origins of FBI Counterintelligence*, 225.

62. Theoharis, *The FBI*, 4. Powers, *Not Without Honor*, 160. Sibley, *Red Spies in America*, 91.

63. General Intelligence Survey in the United States, September 1942, Official File, 10-B, Box 17, FDR PL. General Intelligence Survey, November 1942, Box 17. General Intelligence Survey in the United States, August 1944, Box 18.

64. JEH to Major General Edwin Watson, August 3, 1943, Official File 10B, Justice Department, FBI, Box 18, FDR PL.

65. Theoharis, "Successes and Failures," 57–58. Sibley, *Red Spies in America*, 7.

66. Sibley, *Red Spies in America*, 73. FBI Report, November 27, 1945, 18. Haynes, Klehr, and Vassiliev, *Spies*, 496. At least three American citizens seem also to have been part of this swap.

67. FBI Report, November 27, 1945, 15–16. Haynes, Klehr, and Vassiliev, *Spies*, 205.

68. Sibley, *Red Spies in America*, 75. Peake, "OSS and the Venona Decrypts," 32.

69. FBI Confidential Letter to the Director, NYFO, February 13, 1947, 16. Olmstead, *Red Spy Queen*, 41. Peake, "Afterword," 222.

70. Sibley, *Red Spies in America*, 75. Batvinis, *The Origins of FBI Counterintelligence*, 142, 145. The FBI also failed to capitalize on NKVD general Aleksandr Orlov and Hede Massing.

71. Theoharis, "Successes and Failures," 59–60.

72. Mr. Ladd to the Director, July 31, 1950, 8. Lamphere and Shachtman, *The FBI-KGB War*, 74–75. Mr. Ladd to the Director, February 28, 1951, 19.

73. FBI Report, November 29, 1946, Washington, DC, 67. FBI Report, April 3, 1947, Victor Perlo, 3–4, Vol. 118, ERI.

74. Fox, "What the Spider Did," 219.

75. FBI Report, November 27, 1945, 24–25. Vasily Mironov, one of Zarubin's deputies and a schizophrenic, most likely wrote this letter.

76. Sibley, *Red Spies in America*, 4, 6. These Americans were Steve Nelson, Clarence Hiskey, Arthur Adams, and Joseph Weinberg. Theoharis, "Successes and Failures," 58–59.

77. Leffler, *The Specter of Communism*, 31. Bennett, *Franklin D. Roosevelt*, 57.

78. Hobsbawm, *The Age of Extremes*, 7.

79. Burleigh, *Moral Combat*, 225. Evans, *The Third Reich at War*, 214. Simms, "Stalin Was Both Terrible Tyrant and Essential Ally."

80. Hastings, *Inferno*, 152. "By the Numbers." Andrew and Gordievsky, *KGB*, 329–330.

81. Simms, "Stalin Was Both Terrible Tyrant and Essential Ally." Burleigh, *Moral Combat*, 387. Hastings, *Inferno*, 156, 196. Holborn, *The Political Collapse of Europe*, 163.

82. Burns, *Roosevelt: The Soldier of Freedom*, 379. In November 1941, with the Germans nearing the gates of Moscow, Stalin offered Hitler eastern Poland, the Ukraine, and the Baltic states if he would halt his advance. Hitler declined.

83. Ferguson, *The War of the World*, 529.

84. Bennett, *Franklin D. Roosevelt*, 53. Powers, *Not Without Honor*, 169, 172. Ryan, *Earl Browder*, 205. Starborn, *American Communism in Crisis*, 54.

85. Theoharis, *Chasing Spies*, 52. Blind Memo, April 1, 1944, attached to Memo, JEH to Attorney General, undated, Francis Biddle Papers, FDR PL. Biddle made his statement while the FBI was in the midst of investigating Victor Kravchenko, the Soviet Purchasing Commission official who wanted to defect.

86. Theoharis, *Chasing Spies*, 52. Blind Memo, April 1, 1944, attached to Memo, JEH to Attorney General, undated, Francis Biddle Papers, FDR PL. Vassiliev, WN #3, 108.

Chapter 7 On the Outside Looking In

1. To the Director, from D. M. Ladd, Nathan Gregory Silvermaster, et al., Espionage-R, February 21, 1946. FBI Report, February 21, 1946, Underground Soviet Espionage Organization (NKVD) in Agencies of the United States Government, 6, Vol. 23, ERI.

2. FBI Report, February 21, 1946, Underground Soviet Espionage Organization (NKVD) in Agencies of the United States Government, 6, Vol. 23, ERI. Guy Hottel to Director, FBI, December 6, 1945.

3. Peake, "Afterword," 267. Olmstead, *Red Spy Queen*, 108.

4. Olmstead, *Red Spy Queen*, 109. Underground Soviet Espionage Organization in Agencies of the United States Government, August 24, 1948, 283, Vol. 144, ERI.

5. Peake, "Afterword," 267.

6. FBI Memorandum, from A. H. Belmont to D. M. Ladd, February 19, 1954, 3, Vol. 159, ERI.

7. FBI Report, September 26, 1949, DCL, 9, 3.

8. Underground Soviet Espionage Organization in Agencies of the United States Government, August 24, 1948, 155–156, Vol. 144, ERI.

9. FBI Summary of File References, Subject: DCL, June 3, 1953, 51. Theoharis, "The Truman Administration and the Decline of Civil Liberties," 1012, 1027. Schrecker, *Many Are the Crimes*, 208.

10. FBI Report, October 21, 1946, Underground Soviet Espionage Organization (NKVD) in Agencies of the United States Government, 16, 164, Vol. 82, ERI. Otto Doering to Lieutenant Colonel DCL, February 4, 1946.

11. FBI Summary of File References, Subject: DCL, June 3, 1953, 164, 171. DCL, "The Elizabeth Bentley Matter," 8.

12. FBI Summary of File References, Subject: DCL, June 3, 1953, 155.

13. Shaughnessy Affidavit, June 19, 1951. Hoover Institution, Register of China Defense Supply Records, Historical Notes. McKean, *Tommy the Cork*, 140–141.

14. Shaughnessy Affidavit, June 19, 1951. Hoover Institution, Register of China Defense Supply Records, Historical Notes.

15. Hoover Institution, Papers of William Sterling Youngman, Biographical and Historical Notes. David Acheson, interview with author, June 20, 2008.

16. David Acheson, interview with author, June 20, 2008. FBI Summary of File References, Subject: DCL, June 3, 1953, 176.

17. DCL, "The Elizabeth Bentley Matter," 2.

18. DCL to the AG, DOA, June 22, 1951, 30.

19. DCL to the AG, DOA, June 22, 1951, PHS of DCL, 11.

20. DCL, "The Elizabeth Bentley Matter," 16.

21. Ferrell, *Harry S. Truman and the Modern Presidency*, 94.

22. Byrnes, *The Truman Years*, 32. Powers, *Secrecy and Power*, 284. Fried, *Nightmare in Red*, 73.

23. Ybarra, *Washington Gone Crazy*, 397. Starborn, *American Communism in Crisis*, 113.

24. Byrnes, *The Truman Years*, 15–18. Powers, *Broken*, 202–203, 276.

25. Byrnes, *The Truman Years*, 29–30.

26. Gaddis, *The United States and the Origins of the Cold War*, 336, 348.

27. Vandenberg quoted in Byrnes, *The Truman Years*, 40. Lefeber, *America, Russia, and the Cold War*, 54.

28. Lefeber, *America, Russia, and the Cold War*, 50. Byrnes, *The Truman Years*, 41–42.

29. Powers, *Secrecy and Power*, 276. Troy, *Donovan and the CIA*, 267. Hamby, *Man of the People*, 429.

30. FBI Report, February 26, 1954, A. H. Belmont to D. M. Ladd, 4. FBI Report, October 21, 1946, Underground Soviet Espionage Organization (NKVD) in Agencies of the United States Government, 1, Vol. 82, ERI.

31. Edward A. Tamm to JEH, 1, Gregory Case, January 6, 1947.

32. Memorandum from JEH to Mr. Tolson, Mr. Tamm, Mr. Ladd, Mr. Nichols, January 6, 1947.

33. Edward Scheidt to Director, FBI, January 9, 1947, 2.

34. D. M. Ladd to Edward Tamm, January 8, 1947.

35. Obituary, Edward Pierpont Morgan, *Southeast Missourian*, March 31, 1986. E. P. Morgan to H. H. Clegg, January 14, 1947, 1.

36. FBI Memorandum, E. P. Morgan to H. H. Clegg, Subject: Gregory Case, January 14, 1947, 1.

37. FBI Memorandum, E. P. Morgan to H. H. Clegg, Subject: Gregory Case, January 14, 1947, 1–5.

38. Edward Tamm to JEH, January 15, 1947, Gregory Case, 1.

39. FBI Memorandum, F. L. Jones to D. M. Ladd, Gregory Espionage-R, January 16, 1947, 6.

40. F. L. Jones to D. M. Ladd, 4, 6. NARA, RG 233, IF, Series 1, NF, DCL, Box 193, August 5, 1948. Gentry, *J. Edgar Hoover*, 353–355.

41. Edward Tamm to the Director, Gregory Case, January 23, 1947, 3.

42. Director, FBI, to the Attorney General, Gregory Case, February 12, 1947. Haynes and Klehr, *Venona*, 102.

43. Director, FBI, to the Attorney General, Gregory Case, March 7, 1947. Haynes and Klehr, *Early Cold War Spies*, 72.

44. A. H. Belmont to D. M. Ladd, February 26, 1954, 4. Donegan practiced law in New York City after he left the FBI. One of his clients was Bentley. Underground Soviet Espionage Organization in Agencies of the United States Government, August 24, 1948, 220–221, Vol. 144, ERI.

45. Haynes and Klehr, *Venona*, 411. Underground Soviet Espionage Organization in Agencies of the United States Government, August 24, 1948, 44–45, Vol. 144, ERI.

46. Underground Soviet Espionage Organization in Agencies of the United States Government, August 24, 1948, 99–100, Vol. 144, ERI.

47. Director, FBI, Mary Wolfe Price, April 5, 1947, 2. FBI Report, undated, WFO 100-21412, 17.

48. SAC, Birmingham, to Director, 3–6.

49. D. M. Ladd to the Director, Gregory Case, March 10, 1947.

50. J. K. Mumford to D. M. Ladd, Gregory Case, May 23, 1947, Vol. 118, ERI. D. M. Ladd to the Director, Gregory Espionage-R, February 7, 1947, 2.

51. FBI Report, September 26, 1949, Washington, DC, DCL, 9.

52. D. M. Ladd to the Director, Gregory-Espionage-R, October 21, 1947, Vol. 131, ERI. FBI Report, DCL, 13. Lee may have suffered from benign essential tremors.

53. FBI Report, DCL, 10–13. In April 1952, however, Bentley told the FBI that she remembered only one dinner with Golos and Lee and that it took place in Washington in October 1943. She admitted, though, that Lee's memory of two dinners—one in New York City and one in Washington—could be right.

54. FBI Report, DCL, 13–15.

55. FBI Summary of File References, Subject: DCL, June 3, 1953, 83.

Chapter 8 The Terrible Summer of 1948

1. US HUAC, *Hearings*, August 10, 1948, 740. The testimony of seventy-four witnesses who appeared before the grand jury in its various phases is available to the public at the Harry S. Truman Library. FBI Summary of File References, Subject: DCL, June 3, 1953, 81. FBI Report, Nathan Gregory Silvermaster, with Aliases, et al., 86, Vol. 145, ERI.

2. DCL, "The Elizabeth Bentley Matter," 7. NARA, RG 118, Records of US Attorneys and Marshals, Transcript of Grand Jury Testimony in the Alger Hiss Case, Box 1, Witness File, Mary Price, December 3, 1947, 2574, 2575, 2582. SOHPC, Mary Price Adamson interview, April 19, 1976, 127.

3. Nellor, "Red Spy Ring to Be Broken Soon by US Agencies' Action." Walter, "Jury Expected to Indict 60 as Red Spies." Olmstead, *Red Spy Queen*, 119. Martelle, *The Fear Within*, 21–22.

4. Nathan Gregory Silvermaster with Aliases, et al., August 24, 1948, 221–222, Vol. 145, ERI.

5. Memorandum from JEH to Mr. Tolson, Mr. Tamm, Mr. Ladd, and Mr. Nichols, April 1, 1948, Vol. 137, ERI.

6. H. B. Fletcher to D. M. Ladd, Gregory Case, March 31, 1948. Powers, *Broken*, 214.

7. FBI Report, November 27, 1945, Washington, DC, 51. Powers, *Broken*, 214.

8. Memorandum from JEH to Mr. Tolson, Mr. Tamm, Mr. Ladd, and Mr. Nichols, April 1, 1948, Vol. 137, ERI. Powers, *Broken*, 214. Martelle, *The Fear Within*, 26.

9. Olmstead, *Red Spy Queen*, 122–123.

10. Byrnes, *The Truman Years*, 43–44, 53, 134.

11. Underground Soviet Espionage Organization in Agencies of the United States Government, August 24, 1948, 2, Vol. 144, ERI. Confidential Memorandum to Director, FBI, from Edward Scheidt, October 17, 1948.

12. Olmstead, *Red Spy Queen*, 121–123.

13. Olmstead, *Red Spy Queen*, 124. Director, FBI, to the Attorney General, Gregory Case, April 3, 1948.

14. Olmstead, *Red Spy Queen*, 124. JEH to the Attorney General, Gregory Case, April 5, 1948.

15. Olmstead, *Red Spy Queen*, 124–125.

16. FBI Summary of File References, Subject: DCL, June 3, 1953, 88.

17. Martelle, *The Fear Within*, 31. The grand jury actually handed down two counts: conspiracy to overthrow the American government and conspiracy to teach and advocate the same. FBI Memorandum for Mr. Tolson, July 21, 1948.

18. Frank and Mockridge, "Red Ring Bared by Blond Queen."

19. Frank and Mockridge, "Super-Secrecy Veiled Russia's Spy Cells Here."

20. Olmstead, *Red Spy Queen*, 127–128.

21. Carr, *The House Committee on Un-American Activities*, 55. Fried, *Nightmare in Red*, 77. Haynes, *Red Scare or Red Menace?* 72. Weinstein, *Perjury*, 3.

22. Phillips, *The Truman Presidency*, 161, 225–226.

23. Hamby, *Man of the People*, 450–451.

24. Carr, *The House Committee on Un-American Activities*, 214.

25. Hamby, *Man of the People*, 433.

26. Hamby, *Man of the People*, 433, 448–449. Carr, *The House Committee on Un-American Activities*, 220–227, 229–230, 236, 239–244. Fried, *Nightmare in Red*, 63.

27. Tanenhaus, *Whittaker Chambers*, 215–216. Carr, *The House Committee on Un-American Activities*, 264–265. Harris and Tichenor, *A History of the US Political System*, 354.

28. Phillips, *The Truman Presidency*, 227. Scott quoted in Gentry, *J. Edgar Hoover*, 358.

29. Olmstead, *Red Spy Queen*, 127. Ybarra, *Washington Gone Crazy*, 511–512.

30. O'Reilly, *Hoover and the Un-Americans*, 105–106.

31. Kessler, *Clever Girl*, 164.

32. US Senate, Investigations Subcommittee, *Export Policy and Loyalty*, July 30, 1948, 15, 24.

33. US Senate, Investigations Subcommittee, *Export Policy and Loyalty*, July 30, 1948, 44.

34. US Senate, Investigations Subcommittee, *Export Policy and Loyalty*, July 30, 1948, 44. Official File 264, Communism, "The Communist," May 1943, FDR Presidential Library.

35. US Senate, Investigations Subcommittee, *Export Policy and Loyalty*, July 30, 1948, 19, 40.

36. US HUAC, *Hearings*, July 31, 1948, 501.

37. US HUAC, *Hearings*, July 31, 1948, 529–530. Bentley mistakenly testified that Lee was a member of the Institute of Pacific Relations before the war. Lee did not join that organization until 1946. He was a member of the China Aid Council before the war.

38. "Duncan Lee Denies All Charges Before Congress and in Letter."

39. "Congress to Demand Prosecutions in Spy Case." NARA, RG 233, IF, Series 1, NF, DCL, Box 193, Subpoena for DCL, August 2, 1948.

40. Carr, *The House Committee on Un-American Activities*, 93.

41. Carr, *The House Committee on Un-American Activities*, 96.

42. NARA RG 233, IF, Series 1, NF, DCL, Box 193, August 2, 1948, Summons.

43. NARA RG 233, IF, Series 1, NF, DCL, Box 193, August 5, 1948, Western Union Telegram, O. C. Doering.

44. NARA, RG 233, IF, Series 1, NF, DCL, Box 193, August 6, 1948, Letter from DCL to J. Parnell Thomas.

45. FBI Report, July 26, 1951, WFO, DCL, 5. FBI Summary of File References, Subject: DCL, June 3, 1953, 95. Petrie, *Not a Bowl of Cherries*, 37. John Lee, e-mail to author, October 14, 2012.

46. 18 United States Criminal Code, Section 581 (a) 1946. This statute's penalties ranged from death to thirty years in prison.

47. Goodman, *The Committee*, 251.

48. US HUAC, *Hearings*, 590, 699. Silvermaster testified on August 4, 1948. Perlo testified on August 9.

49. FBI summary of recorded telephone calls between DCL and Michael Quinn Shaughnessy, August 1 and 2, 1948.

50. Office of the Clerk, US House of Representatives, and the Architect of the Capitol, "Cannon House Office Building." Allen, *History of the United States Capitol*, 380–383.

51. Hottel, SAC, WFO, to Director, FBI, Subject: Gregory et al., 1, August 11, 1948.

52. Tanenhaus, *Whittaker Chambers*, 239–240.

53. Healy and Holeman, "3 More Witnesses Balk at Questions."

54. FBI Report, September 26, 1949, Washington, DC, DCL, 19. US HUAC, *Hearings*, August 10, 1948, 717.

55. US HUAC, *Hearings*, August 10, 1948, 717, 719, 723, 740.

56. US HUAC, *Hearings*, August 10, 1948, 720–721, 735.

57. US HUAC, *Hearings*, August 10, 1948, 721–722, 737–738.

58. US HUAC, *Hearings*, August 10, 1948, 723.

59. US HUAC, *Hearings*, August 10, 1948, 725–726.

60. US HUAC, *Hearings*, August 10, 1948, 727–728.

61. US HUAC, *Hearings*, August 10, 1948, 728–729.

62. US HUAC, *Hearings*, August 10, 1948, 732.

63. US HUAC, *Hearings*, August 10, 1948, 733.

64. US HUAC, *Hearings*, August 10, 1948, 734–735.

65. US HUAC, *Hearings*, August 10, 1948, 737.

66. US HUAC, *Hearings*, August 10, 1948, 740.

67. US HUAC, *Hearings*, August 10, 1948, 741–742.

68. US HUAC, *Hearings*, August 10, 1948, 748.

69. US HUAC, *Hearings*, August 10, 1948, 723.

70. Cave-Brown, *Wild Bill Donovan*, 171. Russell Forgan to editor, *New York Times*, February 9, 1959, Papers of Russell J. Forgan, Subject File Miscellany, Hoover Institution, Stanford University.

71. "Donovan Backs Duncan Lee as Loyal in War." Keeley, *The Salonika Bay Murder*, 121.

72. Peake, "Afterword," 298. Pforzheimer told the author the same thing during an interview on June 17, 1999. Waller, *Wild Bill Donovan*, 355.

73. Riebling, *Wedge*, 129.

74. Waller, *Wild Bill Donovan*, 4, 39, 40, 128.

75. US HUAC, *Hearings*, August 10, 1948, 749. Peake to Benson, October 22, 1996, memorandum in author's possession.

76. US HUAC, *Hearings*, August 10, 1948, 754.

77. Hottel to Director, FBI, 2, August 11, 1948.

78. Ottenberg, "Ex-Army Officers Deny Bentley's Charges." "Lee Swears He Never Was Red." Frank and Mockridge, "Spy Says OSS Aide Hinted Atomic Plant Supersecret." "Lee Denies Giving Reds Secrets." DCL, "The Elizabeth Bentley Matter," 7.

79. Andrews, "Miss Bentley Affirms, Lee Denies Spylinks." "Refusing the $64 Question."

80. "The Dilemma." "Facts First."

81. "Duncan Lee Denies All Charges Before Congress and in Letter."

82. DCL to EJL, September 1, 1948. Charles J. Symington to EJL, August 11, 1948. Richard H. Lee to EJL, August 11, 1948.

83. Phillips, *The Truman Presidency*, 228.

84. Elsey quoted in Morgan, *Reds*, 311. Olmstead, *Red Spy Queen*, 142.

85. O'Reilly, *Hoover and the Un-Americans*, 109.

86. O'Reilly, *Hoover and the Un-Americans*, 109–110. Byrnes, *The Truman Years*, 62. Gentry, *J. Edgar Hoover*, 359.

87. NARA, RG 46, Senate Internal Security Subcommittee, Price, Mary, Box 88. SOHPC, Mary Price Adamson interview, April 19, 1976, 122.

88. Kessler, *Clever Girl*, 190.

89. DCL, "The Elizabeth Bentley Matter," 7.

90. DCL, "The Elizabeth Bentley Matter," 15, 17, 34.

Chapter 9 The World's Most Shot-At Airline

1. Container 591, TGC Papers, LOC, MD. McKean, *Tommy the Cork*, 10–14. Saxon, "Thomas Corcoran, Roosevelt Aide, Dies at 80."

2. McKean, *Tommy the Cork*, 14–15, 30–31, 38. Crawford, "Thomas G. (Tommy) Corcoran, Lobbyist of New Deal Era, Dies." Yoffe, "A Fork in the Road," 21.

3. Corcoran quoted in Yoffe, "A Fork in the Road," 22. Lichtman, "Tommy the Cork," 2.

4. McKean, *Tommy the Cork*, 112. Container 586, TGC Papers, LOC, MD. Lichtman, "Tommy the Cork," 2. Corcoran quoted in Lichtman, "Tommy the Cork," 1.

5. Corcoran quoted in Lichtman, "Tommy the Cork," 2. Saxon, "Thomas Corcoran, Roosevelt Aide, Dies at 80." Container 56, TGC Papers, LOC, MD.

6. Leary, *Perilous Missions*, 9.

7. Phillips, *The Truman Presidency*, 277.

8. Container 586, TGC Papers, LOC, MD.

9. Byrd, *Chennault*, 283. Spence, *To Change China*, 228. Leary, *Perilous Missions*, 3.

10. Byrd, *Chennault*, 113–114.

11. Container 594, TGC Papers, LOC, MD. Leary, *Perilous Missions*, 6. Container 594, TGC Papers, LOC, MD.

12. Leary, *Perilous Missions*, 6–7. Container 302, TGC Papers, LOC, MD.

13. Leary, "Portrait of a Cold Warrior," 374–375. Willauer quoted in Leary, "Portrait of a Cold Warrior," 375.

14. Leary, *Perilous Missions*, 9.

15. Leary, *Perilous Missions*, 9–10. Container 594, TGC Papers, LOC, MD.

16. Leary, *Perilous Missions*, 12–14.

17. Leary, *Perilous Missions*, 14, 16, 18, 27. Container 310, TGC Papers, LOC, MD.

18. Leary, "Portrait of a Cold Warrior," 381–382.

19. Claire Chennault to the AG, USA, May 27, 1951.

20. WW Affidavit, May 15, 1951.

21. Willauer quoted in Leary, "Portrait of a Cold Warrior," 383. Container 87, TGC Papers, LOC, MD. Leary, *Perilous Missions*, 38.

22. Spence, *Mao Zedong*, 103.

23. Leary, "Portrait of a Cold Warrior," 384. WW Papers, Box 1, SGMML, Princeton University.

24. Leary, "Portrait of a Cold Warrior," 384. WW Papers, Box 5, SGMML, Princeton University. Container 52, TGC Papers, LOC, MD.

25. Leary, "Portrait of a Cold Warrior," 385.

26. Leary, *Perilous Missions*, 47–48.

27. WW Affidavit, May 15, 1951. Claire Chennault to the AG, USA, May 27, 1951.

28. Byrd, *Chennault*, 307. Claire Chennault Papers, Box 11, Folder 2, Hoover Institution. Byrd, *Chennault*, 312.

29. Container 413, TGC Papers, LOC, MD. Byrd, *Chennault*, 315.

30. Leary, *Perilous Missions*, 67. Claire Chennault Papers, Box 11, Folder 5, Hoover Institution.

31. Leary, *Perilous Missions*, 67–68.

32. Leary and Stueck, "The Chennault Plan to Save China," 355. Container 303, TGC Papers, LOC, MD. Leary, "Portrait of a Cold Warrior," 386–387.

33. Container 303, TGC Papers, LOC, MD.

34. Claire Chennault Papers, Box 11, Folder 9, Hoover Institution. Brinkley, *The Publisher*, 282.

35. NARA, RG 46, Senate Internal Security Subcommittee, Lee, Duncan Chaplin, Box 26. David Acheson, interview with author, June 20, 2008. Container 302, TGC Papers, LOC, MD.

36. Container 306, TGC Papers, LOC, MD.

37. Container 306, TGC Papers, LOC, MD.

38. Leffler, *The Preponderance of Power*, 296. Leary, "Portrait of a Cold Warrior," 387–388.

39. Hamby, *Man of the People*, 398.

40. Leary and Stueck, "The Chennault Plan to Save China," 351. Truman quoted in Phillips, *The Truman Presidency*, 277.

41. Leary and Stueck, "The Chennault Plan to Save China," 353.

42. Lafeber, *America, Russia, and the Cold War*. 88.

43. Leary, "Aircraft and Anti-communists," 654.

44. Excerpt from "Church Committee Report on the Evolution of CIA Covert Action."

45. Gaddis, *George F. Kennan*, 316–317.

46. Gaddis, *George F. Kennan*, 315–317, 319.

47. Excerpt from "Church Committee Report on the Evolution of CIA Covert Action," 181, 185. Thomas, *The Very Best Men*, 19. Wisner graduated from Woodberry Forest in 1927, the year before Lee arrived on campus.

48. Leary, *Perilous Missions*, 71. Excerpt from "Church Committee Report on the Evolution of CIA Covert Action," 186.

49. *CIA's Clandestine Services History*, 1: 12.

50. Leary, *Perilous Missions*, 70. Byrd, *Chennault*, 331.

51. Byrd, *Chennault*, 319. Taylor, *The Generalissimo*, 407, 413. Chiang arrived in Taiwan in early June 1949. He returned briefly to the mainland in November 1949 but was forced to retreat to Taiwan for good on December 10.

52. Leary and Stueck, "The Chennault Plan to Save China," 354.

53. Leary, *Perilous Missions*, 72–73.

54. Byrnes, *The Truman Years*, 134. Gaddis, *George F. Kennan*, 357.

55. Leary and Stueck, "The Chennault Plan to Save China," 357.

56. Leary and Stueck, "The Chennault Plan to Save China," 358.

57. *CIA's Clandestine Services History*, 1: 9. WW Papers, Box 1, SGMML, Princeton University. Container 594, TGC Papers, LOC, MD. Leary, "Aircraft and Anti-communists," 655.

58. WW Affidavit, May 15, 1951.

59. Donovan quoted in Dunlop, *Donovan*, 498.

60. Leary, *Perilous Missions*, 91.

61. Leary, "Aircraft and Anti-communists," 656.

62. Byrd, *Chennault*, 335. Claire Chennault Papers, Box 12, folder 1, Hoover Institution. WW Papers, Box 1, SGMML, Princeton University.

63. *CIA's Clandestine Services History*, 1: 95–96. Leary, "Aircraft and Anti-communists," 656–657. Britain formally recognized Mao's government at 12:01 a.m. on January 6, 1950.

64. Leary, "Aircraft and Anti-communists," 657–658.

65. WW Affidavit, May 15, 1951.

66. Container 302, TGC Papers, LOC, MD.

67. Container 595, TGC Papers, LOC, MD. Leary, *Perilous Missions*, 96.

68. Container 332, TGC Papers, LOC, MD. Leary, "Aircraft and Anti-communists," 659.

69. DCL, PHS, 13, June 22, 1951, the AG, DOA. "Obituary of Lord Shaw-cross." Container 327, TGC Papers, LOC, MD. Shawcross, while attorney general, prosecuted Klaus Fuchs, one of the Soviets' most important atomic spies. WW Papers, Boxes 1 and 3, SGMML, Princeton University. This decision only pertained to forty of the Hong Kong planes. In October 1952, the Hong Kong Supreme Court, following the Privy Council's decision, decided that the remaining CNAC planes belonged to Willauer and Chennault.

70. Gaddis, *George F. Kennan*, 387. Leary, *Perilous Missions*, 104. Lafeber, *America, Russia, and the Cold War*, 93–95.

71. Leffler, *The Specter of Communism*, 104. Claire Chennault Papers, Box 11, folder 12, Hoover Institution. Leffler, *The Preponderance of Power*, 293.

72. Leary, *Perilous Missions*, viii.

73. Chennault quoted in Leary, "Aircraft and Anti-communists," 665. Claire Chennault Papers, Box 11, folder 27, Hoover Institution. From Director, FBI, to SAC, WFO, DCL, January 18, 1951. See also FBI Memorandum, February 29, 1952, DCL.

74. Containers 312, 316, 319, TGC Papers, LOC, MD. Quoted in Leary, "Aircraft and Anti-communists," 668.

75. Taylor, *The Generalissimo*, 430–431. Spector, "The Battle That Saved Taiwan," 98–104.

76. Spector, "The Battle That Saved Taiwan," 104.

77. DCL, "The Elizabeth Bentley Matter," 16.

78. Container 587, TGC Papers, LOC, MD. Bird and Holland, "The Tapping of 'Tommy the Cork,'" 3. McKean, *Tommy the Cork*, 181.

79. Container 597, TGC Papers, LOC, MD. Through these, Hoover also learned that Corcoran was representing Foreign Service officer John Stewart Service in the Justice Department's investigation of the *Amerasia* spy case. Service later became famous as one of the State Department's infamous "China Hands," whom McCarthy accused of losing China. Corcoran quoted in Bird and Holland, "The Tapping of 'Tommy the Cork,'" 2, 4. Gentry, *J. Edgar Hoover*, 322. McKean, "Kerry Chief of Staff McKean."

80. Container 586, TGC Papers, LOC, MD. Bird and Holland, "The Tapping of 'Tommy the Cork,'" 6.

81. Container 588, TGC Papers, LOC, MD. Mrs. Shipley to Mr. MacLeod, Interview with TGC Regarding DCL, January 26, 1954, DCL Passport file.

82. Leary, *Perilous Missions*, 71. Claire Chennault to the AG, USA, May 27, 1951.

83. WW Affidavit, May 15, 1951.

84. James H. Rowe Jr., Affidavit, June 21, 1951.

Chapter 10 A Loyal American

1. Andrew and Mitrokhin, *The Sword and the Shield*, 143. Haynes and Klehr, *Venona*, 25–28.

2. "Venona," 8–9.

3. Theoharis, *Chasing Spies*, 7.

4. Haynes and Klehr, *Venona*, 8. The American effort may also have been spurred by Japan's efforts to break the Soviets' codes. "Venona," 12.

5. "Venona," 13, 46.

6. Haynes and Klehr, *Venona*, 29.

7. "The Soviet Problem," 161.

8. Fox, "In the Enemy's House," 3.

9. Lamphere and Shachtman, *The FBI-KGB War*, 12, 78–79.

10. "Venona Chronology." Of the messages sent from New York to Moscow, 49 percent of the 1944 messages and 15 percent of the 1943 messages were readable. But the Americans were able to read only 1.8 percent of the messages sent in 1942 and only 1.5 percent of those sent in 1945.

11. "Venona," 65. This program was also known throughout its long history as "Jade," "Bride," and "Drug."

12. FBI Report, June 23, 1950, "Study of Code Names in MGB Communications." In all, about 2,900 Soviet messages were partially or completely broken between 1943 and 1981, the last year of this program. These were the easiest to break because of the repeated use of one-time code pads by the Soviets.

13. FBI Report, June 23, 1950, Washington, DC, 3–42. Koh/Koch is discussed on p. 28.

14. FBI Report, July 31, 1950, Washington, DC, Mr. Ladd to the Director, 8.

15. WFO Report, DCL, Mr. A. S. Brent to Mr. C. E. Hennrich, October 30, 1950, 1, 12, Vol. 150, ERI.

16. Hamby, *Man of the People*, 548–549. J. Kahn, "The Extraordinary Mrs. Shipley," 841.

17. Brent to Hennrich, October 30, 1950, 8–9.

18. Brent to Hennrich, October 30, 1950, 11–12.

19. SAC, WFO, to Director, FBI, Subject: DCL, October 27, 1953, 1–2. Venona 1437, New York to Moscow, October 10, 1944. Venona 782, New York to Moscow, May 26, 1943. Venona 880, New York to Moscow, June 8, 1943. Venona 887, New York to Moscow, June 9, 1943. Venona 830, New York to Moscow, June 9, 1944. Venona 1325–1326, New York to Moscow, September 15, 1944. Venona 1354, New York to Moscow, September 22, 1944 (no mention of Lee by name but appears to be a follow-up to 1325–1326). Venona 1353, New York to Moscow, September 23, 1944. Venona 1437, New York to Moscow, October 10, 1944. Venona 954, Moscow to New York, September 20, 1944. The name Lee also appears in Venona 726–729, New York to Moscow, May 22, 1942, but this is before he joined the OSS. The messages pertaining to him have different decoding dates, including 1968, 1974, and 1960. Some were "reissued" after the NSA made more breakthroughs.

20. SAC, WFO, to Director, FBI, Subject: DCL, May 27, 1954, 2. This report contains the date of the reopening of Lee's case. FBI Report, August 14, 1951, Mr. Laughlin to Mr. Ladd. McDonald, "The OSS and Its Records," 78.

21. A. H. Belmont to D. M. Ladd, May 23, 1952, 3; this contained Hoover's handwritten observations on the CIA. Ranelagh, *The Agency*, 28.

22. SAC, NYFO, to Director, FBI, Subject: Joseph Katz, March 15, 1951. FBI Report, May 12, 1951, NYFO, DCL, 4.

23. FBI Report, May 12, 1951, NYFO, 4, 5. Vassiliev, WN #3, 131. Haynes and Klehr, *Venona*, 106–107.

24. FBI Report, July 7, 1954, Washington, DC, DCL, 11. Haynes and Klehr, *Early Cold War Spies*, 295–296. Vassiliev, WN #3, 110. FBI Report, October 27, 1953, SAC, WFO to Director, FBI, Subject: DCL. James M. McInerney to Director, FBI, Subject: Joseph Katz, January 5, 1951, 2. FBI Report, May 12, 1951, NYFO, DCL, 6.

25. Chambers, *Witness*, 546.

26. FBI Report, May 12, 1951, NYFO, 4–6.

27. FBI Report, September 26, 1949, Washington, DC, DCL, 3.

28. FBI Report, August 16, 1949, DCL. The AG, DOA, to DCL, June 22, 1951, citing the adjutant general's April 23, 1951, letter to DCL.

29. DCL to AG, June 22, 1951, 1–2, 32.

30. PHS of DCL, June 22, 1951, 6.

31. RTA of DCL to AG, June 22, 1951, 6–15.

32. RTA of DCL to AG, June 22, 1951, 7–8.

33. RTA of DCL to AG, June 22, 1951, 8–10.

34. RTA of DCL to AG, June 22, 1951, 6–8, 10–11, 15.

35. RTA of DCL to AG, June 22, 1951, 15.

36. RTA of DCL to AG, June 22, 1951, 15, 34.

37. Doering Affidavit, June 20, 1951.

38. Doering Affidavit, June 20, 1951.

39. Archbold Van Beuren Affidavit, June 18, 1951.

40. DCL, PHS of DCL, 11–13.

41. Container 70, TGC Papers, LOC, MD. Olmstead, *Red Spy Queen*, 146.

42. From Director, FBI, to SAC, WFO, Subject: DCL, October 10, 1951. Colonel Gordon E. Dawson, Chief, Security Division, to JEH, May 1, 1952. Lee was discharged under 6(a)9, SR 140–175.1.

43. FBI Report, July 26, 1951, Washington, DC, DCL, 5. This act was amended in 1950 by the ISA of that same year. The Immigration and Nationality Act extended this bar to members of the CPUSA and prohibited aliens who were members from entering the United States.

44. Ybarra, *Washington Gone Crazy*, 569–570. Fried, *Nightmare in Red*, 145–146.

45. Ybarra, *Washington Gone Crazy*, 509, 570.

46. US Senate, Subcommittee to Investigate the Administration, *The Institute of Pacific Relations*.

47. SAC, WFO, to Director, FBI, Subject: DCL, November 6, 1951. By the end of 1954, Lee's was one of 11,033 names carried on these two lists. Theoharis, "The Truman Administration and the Decline of Civil Liberties," 1021.

48. Ybarra, *Washington Gone Crazy*, 577–578. Olmstead, *Red Spy Queen*, 168.

49. DCL, "The Elizabeth Bentley Matter," 32.

50. Olmstead, *Red Spy Queen*, 130, 145. Peake, "Afterword," 248.

51. Peake, "Afterword," 250. Haynes and Klehr, *Early Cold War Spies*, 75–76.

52. Haynes and Klehr, *Early Cold War Spies*, 78–79. Haynes and Klehr point out that only two of the people Bentley claimed to be Soviet spies were ever convicted: William Remington for perjury and Edward Fitzgerald for contempt of court. See G. May, *Un-American Activities*, 8, for an account of the attack on Remington.

53. SAC, WFO, to Director, FBI, Subject: DCL, September 20, 1951.

54. SAC, WFO, to Director, FBI, Subject: DCL, June 2, 1952, 1–2.

55. SAC, WFO, to Director, FBI, Subject: DCL, June 2, 1952, 1–2.

56. SAC, WFO, to Director, FBI, Subject: DCL, June 2, 1952, 1–2. SAC, WFO, to Director, FBI, Subject: DCL, May 16, 1952. FBI Report, August 15, 1952, WFO, DCL, 22.

57. Director, FBI, to SAC, WFO, DCL, March 25, 1952.

58. FBI Report, November 17, 1952, Los Angeles, California, DCL, 1–2. John Espey, letter to the author, July 19, 1999. *A Register of Rhodes Scholars, 1903–1981*, 258. Espey died in September 2000.

59. FBI Report, March 12, 1952, Baltimore, Maryland, DCL, 2. FBI Report, April 27, 1953, Boston, Massachusetts, DCL, 1. FBI Report, September 15, 1952, Buffalo, New York, DCL, 1. FBI Report, August 15, 1952, Washington, DC, DCL, 10.

60. FBI Report, August 15, 1952, Washington, DC, DCL, 10. Stahr died on November 11, 1998.

61. FBI Report, August 15, 1952, Washington, DC, DCL, 12–13. *A Register of Rhodes Scholars, 1903–1981*, 276. Williams died in April 1994. FBI Report, August 15, 1952, Washington, DC, DCL, 13.

62. *A Register of Rhodes Scholars, 1903–1981*, 246. NARA, RG 233, IF, Series 1, NF, Daniel Boorstin, Box 2. Boorstin died on February 28, 2004.

63. SAC, Chicago to Director, FBI, Subject: DCL, 1, November 28, 1952. NARA, RG 233, IF, Series 1, NF, Daniel Joseph Boorstin, Box 7. See also Boorstin's file in the same RG, Box 22, in the F&RS. Wiener, *Professors, Politics, and Pops*, 55–56. The FBI also interviewed Boorstin in April 1950.

64. NARA, RG 233, IF, Series 1, NF, DCL, Box 193.

65. FBI Report, January 21, 1953, Chicago, Illinois, DCL, 2–4. See State Department summaries of this interview and the bureau's January 12, 1953, report in DCL Passport file.

66. FBI Report, January 20, 1953, NYFO, DCL.

67. FBI Report, March 5, 1952, New Haven, Connecticut, DCL, Espionage-R, ISA of 1950, 2. Osborn is named in FBI Report, August 4, 1952, NYFO, DCL, 3. Osborn died on October 17, 1976.

68. FBI Report, July 22, 1952, New Haven, Connecticut, DCL.

69. NARA RG 233, IF, Series 1, NF, DCL, Box 193, Robert B. Barker to Louis J. Russell, May 22, 1952.

70. Dixon, "Washington Scene," DCL Passport file.

71. Gavin Lee, e-mail to author, July 5, 2011.

72. FBI Report, August 4, 1952, NYFO, DCL, 9.

73. Waller, *Wild Bill Donovan*, 355, 360. Mrs. Shipley to Mr. MacLeod, Interview with TGC Regarding DCL, January 26, 1954, DCL Passport file. Container 187, TGC Papers, LOC, MD.

74. Schrecker, *The Age of McCarthyism*, 73.

75. Leffler, *The Specter of Communism*, 91. Spence, *Mao Zedong*, 108.

76. Fried, *Nightmare in Red*, 123. McCarthy was no stranger to anticommunism. When he ran for the Senate in 1946, he denounced Yalta and accused Robert La Follette Jr. of being "communistically inclined." See Powers, *Not Without Honor*, 236–237.

77. Operations Memorandum, from AmConsul, Bermuda, to DOS, Investigation of Ishbel S. G. Lee, October 6, 1953, DCL Passport file.

78. FBI Report, December 28, 1953, DCL, WFO. John Lee, e-mail to author, June 19, 2011.

Chapter 11 Ishmael

1. Alice I. Gady to DCL, August 28, 1953. SAC, NYFO to Director, FBI, Subject: DCL, September 17, 1953. This company became AIG in 1967. Container 70, TGC Papers, LOC, MD.

2. John Lee, e-mail to author, June 19, 2011.

3. SAC, WFO, to Director, FBI, Subject: DCL, July 14, 1953. JEH to John Horan, DCL, August 25, 1953, DCL Passport file. Kutler, *The American Inquisition*, 97.

4. R. B. Hood to Shipley, DCL, July 8, 1953, DCL Passport file. The Passport Division became the Passport Office in 1952. JEH to John Horan, August 25, 1953, DCL Passport file.

5. John Foster Dulles to American Consul General, DCL, August 12, 1953, DCL Passport file.

6. DOS Passport Application, DCL, July 22, 1949, DCL Passport file. Mr. Nicholson to Mrs. Shipley, DCL, December 14, 1950.

7. J. Kahn, "The Extraordinary Mrs. Shipley," 829, 832–833, 843.

8. Kutler, *The American Inquisition*, 92.

9. J. Kahn, "The Extraordinary Mrs. Shipley," 821–822.

10. J. Kahn, "The Extraordinary Mrs. Shipley," 840, 865. Kutler, *The American Inquisition*, 92–93.

11. Shipley quoted in Kutler, *The American Inquisition*, 93. DOS Reference Slip, March 11, 1955, DCL Passport file.

12. TGC to Shipley, February 18, 1952, DCL Passport file. TGC to Ashley Nicholas, February 25, 1952, DCL Passport file.

13. Shipley to Mr. Nicholson, "Case of DCL," February 25, 1952, DCL Passport file. Shipley, Passport Division, February 25, 1952, DCL Passport file.

14. Passport Renewal Application, DCL, February 19, 1952, DCL Passport file. Memo to Mr. Russell, February 26, 1952, NARA RG 233, IF, Series 1, NF, DCL, Box 193.

15. JEH to John N. Horan, "DCL," August 25, 1953, DCL Passport file. Operations Memorandum, from AmConsul, Bermuda, to DOS, Investigation of Ishbel S. G. Lee, October 6, 1953, DCL Passport file.

16. Incoming Telegram, from Hamilton to Secretary of State, December 21, 1953, DCL Passport file.

17. Outgoing WIROM, AmConsul, Hamilton, "DCL," December 22, 1953, DCL Passport file.

18. DCL, "The Elizabeth Bentley Matter," 9. Boyle, *The Churchill-Eisenhower Correspondence*, 109. AmConsul, Bermuda, to DOS, Deportation Order Against DCL, February 5, 1954, DCL Passport file.

19. "Colony Is Administrative Centre of World-Wide Insurance Business." AmConsul, Bermuda, to DOS, Deportation Order Against DCL, February 5, 1954, DCL Passport file.

20. "Chapter 4: McCarthyism and Cold War, Diplomatic Security in the 1950s."

21. Shipley to MacLeod, Interview with TGC Regarding DCL, January 26, 1954, DCL Passport file.

22. Shipley to MacLeod, Interview with TGC Regarding DCL, January 26, 1954, DCL Passport file.

23. AmConsul, Bermuda, to DOS, Deportation Order Against DCL, February 5, 1954, DCL Passport file.

24. AmConsul, Bermuda, to DOS, Deportation Order Against DCL, February 5, 1954, DCL Passport file.

25. AmConsul, Bermuda, to DOS, Deportation Order Against DCL, February 5, 1954, DCL Passport file.

26. AmConsul, Bermuda, to DOS, Deportation Order Against DCL, February 5, 1954, DCL Passport file.

27. Flinn to Shipley, "DCL," May 20, 1954, DCL Passport file. DCL, "The Elizabeth Bentley Matter," 9.

28. FBI Report, May 24, 1955, NYFO, DCL, 2. DCL, "The Elizabeth Bentley Matter," 10.

29. In 1947, United Fruit, which was primarily based in Guatemala, retained Corcoran to be its chief lobbyist in Washington. By 1951–1952, he was acting as the company's secret go-between in a CIA plot to overthrow that country's left-wing government. The DOS stifled that particular plot, but another succeeded in June 1954. Office Memorandum, "Case of DCL," March 4, 1954, DCL Passport file.

30. Office Memorandum, March 4, 1954, DCL Passport file. Kutler, *The American Inquisition*, 98.

31. Office Memorandum, March 4, 1954, DCL Passport file.

32. WFO to Immigration and Naturalization Service, DCL, May 4, 1954.

33. William Youngman to Shipley, July 12, 1954, DCL Passport file.

34. From Shipley, "For the Record," July 16, 1954, DCL Passport file.

35. Passport Office, September 13, 1954. 18 United States Criminal Code, Sections 1001 and 1542.

36. DOS Passport Application, DCL, July 19, 1954, DCL Passport file.

37. DOS Telephone Inquiry, "Miss Sime of Sen. Byrd's Office," July 22, 1954.

38. Shipley to Warren Olney III, "DCL," September 10, 1954.

39. EJL to Shipley, September 15, 1954, DCL Passport file.

40. William P. Rogers to Shipley, DCL, October 5, 1954. Thomas K. Hall to Shipley, DCL, October 19, 1954, DCL Passport file. Hall to Shipley, October 19, 1954, DCL Passport file.

41. William F. Tompkins to Director, FBI, Subject: DCL, November 17, 1954.

42. Olmstead, *Red Spy Queen*, 146. Budenz became a Catholic and Chambers, ultimately, a Quaker.

43. Olmstead, *Red Spy Queen*, 154. Kessler, *Clever Girl*, 202.

44. Peake, "Afterword," 269.

45. Peake, "Afterword," 269. Olmstead, *Red Spy Queen*, 175.

46. Special agent in charge quoted in Peake, "Afterword," 270.

47. Olmstead, *Red Spy Queen*, 195–196. Peake, "Afterword," 271.

48. Olmstead, *Red Spy Queen*, 162, 169–171, 182, 193–194. Vassiliev, WN #2, 34.

49. Olmstead, *Red Spy Queen*, 187.

50. SAC, WFO, to Director, FBI, DCL, November 26, 1952. FBI Report, December 28, 1953, Washington, DC, DCL, DCL Passport file.

51. FBI Report, December 28, 1953, Washington, DC, 8. Julius Joseph joined the OSS in 1943. An example of what Lee told Bentley about Donovan's proposal can be found in Vassiliev, WN #1, 88.

52. Sparrow was first tentatively proposed in July 1943. On January 20, 1944, Lee transmitted to Colonel Edward Buxton, who was the acting head of the OSS while Donovan was traveling overseas, "Implementation Study for the Over-All and Special Programs for Strategic Services in the Balkans as They Pertain to Hungary." The Secretariat also transmitted Donovan's approval for the mission and received the news that it had failed. William J. Donovan Papers, MHI, Carlisle, Pennsylvania, Box 90C; NARA RG 226, Entry 190C, Box 5, Dulles Files, Sparrow; "Burns from Donovan," January 17, 1944, Box 191, Folder 2704; July 20, 1944, the Secretariat to the Director, "Report of Branches of the OSS for the Month of May 1944"; and General Donovan, Secretariat, "Plan for Hungary," October 14, 1943, Box 194, Folder 2757. FBI Report, December 28, 1953, Washington, DC, DCL. Vassiliev, WN #3, 106. None of the nine Venona cables that pertain to Lee discusses Operation Sparrow.

53. It is also unclear how the Department of Justice, even if it had had OSS documents that it could have used against Lee, would have gotten them into evidence. There is no indication in his file that the CIA was willing to declassify any of those it found that related to Bentley's allegations, and the Classified Information Procedures Act did not yet exist.

54. Cave Brown, *Wild Bill Donovan*, 172.

55. FBI Report, November 9, 1954, Washington, DC, DCL, DCL Passport file. FBI Report, November 9, 1954, Washington, DC, DCL Passport file.

56. Lamphere and Shachtman, *The FBI-KGB War*, 280–281.

57. FBI Report, H. W. Schweppe to W. A. Branigan, DCL, October 17, 1955, 3. DCL, "The Elizabeth Bentley Matter," 7. Armstrong, "The Spirit of the Fifth Amendment Privilege," 75–83. The statute applied to criminal cases that involved charges of espionage, treason, sedition, and the Atomic Energy Act.

58. DCL to William F. Tompkins, November 2, 1954, DCL Passport file. Tompkins to DCL, December 8, 1954. Tweedy to Alan Geoffrey Tunstal Chaplin, December 10, 1954, DCL Passport file.

59. Donovan to Harry Durham Butterfield, December 10, 1954, DCL Passport file.

60. G. Lewis to AmConsul, Hamilton, December 21, 1954. Clare to Shipley, DCL, October 28, 1954.

61. Flinn to Shipley, DCL, March 1, 1955, DCL Passport file.

62. SAC, NYFO, to Director, FBI, Subject: DCL, December 16, 1954. Flinn to Shipley, March 1, 1955. FBI Report, January 14, 1955, NYFO, DCL, DCL Passport file.

63. FBI AIR-Tel, NYFO, April 14, 1955, DCL.

64. F. E. Lintilhac to Shipley, January 28, 1955. Telegram from William Youngman to Shipley, February 14, 1955, DCL Passport file.

65. "Typescript of the Autobiography of Sir Alexander Hood," Part 2, 20, Box 290, Wellcome Library, London. Lord Moran's description of Hood can be found at Janus: Sir Raynor Arthur Collection of Photographs (http://janus.lib .cam.ac.uk/db/node.xsp?id=EAD%2FGBR%2F0115%2FY3011XX).

66. Youngman Memorandum, April 4, 1955, DCL Passport file.

67. "Conversation Between Gwen Lewis and TGC," April 11, 1955, DCL Passport file.

68. J. Kahn, "The Extraordinary Mrs. Shipley," 823. Shipley quoted in Kutler, *The American Inquisition*, 93.

69. Rauh quoted in Kutler, *The American Inquisition*, 94.

70. Honan, "Frances Knight, 94, Director of Passport Office for Decades," September 18, 1999.

71. J. Kahn, "The Extraordinary Mrs. Shipley," 872.

72. Isserman, "Disloyalty as a Principle," 7. Klehr, "Was Joe McCarthy Right?"

73. Powers, *Not Without Honor*, 265. Eisenhower, however, had done a bit of red baiting himself. In November 1953, he let Herbert Brownell, his attorney general, accuse Harry Truman of allowing Harry Dexter White to become the American director of the International Monetary Fund, even though Bentley had claimed that White was one of her subsources.

74. Senate Resolution 301: Censure of Senator Joseph McCarthy, December 2, 1954.

75. Powers, *Broken*, 235–236, 265–271. Benson and Warner, *Venona*, xxx.

76. Powers, *Not Without Honor*, 272.

77. Frances G. Knight to Robert Streeper, May 23, 1955, DCL Passport file. DOS WIROM, American Counsel General, Hamilton, Bermuda, June 8. Thruston B. Morton to Frances G. Knight, "Denial of Passport for DCL," June 3, 1955. Memorandum of Conversation, "Passport of DCL," May 24, 1955, DCL Passport file.

78. Telegram, Maleady to Secretary of State, June 28, 1955, DCL Passport file.

79. Colonial Secretary's Office, Bermuda, July 8, 1955, to William S. Youngman, DCL Passport file. FBI Report, October 6, 1955, NYFO, DCL.

Chapter 12 The Irony of My Life

1. Eleanore Lee, e-mail to author, January 28, 2011. Kathy Cole, e-mail to author, January 3, 2013. Ishbel's second husband was Edward Petrie, a retired member of the British Colonial Service. Ishbel married him in 1973. See "Brian Berkeley Burland."

2. John Lee, e-mail to author, December 12, 2012. Petrie, *Not a Bowl of Cherries*, 40.

3. DCL, "The Elizabeth Bentley Matter," 13. Agreement Between DCL and Isabella Scott Lee, September 28, 1958. Questionnaire, August 14, 1959, in author's possession. They divorced on October 5, 1959.

4. Medical Examination, DCL, November 26, 1956. Medical Examinations, DCL, January 14, 1958, and December 9, 1958.

5. *A Register of Rhodes Scholars, 1903–1981*, 293.

6. Eleanore Lee, e-mail to author, January 28, 2011. The Foreign Affairs Oral History Collection of the Association for Diplomatic Studies and Training, Interview with Eleanore Cobb Lee, May 30, 1990, 8–9. Eleanore Lee, e-mail to author, January 28, 2011.

7. The Foreign Affairs Oral History Collection of the Association for Diplomatic Studies and Training, Interview with Eleanore Cobb Lee, May 30, 1990. See also *A Register of Rhodes Scholars, 1903–1995*, 112.

8. AL to Shipley, February 2, 1955, DCL Passport file. Shipley to AL, March 11, 1955, DCL Passport file. Armistead, realizing his career at the State Department was stalled, retired in 1967, the same year he went to work for the Pharmaceutical Manufacturers Association. He died on August 4, 1998.

9. Waller, *Wild Bill Donovan*, 360, 363. John Foster Dulles to JEH, June 12, 1953.

10. FBI Report, July 7, 1953, Rosen to Ladd, Eisenhower Investigations. Waller, *Wild Bill Donovan*, 364. FBI Teletype from NYFO to FBI Headquarters and SAC, WFO, William Joseph Donovan, June 15, 1953.

11. Powers, *Broken*, 234. H. W. Schweppe to W. A. Branigan, DCL, October 17, 1955.

12. A. H. Belmont to L. V. Boardman, February 1, 1956.

13. A. H. Belmont to L. V. Boardman, February 1, 1956.

14. Haynes and Klehr, *Early Cold War Spies*, 83. As Haynes and Klehr point out, a substantial number of Venona intercepts were not successfully cracked and read until the 1960s and 1970s. Andrew and Mitrokhin, *The Sword and the Shield*, 144, 155, 160. Philby was recalled to London in 1951 and fled to the Soviet Union in 1963. Weisband was convicted of contempt in 1950 and spent a year in federal prison. Haynes and Klehr, *Early Cold War Spies*, 83–86. Thanks most likely to Weisband's information, the Soviets changed their codes in 1948, making them again unreadable.

15. A. H. Belmont to L. V. Boardman, February 1, 1956.

16. A. H. Belmont to L. V. Boardman, February 1, 1956.

17. Powers, *Broken*, 234. In 1957, the US Supreme Court dealt the Smith Act a fatal blow in *Yates v. United States*, 354 US 298 (1957).

18. Powers, *Broken*, 237.

19. Gentry, *J. Edgar Hoover*, 442–443.

20. Powers, *Broken*, 233. Schrecker, *Many Are the Crimes*, 227, 232.

21. SAC, NYFO, to Director, FBI, Subject: DCL, March 26, 1957. FBI Report, January 16, 1957, NYFO, DCL.

22. Gordon B. Tweedy to Charlotte [*sic*] Knight, January 31, 1958, DCL Passport file. Robert D. Johnson to Passport Files, "Passport Case of DCL," February 19, 1958. Affidavit, DCL, February 25, 1958, DCL Passport file. Roderic O'Connor to Frances G. Knight, Passport Matter of DCL, April 1, 1958, DCL Passport file.

23. Thomas I. Mall to Harris Houston, DCL, May 7, 1958. Frances Knight to JEH, May 16, 1958, DCL Passport file. *Kent v. Dulles*, 357, US 116 (1958).

24. SAC, NYFO, to Director, FBI, Subject: DCL, June 24, 1958. T. J. McAndrews to Frances Knight, DCL, July 10, 1958, DCL Passport file. FBI Liaison, "DCL," May 1, 1967, DCL Passport file.

25. Petrie, *Not a Bowl of Cherries*, 40.

26. Peake, "OSS and the Venona Decrypts," 24, 33. Ishbel Petrie to DCL, July 18, 1977. Kathy Cole, e-mail to author, January 3, 2013.

27. American International Underwriters consisted of over one hundred insurance companies. John Lee, e-mail to author, February 20, 2013. Gavin Lee, e-mail to author, July 5, 2011. John Lee, e-mails to author, June 19, 2011, September 15, 2013.

28. Gavin Lee, e-mail to author, July 5, 2011.

29. John Lee, e-mail to author, June 19, 2011. Eleanore Lee, e-mail to author, January 28, 2011.

30. Passport Application of DCL, April 20, 1967, DCL Passport file. William S. Youngman to Staff, June 8, 1965. Gavin Lee, e-mail to author, July 5, 2011. The stock was in American International Underwriters.

31. DCL, Application for Permanent Residence in Canada, December 3, 1973. John Lee, e-mail to author, June 19, 2011.

32. Rarick, "The Untouchables Unfinished." DCL, "The Elizabeth Bentley Matter," 11.

33. SAC, WFO, to Director, FBI, March 6, 1970. These logs also applied to Alger Hiss, who was then suing the federal government.

34. John Lee, e-mail to author, June 19, 2011. DCL to Arnold Smith, September 14, 1974. Freeman, "Insurer to the World."

35. DCL to Arnold Smith, March 31, 1974. DCL to Canadian Consulate General, November 28, 1972.

36. Hamilton Cassels to DCL, December 2, 1973.

37. DCL to Hamilton Cassels, Reply to Question 31 (2) (d), October 8, 1973.

38. DCL to Hamilton Cassels, October 11, 1973. DCL to Hamilton Cassels, January 17, 1974. DCL, Application for Permanent Residence in Canada, December 3, 1973.

39. DCL to Arnold Smith, September 14, 1974. AL to Francis Lee, April 22, 1988. Canadian Association of Rhodes Scholars. DCL membership card, Veterans of the OSS, 1977. DCL, "Some Thoughts on Faith and Belief," February 1, 1983. DCL, "My Family," November 1, 1984. DCL to the editor, *Globe and Mail*, May 29, 1977.

40. DCL, "The Elizabeth Bentley Matter," 17. John Lee, e-mail to author, June 19, 2011.

41. John Lee, e-mail to author, June 19, 2011.

42. EJL to DCL, December 19, 1960. "Lucy Chaplin Lee, January 22, 1884– February 25, 1971," 6.

43. SOHPC, Mary Price Adamson interview, April 19, 1976, 130–131, 133–134.

44. McKinley, "Maurice Halperin, 88, a Scholar Who Chronicled Castro's Career."

45. NARA RG 233, IF, Series 1, NF, Donald Niven Wheeler, Box 50. See also F&RS, Box 368, in the same RG. *A Register of Rhodes Scholars, 1903–1995*, 94. Alarcon, "Donald Wheeler, Communist, Dies at 89.

46. Cave Brown, *Wild Bill Donovan*, 830, 833. Dunlop, *Donovan*, 506.

47. Leary, *Perilous Missions*, 211.

48. Leary, *Perilous Missions*, 211. Wise and Ross, *The Invisible Government*, 179.

49. Saxon, "Thomas Corcoran, Roosevelt Aide, Dies at 80." Crawford, "Thomas G. (Tommy) Corcoran, Lobbyist of New Deal Era, Dies." David Corcoran to DCL, January 27, 1982.

50. Olmstead, *Red Spy Queen*, 197, 199–200, 202. Cablegram to Director and SAC, NYFO, from SAC, New Haven, December 3, 1963.

51. Powers, *Secrecy and Power*, 486.

52. Powers, *Secrecy and Power*, 487.

53. Carr, *The House Committee on Un-American Activities*, 218.

54. Rundquist, "Abolition of the House Internal Security Committee," 5, 6, 8, 12, 16.

55. DCL to AL and Eleanore Cobb Lee, December 23, 1977.

56. AL to DCL, January 1, 1978.

57. "DCL—Biographical Synopsis," June 30, 1979. "DCL—Outline of Memoirs, Items Not Refer [*sic*] to [in] Synopsis," June 30, 1979, in author's possession.

58. "DCL—Outline of Memoirs, Items Not Refer [*sic*] to [in] Synopsis," February 1982.

59. DCL Memoirs, "Foreword," February 8, 1982, in author's possession.

60. DCL, "The Elizabeth Bentley Matter," September 15, 1983, 1–5, 12.

61. DCL, "The Elizabeth Bentley Matter," 28–29, 31.

62. DCL, "The Elizabeth Bentley Matter," 2, 22, 27, 33.

63. DCL, "The Elizabeth Bentley Matter," 18–21, 34.

64. Isserman, "Disloyalty as a Principle," 3.

65. The Venona program was officially declassified on July 11, 1995. John Lee, e-mail to author, January 6, 2011.

66. For those critical of Venona, see Schnier and Schnier, "Cables Coming in from the Cold," 25–30. Nelson, "Illuminating the Twilight Struggle," B4–B6. Schrecker, "The Spies Who Loved Us?" 28–31. For the opposite view, see Isserman, "They Led Two Lives," 1–5, and Haynes and Klehr, *In Denial*, esp. 89–91, 95–101.

67. DCL Obituary, April 19, 1988, *New York Times*.

68. Aaron, "A Decade of Convictions," 738, 741.

69. Andrew, *Defend the Realm*, 368.

70. Le Carré, "Introduction," 27. Lamphere and Shachtman, *The FBI-KGB War*, 246.

71. Le Carré, "Introduction," 31–32.

72. Post, "The Anatomy of Treason," 2–3. Marbles, "Psychology of Treason," 74–75.

73. Schlesinger, *A Life in the 20th Century*, 305.

74. Haynes and Klehr, *Venona*, 408. Ironically, Goldberg's name appeared first on the list of suspected communists inside the OSS that Lee handed to Bentley in September 1944. For the list, see Vassiliev, WN #3, 110. Sparrow seems to have been betrayed to the Germans, not by Lee. Double agents inside one of the OSS's spy networks in Turkey alerted the Germans to Sparrow. See Waller, *Wild Bill Donovan*, 254–255, for an explanation of this betrayal.

75. Haynes, Klehr, and Vassiliev, *Spies*, 308–310. Ranelagh, *The Agency*, 28. Four Central Intelligence directors, Allen Dulles, Richard Helms, William Colby, and William Casey, all served in the OSS.

76. Peake, "Soviet Espionage and the Office of Strategic Services," 125. Le Carré, "Introduction," 40.

77. Peake, "Soviet Espionage and the Office of Strategic Services," 127–128. The CIA formally established a Counterintelligence Staff on December 20, 1954.

Bibliography

Archives

Chennault, Claire Lee, papers, Hoover Institution, Stanford University, Palo Alto, California.

Corcoran, Thomas Gardiner, papers, Manuscript Division, Library of Congress, Washington, DC.

Donovan, William J., papers, Military History Institute, Carlisle, Pennsylvania.

Foreign Affairs Oral History Collection for Diplomatic Studies and Training, interview with Eleanore Cobb Lee, May 30, 1990.

Forgan, Russell D., papers, Hoover Institution, Stanford University, Palo Alto, California.

Hickler, David, collection, Department of Special Collections, Eugene McDermott Library, University of Texas, Dallas.

Hood, Alexander, typescript of the autobiography of Sir Alexander Hood, Wellcome Library, London.

Lee, Duncan Chaplin, FBI files, Freedom of Information Act.

Lee, Duncan Chaplin, file, Rhodes House, Oxford, England.

Lee, Duncan Chaplin, lectures/tutorial reports and evaluations, Christ Church, Oxford.

Lee, Duncan Chaplin, OSS personnel file.

Lee, Duncan Chaplin, personal papers, on loan to the author by the Lee Family.

Lee Family Digital Archive, Washington and Lee University, Lexington, Virginia.

NARA, File Unit 130, Lee, Duncan Chaplin, classified passport applications, A-Le, 1950–1959, RG 59, General Records of the State Department, Box 23. Declassified by NARA on August 28, 2012.

NARA, RG 226, Records of the Office of Strategic Services, College Park, Maryland.

NARA, RG 233, HUAC, Washington, DC.

NARA, RG 46, Senate Internal Security Subcommittee, Washington, DC.

Official File 1661, Espionage; Official File 263, Communism; President's Personal File 3960, Communism; Official File 10B, Justice Department: Federal Bureau of Investigation: Numbered Reports, and Office of Strategic

Services Reports in the President's Secretary File, at the Franklin D. Roosevelt Library, Hyde Park, New York.

Records of United States Attorneys and Marshals, transcripts of grand jury testimony in Alger Hiss, RG 118, 1947–1949, Harry S. Truman Library, Independence, Missouri.

Silvermaster Files, volumes 1–162, ERI, Washington, DC.

Southern Oral History Program Collection, Center for the Study of the American South, Wilson Library, University of North Carolina, Chapel Hill, interview with Mary Price Adamson, April 19, 1976.

Williams Family Papers (Murat Williams), Albert and Shirley Small Special Collections Library, University of Virginia, Charlottesville.

Congressional Hearings

US House, Committee on Un-American Activities. *Hearings Regarding Communist Espionage in the United States*. 80th Cong., 2d Sess. Washington, DC, 1948.

US House, Committee on Un-American Activities. *Investigation of Communist Activities in New Haven, Conn., Area—Part 1*. 84th Cong. 2d sess. Washington, DC, 1956.

US Senate, Investigations Subcommittee of the Committee on Expenditures in the Executive Departments. *Export Policy and Loyalty*. 80th Cong., 2d Sess. Washington, DC, 1948.

US Senate, Subcommittee to Investigate the Administration of the Internal Security Act and Other Internal Security Laws of the Committee on the Judiciary. *The Institute of Pacific Relations*. 82d Cong., 2d Sess. Washington, DC, 1951–1952.

Articles and Books

Aaron, Daniel. "A Decade of Convictions: The Appeal of Communism in the 1930s." *Massachusetts Review* 2, no. 4 (Summer 1961): 736–747.

Ackerman, Kenneth D. *Young J. Edgar*. New York: Carroll and Graf, 2007.

Allen, William C. *History of the United States Capitol: A Chronicle of Design, Construction, and Politics*. Washington, DC: US Government Printing Office, 2002.

Andrew, Christopher. *Defend the Realm: The Authorized History of MI5*. New York: Alfred A. Knopf, 2009.

Andrew, Christopher, and Oleg Gordievsky. *KGB: The Inside Story*. New York: HarperPerennial, 1991.

Andrew, Christopher, and Vasili Mitrokhin. *The Sword and the Shield: The Mitrokhin Archive and the Secret History of the KGB*. New York: Basic Books, 1991.

Armstrong, J. Elwood. "The Spirit of the Fifth Amendment Privilege—a Study in Judicial Method—*Ullman v. United States*." *Maryland Law Review* 17 (1957): 75–83.

"Arnold Cantwell Smith." Canadian Encyclopedia. www.thecanadian encyclopedia.com/articles/arnold-cantwell-smith.

Ascherson, Neal. "What Sort of Traitors?" *London Review of Books*, February 7, 1980. www.lrb.co.uk/V02/n02/neal-ascherson/what-sort-of-traitors.

Aydelotte, Frank. *The American Rhodes Scholarships: A Review of the First Forty Years*. Princeton, NJ: Princeton University Press, 1946.

Bates, M. Searle. "The Theology of American Missionaries in China, 1900–1950." In *The Missionary Enterprise in China and America*, edited by John King Fairbank. Cambridge, MA: Harvard University Press, 1974.

Batvinis, Raymond. *The Origins of FBI Counterintelligence*. Lawrence: University Press of Kansas, 2007.

Bennet, Edward. *Franklin D. Roosevelt and the Search for Victory: American-Soviet Relations, 1939–1945*. Wilmington, DE: SR Books, 1984.

Benson, Robert Louis, and Michael Warner. *Venona: Soviet Espionage and the American Response, 1939–1957*. Washington, DC: National Security Agency, Central Intelligence Agency, 1996.

Bentley, Elizabeth. *Out of Bondage*. New York: Ivy Books, 1988.

Bernstein, Marver. "The Loyalty of Federal Employees." *Political Research Quarterly* 2 (1949): 254–264.

Bird, Kai, and Max Holland. "The Tapping of 'Tommy the Cork.'" *Nation* 8 (1986).

Boyle, Andrew. *The Climate of Treason*. London: Coronet, 1980.

Boyle, Peter. *The Churchill-Eisenhower Correspondence*. Chapel Hill: University of North Carolina Press, 1990.

Brands, H. W. *A Traitor to His Class: The Privileged Life and Radical Presidency of Franklin Delano Roosevelt*. New York: Anchor Books, 2008.

Brendon, Piers. *The Decline and Fall of the British Empire, 1781–1997*. New York: Alfred A. Knopf, 2008.

"Brian Berkeley Burland." Bermudabiographies. www.bermudabiographies .bm/Bios/Biography-Brian%20Burland.html.

Brinkley, Alan. *The Publisher: Henry Luce and His American Century*. New York: Alfred A. Knopf, 2010.

Brody, David. *Workers in Industrial America: Essays on the 20th Century Struggle*. New York: Oxford University Press, 1980.

Burleigh, Michael. *Moral Combat: A History of World War II*. London: HarperPress, 2011.

Burns, James McGregor. *Roosevelt: The Soldier of Freedom, 1940–1945*. New York: History Book Club, 2006.

"By the Numbers: The US Military." National WWII Museum. www.national ww2museum.org/learn/education/for-students/ww2-history/ww2-by -the-numbers/us-military.html.

Byrd, Martha. *Chennault: Giving Wings to the Tiger.* Tuscaloosa: University of Alabama Press, 1987.

Byrnes, Mark. *The Truman Years: 1945–1953.* Essex, UK: Pearson Education Limited, 2000.

Cameron-Watt, Donald. *How War Came.* New York: Pantheon Books, 1986.

Carr, Robert. *The House Committee on Un-American Activities, 1945–1950.* Ithaca, NY: Cornell University Press, 1952.

Carter, Carolle J. "Mission to Yennan: The OSS and the Dixie Mission." In *The Secrets War: The Office of Strategic Services in World War II,* edited by George C. Chalou. Washington, DC: National Archives and Records Administration, 1992.

Cave Brown, Anthony. *Wild Bill Donovan: The Last Hero.* New York: Times Books, 1982.

Cave Brown, Anthony, and Charles MacDonald. *On a Field of Red: The Communist International and the Coming of World War II.* New York: G. P. Putnam's Sons, 1981.

Chambers, Whittaker. *Witness.* New York: Random House, 1952.

"Chapter 4: McCarthyism and Cold War, Diplomatic Security in the 1950s." Department of State. www.state.gov/documents/organization/176702 .pdf.

Chervonnaya, Svetlana. "Golos, Jacob (1889–1943)." DocumentsTalk.com. www.documentstalk.com/wp/golos-jacob.

———. "Katz, Joseph." DocumentsTalk.com. www.documentstalk.com/wp /katz-jospeh.

———. "Zarubin, Vassili Mikhailovich (1894–1974)." DocumentsTalk.com. www.documentstalk.com/wp/zarubin-vassili-mikhailovich-1894-1974.

"Church Committee Report on the Evolution of CIA Covert Action." In *Covert Action,* edited by Loch K. Johnson. Vol. 3 of *Strategic Intelligence.* Westport, CT: Praeger International, 2007.

Cline, Ray. *Secrets, Spies, and Scholars: The Essential CIA.* Washington: Acropolis Books, 1976.

Collard, Dudley. *Soviet Justice and the Trial of Radek and Others.* London: Victor Gollancz Ltd., 1937.

Conquest, Robert. *The Great Terror: A Reassessment.* New York: Oxford University Press, 2008.

———. *Inside Stalin's Secret Police: NKVD Politics, 1936–39.* Stanford, CA: Hoover Institution Press, 1985.

Crosby, Laurence A., Frank Aydelotte, and Alan C. Valentine. *Oxford of Today.* New York: Oxford University Press, 1927.

Dallin, David. *Soviet Espionage.* New Haven, CT: Yale University Press, 1955.

Divine, Robert. *Roosevelt and World War II.* New York: Penguin Books, 1975.

Dunlop, Richard. *Donovan: America's Master Spy.* New York: Rand McNally, 1982.

Espey, John. *Tales out of School*. New York: Alfred A. Knopf, 1947.

Evans, Richard. *The Third Reich at War*. New York: Penguin Group, 2008.

———. *The Third Reich in Power*. New York: Penguin Group, 2005.

Feklisov, Alexander, and Sergei Kostin. *The Man Behind the Rosenbergs*. New York: Enigma Books, 2001.

Ferguson, Niall. *The War of the World: Twentieth-Century Conflict and the Descent of the West*. New York: Penguin Press, 2006.

Ferrell, Robert. *Harry S. Truman and the Modern Presidency*. Boston: Little, Brown, 1983.

Fitzgerald, Frances. *Way out There in the Blue*. New York: Simon and Schuster, 2000.

Fox, John. "In the Enemy's House: Venona and the Maturation of American Counterintelligence." Paper presented at the 2005 Symposium on Cryptologic History, October 27, 2005. www.fbi.gov/about-us/history /highlights-of-history/articles/venona.

———. "What the Spider Did: US and Soviet Counterintelligence Before the Cold War." *Journal of Cold War Studies* 2, no. 3 (Summer 2009): 206–224.

Fried, Albert. *Communism in America: A History in Documents*. New York: Columbia University Press, 1997.

Fried, Richard. *Nightmare in Red: The McCarthy Era in Perspective*. New York: Oxford University Press, 1990.

Gaddis, John Lewis. *George F. Kennan: An American Life*. New York: Penguin Press, 2011.

———. *The United States and the Origins of the Cold War, 1941–1947*. New York: Columbia University Press, 1972.

Gage, Beverly. *The Day Wall Street Exploded: A Story of America in Its First Age of Terror*. New York: Oxford University Press, 2009.

Gardiner, Juliet. *The Thirties: An Intimate History*. London: HarperPress, 2011.

Garrow, David. *The FBI and Martin Luther King: From Solo to Memphis*. New York: W. W. Norton, 1981.

Gentry, Curt. *J. Edgar Hoover: The Man and the Secrets*. New York: Penguin Group, 1992.

Goldstein, Robert. *American Blacklist: The Attorney General's List of Subversive Organizations*. Lawrence: University Press of Kansas, 2008.

Goodman, Walter. *The Committee: The Extraordinary Career of the House Committee on Un-American Activities*. New York: Farrar, Straus, and Giroux, 1968.

Gregory, Adrian. *The Last Great War: British Society and the First World War*. Cambridge: Cambridge University Press, 2008.

Grose, Peter. *Gentlemen Spy: The Life of Allen Dulles*. New York: Houghton Mifflin, 1994.

Hamby, Alonzo. *Man of the People: A Life of Harry S. Truman*. New York: Oxford University Press, 1995.

Harris, Richard, and Daniel J. Tichenor. *A History of the US Political System: Ideas, Interests, and Institutions.* Santa Barbara, CA: ABC-CLIO, 2010.

Hastings, Max. *Inferno: The World at War, 1939–1945.* New York: Alfred A. Knopf, 2011.

Haynes, John Earle. "Adolph Berle's Notes on His Meeting with Whittaker Chambers." John Earl Haynes: Historical Writings. www.johnearlhaynes .org/page100.html.

————. "The Mental Comintern and the Self-Destruction Politics of the CPUSA, 1945–1958." John Earl Haynes: Historical Writings. www.john earlhaynes.org/page65.html.

————. *Red Scare or Red Menace? American Communism and Anti-Communism in the Cold War Era.* Chicago: Ivan Dee, 1996.

Haynes, John Earle, and Harvey Klehr. "Alexander Vassiliev's Notebooks: Provenance and Documentation of Soviet Intelligence Activities in the United States." Wilson Center. www.wilsoncenter.org/sites/default/files/Vassiliev Notebooks_Web_intro_Final1.pdf.

————. *Early Cold War Spies: The Espionage Trials That Shaped American Politics.* New York: Cambridge University Press, 2006.

————. *In Denial: Historians, Communism, and Espionage.* San Francisco: Encounter Books, 2003.

————. "J. Robert Oppenheimer: A Spy? No. But a Communist Once? Yes." Washington Decoded, February 11, 2012. www.washingtondecoded.com /site/2012/02/jro.html.

————. *Venona: Decoding Soviet Espionage in America.* New Haven, CT: Yale University Press, 1999.

Haynes, John Earle, Harvey Klehr, and Alexander Vassiliev. *Spies: The Rise and Fall of the KGB in America.* New Haven, CT: Yale University Press, 2009.

Heinrichs, Waldo. "The United States Prepares for War." In *The Secrets War: The Office of Strategic Services in World War II*, edited by George C. Chalou. Washington, DC: National Archives and Records Administration, 1992.

Hess, Jerry N. "Oral History Interview with Stephen J. Spingarn." Harry S. Truman Library and Museum, March 29, 1967. www.trumanlibrary.org /oralhist/sping8.htm

"The History of Christ Church." Christ Church. www.chch.ox.ac.uk/visiting /history.

Hobsbawm, Eric. *The Age of Extremes: A History of the World, 1914–1991.* New York: Vintage Books, 1996.

Holborn, Hajo. *The Political Collapse of Europe.* New York: Alfred A. Knopf, 1951.

Hopkins, June. "Christodora Settlement House." Social Welfare History Project. www.socialwelfarehistory.com/organizations/christodora-settlement-house.

Hyde, Earl, Jr. "Bernard Schuster and Joseph Katz: KGB Master Spies in the United States." *International Journal of Intelligence and Counterintelligence* 12, no. 1 (1999): 35–57.

Isserman, Maurice. "Disloyalty as a Principle: Why Communists Spied in the 1930s." Internet Archive. web.archive.org/web/20030405124423/http://www.afsa.org/fsj/oct00/isserman.cfm.

———. "They Led Two Lives." *New York Times*, May 9, 1999. www.nytimes.com/books/99/05/09/reviews.

———. *Which Side Were You On? The American Communist Party During the Second World War*. Middletown, CT: Wesleyan University Press, 1982.

Kahn, E. J. *The China Hands: America's Foreign Service Officers and What Befell Them*. New York: Viking Press, 1975.

Kahn, Jeffrey. "The Extraordinary Mrs. Shipley: How the United States Controlled International Travel Before the Age of Terrorism." *Connecticut Law Review* 43, no. 3 (February 2011): 821–888.

Keeley, Edward. *The Salonika Bay Murder, Cold War Politics and the Polk Affair*. Princeton, NJ: Princeton University Press, 1989.

Kelley, Brooks. *Yale: A History*. New Haven, CT: Yale University Press, 1974.

Kennedy, David. *Freedom from Fear: The American People in Depression and War, 1929–1945*. New York: Oxford University Press, 1999.

Kessler, Laura. *Clever Girl: Elizabeth Bentley, the Spy Who Ushered in the McCarthy Era*. New York: Harper Collins, 2003.

Kimball, Warren. *The Juggler: Franklin Roosevelt as Wartime Statesman*. Princeton, NJ: Princeton University Press, 1991.

Klehr, Harvey. "Was Joe McCarthy Right?" Raleigh Spy Conference. www.raleighspyconference.com/docs/joe_mccarthy_klehr.pdf.

Klehr, Harvey, John Earle Haynes, and Fridrikh Firsov. *The Secret World of American Communism*. New Haven, CT: Yale University Press, 1995.

Klehr, Harvey, and Ronald Radosh. *The Amerasia Spy Case: Prelude to McCarthyism*. Chapel Hill: University of North Carolina Press, 1996.

Kutler, Stanley. *The American Inquisition: Justice and Injustice in the Cold War*. New York: Hill and Wang, 1982.

Lamphere, Robert, and Tom Shachtman. *The FBI-KGB War: A Special Agent's Story*. New York: Random House, 1986.

Le Carré, John. "Introduction." In *Philby: The Spy Who Betrayed a Generation*, by Bruce Page, David Leitch, and Phillip Knightley. London: Sphere Books Limited, 1977.

Leary, William. "Aircraft and Anti-Communists: CAT in Action, 1949–1952." *China Quarterly* 52 (1972): 654–669.

———. *Perilous Missions: Civil Air Transport and CIA Covert Operations in Asia*. Washington, DC: Smithsonian Institution Press, 2002.

———. "Portrait of a Cold Warrior: Whiting Willauer and Civil Air Transport." *Modern Asian Studies* 5 (1971): 378–388.

Leary, William, and William Stueck. "The Chennault Plan to Save China: US Containment in Asia and the Origins of the CIA's Aerial Empire, 1949–1950." *Diplomatic History* 8, no. 4 (October 1984): 349–364.

Lee, Armistead. "Kinsmen in the Clergy." Society of Lees of Virginia, May 12, 1978. In author's possession.

———. "Memories of My Parents." 1990.

———. "Reflections on a Crowded Life." April 3, 1990.

———. "Some Reminiscences of My Father, Edmund J. Lee, D.D., 1877–1962." December 8, 1981.

Lee, Duncan Chaplin. "DCL—Biographical Synopsis, June 30, 1979." In author's possession.

———. "The Elizabeth Bentley Matter (A Memorandum for My Children)." September 15, 1983. In author's possession.

———. "My Family: A Memorandum for My Children and Grandchildren." November 1, 1984.

———. "Some Thoughts on Faith and Belief." February 1, 1983.

Lee, Lucy Chaplin. *An American Sojourn in China: Family Memories.* Annandale, VA: Turnpike Press, 1968.

"The Lees of Virginia: An American Legacy." Lee Family Digital Archive, Washington and Lee University. http://leearchive.wlu.edu/legacy/index.html.

Lefeber, Walter. *America, Russia, and the Cold War, 1945–1975.* New York: John Wiley and Sons, 1976.

Leffler, Melvyn. *The Preponderance of Power: National Security, the Truman Administration, and the Cold War.* Stanford, CA: Stanford University Press, 1992.

———. *The Specter of Communism: The United States and the Origins of the Cold War, 1917–1953.* New York: Hill and Wang, 1994.

Lichtman, Allan. "Tommy the Cork: The Secret World of America's First Modern Lobbyist." *Washington Monthly* (February 1987): 41–49.

"Lucy Chaplin Lee, January 22, 1884–February 25, 1971." *The Chat* (April 1971): 6–7.

Mangold, Tom. *Cold Warrior, James Jesus Angleton: The CIA's Master Spy Hunter.* New York: Simon and Schuster, 1991.

Marbles, William. "Psychology of Treason." In *Inside the CIA's Private World: Declassified Articles from the Agency's Internal Journal, 1955–1992,* edited by H. Bradford Westerfield. New Haven, CT: Yale University Press, 1997.

Martelle, Scott. *The Fear Within: Spies, Commies, and American Democracy on Trial.* New Brunswick, NJ: Rutgers University Press, 2011.

May, Gary. *China Scapegoat: The Diplomatic Ordeal of John Carter Vincent.* Washington, DC: New Republic Books, 1979.

———. *Un-American Activities: The Trials of William Remington.* New York: Oxford University Press, 1994.

May, Henry. *Protestant Churches and Industrial America.* New York: Harper Torch Books, 1967.

McDonald, Lawrence. "The OSS and Its Records." In *The Secrets War: The Office of Strategic Services in World War II,* edited by George C. Chalou. Washington, DC: National Archives and Records Administration, 1992.

McElwee, William. *Britain's Locust Years: 1918–1940*. London: Faber and Faber, 1962.

McKean, David. "Kerry Chief of Staff McKean: Tommy the Cork's Legacy." National Journal, January 21, 2004. www.nationaljournal.com.

———. *Tommy the Cork: Washington's Ultimate Insider from Roosevelt to Reagan*. South Royalton, VT: Steerforth Press, 2004.

Middlekauff, Robert. *The Glorious Cause: The American Revolution, 1763–1789*. Oxford History of the United States. New York: Oxford University Press, 1982.

"Milestones: 1937–1945: The Tehran Conference, 1943." Office of the Historian, US State Department. http://history.state.gov/milestones/1937-1945 /TehranConf.

Morgan, Ted. *Reds: McCarthyism in Twentieth-Century America*. New York: Random House, 2003.

Morris, James. *Oxford*. London: Faber and Faber, 1965.

Nelson, Anna Kasten. "Illuminating the Twilight Struggle: New Interpretations of the Cold War." *Chronicle of Higher Education*, June 25, 1999, B4–B6.

Newton, Verne. *The Cambridge Spies: The Untold Story of MacLean, Philby, and Burgess in America*. Lanham, MD: Madison Books, 1991.

Norfleet, Elizabeth. *Woodberry Forest: A Venture in Faith*. New York: Georgian Press, 1955.

Office of the Clerk, US House of Representatives, and Architect of the Capitol. "Cannon Office Building: A Congressional First." 2006. Architect of the Capitol brochure.

Olmstead, Kathryn. *Red Spy Queen: A Biography of Elizabeth Bentley*. Chapel Hill: University of North Carolina Press, 2002.

O'Reilly, Kenneth. *Hoover and the Un-Americans: The FBI, HUAC, and the Red Menace*. Philadelphia: Temple University Press, 1983.

"Our History." The Masters School. www.mastersny.org/about-us/history/index .aspx.

Overy, Richard. *The Morbid Age: Britain Between the Wars*. London: Allen Lane, 2009.

Peake, Hayden. "Afterword." In *Out of Bondage*, by Elizabeth Bentley. New York: Ivy Books, 1988.

———. "OSS and the Venona Decrypts." *Intelligence and National Security* 12, no. 3 (July 1997): 14–34.

———. "Soviet Espionage and the Office of Strategic Services." In *America Unbound: World War II and the Making of a Superpower*, edited by Warren F. Kimball, 107–138. New York: St. Martin's Press, 1992.

Pelling, Henry. *The British Communist Party: A Historical Profile*. London: Adam and Charles Black, 1975.

Perry, Roland. *Last of the Cold War Spies: The Life of Michael Straight—the Only American in Britain's Cambridge Spy Ring*. Cambridge, MA: Da Capo Press, 2005.

Persico, Joseph. *Roosevelt's Secret War: FDR and World War II Espionage*. New York: Random House Trade Books, 2001.

Petrie, Ishbel. *Not a Bowl of Cherries*. County Durham, UK: Pentland Press, 1997.

Phillips, Cabell. *The Truman Presidency: A History of a Triumphant Succession*. New York: Penguin Books, 1966.

Phillips, Clifton. "The Student Volunteer Movement and Its Role in China Missions, 1886–1920." In *The Missionary Enterprise in China and America*, edited by John King Fairbank. Cambridge, MA: Harvard University Press, 1974.

Pierson, George. *Yale Book of Numbers: Historical Statistics of the College and University, 1701–1977*. Yale University Office of Institutional Research. http://oir.yale.edu/1701-1976-yale-book-numbers.

Pincher, Chapman. *Traitors: The Anatomy of Treason*. New York: St. Martin's Press, 1987.

Post, Jerrold. "The Anatomy of Treason." *Studies in Intelligence* 19, no. 2 (Spring 1975): 37–47.

Powers, Richard Gid. *Broken: The Troubled Past and Uncertain Future of the FBI*. New York: Free Press, 2004.

———. *Not Without Honor: The History of American Anticommunism*. New York: Free Press, 1995.

———. *Secrecy and Power: The Life of J. Edgar Hoover*. New York: Free Press, 1987.

Rafalko, Frank J. *Counterintelligence in World War II*. A Counterintelligence Reader 2. Washington, DC: National Counterintelligence Center, 1994.

Ranelagh, John. *The Agency: The Rise and Decline of the CIA*. New York: Simon and Schuster, 1987.

Rarick, John. "The Untouchables Unfinished." *Congressional Record*, Extension of Remarks, March 25, 1958.

A Register of Rhodes Scholars, 1903–1981. Oxford: Alden Press, 1981.

A Register of Rhodes Scholars, 1903–1995. Oxford: Information Press Ltd., 1995.

Riebling, Mark. *Wedge: From Pearl Harbor to 9/11—How the Secret War Between the FBI and CIA Has Endangered National Security*. New York: Simon and Schuster, 2002.

Robert, Dana. *Occupy Until I Come: A. T. Pierson and the Evangelization of the World*. Grand Rapids: William B. Eerdmans Publishing, 2003.

Romerstein, Herbert, and Eric Breindel. *The Venona Secrets: Exposing Soviet Espionage and America's Traitors*. Washington, DC: Regnery Publishing, 2000.

Rundquist, Paul. "Abolition of the House Internal Security Committee." Congressional Research Service, March 9, 1988, 1–20.

Ryan, James. *Earl Browder: The Failure of American Communism*. Tuscaloosa: University of Alabama Press, 1997.

Schiff, Judith. "The Hoot Heard Round the World." *Yale Alumni Magazine* 69, no. 4 (March/April 2006): 22–23.

Schlatter, Richard. "On Being a Communist at Harvard." *Partisan Review* 44 (December 1977): 605–617.

Schlesinger, Arthur M., Jr. *A Life in the 20th Century: Innocent Beginnings, 1917–1950*. Boston: Houghton Mifflin, 2000.

―――. "The Missionary Enterprise and Theories of Imperialism." In *The Missionary Enterprise in China and America*, edited by John King Fairbank. Cambridge, MA: Harvard University Press, 1974.

Schneir, Walter, and Miriam Schnier. "Cables Coming in from the Cold." *Nation*, July 5, 1999, 25–30.

Schrecker, Ellen. *The Age of McCarthyism: A Brief History with Documents*. Boston: Bedford/St. Martin's, 2002.

―――. *Many Are the Crimes: McCarthyism in America*. Boston: Little, Brown, 1998.

―――. "The Spies Who Loved Us?" *Nation*, May 24, 1999, 28–31.

Service, Robert. *Stalin: A Biography*. Cambridge, MA: Belknap Press of Harvard University Press, 2004.

Sevareid, Eric. *Not So Wild a Dream*. New York: Alfred A. Knopf, 1946.

―――. "Our Good Friends, the Head-Hunters." *Reader's Digest*, February 1944, 121–131.

Sibley, Katherine A. S. "Catching Spies in the United States." In *Counterintelligence and Counterterrorism: Defending the Nation Against Hostile Forces*, edited by Loch K. Johnson. Vol. 4 of *Strategic Intelligence*. Westport, CT: Praeger Security International, 2007.

―――. *Red Spies in America: Stolen Secrets and the Dawn of the Cold War*. Lawrence: University Press of Kansas, 2004.

Simms, James. "Stalin Was a Terrible Tyrant and Essential Ally." *Roanoke Times*, September 4, 2010.

Sinclair, Andrew. *The Red and the Blue: Cambridge, Treason, and Intelligence*. Boston: Little, Brown and Company, 1986.

Smith, Bradley. *The Shadow Warriors: OSS and the Origins of the CIA*. New York: Basic Books, 1983.

―――. *Sharing Secrets with Stalin: How the Allies Traded Intelligence, 1941–1945*. Lawrence: University Press of Kansas, 1996.

Smith, Gaddis. "Life at Yale During the Great Depression." *Yale Alumni Magazine* (November–December 2009): www.yalealumnimagazine.com/articles /2644.

Snyder, Timothy. *Bloodlands: Europe Between Hitler and Stalin*. New York: Basic Books, 2010.

"The Soviet Problem." George Washington University. www2.gwu.edu/~nsa archive/NSAEBB/NSAEBB260/NSA-2.pdf.

Spector, Ronald. "The Battle That Saved Taiwan." *MHQ* (Autumn 2012): 98–104.

Spence, Jonathan. *Mao Zedong: A Life*. New York: A Lipper/Penguin Book, 1999.

———. *The Search for Modern China*. New York: W. W. Norton, 1990.

———. *To Change China: Western Advisers in China, 1620–1960*. New York: Penguin Books, 1986.

Starborn, Joseph. *American Communism in Crisis, 1943–1957*. Berkeley: University of California Press, 1972.

Swanberg, W. A. *Luce and His Empire*. New York: Charles Scribner's Sons, 1972.

Tanenhaus, Sam. "Tangled Treason." *New Republic*, July 5, 1999, 29–33.

———. *Whittaker Chambers: A Biography*. New York: Modern Library Edition, 1998.

Taylor, Jay. *The Generalissimo: Chiang Kai-shek and the Struggle for Modern China*. Cambridge, MA: Belknap Press of Harvard University Press, 2009.

Theoharis, Athan. *Chasing Spies: How the FBI Failed in Counterintelligence but Promoted the Politics of McCarthyism in the Cold War Years*. Chicago: Ivan Dee, 2002.

———. *The FBI and American Democracy: A Brief Critical History*. Lawrence: University Press of Kansas, 2004.

———. "The Successes and Failures of FBI Counterintelligence." In *Counterintelligence and Counterterrorism: Defending the Nation Against Hostile Forces*, edited by Loch K. Johnson. Vol. 4 of *Strategic Intelligence*. Westport, CT: Praeger Security International, 2007.

———. "The Truman Administration and the Decline of Civil Liberties: The FBI's Success in Securing Authorization for a Preventive Detention Program." *Journal of American History* 64, no. 4 (March 1978): 1010–1030.

Theoharis, Athan, and John Cox. *The Boss: J. Edgar Hoover and the Great American Inquisition*. Philadelphia: Temple University Press, 1988.

Theoharis, Athan, with Tony Poveda, Susan Rosnefeld, and Richard Gid Powers. *The FBI: A Comprehensive Guide from J. Edgar Hoover to the X-Files*. New York: Checkmark Books, 2000.

Thomas, Evan. *The Very Best Men: Four Who Dared—The Early Years of the CIA*. New York: Simon and Schuster, 1995.

Thomson, David. *England in the Twentieth Century*. Middlesex, UK: Penguin Books, 1965.

Trevor-Roper, Hugh. *Christ Church, Oxford: The Portrait of a College*. Published by authority of the Governing Body of Christ Church, 1989.

Troy, Thomas. *Donovan and the CIA: A History of the Establishment of the Central Intelligence Agency*. Frederick, MD: Aletheia Books, 1981.

———. *Wild Bill and Intrepid: Donovan, Stephenson, and the Origin of CIA*. New Haven, CT: Yale University Press, 1996.

US Government, US Department of State, and Bureau of Diplomatic Security. "The Vital Function, World War II and Diplomatic Security." In *History of the Bureau of Diplomatic Security*. Wiltshire, UK: Global Publishing Solutions, 2011. www.state.gov/documents/organization/176704.pdf.

US Senate. *Supplementary Detailed Staff Reports on Intelligence Activities and the Rights of Americans, Book III, Final Report of the Select Committee to Study Governmental Operations with Respect to Intelligence Activities*. It's About Time, April 23, 1976. www.itsabouttimebpp.com/cointelpro/pdf/COINTELPRO_Action.pdf.

"Venona." George Washington University. www2.gwu.edu/~nsarchiv/NSAEBB/NSAEBB278/01.PDF.

"Venona Chronology." National Security Agency. www.nsa.gov/public_info/declass/venona/chronology.shtml.

Waller, Douglas. *Wild Bill Donovan: The Spymaster Who Created the OSS and Modern American Espionage*. New York: Free Press, 2011.

Warner, Michael. *The Office of Strategic Services: America's First Intelligence Agency*. Washington, DC: Public Affairs, Central Intelligence Agency, 2007.

Weinstein, Allen. *Perjury: The Hiss-Chambers Case*. New York: Random House, 1997.

Weinstein, Allen, and Alexander Vassiliev. *The Haunted Wood*. New York: Random House, 1999.

White, G. Edward. *Alger Hiss's Looking Glass Wars: The Covert Life of a Soviet Spy*. Oxford: Oxford University Press, 2004.

Wiener, Jon. *Professors, Politics, and Pop*. London: Verso, 1991.

Willey, John, and Dan Dry. *Woodberry Forest*. Louisville, KY: Harmony House Publishers, 1999.

Winter, Jay. *The Great War and the British People*. Cambridge: Cambridge University Press, 1986.

Wise, David, and Thomas Ross. *The Invisible Government*. New York: Bantam Books, 1965.

Yale Banner 1935. New Haven, CT: Yale University, 1935.

Ybarra, Michael. *Washington Gone Crazy: Senator Pat McCarran and the Great American Communist Hunt*. Hanover, NH: Steerforth Press, 2004.

Yoffe, Emily. "A Fork in the Road." *New Republic*, September 17, 1977, 21–22.

Ziegler, Philip. *Legacy: Cecil Rhodes, the Rhodes Trust and Rhodes Scholarships*. New Haven, CT: Yale University Press, 2008.

Press Articles

Alarcon, Evelina. "Donald Wheeler, Communist, Dies at 89." *People's World*, November 22, 2002.

Andrews, Bert. "Miss Bentley Affirms, Lee Denies Spylinks; Perjury Inquiry Asked." *New York Herald Tribune*, August 11, 1948.

"Angell Welcomes Freshmen to Yale." Special to the *New York Times*, October 2, 1931.

"Colony Is Administrative Centre of World-Wide Insurance Business." *Royal Gazette Weekly*, January 17, 1954.

"Congress to Demand Prosecutions in Spy Case." *Washington Post*, August 2, 1948.

Crawford, Kenneth. "Thomas G. (Tommy) Corcoran, Lobbyist of New Deal Era, Dies." *Washington Post*, December 7, 1981.

"The Dilemma." *Washington Post*, August 4, 1948.

"Donovan Backs Duncan Lee as Loyal in War." *New York Times*, August 31.

"Duncan Lee Denies All Charges Before Congress and in Letter." *Pittsylvania Tribune*, August 12, 1948.

"Engagement Announced." *Danville Register*, April 24, 1938.

"Facts First." *Washington Post*, September 17, 1948.

"4 Yale Students Rhodes Scholars." Special to the *New York Times*, January 9, 1935.

Frank, Nelson, and Norton Mockridge. "Red Ring Bared by Blond Queen." *New York World-Telegram*, July 21, 1948.

———. "Spy Says OSS Aide Hinted Atomic Plant Supersecret." *New York World-Telegram*, August 10, 1948.

———. "Super-Secrecy Veiled Russia's Spy Cells Here." *New York World-Telegram*, July 22, 19, 1948.

Freeman, James. "Insurer to the World." *Wall Street Journal*, February 6, 2013.

Ghio, Bob. "Lost in Head-Hunter Country." *Yank: The Army Weekly*, December 31, 1943.

Healy, Paul, and Frank Holeman. "3 More Witnesses Balk at Questions." *Washington Times-Herald*, August 11, 1948.

Honan, William. "Frances Knight, 94, Director of Passport Office for Decades." *New York Times*, September 18, 1999.

"Lee Denies Giving Reds Secrets." *Danville Bee*, August 10, 1948.

"Lee Swears He Never Was Red." *Washington Evening Star*, August 10, 1948.

Mckinley, James, Jr. "Maurice Halperin, 88, a Scholar Who Chronicled Castro's Career." *New York Times*, February 12, 1995.

Nellor, Edward. "Red Spy Ring to Be Broken Soon by US Agencies' Action." *New York Sun*, October 16, 1947.

"Obituary of Edward Pierpont Morgan." *Southeast Missourian*, March 31, 1986.

"Obituary of Lord Shawcross." *Telegraph*, July 11, 2003.

Ottenberg, Miriam. "Ex-Army Officers Deny Bentley's Charges, Lee Swears He Was Never Red." *Washington Evening Star*, August 10, 1948.

"Refusing the $64 Question." *Danville Register*, August 12, 1948.

"Report on [Harry Dexter] White." *Sunday (Washington) Star*, November 8, 1953.

Saxon, Wolfgang. "Thomas Corcoran, Roosevelt Aide, Dies at 80." *New York Times*, December 7, 1981.

"Seniors Elect 86 Juniors to Yale Societies." Special to the *New York Times*, May 10, 1934.

Walter, James. "Jury Expected to Indict 60 as Red Spies." *Washington Times-Herald*, October 17, 1947.

"Yale Lists Honors for 704 Students." Special to the *New York Times*, September 22, 1933.

Letters, E-Mails, and Interviews

Acheson, David, interviews, June 20, 2008; October 14, 2008.

Black, William, telephone interview, April 22, 1999.

Cole, Kathy, e-mail, January 3, 2013.

Espey, John, letter, July 19, 1999.

Fidell, Eugene, e-mail, October 25, 2011.

Haynes, John Earl, e-mail, May 14, 2012.

Horowitz, Dr. Daniel, e-mail, March 30, 2013.

Lee, Eleanore, e-mail, "Notes on My Memories of Duncan," January 28, 2011.

Lee, Gavin, e-mail, July 5, 2011.

Lee, John, e-mails, June 19, 2011; December 12, 2011; October 14, 2012; February 20, 2013; September 15, 2013.

McIntosh, Elizabeth, telephone interviews, April 17, 2008; May 14, 2008.

Merillat, Christopher, interview, June 20, 2005.

Nangle, Robert, telephone interviews, October 17, 2011; December 9, 2011.

Peake, Hayden B., to Robert Louis Benson, memorandum, October 22, 1996.

Pforzheimer, Walter, interview, June 17, 1999.

Scully, Dr. John, letter, June 8, 1999.

Websites

Canadian Encyclopedia: www.thecanadianencyclopedia.com.

CIA's Clandestine Services History of Civil Air Transport: https://www.cia.gov/library/publications/historical-collection-publications/clandestine-services-histories-of-civil-air-transport/index.html.

John Earl Haynes: Historical Writings: www.johnearlhaynes.org.

Lee Family Digital Archive: http://leearchive.wlu.edu.

Letting Documents Talk: A "Non-Definitive" History, Svetlana Chervonnaya: www.documentstalk.com/wp.

Nangle, Benjamin Christie, Yale University Manuscripts and Archive, Historical Register online: http://avideo.library.yale.edu/hro/details.php?varPriNum=2804&varSearchVal=Nangle.

National WWII Museum: www.nationalww2museum.com.

Wilson Center Digital Archive, Vassiliev Notebooks: http://digitalarchive.wilsoncenter.org/collection/86/Vassiliev-Notebooks.

Index